A STATE
of CHANGE

Chinook jumping rapids on the Merced River before the Age of Dams.
OIL ON COTTON RAG PAPER, 9 X 6 1/2 INCHES, 2005

A STATE of CHANGE

Forgotten Landscapes of California

Laura Cunningham

Heyday, Berkeley, California

The publisher wishes to thank the BayTree Fund, the Candelaria Fund, the Christensen Fund, the Moore Family Foundation, and TomKat Charitable Trust for their generous contributions to this project.

Library of Congress Cataloging-in-Publication Data

    Cunningham, Laura, 1966-
      A state of change : forgotten landscapes of California / Laura Cunningham.
        p. cm.
      Includes bibliographical references and index.
      ISBN 978-1-59714-136-9 (pbk. : alk. paper)
      1. Natural history--California. 2. Landscape changes--California. 3. Historical geology--California. I. Title.
      QH105.C2C86 2010
      508.794--dc22

                          2010005766
ISBN 978-1-59714-306-6
First paperback printing 2015

Cover Art: Grizzly bear in "beargrass"—purple needlegrass. Pencil on paper, 2005.
Cover Design: Ashley Ingram
Interior Design/Typesetting: J. Spittler/Jamison Design
Printed in China by Imago
Orders, inquiries, and correspondence should be addressed to:
    Heyday
    P. O. Box 9145, Berkeley, CA 94709
    (510) 549-3564, Fax (510) 549-1889
    www.heydaybooks.com

10 9 8 7 6 5 4 3 2 1

FSC
www.fsc.org

MIX
Paper from
responsible sources
FSC® C005748

To my father, Jay
and my mother, Marcia

Manzanita study, September

Tule world: a pair of wood ducks, and a pied-billed grebe in the background

CONTENTS

Chinook salmon. OIL ON PAPER, 4 X 8 1/2 INCHES, 2005

"Each succeeding generation accepts less and less of the real thing because it has no way of understanding what has been lost....each generation doesn't know what it's missing—it's as though eagle and osprey were never present."

—Michael Frome, *Regreening the National Parks*, 1992

"The uniqueness of phylogenetic lineages makes history all-important, and history in turn generates a sense of the sacredness of place and life—not general and abstract but concerned with a single organism in a particular habitat, watched for an explicit span of time."

—Edward O. Wilson, *In Search of Nature*, 1996

Chinook ocean colors. Oil on paper, 3 x 9 inches, 2005

ACKNOWLEDGMENTS

Though there are too many to mention by name, I would like to thank all those experts, naturalists, and specialists who took the time to talk with me about the past and present. Malcolm Margolin has my special thanks for taking on this project, patiently urging me in fruitful directions while sharing a vision of the beauty and wonder of early California. Jeannine Gendar's careful attention has been crucial in steering an overly large mass of material into something more readable and organized, and I have benefited from her knowledge of California history and traditions throughout. Also, huge thanks to my supportive family, who never stopped me from exploring natural history, no matter how many grass stems and animal skulls I brought home to sketch. My sister, Margot, and her husband, Pierre, provided interesting conversations about restoring early California plant and animal communities. And thank you to my husband, Kevin, for his endless encouragement.

Acres of spreading, leafy creeping wildrye cover parts of a Coast Range valley.
Willows and cottonwoods line a stream, valley oaks dot the valley beyond.

OIL ON PANEL, 5 X 6 INCHES, 2003

INTRODUCTION

Broad Valleys, Rolling Hills

"Boulders the size of Volkswagens came down right there," George yelled, motioning with both arms across the canyon. "The noise was so loud, I couldn't hear Rocky talk right next to me."

We stood in the lower part of a desert canyon of the Panamint Mountains, looking out over a stream that came down next to the shack where the two gold miners lived. A lanky man with gray stubble beard, George took his hat off to show us the little gold nugget embedded in glass attached to his hatband. He was proud of how he and his son lived on the mountain and extracted just enough of the shiny mineral from a crawl-hole up-canyon to make a living. Looking around, I could think of no better historical reenactment of 1850s living than their camp with no electricity or running water, but complete with a little garden of squash, corn, and big-leaved tobacco.

"Here, have some," George said, handing me a bag of cured leaves. I didn't smoke but accepted his generosity and took the bag, happy that he was willing to share with us the history of the local land.

I steered the conversation back to the great flood that had wiped out the old road and changed the geography of the canyon twenty years ago.

"Yup, that was a hundred-year flood. We've had to walk up the canyon since the road was taken out," George explained.

Walking up the canyon was my job that summer, on a team led by herpetologist David Morafka to survey for the elusive Panamint alligator lizard, a slim, snakelike reptile that hunts insects in rocky talus slopes and desert stream thickets, only in ranges between the Sierra Nevada and Death Valley. No one knew how common or rare these animals were—few people had seen them. Were they nearly extinct or merely secretive? We hiked up the canyon probably a hundred times, twice a week or more, to turn over stones, search in wild grape and willow thickets, and set live traps. Through the spring high water, into the summer heat and the fall yellowing of the willows and cottonwoods, we saw the subtle seasonal changes.

Up the rocky canyon, past barrel cactus and steep cliffs where bighorn sheep came down to drink, a wonderful gorge of white marble towered over the trail, polished from past floodwaters, where ten-foot-high cascading waterfalls poured over the trail. The place seemed incredibly wild and remote, although someone had recently found an old Shoshone lodge frame of branches still standing in a deep side canyon—people had lived here long before we were born. Old rusted vehicles sat in places in the stream, relicts from a previous era, before the great flood, when folks ascended 6,000 feet to a miners' ghost town. All through the canyon, the water was alive with green moss, maidenhair ferns, flowering stream orchids, pools of Pacific treefrogs and half-dollar-sized water beetles—an oasis in the harsh desert. And we memorized every footstep of it.

All through the summer our work progressed as we recorded notes on plant life, habitat types, rainfall, and water quality, and made a digital photo file of the area. We found our gold: three

Panamint alligator lizards with beautiful cream-and-orange banded bodies and inquisitive amber eyes. But we did not expect what was to come at the end of the season—we would witness how suddenly a landscape can change.

It came in the night. At the time, I lived in park housing on the Death Valley side of the Panamints, in view of the pinyon woodlands covering the mountain. The fiercest September thunderstorm I can remember pounded our roof, sending slurries of water down the street in the otherwise arid, barren badlands. Then it moved on. I went outside to look at it, a dark floating cell like some monstrous being, throwing off tremendous amounts of lightning as it blew slowly across the starry sky over the valley. I watched as it aimed directly for the top of our canyon. Dead on, the lightning illuminated the crags and peaks above our stream.

The next day we drove out to the canyon and could barely believe what we saw. A massive new avalanche of boulders and debris filled the old streambed, carving out the canyon walls, destroying the willows and tall cottonwoods, and spilling out the fan at the base of the canyon. A new channel took out the road to the trailhead (again). Car-sized boulders lay where none had been the week before. Jagged rock-rubble and broken tree trunks lay everywhere in a chaotic mass. The old junk vehicles had been carried a mile down-canyon and dumped by George and Rocky's place. The miners had survived fine, having known to build up on the inside curve terrace of the river channel. The floodwaters had pummeled the outside curve, throwing mud fifty feet up on the cliff.

We all stood around scratching our heads.

"Looks like we got another hundred-year flood," Rocky offered.

Five years later, we returned to the canyon. It had changed again. New willows and cottonwoods had seeded themselves and already grew over our heads. The rocks had settled, some soil had formed, and the stream meandered through lush, green thickets. Even the orchids returned. The treefrogs and water beetles recolonized the devastation, having survived in springs up on the canyonsides. Bighorn sheep sign littered the ground; the animals took advantage of the fresh pioneer vegetation to dine on. Alligator lizards still crawled over the rocks; perhaps a few were swept away by the flood, but most had probably survived.

Rivers and streams have taught me a lot about larger cycles of time, events that take place over decades, changes that can only be seen if you watch for more than a year. Then some of the secrets begin to show themselves to you, slightly, not always clearly. This book is about some of the changes that have shaped California in our own lifetime, but also beyond historical memory, back into deep time.

Historical Ecology

Historical ecology is the study of the history of a landscape and the life-forms that live on it, including ourselves and our experiences. I have approached this work as an artist-naturalist might if she could visit Old California to explore, take notes, sketch, paint, and listen to the stories told about the changing landscape and wildlife.

Although it was speculative, I felt that enough information existed to attempt a reconstruction of the past world of early California. Perhaps it would be best brought back to life through pictures, imperfect as they might be. Our libraries and museums contain so many historical accounts by explorers, pioneers, native people, and naturalists; scholarly studies of fluctuating wildlife populations during the colonization period; ecological research into present California systems; archaeology and paleontology; old photographs of the state on the edge of pristine times;

and magnificent paintings of early landscapes. Surely, I thought, a comprehensive re-creation can be attempted. Bolstered by this thought, since 1980 I have traveled all over the state, tracking the remaining vestiges and relictual pieces of semi-pristine landscapes in order to flesh out the narratives that I found. The clues to the past yet remain, if one is willing to patiently seek them in the field.

Learning from the long line of artists who have sought to study the land and encode its colors, shapes, and moods in paint, I chose the classical techniques of graphite, charcoal, and ink studies, and most especially oil sketching, to bring alive the richness of early California. The technique of oil sketching on paper, board, and canvas was perfected by artists of the eighteenth, nineteenth, and twentieth centuries on their explorations of wild lands and country lanes.

French painters traveled out of the city early on: Pierre-Henri de Valenciennes left the first text on the serious study of open-air painting in 1820. He wrote that the essentials of landscape painting include "invention," the ability to imagine a subject; "composition"— the grace, harmony, and "timing-rhythm" of a painting—which he said depends on learning; and "execution," employing colors well, also dependent on practice.[1] Valenciennes was a member of two scientific societies, and he stressed the importance of studying nature to his students—the importance of understanding geology, the weather, how rivers and trees move and grow. To him the oil study was a kind of scientific specimen collected, a record of a phenomenon.[2]

California grizzly in summer-gold blue oak savanna

Out of these methods came American painters who took their paint boxes into what they described as the "wilderness" of North America: Frederic Church, Albert Bierstadt, Worthington Whittredge, Thomas Moran, and many others now known as the Hudson River School. Sometimes accompanying survey parties or scientific expeditions, at other times mounting their own trips to paint out of doors during the summer months, these artists recorded scenes that were highly developed in beauty and accurate observation of elements of the natural world. I found no better teachers of art than their canvases.

I modeled my researches on their examples: I carried a paint box and traveled through California as an artist-naturalist. Like them, I endeavored to spend hours sketching in the wild. These field studies were by far the most crucial part of this project. I have made expeditions to locate, observe, and sketch declining species, such as the sea otter and least Bell's vireo. If a species, such as the grizzly, is best studied outside of California, I have made an effort to travel to those last areas where they still roam wild. I have also spent much time studying relict habitats and populations of particular plants, such as native grasses and vernal pool endemics.

Sunset view in November, a thousand years ago, looking west from the Berkeley Hills across the glinting stems of purple needlegrass bunches and the San Francisco Bay, toward Mount Tamalpais on the right and the Golden Gate on the left. El Cerrito and Albany Hill lie below the ridge on the left. OIL ON COTTON RAG PAPER, 9 ¾ x 13 ¾ INCHES, 1997

Back in the studio I took the notes, photos, sketches, and color studies that I gathered on my travels and reconstructed larger, more refined scenes of Old California landscapes and wildlife as a method for visualizing the changes that have swept over our state. Paintings of past landscapes and wildlife can be thought of as interpretations of raw data, enhanced by specific observations and general laws of ecological and cultural processes. They are possibilities, subject to change with new information.

In writing this book, however, the limitations of size quickly became apparent, and my original aim at a comprehensive, encyclopedic work on California's early natural history had to be modified toward a presentation of a few examples for each chapter, "teasers" to the topic. I chose stories which I thought best explained the state's wonderful and sometimes unfamiliar landscapes and the processes that shape them. And I concentrated on California's core geography and habitats of the west-central and southern parts of the state. As much as I would have liked to include the desert, the Owens Valley, more of the Sierra Nevada, the sagebrush basins and Cascades, the redwood country and northern California woodlands, I had to limit this study. Much more could be told.

As I dove deeper into the richness of California landscapes, what struck me most were not the individual animals and plants, nor even the vision of cityscapes erased back to natural habitats, but the processes that affect the world, including us. Things such as fire, climate change, disturbance, and species interactions. Things that ecologists are wrestling with, trying to study and define. Things that Native Californians have understood for countless generations. Look for these ecological processes through each chapter.

The wonderful aspect of discovering old landscapes is that anyone can do it. You do not have to have a Ph.D., simply good powers of observation and a lot of curiosity. I describe activities throughout the book for the landscape detective, and the beneficial side effects include getting us closer to the land itself.

The term "pristine" is used here in the rather arbitrary sense of the time before massive European colonization during the eighteenth and nineteenth centuries. California's environments have always been in a state of flux, due to climatic and geologic events, and were for thousands of years managed by Native peoples. But the distinction is useful. Standing in the middle of a valley or on a mountain, seemingly unaffected by modern civilization, I have often been struck by how unrecognizable the landscape would be when compared to an early description of the same spot. The lack of animals that were once called abundant, the new weedy plants, even the lowered water tables all call attention to profound changes that mark a major discontinuity in the long flow of California's ecology. One can speculate that in some important respects, the natural world of the state during the fifteenth century, say, was more similar to a time one hundred thousand years ago than it is to the modern world. Fossil fuel burning, pesticides and herbicides, pavement and asphalt, dumped pollutants, and greatly lowered biodiversity are novel in geologic history.

A few years ago at an art show in San Francisco a man walked up to one of my paintings showing the city as it might have appeared four hundred years ago with prairie and elk sign. He silently studied the piece, then looked at me and asked, "Why do you want to go back to this? Isn't our civilization good enough?"

He had assumed I hated the twenty-first century, with its technology and fast pace. I am occasionally annoyed by it, but he was wrong.

I did not advocate returning to this lost world wholesale, I told him, but recognizing it, studying it as a part of our heritage, a prehistory that has helped shape the California myth: rolling, bright yellow hills, sun-drenched poppy fields, sapphire blue skies, great forests that awed the world, glacial valleys, and of course, the golden bear. Knowing some of the ways in which older, healthier ecosystems operated can surely aid us in making our present land more habitable. I tried to explain to the man that I simply enjoy history: the Old World has its Roman ruins to look back on in awe; Californians have a natural legacy of equal interest, much of it similarly in ruins, awaiting careful students to gaze upon it, get closer to it, imagine it, restore it to beauty.

As we walk through the hills and valleys of California to see what secrets we might be able to uncover about the past, and the future, what we will see is that change is always happening. Change is the most natural part of our landscape, and change is what we must embrace and learn to live with, for our future California landscape will be swept along in its continuing currents.

A Note about Names

Most plant scientific names follow *The Jepson Manual of Higher Plants of California*. Bird names are taken from the National Audubon Society's *The Sibley Guide to Birds*. No single standard exists for invertebrate, amphibian, reptile, or mammal names, and thus these follow several recent authors. (See Appendix for a list of scientific names for species in this book.)

ONE

GOLDEN BEAR

Back in Time

To gain some sort of insight into how Old California "felt," I camped for several weeks in Yellowstone National Park, a place where bears of all sorts still behave in a seminatural way, a place where I could sketch them in the field—at a respectful distance, with a spotting scope—and watch them interact with the wide landscape.

I was lucky enough to watch many bears for days on end, albeit as dots from the roadside, and I admit to being on edge when hiking out into their realm, for grizzlies can be dangerous. They seem to think of us as flimsy bear cousins that might be invading their optimum feeding spots. And when bears have a territorial tiff, they stand ten feet tall and bite their opponents' furry cheek ruffs, with audible tooth clashes and roars echoing across valleys—humans do not fare well in this situation.

So I gave them my respect and refrained from leaving my picnic strewn about, and soon their fascinating behavior opened up to me.

Back in California, where only the ghosts of grizzlies roam, I visited the shopping mall near my childhood home in the East Bay. Decades had passed since I visited the place. Everything had changed, I saw, as I walked between ornamental parking lot islands and new café franchises, dress-for-less stores, and pet supply centers, all built in a style that might be called desert Tuscan. I stood on ground I had walked on as a child, the parking lot where I had learned to drive, and yet only the view of Albany Hill and the bayshore remained somewhat similar to my memories.

A grizzly, long ago, wanders the blue oak and feathergrass hills of the South Coast Range. OIL ON PAPER, 10 X 7 INCHES, 1997

I had always been fascinated by the floras and faunas of past epochs, evolving landforms, and what the gathered fossils of a place might reveal. Not so long ago, strange animals had wandered the shores of this landscape and communities had thrived that we, using the slim evidence remaining, can only speculate about. I contemplated the possibility of grizzly bears digging tubers in this plaza ground—difficult to imagine. But paleontology was my hobby and chosen topic of study, and paleoart would help me imagine these past environments and journey back in time, to try to learn from the past.

At the nursery where my sister Margot works, I talked with a volunteer who was busy potting seedlings.

"All the shopping plazas look alike now," I commented.

Gordon responded, "Yeah, and I remember playing in El Cerrito Plaza when it was all fields."

This was the mall I had just revisited. I was caught by surprise as I found a living link to the history of a place I had only known as blacktop.

He told us stories of how, as a boy in the 1940s, he had collected frogs and stickleback fish in the creek that ran through the fields and taken them home in jars. "The creek was loaded with pollywogs back then," he said.

I was amazed—I could actually interact with an extinct landscape through this man's memories. I asked him questions.

"Were there any wildflowers in the fields?"

"Well," he answered, "I was just a kid, and I didn't know botany, of course. But there were oaks, big oaks."

He described tall, shapely oaks that he thought were valley oaks, as well as coast live oaks hung with lichens, and arroyo willows lining the creek. A low, swampy spot existed towards the bay nearby. Margot and I listened to the only oral history we had ever heard of the area.

"They started to build the old mall in the 1950s—built the parking lot right up to the old creek."

Armed with this newfound knowledge of the local plaza, I was determined to dig deeper into the past. I went back and "field walked" the area as an archaeologist would, looking for artifacts. Sure enough, there were relicts. An old, spreading live oak grew out of the courtyard of a dentist's office; the creek still ran there, out of a pipe now, with houses on the other bank and English ivy lining my side. A few willows held onto their dirt-bank existence. I even found sticklebacks in a pool farther west, near the bayshore, freeways arching overhead.

The next phase was to search for empty lots in the surrounding suburbs. Within a mile of the plaza I found relict native plants in weedy squares of property between homes: California poppies, a small lupine, and bunches of native California oatgrass. A valley oak, rare on the coast, towered out of a backyard residence to the south, in Berkeley. Old photographs in the library showed that the area was once a nearly treeless grassland.

Back at the plaza, wading through rows of parked cars, I found a plaque along San Pablo Avenue, placed by the Oakland Junior Chamber of Commerce and the Boy Scouts of America in 1937, that read, "This monument marks the southern boundary of the Rancho San Pablo; 17,938 acres granted by Governor Jose Figueroa to Don Francisco Maria Castro, June 12, 1834." This was the only onsite clue to a further layer of history, beyond the reach of oral history or photographs now. A small adobe house still stands about three miles to the north, eroded brown bricks and wooden beams surrounded by fast-food restaurants. I tried to imagine herds of horned Spanish cattle spread out over the hills and flats, and fine horsemen galloping out to hunt or lasso stock on the wide grasslands by the little hill here.

Documentary evidence became necessary now to reconstruct these deeper layers of time. Father Juan Crespí's diary of the Fages exploratory expedition up California in 1772 described, on March 27 and 28, how the Spanish walked along a grassy plain of the East Bay, crossing many arroyos emptying into the estuary. The hills to the east were treeless and grass-covered. Lilies and an abundance of "very leafy sweet marjorum" grew on the plain. Was this hedge nettle? They killed

The site of El Cerrito Plaza, five hundred years ago. Grizzlies gather around a coast live oak to eat acorns. "Bear diggings" can be seen in the foreground, where grizzlies have been digging for ground squirrels and gophers. The dusk light silhouettes Albany Hill and reflects on the bay. Stems of California oatgrass bend in the grassland.   OIL ON COTTON RAG PAPER, 7½ X 8 INCHES, 2005

a grizzly at Strawberry Creek (in present Berkeley) and must have passed within a mile of El Cerrito Plaza.[1]

To the north the explorers encountered a village of Indians on the bank of Wildcat Creek, near San Pablo Bay. Bedrock mortars in several small ravines in the nearby hills attested to acorn gathering and pounding activities that took place in small live oak groves in some past era.

But local histories state that grizzlies were particularly numerous in the El Cerrito–Berkeley area; names of nearby places, such as Grizzly Peak and Bear Creek, back up this assertion. Three or four hundred years ago, bears might be uppermost in my mind if I could walk across the field that once occupied the parking lot—I might see well-worn bear trails across the bunchgrass flat, leading to a massive oak where bears would gorge on acorns. The oak trunk might be rubbed by bears, and I would find rounded, sunken areas in the wildrye under the willows along the creek, day beds for bears escaping the midday sun. Settlers in Orange County described finding claw marks on alder and maple trunks years after grizzlies were gone from the region, and worn trails winding through the brush of canyons.[2] Now, all hints that grizzlies once dominated the El Cerrito landscape have been erased. Picturing large bears around the neighborhood was difficult, and I wished to know more about this hidden world beyond living memory.

Big Bears

The largest bears in the lower forty-eight states were found in California until just after 1900. Jim Sleeper, who grew up in southern California at Santa Ana, said the average size of grizzlies there was around six hundred pounds.[3] But a mammoth male bear came out of San Onofre Canyon, in the low, coastal Santa Ana Range, that weighed in at fourteen hundred pounds, larger even than the great buffalo-killing grizzlies of the Plains states and equaled only by the largest Kenai Peninsula brown bears of Alaska.[4] Females were often half the bulk of these giants. And there were tales of even larger bears: in 1873 John Lang shot the animal the locals called "the California King" in Soledad Canyon, on the north flank of the San Gabriel Mountains. "One of the grizzliest grizzlies ever seen on the coast," it was said to tip the scales at an incredible twenty-two hundred pounds, and its feet were sixteen and a half inches long. One San Diego County bear brought down with several shots was "bigger than a Durham bull"; two horses were needed to turn it over, and it measured seven feet from nose to tail and was estimated to have stood nine and a half feet tall. Super-sized California grizzlies also came from the Santa Rosa Mountains, San Jacinto Mountains, and Cuyamaca Mountains, all in southern California. Hunters claimed to have found equally gargantuan bears as far north as Monterey and Hollister, in the South Coast Ranges.[5]

Grizzlies were somewhat smaller in the North Coast Ranges and Sacramento Valley, and the smallest specimens came from the lower slope of the southern Sierra Nevada in Kern County.[6]

California grizzly pelage color was quite varied, from gray to brown, yellowish, red, silvery, or white-patched, and often with multicolored long hairs or "grizzled" whitish tips. Bears could sport uniform tones or patterns, such as a dark dorsal stripe, light-tipped side bands, and black legs and underparts.[7] Several Santa Ana grizzlies were black with whitish faces and necks.[8] Such was the color variety of these bears that they earned any number of descriptive names, such as cinnamon bear, silver-tip, gray bear, brown bear, little black bear, and oso gris—grizzled bear.[9]

During my "bear-watching" seasons at Yellowstone National Park, I sat on roadsides with a like-minded international group gathered to spot bears and other wildlife in one of the few places left where a nearly complete ecosystem full of Holocene megafauna still exists, interacting as they once did in California. We were gratified to see grizzlies often, and I sketched bears of brown-coppery hues with light sheens on their midsections, huge dark brown males with potbellies, and even blonde bears.

Distribution and Abundance

So pervasive was the golden bear in Old California that it earned a place on the state flag. Southern California historian Jim Sleeper wrote, "He was the one creature in the range which every gulch, hogback, peak and potrero at some time shared in common."[10] Naturalists Tracy Storer and L. Tevis found records of grizzlies across the state in nearly every habitat, except deep in the Mojave and Colorado Deserts.[11]

Grizzlies were found on the west slope of the Sierra Nevada, even to the summits—one was killed around 1902 at 10,000 feet, near Carson Pass, Amador County.[12] They lived abundantly in southern California, across the grassy plains and valleys, the sycamore-lined creeks, the sweet-smelling sage ridges, and the boulder gorges. Cahuilla people near Palm Springs and Indian Wells reported that grizzlies sometimes wandered to the western edge of the Colorado Desert.[13] But gradually, hunting pressures pushed the southern California bears into the backcountry mountains, into open pine forests and chaparral.[14]

Prior to 1850 the bears were numerous in the Sacramento Valley, roaming the tule marshes, slough edges, and great riparian woodlands of willow and cottonwood. In the Napa Valley area in 1831, a settler said bears were everywhere on the valley floors and in the ranges, and as many as sixty could be seen in a twenty-four-hour period.[15] They hunted the brush and deep coast live oak woodlands of the San Francisco Bay Area, and they also lived in arid grasslands, such as Corral Hollow, in the Interior Coast Range hills of Alameda County.[16] "Herds" of bears were reported on the coastal prairies of the San Francisco peninsula. A grizzly was found swimming to Angel Island in the San Francisco Estuary in 1827.[17] In the 1860s settler Jonathan Watson once saw three hundred grizzlies in a single valley in the Santa Cruz Mountains.[18]

The Food Quest

The bounteous acorn crop provided by the abundant and diverse oaks around the state surely helped to account for the large numbers of huge bears. John Xantus, a medic stationed at Fort Tejon, in the Tehachapi Mountains, described the glens of valley oaks there as "great rendezvous" spots for grizzlies seeking ripe acorns.[19] In 1840 at Cholame Valley, in the South Coast Range, eighteen grizzlies were seen eating acorns under the oaks in one fall afternoon.[20] Though large adult grizzlies cannot climb well, old-timers watched them nevertheless get up into the bowed and twisted giant limbs in their efforts to reach acorns. Homesteader S. T. Miller, near Irvine in 1874, described them:

> Every fall...for a while after I went to the Bell Canyon Place, bears used to come down into the oaks in Crow Canyon....They would climbe the oaks and feed on the acorns.... The bears were so heavy that in climbing to the topmost limbs they'd break out the tops. I have seen lots of oaks broken.[21]

Young bears climbed well and went up into the acorn-laden branches to shake and break the twigs and relieve them of their bounty.[22] In good pine-nut years in the Rocky Mountains, grizzlies can gain more than three pounds per day as they gobble up this rich food[23]—I can imagine California grizzlies gaining much weight in good acorn years.

Grizzlies in the past must have commonly fished for river salmon, probably most often on spawning reaches and waterfalls or rapids where migrating salmon were vulnerable. For instance, bears were said to come down at night to San Jose–area streams, such as Stevens Creek, when the salmon and steelhead ran.[24] Grizzlies were occasionally seen fishing for steelhead in south coastal streams, such as at Trabuco Canyon.[25] Other early observers saw grizzlies scavenging for fish along coastal shores, and even using their paws to catch live marine fish.[26]

The complex interconnections of the various life-forms and processes of a given piece of land fascinate me, and I have pondered how the recent changes to California have affected this bear-fish network. In the forests of the Pacific Northwest, where salmon abound and bears still feed on them, researchers have noticed interesting links between the ocean nutrients contained in salmon bodies and forest growth. Bears swiping up salmon usually carry off the larger fish as far as two hundred yards into the forest to feed, avoiding such competitive scavengers as gulls, ravens, and eagles. The bears often do not finish the carcass, preferring the fattest flesh and especially the eggs of females. The fish remains gradually decay into the forest floor, adding nitrogen and other nutrients that increase vegetative growth, and allow streamside trees to grow faster and larger than trees away from the streams, or on streams where salmon have been extirpated. The tree rings of salmon-fertilized trees are thicker after good fish-run years, although with a delay of one to three years. As much as half the nitrogen in these rings was found to come from salmon. In addition, bears deposit scat and urine, also rich in nitrogen, in the vicinity of salmon streams, cycling ocean nutrients far into the mountains. On the Columbia River bears eat salmon—up to 58 percent of their diet—even eight hundred miles inland. Grizzlies have been shown to grow larger and have more cubs per litter when living around salmon streams. After finding these links, researcher Thomas E. Reimchen observed that there is really no such thing as surplus, that everything is used—food for thought about Old California ecosystems.[27]

Russian explorer Otto von Kotzebue, traveling up the Sacramento River in the 1820s, witnessed a predatory grizzly trying to catch a deer for dinner:

> In the night we were much disturbed by bears, which pursued the deer quite close to our tents; and by the clear moonlight we plainly saw a stag spring into the river to escape the bear; the latter, however, jumped after him, and both swam down the stream till they were out of sight.[28]

In the past grizzlies were known to follow the buffalo herds of the Great Plains, and today they will follow caribou along parts of their migrations, looking for on opportunity to make a kill or scavenge a carcass after an accident or a wolf predation; undoubtedly grizzlies also interacted with the large elk herds in California's grasslands and savannas, although the swift-footed elk could usually outrun the big bears easily.

It would be more profitable for the grizzlies to scent out baby elk on their traditional calving grounds. In June our group watched a grizzly in Yellowstone zigzag across a valley flat, trying to scent out elk calves hiding low in the grass while their mothers grazed. Nearby elk cows, with

*A huge southern California bear wanders through the foothills above the San Fernando Valley five hundred years ago.
The slopes are covered with giant needlegrass, one-sided bluegrass, prickly pear, California buckwheat and other flowering
buckwheats, black sage, and lemonadeberry.* OIL ON PANEL, 12 X 24 INCHES, 2005

heads high, watched the bear's busy meanderings. We were sure the grizzly would suddenly pounce on a calf, but it failed to find one. It walked away into a ravine and turned over logs and searched among serviceberry bushes, the cows still watching it. Another bear succeeded in finding an elk calf hunkered down, killed it, and dragged it a quarter-mile to a boulder pile, where it ate the calf, then rested and guarded the carcass from scavengers.

Bears may test a group of elk and calves by loping towards them and rushing in if a calf is slow to run. The bear's front claws are "exceedingly long, strongly curved"—two to six inches or more—though often worn down from digging.[29] But big ungulates have the wherewithal to defend themselves: elk bulls have been known to gore grizzlies with their sharp antlers. And visitors at Yellowstone told me they had seen a group of bison surrounding an elk calf, not allowing even its mother to approach it; a grizzly lingered at the edge of the nearby forest, unwilling to brave the horned adult herd guarding his prey. The grizzly left, and the bison then wandered off, allowing the elk cow to reunite with her calf. I was amazed to hear that the bison applied their protective behavior toward the young of another species.

Back in Old California, grizzlies also chased livestock, raiding cattle at places like Half Moon Bay and Santa Cruz. Sometimes a bear was seen to roll about on the ground to attract curious cattle, which circled the strange sight—then the grizzly jumped out, grabbed a young bull, and whacked it on the back with a paw, breaking its back and bringing it down. (This was a common story among cowboys in California, and the amount of truth in its telling is up for debate.) These amazingly powerful animals showed their strength, as when a four-hundred-and-fifty-pound sow bear was reported to have dragged a two-hundred-pound heifer for three miles across jagged rocks, over fallen logs, and up a narrow trail on a steep mountain in Monterey County.[30] One grizzly snatched a three-hundred-pound hog from its pen on Ben Lomond Mountain.[31]

Today grizzlies in Alaska often dig for ground squirrels. Big "piano-sized" holes dot slopes as the bears pursue the rodents.[32] The abundant California ground squirrel probably provided bears with much prey in the grasslands at all times of year. Perhaps grizzlies, as well as wolves, coyotes, foxes, and eagles, kept ground squirrels in check during the early days, not allowing them to

ATTACKING BULL ELK: JUMPING ON ELK'S BACK WITH A SLAM, BRINGING IT DOWN WITH ITS WEIGHT.

Field sketches

overpopulate and eat themselves out of plant food. Biologist Adolph Murie found that this could be the case for Arctic ground squirrels.[33]

Grizzlies also chase voles through their grassy haunts, and pocket gopher hunting is revealed by signs of the bears' widespread digging and scraping. All these rodents probably provided valuable food for the California grizzly.

Carrion is a perennial favorite. One early morning at Yellowstone, our bear-watching group noticed a huge male grizzly walking through a valley floor, its nose constantly to the ground. We moved up the hill, closer to our parked cars, to give him plenty of room. As we watched with binoculars and spotting scopes, one of our group suggested the bear was scenting out female bears in estrus. But the bear suddenly stopped, having found a winter-killed elk carcass hidden in a sagebrush clump. He chewed at it, his head and shoulder hump bobbing above the sagebrush; then he moved off, continuing to sniff the ground.

I talked with biologist Ryan Young, who works with sniffer dogs, and his observations gave me a possible glimpse of the world of the bear: Ryan noticed that scent moves like a liquid along the ground. He watched the dogs follow the scent as it whirled into eddies behind bushes. Early in the morning the scent pooled up in depressions until a breeze blew it out and it flowed out across the ground. I could imagine bears, with their exquisite sense of smell, following these "streams."

As the early Spanish explorer Vizcaíno saw in Monterey in 1602, grizzlies scavenged beached whales: they came at night to feed on the carcass of a very large whale. William Brewer, botanist for the California Geological Survey in the 1860s, found at Monterey "a whale...stranded on the beach, and the tracks of grizzlies were thick about it."[34]

The great bears were also said to steal prey killed by mountain lions and jaguars around Fort Tejon.[35] Wolf kills are often visited by grizzlies today in areas where the two share ranges (see chapter eleven)—in 1968 a total of twenty-three grizzlies were seen at a single bison carcass in the Yellowstone area.[36]

California bears probably ate grasshoppers, ants, moths, and insect larvae such as wood-boring beetle grubs, tearing apart logs in their search for these morsels.

Besides acorns, grizzlies are known to eat an extremely wide variety of plant foods, and evidence from the past indicates California bears were no different.

Botanist Willis Jepson referred to purple needlegrass as "beargrass" in his early botanical guide to California,[37] perhaps indicating that this common bunchgrass was eaten by grizzlies—it would be most palatable in the early spring. Grizzlies today graze the green leaves of grasses in Wyoming and

Field notes: "Grizzly bear in 'beargrass'—purple needlegrass"

Hundreds of years ago on a bay mudflat, bears feast on a gray whale carcass. Seabirds flock to join in: ring-billed gulls, herring gulls, California gulls, Thayer's gulls, glaucous-winged gulls, western gulls, and a bald eagle.
ACRYLIC ON PAPER, 11 X 17 INCHES, 1988

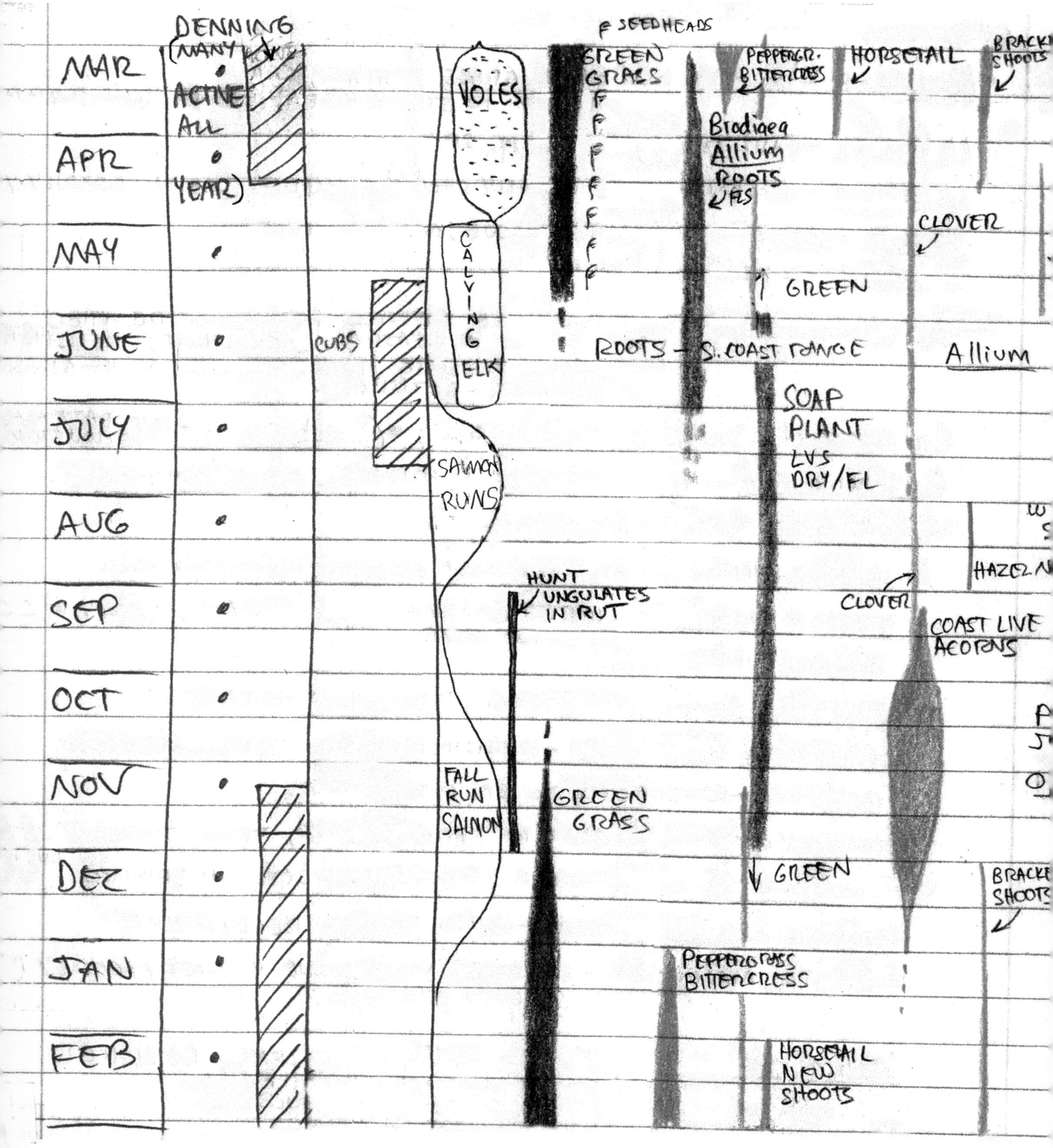

DENNING
(MANY

@ SEEDHEADS

MAR — ACTIVE ALL — VOLES — GREEN GRASS — F — PEPPERGR. BITTERCRESS — HORSETAIL — BRACKEN SHOOTS

APR — • YEAR) — Brodiaea Allium ROOTS FLS

MAY — • — CALVING ELK — CLOVER — GREEN

JUNE — • — CUBS — ROOTS - S. COAST RANGE — Allium

JULY — • — SALMON — SOAP PLANT LVS DRY/FL

AUG — • — RUNS — HAZEL N

SEP — • — HUNT UNGULATES IN RUT — CLOVER — COAST LIVE ACORNS

OCT — • — P J O

NOV — • — FALL RUN SALMON — GREEN GRASS

DEC — • — GREEN — BRACKEN SHOOTS

JAN — • — PEPPERGRASS BITTERCRESS

FEB — • — HORSETAIL NEW SHOOTS

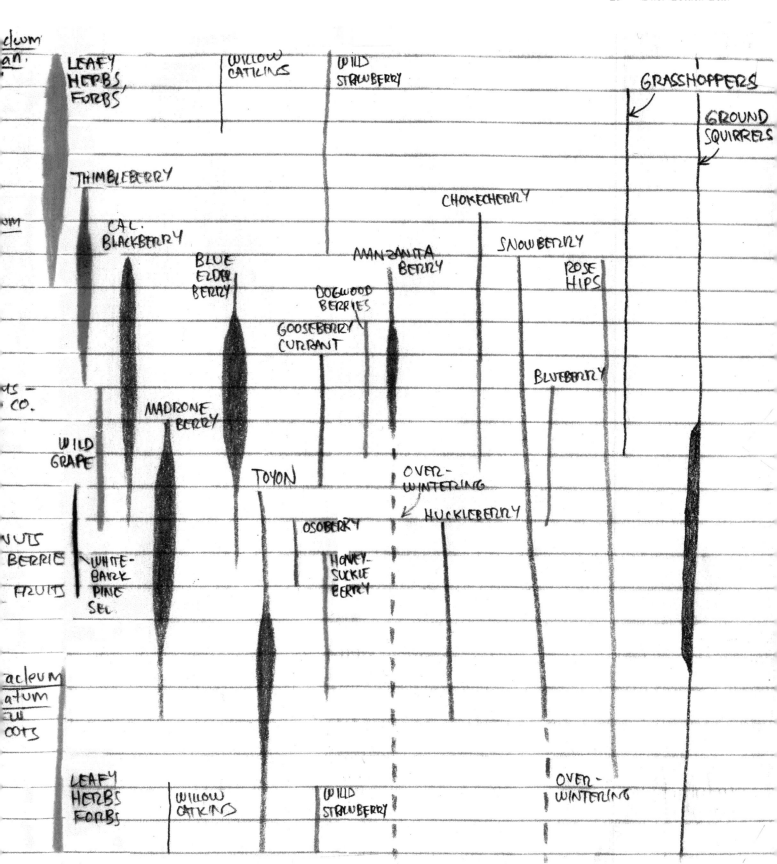

Hypothetical central California grizzly food calendar

Montana, including brome grass, bluegrass, and Idaho fescue. They also eat sedges and rushes. In fact, in Yellowstone National Park green grasses and sedges were found to be dietary staples of the grizzly,[38] and the bears can look like grazing cattle. Groups of bears in California's past might have congregated on burns to feed on new plant growth.

Grizzlies were very fond of fresh, green clover leaves and flowers growing in grassy areas, according to many early reports. In the Sacramento Valley in spring and early summer, bears were reported to come out of the hills and river thickets to graze on green clover "like herds of swine."[39]

Studies of living bears in the various parts of North America where they still roam indicate that grizzlies probably ate dozens of other wild greens. Just a few examples could be listed to show the huge range of bear food—the soft lettuce-like miner's lettuce, or claytonia, as well as yellowcarrot, thistles, willow herb, peppergrass, owl's clover, and native dandelion. I can picture myself hiking down a narrow trail in the past in what is now Tilden Regional Park, in the East Bay, and running into a large grizzly breaking down stalks of cow parsnip, crunching on the juicy stems—and I would have to reverse my course.

The Spanish explorer Pedro Fages, a few miles west of San Luis Obispo in the summer of 1769, noted: "In this canyon were seen whole troops of bears; they have the ground all plowed up from digging in it to find their sustenance in the roots which the land produces."[40] Roots and bulbs are an abundant, high-quality food source in the state, and grizzlies took advantage of this. They could dig up various species of the lily family with their long front claws: Mariposa lilies, wild onions, brodiaeas, and perhaps soap plant bulbs.

Exploring the grassy Inner Coast Range hills on the western edge of the San Joaquin Valley in Stanislaus County, William Brewer in 1862 found grizzly tracks in "exceeding abundance," as he wandered about on moonlit nights near his camp. On Mount Oso he found the whole summit dug over by bears for roots, and the trees scratched and broken.[41]

On the south coastal plains and hills, around Pasadena for example, bears may have fed on beavertail cactus fruits in fall.

Bears will travel miles to dine on huckleberries or similar delights, and in California the berry crops are diverse, most likely attracting bears in the past to the oak woodlands, redwood forests, and shrublands to feed on rose hips, osoberries—"bear berry" in Spanish—thimbleberries, blackberries, salmonberries, snowberries, wild strawberries, huckleberries, madrone berries, choke-cherries, serviceberries, dogwood berries, gooseberries, and currants. Nearly every season had its berries—elderberries and wild grape thickets probably attracted bears in the summer, and in winter they could feast on the berries of manzanita and toyon.

The bear biologists John Craighead, Jay Sumner, and John Mitchell, studying bears in the Yellowstone region, described important sites on the landscape they called "ecocenters," where large amounts of dependable, high-quality food were located seasonally.[42] Grizzlies congregated at these spots, sometimes to over one hundred individuals, and regular trails might radiate out like spokes on a wagon wheel as bears traveled in from distant surroundings. I am tempted to think Old California had many such ecocenters: berry patches, oak groves, salmon rivers, coastlines where whale carcasses were likely to turn up. The rich diversity of available food partly explains the presence of so many grizzlies, although many of the foods, such as acorn crops and rodent populations, would vary in quantity from year to year, keeping the bears on the move over large ranges.

Some Old Bear Behavior

All this abundance of food may also explain why many grizzlies in California did not hibernate like their Rocky Mountain cousins. The mast-rich California woodlands could keep bears feeding all winter; where acorns and beechnuts are common in eastern North America, black bears will forgo denning as well.[43] Famous trapper Grizzly Adams saw bears through the winter in the central Sierra below 5,000 feet.[44] In Orange County grizzlies were sighted in every month of the year.[45]

Dens of grizzlies that did hibernate, or dens of sow bears with cubs, occurred in such sites as natural caves, boulder-formed hollows, or dug-out holes, often in thick chaparral. In the San Joaquin Valley bears dug burrows four feet in diameter, acting like giant ground squirrels.[46]

The signs of these huge beasts would be evident to a hiker two hundred years ago: trails were common along streams, leading to oak groves from thickets, and all over the chaparral. Some paths were worn down five to six inches deep into the ground surface. The bears would often place their steps into the same spot each time they passed, creating a series of pits in the trail.[47] Tubes through dense chaparral may have been formed as the grizzlies passed under the canopies of taller shrubs.

Grizzlies seem to enjoy rubbing their hides on rocks and trees, and claw scratches and bite marks may also serve as communication points for the bear population. In California claw scratches and rub marks were seen on pine and manzanita trunks and downed logs;[48] undoubtedly oaks were much used. Some places where bears rub their hides become smooth and worn from centuries of use.[49]

California grizzly females were observed to have from one to three cubs, two usually, which corresponds to what is observed today at Yellowstone. When breeding coincides with ecocenter groupings, mating occurs at these sites; if not, the bears breed as isolated, dispersed individuals.[50]

Knowledge of the interactions of different animal species on the landscape can be as important in reconstructing the past as individual species accounts. While watching wildlife in Yellowstone National Park, I saw a coyote following a mother grizzly who was feeding on a grassy slope with her two cubs. Perhaps the coyote was hoping they would disturb a rodent out of its burrow. The sow took a few steps toward the coyote to chase it off. It was like a vignette from Old California.

Where the smaller black bears dwelled side by side with grizzlies, as in the Yosemite area of the Sierra Nevada, hunters observed that black bears deferred to grizzlies on carcasses.[51] An ecological "release" may have happened to black bears after the extirpation of their larger cousins, as in the Tehachapi Mountains, where no black bears were reported until after the disappearance of the dominant grizzly.[52] In the 1960s and 1970s, with grizzlies no longer ranging there, black bear numbers were observed to have increases in the southern California ranges.[53]

Jim Sleeper said, of the Santa Ana Mountains of Orange and San Diego Counties, that Indians avoided canyons with dense grizzly concentrations when establishing villages. People and bears must have been in competition for food at acorn trees, hazelnut thickets, and good root areas, but many tribes also hunted grizzlies. The Hupa called the grizzly "Great Big Brown,"[54] and this reminds me of the parallel in the English language: the words "bear" and "bruin" come from an old Indo-European root meaning "brown," a word of respect Eurasian hunters once used so as not to offend the animal— people and bears have an ancient connection in the Northern Hemisphere.

Bear biologist Barrie Gilbert, however, thinks the "demonic" reputation of grizzlies as unpredictable and dangerous is undeserved: working with the bears for decades and studying historic accounts such as those of the Lewis and Clark expedition, he believes Indians and grizzlies coexisted well

for thousands of years.[55] Bear attacks may have been, more often than not, defensive behavior by hunted or provoked bears.

The End of the Bear

"Suddenly we heard a crackling of brush and a puffing, angry sound like the blowing of a frightened hog, not fifty yards away, and we knew the bear had scented us."[56] William Brewer noted that the California grizzly generally left men alone if not bothered or shot at. But as one might guess from the dramatic description from an 1859 hunting party quoted here, this was not to be.

Mexican rancheros usually slaughtered cattle on the *matanza* grounds out on the range, taking the hides and fat and leaving much of the meat—a boon to the carrion-seeking grizzlies. The *matanzas* probably became new ecocenters, attracting bears from long distances. But not all was easy for the bruins. Vaqueros took sport in chasing and lassoing bears, transporting them back to the corrals to face a well-chosen wild bull in battle.

RUBBING BACK ON TREE

For a year I lived in the town of Corralitos, east of Santa Cruz, so named for the "little corral" used for bear-and-bull fights during California's Mexican era. Looking out over the rural, peaceful horse fields and housing developments, I could barely visualize a bear hunt: soldiers and gentlemen armed with riatas would ride out from the rancho on gennet horses, lasso a grizzly up in Loma Prieta by the paws and neck, muzzle it, and drag it back to the bull pit to celebrate Easter or some special occasion, such as the inauguration of the governor. The bear's leg would be tied to a pole, or to the leg of the bull, and a fight would erupt. Sometimes the long-horned bull would win, goring the bear. But another time, the bear would swing a mighty paw and knock the bull off its feet, killing it. See Ray Chapin's *The Grizzly Bear in the Land of the Ohlone Indians* for eyewitness descriptions from this time in history.[57]

The California legislature outlawed bear-and-bull fights in 1854, "to prevent noisy or barbarous amusements on the Sabbath."[58] By then American settlers had been pushing into the fertile valleys, forcing most bears into the mountains and remote hills. But grizzlies continued to raid farms and ranches for honey, corn, and domestic sheep and calves.

Grizzlies quickly gained individual names and fame: "White

Face," "Moccasin John," who lost his claws in a trap, "Baldy," and "Old Clubfoot," who raided bee farms in Orange County. Folk tradition often gave this last name to bears who had wrenched a foot out of a trap. The largest bear killed in the Santa Ana Mountains was simply known as "The Big Bear."[59]

"Market hunters" in southern and central California concentrated on quail, geese, ducks, and deer to supply markets, but in the late 1870s they turned to grizzlies. Bear meat was considered a tasty offering in San Francisco and was shipped from ports as far away as San Diego. Dried bear meat was equally profitable to supply to gold miners, and so "jerky hunters" helped reduce the bear population in the last decades of the nineteenth century. Bear hides were often sold Back East, and gall bladders to Chinese immigrants. An Oakland resident noticed bears were rare in the Diablo Range, from hunting, as early as 1857.[60] "They are scarcer now," said Colin Preston, a San Luis Obispo hunter, in an 1857 interview. "When I came here first we saw them every day. Now we ride sometimes fifty miles to find a bear." He claimed to have killed seventy large bears and one hundred and forty smaller ones in ten years.[61] Many bears were poisoned with strychnine and trapped by stockmen. In the Santa Cruz Mountains, grizzlies held out into the 1880s, then were gone.[62] By 1888 grizzly numbers had declined noticeably in the Santa Ana stronghold, and by 1898 bears were considered "shot out," though isolated reports of grizzlies continued there until 1913.[63]

Possibly the last California grizzly strongholds were the rugged canyons and tall ridges of the southern Sierra, where a few bears were sighted and shot in the 1920s, and the remote wilderness of what is now the Los Padres National Forest in the South Coast Range. When I visited these still-remote places I couldn't help but imagine large bear tracks in the mud of a streambank, a tuft of long multicolored fur caught in a gooseberry thorn, clawed-up diggings in a meadow, or a distant dot moving along a grassy ridge—the ghost of a California grizzly now beyond our living memory.

DIGGING UP
GROUND SQUIRREL

TWO

MYSTERIES
OF TIME AND CLIMATE

Seeing the Big Cycles

When I traveled back in time to imagine the lives of California grizzlies, I realized that the period we live in is a sliver from a giant block of time in continuous flux. According to archaeological and paleontological remains and eyewitness records, the landscape is always changing, animal and plant numbers and distributions always fluctuating. And most glaringly, the climate has never been static; there have been drought years and wet years; cooler, moister centuries and times of aridity lasting for hundreds or thousands of years.

One thing that seems to remain constant is the cyclic nature of this flux. Cycles within cycles can be detected from various sources: pollen preserved in lake muds, tree ring data, glacial till patterns, alpine tree-line fluctuations, fossils, historic precipitations, and others. Varying amounts of oxygen isotopes in foraminifera (microscopic planktonic organisms) can indicate changes in ocean temperature.

Huge planetary supercycles of four hundred million years may be based on differential heat welling up from the earth's core into varied parts of the molten zone below the crust, shaping large landmasses and breaking them apart, and ripping through sea floors at times to release carbon dioxide, which warms the planet. Thus our climate has moved between "greenhouse" and "icehouse" phases during the last billion years.[1] We are currently in one of the icehouse phases; the poles are covered with ice, and glacial-interglacial cycles dominate the climate. The dinosaurs of the late Cretaceous period, eighty to sixty-five million years ago, and mammals of the early Cenozoic era, peaking during the Eocene epoch forty million years ago, lived in a greenhouse phase: the poles had no ice cover, and world temperatures averaged much warmer than today—there were tropical forests and crocodiles as far north as Alaska.

Smaller Cycles

Great astronomical events that we in our everyday lives are not aware of pull and shift the earth in subtle ways that cause profound ripple effects in climate, vegetation, and faunas: gravitational interactions with the moon and the planets give rise to cyclic variations in Earth's orbital eccentricity, causing hundred-thousand-year cycles; variations in Earth's obliquity cause forty-one-thousand-year cycles; variations in Earth's precession cause a twenty-three-thousand to nineteen-thousand-year cycle. These cycles affect climate by slightly changing the latitudes that receive solar insolation (warmth from the sun's rays hitting Earth's surface).[2]

The changes may seem subtle, but even slight decreases in solar warmth over the Northern Hemisphere, perhaps triggered by an increase in the forty-one-thousand-year cycle, caused major sheets of ice to grow over the northern continents 2.37 million years ago.[3] Glaciers capped the Sierra Nevada. Of perhaps nine ice ages, the latest and apparently one of the strongest ice advances was the Wisconsin Glacial (called the Tioga in the Sierra), which peaked at about eighteen thousand years ago. During this time ice scoured the central and northern Sierra; glaciers coalesced into great ice fields, overtopping the canyon divides and blanketing the Sierra down to 8,000 or 6,000 feet. Valley glaciers at times flowed down their west-slope canyons to as low as 1,900 feet. In the southern Sierra the glaciers existed mostly above 13,000 feet. On the east side glaciers crept down to 7,000 to 4,200 feet. At times during the Pleistocene, they calved icebergs into Mono Lake. High-velocity meltwater rivers poured into the Central Valley. Pollen of giant sequoias found in the San Joaquin Valley and by Mono Lake tells us that the scene must have been quite different from that of today. The last large glacial tongues began melting off the west side of the Sierra about fifteen thousand years ago, and soon the great glaciers were gone, leaving scoured granite basins and carved peaks by eleven thousand years.[4]

During this last ice age, mean annual temperatures dropped as much as 10 to 15 degrees Fahrenheit, central latitudes of the United States had a precipitation increase of ten to fifteen inches (but the Pacific Northwest became a dry steppe-tundra), vegetation zones dropped 1,000 to 3,000 feet, and some species grew one hundred to two hundred miles south of their present distributional limits.[5]

During interglacial phases the climate is warmer and drier, as in our time. The last interglacial, the Sangamon, occurred from about 127,000 to 110,000 years ago.[6] The period of time covered by this book includes our present interglacial, the Holocene epoch, which dates back about 10,000 or 11,000 years.

The early Holocene was somewhat cooler than today, as shrinking continental ice sheets still menaced. Continental glaciers did not completely disappear from eastern Canada, for example, until thirty-four hundred years ago. Some regions, such as the southwestern United States, may have been moister than today.

Middle Holocene Warming

From about 8,000 to 4,000 years B.P. (before present), a dry, hot phase clenched California and much of the Northern Hemisphere. Mean annual temperatures increased 2 to 5 degrees and rainfall decreased four to five inches.[7] During this time, called the Altithermal (high temperature) or Xerothermic (dry temperature) phase, the warmth-loving basswood plant spread farther north in England than today. Hazelnuts grew north of their present limit in Scandinavia, and the European land tortoise spread north into Denmark, then disappeared three thousand years ago. In the central Great Plains of North America, grasslands invaded eastward into the woodland, but they have since retreated. Charcoal deposits in swamps reveal that wildfires almost doubled in frequency in the spruce forests around the Great Lakes from seven thousand to four thousand years ago.[8]

In California many xeric, or arid-adapted, plants spread northward or coastward, leaving relict populations behind today: sycamore went westward into the Bay Area, honey mesquite northward into the Central Valley, blue oak westward into Marin County, and black sage northward into the Diablo Range.[9] Tree lines in the mountains rose.

After the intense warming of the Xerothermic interval, temperatures cooled in a slow, oscillatory way between dry and moist phases, approaching our present condition. Short episodes of cold and renewed mountain glaciation have been recorded at about 4,500 years B.P., 3,000 B.P., and 1,000 B.P.[10]

The Medieval Warm Period

Another phase, called the Medieval Warm Period, took place from about twelve hundred to seven hundred years ago. Alpine glaciers retreated. Tree line moved upslope again. In Canada fossil forests are found 150 miles north of the present species limits, radiocarbon dated at A.D. 870 to 1140.[11] In medieval England grapes were cultivated for fine wines—and have not been since. Vikings colonized Greenland in wooden ships unhindered by sea ice.[12] Maize agriculture by Native Americans spread into favorable areas of the upper Mississippi Valley and Northeast.[13] In California and much of the West, epic droughts hit during this period, apparently the harshest and driest of the entire Holocene: many streams and springs in southern California dried up, fires became more frequent in the Sierra, the water level of Mono Lake dropped, and people abandoned parts of the arid Great Basin and Colorado Plateau.[14]

Climate researchers argue whether this warm period was widespread across the globe, and some say there is not enough documentation to call this a true climatic "phase."[15] But with the onset of the fourteenth century, everything changed, and the evidence becomes clearer.

The Little Ice Age

After the Medieval Warm Period, the climate surged into a colder and wetter oscillation. Tree lines fell, the grape harvests failed in England, and sea ice gripped the coasts of Greenland, forcing the Vikings to abandon their colonies there. Frosts in wildly fluctuating cold years killed the olive trees in France.[16] The "Little Ice Age" had arrived. It lasted from A.D. 1300 to 1850.

In the Sierra, the Dana, Lyell, and McClure Glaciers grew and peaked in size by 1850 to 1855.[17] The polar jet stream moved and storm tracks from the North Pacific shifted south in California. Big storms hit, stream flows increased in southern California, erosion resumed in the deserts, and lakes formed on many playas in the Mojave Desert. As it had during the big Ice Age, the Pacific Northwest became drier.[18]

The Little Ice Age may have played a part in bringing some strange animals into California, such as tropical birds and fish from the south. Let us take a closer look for clues about how this climatic age differed from today.

John Xantus had an eye for nature. He traveled to America just as the gold rush was starting. After joining the U.S. Army, he was stationed in 1857 as a medic at Fort Tejon. The Smithsonian Institution hired him to collect specimens for their growing catalog, and he wrote a series of letters about the astonishing array of birds, reptiles, amphibians, and mammals he observed and collected there. He described, in vivid detail, parts of southern California that have since changed dramatically. Not a small lizard nor a beetle missed his attention. Despite his flowery prose and the nearly audible Hungarian accent in his writings, they open a window to the past, a view that is remarkably broad in scope and detail for so early a date.

I set off with notebooks and sketchpads to visit Fort Tejon, a lonely Army outpost from 1854 to 1864, now a state historic park along busy Highway 5 in the Tehachapi Mountains. My goal was to retrace some of Xantus's explorations. The September day was hazy and clear, hot sunlight drying the grass crisp and turning the buckeyes brown on the north-facing canyonside. Only the native

RECENT INTERGLACIAL (HOLOCENE)

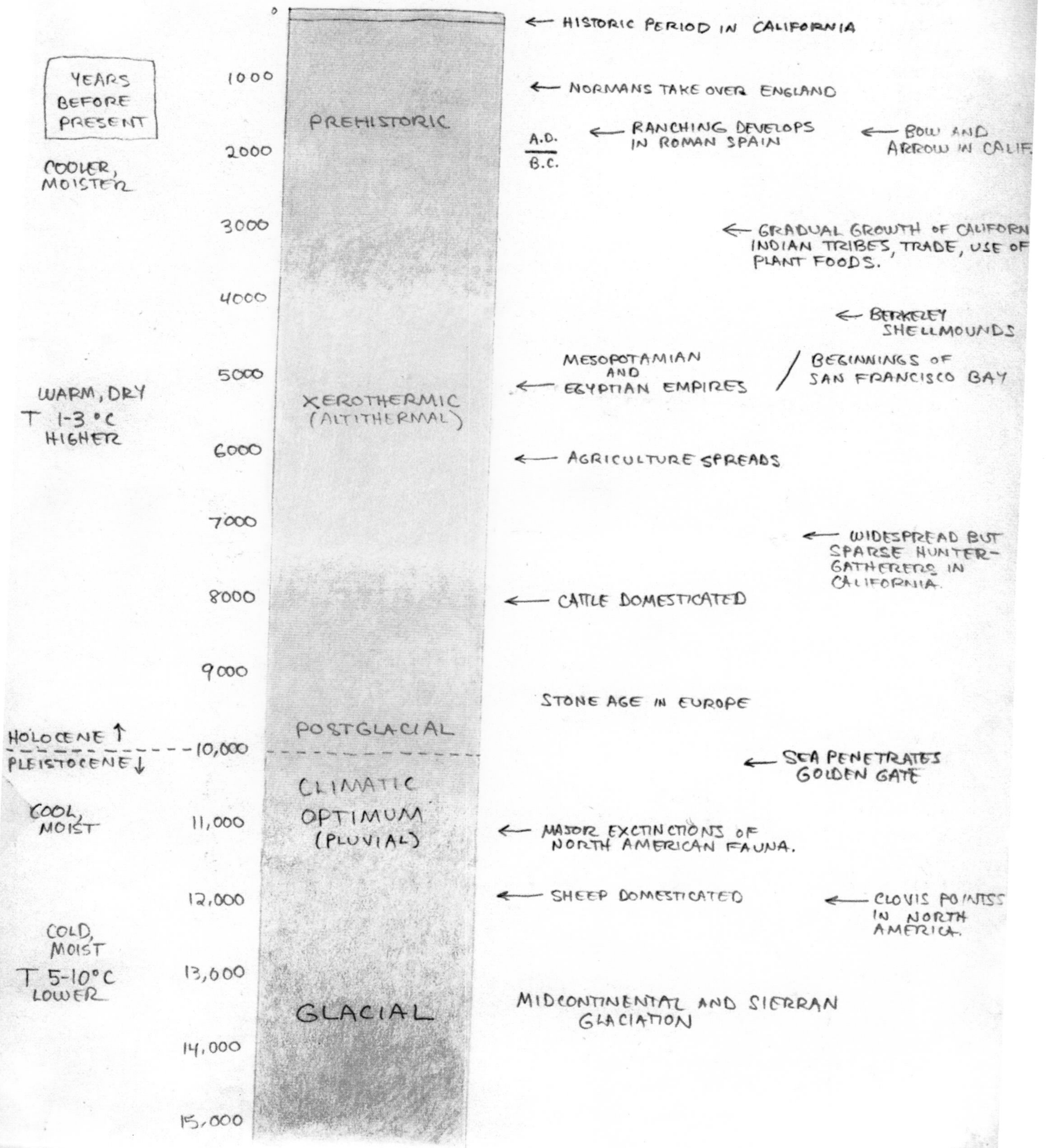

← HISTORIC PERIOD IN CALIFORNIA

YEARS
BEFORE
PRESENT

1000 ← NORMANS TAKE OVER ENGLAND

PREHISTORIC

A.D. ← RANCHING DEVELOPS IN ROMAN SPAIN   ← BOW AND ARROW IN CALIF.

2000

B.C.

COOLER, MOISTER

3000 ← GRADUAL GROWTH OF CALIFORN. INDIAN TRIBES, TRADE, USE OF PLANT FOODS.

4000 ← BERKELEY SHELLMOUNDS

MESOPOTAMIAN AND   BEGINNINGS OF
5000 ← EGYPTIAN EMPIRES   / SAN FRANCISCO BAY

WARM, DRY
T 1-3°C HIGHER

XEROTHERMIC (ALTITHERMAL)

6000 ← AGRICULTURE SPREADS

7000 ← WIDESPREAD BUT SPARSE HUNTER-GATHERERS IN CALIFORNIA.

8000 ← CATTLE DOMESTICATED

9000

STONE AGE IN EUROPE

HOLOCENE ↑
POSTGLACIAL
PLEISTOCENE ↓ -- -10,000

← SEA PENETRATES GOLDEN GATE

COOL, MOIST

CLIMATIC OPTIMUM (PLUVIAL)

11,000 ← MAJOR EXTINCTIONS OF NORTH AMERICAN FAUNA.

12,000 ← SHEEP DOMESTICATED   ← CLOVIS POINTS IN NORTH AMERICA.

COLD, MOIST

T 5-10°C LOWER

13,600

GLACIAL

MIDCONTINENTAL AND SIERRAN GLACIATION

14,000

15,000

Tehachapi Mountains: did thick-billed parrots sometimes visit southern California mountains to dine on pinyon nut crops?
OIL ON CANVAS, 6 ¾ X 9 INCHES, 2003

buckwheats flowered, a white fuzz on the dry, brushy slopes of scrub oak and mountain mahogany. Standing next to the old barracks and looking up with binoculars into tall valley oaks draped with green grapevines, I could see many of the birds that Xantus described so well a hundred and fifty years ago: "ultramarine" jays (scrub jays) and "red-breasted Carduelis" (house finches), which he called "quite common here," and they still were; Anna's hummingbirds feeding on pink thistle flowers; and the noisy, ever present acorn woodpeckers, which Xantus saw "in immense numbers" and which were still flocking about the oaks, hammering acorns into the trunks for storage.

Anomalies of the Little Ice Age

Collecting through several seasons, Xantus catalogued nests and eggs and made a long bird list for the area.[19] But what struck me most were the few anomalies in his observations. Even after I had worked through the tangled and myriad changes in names and taxonomy, they remained mysterious. These birds, not found in the region, nor even in the U.S., live far to the south, in Mexico or tropical America. For instance, on June 5, 1857, he wrote to Spencer F. Baird of the Smithsonian:

> Yesterday I noticed a very important thing. I climbed a [tree] for a hawks nest and
> found amongst the young ones a parrots head, feet, and scattered round long blue and
> red feathers; this circumstance gave me a hint, to hunt for the parrott and procure him if
> possible, because to my knowledge there is only one parrott in the U.S. until now known,
> and the remains in the nest, were decidedly of an other, quite different and larger species.[20]

Natural history writer Ann Zwinger thinks it was an escaped pet, but later Xantus writes:

> I am extremely sorry now, that I did not keep the wrecks of the parrot, I find in a nest, and mentioned to you. I see it was carelessness, but to late to philosophise about now. I never have seen the bird itself, although I heard that around San Gorgonio, and San Bernardino, even on the timbered lands SE of San Diego, they are sometimes met with. I didn't give up the hope altogether to get one, but the chances are few I see it so well![21]

What did he see? Xantus thought it was not the "one native parrot," probably referring to the extinct Carolina parakeet. No, this parrot was larger. I searched university libraries for illustrations and descriptions, but none exactly matched. Did native parrots wander up from Mexico in the past? The nearest possibility could be thick-billed parrots, which today breed in the mountains of north and central Mexico, and which historically were noted to wander to southeastern Arizona and southwestern New Mexico in irregular, irruptive movements. Further, the Espejo expedition of 1582-83 saw parrots in northern Arizona.

Thick-billed parrots live in oak-pine forests, usually in rugged mountain areas, where they feed mostly on pine nuts but also acorns, agave seeds, and even nectar from agave flowers. They need large, dead trees with holes for nesting, although one population uses limestone cliffs. Flocks of a thousand parrots or more wander widely in search of seed crops, which they strip clean from the pines and then move on. Although these birds are green with maroon foreheads, not the red and blue described by Xantus, I can only speculate that in the past, perhaps large parrots of some kind periodically wandered up from the south into the rugged, pine-covered mountain ranges of southern California after nut crops, leaving only a few eyewitness accounts as to their presence.

Then there is the mystery of the giant woodpecker reported by several observers. Early ornithologists reported that in a "little explored district of California which borders the territory of Mexico," specimens of a woodpecker the size of an ivory-billed woodpecker were obtained.[22] They had a crest of silky feathers four inches long, black in the female and scarlet in the male, and black bristles around the bill (these are white in the ivory-billed). The back was a glossy, greenish black and the wings had large white patches. They were seen not only in California, but in the Rocky Mountains, where in August 1834 ornithologist John Townsend saw several, "very shy," in tall pines.

Xantus as well saw them, in his travels through the San Gabriel Mountains above San Fernando Valley, in lush forests with abundant Nuttall's woodpeckers, acorn woodpeckers, and red-breasted sapsuckers. He described the mystery bird as twenty-seven inches long, iridescent blue and green mixed with black, and wings snow white, "the largest and rarest woodpecker known."[23]

These specimens and descriptions are surely of the imperial woodpecker, the largest woodpecker in the world and a close relative of the ivory-billed. Today the species is restricted to remote, old-growth pine forests above 7,000 feet in northwestern Mexico, where it may be recently extinct due to logging. The birds lived in family groups in giant old pine groves, where they excavated deep pits in bark to find beetle larvae. Thick-billed parrots competed with these woodpeckers for nest holes.[24]

From old photos of imperial woodpeckers, I reconstructed a possible scene of a flock in the San Jacinto Mountains of southern California. Perhaps the primeval forest haunts of this shy giant became too disturbed by settlers, miners, lumbermen, and road builders in the late 1800s, precipitating a large range shrinkage, but I wonder if other reasons caused its disappearance from western North America.

Stranger birds still were reported. John James Audubon wrote and illustrated his massive Birds of America series from 1840 to 1844. He could not travel to all parts of the country, so he gathered all the reports he could from exploring ornithologists. In accounts from California he learned of the "Columbia magpie or jay," which he illustrated from a specimen collected at the Columbia River. It was recorded as occurring in "the woody portions of Northern California."[25] This bird is now known as the magpie-jay, common in Mexico and south into the Tropics. I saw these dazzling blue birds with dainty feather crests in the Pacific dry tropical forests of Costa Rica one day, a pair hopping about, eating nutlets from a tree and making querulous calls in typical jay fashion. Perhaps in Old California they dined on acorns and the miniature avocado fruits of the California bay.

Several birds have changed their ranges due to obvious factors associated with modern civilization: mockingbirds spread into suburbia after good ornamental berry crops and nesting trees created a new habitat, and doubled their population in the twentieth century. European starlings were brought to North America as pets but escaped and increased explosively all over the country, apparently reaching California by the 1940s.[26] Cattle egrets apparently introduced themselves, straying from Africa across the Atlantic to South America during a storm in the 1930s; they found agricultural fields and cattle herds much to their liking and had spread to the Salton Sea and Central Valley by 1962.

A pair of magpie-jays feed on California bay fruits in the past. OIL ON TONED COTTON RAG PAPER, 6 ½ X 8 INCHES, 2003

But the birds Xantus and other early biologists recorded follow a different pattern, one possibly related to climate change.

Changes in Climate, Changes in Range

Looking at deep time, we can see that large-scale climatic fluctuations during the last million years have caused major changes in the distributions of plant and animal species. Full glacial conditions in California caused an overall cooling of 10 degrees Fahrenheit and more moisture but also, apparently, less extreme temperatures—winters were warmer and summers cooler than today. This allowed a peculiar mixing of northern and southern species whose ranges do not come close during our time. During the Pleistocene epoch (1.8 million to ten thousand years ago), spruce voles were found well south of their modern range in Canada and the Rocky Mountains, to Arkansas and Tennessee; conversely, those riverine rodents the capybaras, now associated with South America, were found north into Florida during the ice ages.[27] These non-analog conditions make paleoenvironmental reconstructions interestingly complex.

Left: An imperial woodpecker flock in giant ponderosa pines and bigcone spruces, San Jacinto Mountains overlooking the Colorado Desert. Black-crested females hammer on trunks and branches while a red-crested male clings to the trunk above. A hairy woodpecker is dwarfed, top left. OIL ON COTTON RAG PAPER, 16 X 12 INCHES, 1998

Although the Little Ice Age was a period of worldwide neoglaciation, little is known of its biological consequences. In the American Southwest, climate may have become rainier. At the time of the gold rush, California was just coming out of the Little Ice Age, and I believe keen naturalists of the day picked up evidence of it. On the cusp of climate change in 1869, John Xantus told of rain "for weeks in torrents" in March.[28] Severe snows in February in the mountains blocked the road to Los Angeles.

Xantus may have seen Mexican birds that ranged north into California with moister conditions. A drying phase followed that culminated in the Dust Bowl years of the 1930s.[29] These birds may then have contracted their ranges back to core areas in the Tropics or to the monsoonal mountains of Mexico.

Enter El Niño

The intense winter storms Xantus witnessed may have been related not only to the Little Ice Age but to the El Niño cycle. During the winter of 1982-83, storm upon storm beat rain down upon the windows of my house, which faced the San Francisco Bay. The rain was fierce, I recall—mudslides slumped down hill slopes, and local streams flooded higher than I had ever seen. This is what happens during an El Niño event, when sea temperatures jump in the eastern Pacific as much as 10 degrees, and warm equatorial waters flow west. The air pressure drops in the eastern Pacific, while it rises in the western Pacific; this is termed the "Southern Oscillation" and linked with El Niño as the El Niño–Southern Oscillation (ENSO).

El Niño years are really the warm extreme of the normal oscillation of winds and sea currents. Cold extremes, or La Niñas, occur when the easterly trade winds become stronger across the Pacific. In warm ENSO phases, the Pacific Northwest, often but not always including northern California, becomes warmer in winter, sometimes drier and sometimes moister. Central California often becomes much rainier in winter. The Southwest becomes cooler and wetter. The Great Basin may have increased summer rains.[30] These ENSO events show how interconnected our world is: small instabilities in sea surface temperature and convection over the tropical Pacific will impact distant locations and ultimately alter global climate within months. This is called the "teleconnection pattern."

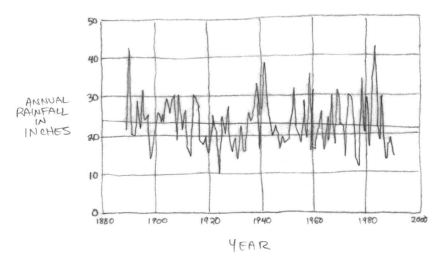

Average Annual Rainfall for California (from J. D. Goodridge's "One Hundred Years of Rainfall Trends in California")

ENSO events of varying intensity have recurred throughout the Holocene epoch: moderate to strong ENSO events occur about every five to six years, and every twelve to fourteen years, very strong events happen.[31] Evidence of giant floods associated with extreme ENSO episodes cycling about every one thousand years was found in Peru: in A.D. 1325 gigantic floods apparently caused huge trouble for the Inca dynasty of Nyamlap—this may have been a worldwide climatic event.[32]

Sea and Surf

Just as changing climate affected birdlife in the mountains and valleys, the warm-cold fluctuations of seawater off California's coast have had drastic effects on fish faunas through time, causing awe-inspiring abundance as well as catastrophic declines that have swung the economy of the state. As blue-filtered light illuminated the water column, rushing schools of fish responded not only to El Niños and La Niñas, but to even more complex cycles that reveal how little we know about the climate and its grip on our lives.

In 1889 Dr. Charles Holder, a zoologist and sport fisherman from Massachusetts, went to Santa Catalina Island, specifically a little hotel at Avalon in a small cove. The fish impressed him. "It was a common sight to see schools of sardines and anchovies being cleverly crowded into the shallow water along the shoreline by ravenous yellowtail and white sea bass."[33]

The warm waters of certain years brought great schools of the famous "leaping tuna," the bluefins. They fed on sardines and anchovies in breathtaking frenzies, churning the water white. Flocks of California flying fish cheered by boating tourists leapt out of the water to escape the onrushes of the tuna. After Holder caught a 183-pound leaping tuna on a modified rod and reel, the anglers came in droves for the excitement, and Holder helped to form the Tuna Club in 1898 in order to protect game fishes.[34]

The famous "leaping tuna" chasing flying fish, off Catalina Island. OIL ON TONED COTTON RAG PAPER, 9 X 4 ¼ INCHES, 2006

The Chumash had been deep-sea fishing in the Santa Barbara Channel at least since A.D. 500 in sea-canoes (*tomols*) made of wooden planks. Now, other boats went out from the southern California shores. Longtime San Diego resident Herbert Minshall recalled with fondness the beginning, in the 1920s, of deep-sea sport fishing adventures off the South Coast.[35] The kelp forests teemed with big game fish feeding on abundant sardines after April, when the waters warmed. From "Albacore City," boats took fishermen to barges parked in the kelp beds, where rods and reels, or long Calcutta cane poles with piano wire and large hooks were set up. The fishing was spectacular. "Schools of game fish boiled around the barge, competing frantically for the bait," Minshall recalled.[36] Yellowtail tunas surged after the sardines and "[s]uddenly the green depths were filled with dark, hurrying shapes with bright yellow tails," wildly threshing and jerking the rods. Eighteen-pounders were gaffed and pulled on board. The yellowtails taken from the water were blue-purple and silver on their sides, fading as the fish died. After a lull, a California barracuda might then strike at the bait.

At the same time, commercial ships trolled the kelp beds for the big fish. In 1916, thirty million pounds of tuna, mostly albacore, were canned in California. As warm-water cycles turned to cold, sardines—a favorite prey fish—declined, and pollution also helped to reduce sport fishing in southern California.

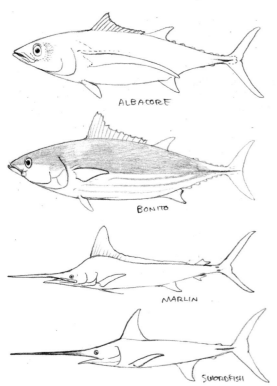

ALBACORE

BONITO

MARLIN

SWORDFISH

Sometimes the tropical waters return. During the 1982-83 El Niño, swarms of Pacific bonito—small, near-shore tunas rarely found north of Point Conception—were seen in San Francisco Bay. In 1997 other rarely seen fish appeared along the southern and central California coast. Skipjack tuna, albacore, and sheephead headed to Santa Catalina Island. El Niños have brought tropical exotics such as mahi mahi as far north as the Farallon Islands, as well as bluefin tuna and swordfish. Striped marlin, usually found in southern Baja California, have checked out lures from boats off Santa Cruz.[37]

But nonclimatic trends counter the effects of El Niños. Worldwide, big ocean fish—tunas, sharks, halibut, swordfish, and others—have decreased 90 percent in numbers since the early days of commercial fishing, and body sizes have become smaller everywhere from the Tropics to the Arctic, and even in the middle of the Pacific. The U.S. has curtailed overharvesting, but many other countries are still in denial about the situation, sometimes stretching nets out sixty miles long. Thus, when fish landings are plotted against sea surface temperatures, white sea bass, bluefin tuna, and barracuda spike in numbers during warm-water years, but overall they have declined due to commercial overfishing. The spikes may be due to increased accessibility of the fish populations, rather than to increased stocks. The exception to this pattern is shown by swordfish, which have been landed in greater numbers since 1976. As is usual for the natural world in which we are embedded, the situation is complex: this date marked both a broad oceanic warming shift and, simultaneously, a switch from traditional harpoon fishing to gill netting for swordfish, which greatly increased the catch of that in-demand delicacy.[38] Environment and exploitation are sometimes difficult to separate in the game of cause and effect.

Regime Change in the Sea

Populations of big fish are driven not just by ocean temperatures but by the numbers of prey fish, which also fluctuate with climate. The entangled ways that species interact with the physical environment, with climate, and with each other have recently become strikingly apparent among some of the world's most important fisheries, those of the "small pelagics," such as California sardines and northern anchovies.

"Sardines are...so abundant in San Francisco Bay that they literally obstruct the passage of boats through the water," said one 1892 observer.[39] The first West Coast sardine cannery opened in San Francisco in 1890; by 1915 the sardine industry had become the largest single fishery in California, measured by poundage landed. The peak hit in 1941—over a billion pounds caught off California.[40] Abruptly, in the mid 1940s, the sardine population crashed, forcing the canneries to close in the 1950s.[41]

What caused the crash? The short answer is that the effects of climate change were exacerbated by intense overfishing. But the deeper researchers go, trying to determine exactly how these factors affect economically important fish—trying to understand ecosystems and their changes—the more questions seem to come up. Cycles within cycles of climatic variation surface, each influencing the upwelling associated with the California Current ecosystem that extends from Baja California to British Columbia and from seventy miles to sixteen hundred miles out into the Pacific.

What is upwelling? In the Northern Hemisphere, the rotation of the earth deflects the wind-driven surface currents in one direction, while deeper layers of seawater are deflected more slowly, dragging along and then spiraling back on themselves so that at three hundred feet down, the currents actually flow opposite to their direction on the surface. The top layer of blue-green ocean is pushed away from the coast and is replaced by an upwelling of deep, cold water.[42]

Yearly seasonal cycles in the California Current are dominated by the Aleutian Low Pressure system, which brings winter storms, and the North Pacific High Pressure system, which brings dry summers. The California Current is generally strongest during the spring and summer (off southern California it is stronger in winter and early spring).

Sardines lay their eggs floating in the upper seawater layers, stirred by the winds and rich with nutrients and plankton, around the inshore areas off Mexico and southern California. El Niño events favor the floating sardine eggs and larvae—upwelling is weakened or turned off, and the warmth reduces populations of pelagic small invertebrates, such as tunicates, that prey on the tiny new fish: more sardines survive to adulthood. During cold years, when upwelling is strong, sardine eggs and hatched larvae may be blown out to sea by the churning currents and lost, and cold-loving planktonic predators are more numerous. One good year of warm seas is not enough to produce an increase in the sardine population; only many warm years in a row or an increased frequency in El Niños will allow the sardine population to surge in numbers.[43]

Not only do yearly fluctuations in climate affect the sardines, there is also interdecadal variation (multi-decade cycles), such as the Pacific Decadal Oscillation (PDO). These long-lived (about thirty years), El Niño-like patterns were discovered by science in 1996 but their causes are still unknown. There was a cold phase from 1890 to 1924, and warm phases from 1925 to 1946 and 1977 to about 1999, when sea surface temperatures increased in the California Current, the number of El Niño events increased, and the Aleutian Low Pressure system deepened and moved eastward, changing winds and currents off California. This allowed the sardine biomass to grow again (and swordfish did well too). Spawning grounds increased north of Point Conception, and feeding migrations went farther north.

The habitats and climatic triggers of the California Current vary geographically, and effects on the current change with depth: the PDO appears to dominate upper layers, while ENSO changes dominate below. Some fish appear to be more influenced by interannual climate cycles, while sardines are more affected by interdecadal changes.[44] Apparently salmon and flatfish respond more to PDO variations, while white sea bass respond more to El Niño patterns.[45]

And these cycles go back in time. Sea-dwelling microalgae that leave minute cells, known as diatoms, buried in the seafloor oozes reveal what the temperatures were in past ages in the Pacific, and they can tell a lot about the state of coastal upwelling. Banded layers of ocean sediments off California show that El Niño conditions weakened or turned off upwelling in three- to seven-year cycles, and that these cycles occurred within variable decadal and millennial cycles back into the Pleistocene.[46]

But the Pleistocene world must have been very different, as cold, dry winds blew from the east off the continent, depositing silt and loess (fine, wind-carried "rock flour" produced by runoff from the great glaciers) into the oceans, and apparently no upwelling happened off central California. By thirteen thousand years ago, atmospheric temperatures had warmed and summer fogs were bathing the California coasts with their cool mists. In the early Holocene, upwelling was irregular and often shut off, as indicated by the presence of tropical diatoms that favor warmer waters with low nutrient availability.[47] By seven thousand years ago, the cold upwelling currents had fully developed, attracting burgeoning populations of anchovies and other cold-water fish as well as seabirds and sea mammals.

So the Pacific Ocean may shift, in places, to a "sardine regime" or an "anchovy regime," with varying sea temperatures and current patterns. Anchovies decline during warm ENSO phases. When sardines are abundant, anchovies are not, and vice versa. Archaeological remains on Peru's coast show anchovies were much more abundant eight thousand years ago, when El Niños were less frequent.[48] Strangely, the reverse pattern happens on the other side of the Pacific, in rich waters off Japan: Japanese anchovies increase in warm-water climate phases while the cold-favoring eastern sardines decrease.[49]

What happens in California is related to planetwide climate oscillations. Fishery managers today have had to take a more holistic view of marine life than in the past, taking into account the ways that species interact with each other, and new information about the physical environment they occupy. This is quite a challenge: habitat is a dynamic entity whose boundaries change with climate, and climate is still not well understood. There may exist what ecologists call "multiple alternative steady states," many ways in which an ecosystem can run smoothly and sustainably.

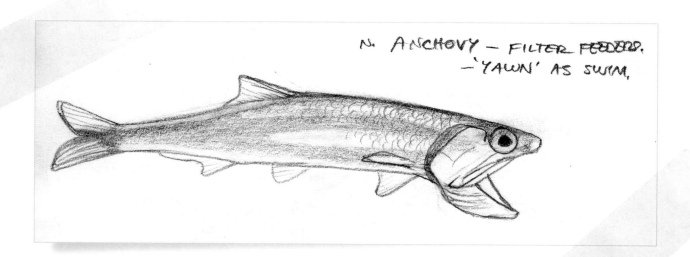

N. ANCHOVY — FILTER FEEDERS. — 'YAWN' AS SWIM.

Climate Change

"The farther backward you can look, the farther forward you are likely
to see."

—*Winston Churchill*

Because they are so sensitive to temperature, sardines have been labeled a "sentinel species"; they can alert humans to environmental changes and help us to understand climate-ecosystem links, a net in which we are unavoidably enmeshed. Key to this understanding is observation, watching the changing ocean habitats and other sensitive landscapes, such as ice sheets.

By the 1880s the Sierran glaciers were in full retreat, as the Industrial Revolution swung into high gear and greenhouse gases filled the skies. The Palisades Glacier alone, during the years 1933 to 1938, thinned twenty-seven feet,[50] and it continues to shrink today. The twentieth century experienced a steep warming trend that culminated in the warmest decade since temperature measurements began, in the mid-1800s. All ten of the warmest years in the global record occurred in the 1990s.[51]

What's more, the consensus among climate scientists is that these unusually high temperatures have not been matched in recent centuries. Temperature curves reconstructed from proxy data (such as tree rings and sediment records) show that the last fifteen years have been the warmest the earth has seen in the last one thousand years, and possibly the last two thousand[52]—warmer than the Medieval Warm Period and beginning to match the heat of the mid-Holocene Xerothermic period. But our current warm epoch is not due to orbital changes, as was the Xerothermic. So what is going on here?

Understanding climate change is very difficult, and the researcher's ever present mantra is "more work is needed." Often theories seem to boil down to a battle between radically different computer models. Trying to measure the relevant factors over a long enough time to see patterns is tough, but strides are being made. In recent years longer and finer ice cores have been pulled out of Greenland and Antarctica, allowing a greater understanding of paleoclimates.

Global warming has come to be recognized as due to the artificial input of carbon dioxide into the atmosphere from coal burning, beginning in the Industrial Revolution, and lately from car exhaust too. Subtle changes are continually happening due to global warming—some, for example in the high talus slopes and alpine summits of the Sierra, deduced by good old-fashioned naturalists. I have been scolded by certain biologists who believe that the study of natural history is "passé," that genetic research is all the rage. But this is mostly lab work. Only by spending hours, days, weeks in the field can we see important trends in our changing landscape.

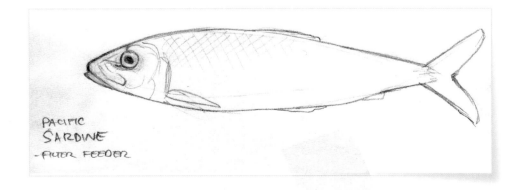

PACIFIC
SARDINE
- FILTER FEEDER

In 1911 Joseph Grinnell of the Museum of Vertebrate Zoology at UC Berkeley launched a survey of animals along a huge transect across the Sierra Nevada, starting at Yosemite Valley. He was already seeing, nearly a century ago, changes to the biota of the mountains, and he had the patience and foresight to begin carefully collecting and recording data that he knew would be useful a hundred years in the future. He was right. In 2003 the staff of the Museum of Vertebrate Zoology, including mammalogist Jim Patton, resurveyed and retrapped Grinnell's localities in the Sierra.

I can well imagine such a field survey, as I took Patton's class years ago. We tried to keep up with him on field trips as he marched up the steepest hills with great endurance, tirelessly setting traplines through forest and brush. We handled hundreds of rodent live traps—small, metal boxes baited with oats: a kangaroo rat or pocket mouse would enter the door at night and step on a hinged plate that triggered the door to snap shut behind it. The next morning we would weigh each rodent and take measurements of such anatomical parts as the hind foot and ear, which aided in identifying the often similar-appearing species. We recorded our notes in field books of the same design that Grinnell developed during his surveys.

Patton and his 2003 team found that many small mammals had moved their range upwards in elevation in the Sierra during the last hundred years. California voles had invaded Yosemite Valley from the lower grassland belt. Pinyon mice had gained 2,000 feet of elevation on both the west slope and east slope, compared to Grinnell's findings. Grinnell found alpine chipmunks abundant above 8,000 feet around Tuolumne Meadows, and they were the dominant chipmunk in Lyell Canyon; Patton's team found only three, all above 10,200 feet. That noisy chirper the pika, found in talus slopes of Glen Aulin and other alpine country in Grinnell's day, was also moving up in elevation and is no longer found that low—they cannot tolerate the increased summer temperatures of the last century. Global warming is forcing animals to shift their ranges before our eyes.[53] What will the Sierra be like in the future?

Into the Future

Paleoclimatic information can help us understand how climate change will affect our world today and in the future, but we are racing far beyond the known natural range of variation for carbon dioxide levels. What is not yet known is where this trend is going. What will the climate be like in a hundred years? Some climate scientists have modeled the next century for California as having a 3 to 10 degree Fahrenheit rise in temperature, depending on carbon dioxide emission rates. Central California may have warmer, wetter winters, with increased ENSO activity, and slightly warmer summers,[54] but the rainfall trend is difficult to anticipate. Most models for the Mojave Desert predict increasing rainfall with warming in southern California.[55]

As we have seen, animal and plant ranges change with climate, and this will most likely happen in the future, although with attendant difficulties because of the habitat destruction, fragmentation, and loss of migration corridors that have gone hand-in-hand with global industrialization. Humans, too, will undergo difficult changes, as history and prehistory have indicated. Observing and understanding the changing landscape we live on, so that we can adapt with it, may be our best survival behavior. The field of historical ecology is quite relevant for the future. Perhaps in a hundred and fifty years someone will look at my field notes, discern changes in mammal or bird ranges, and begin to decipher the mysteries of time and climate.

Pika

THREE

SHORELINE STORIES

Methods of the Landscape Detective

More than one person's history, more than the study of a single plant or animal, historical ecology reveals how a whole landscape or water body changes over time: how the geology, climate, and geography interact with the vegetation, animals, and humans of a place. A multidisciplinary study, it combines the physical, biological, and social sciences with history, seeking to explain particular events and relationships and how they vary through time.

This is no easy feat. Several years ago, when I was studying under conservation biologist Dick Richardson, we discussed how to observe the natural world. "Ecological communities are very complex, too complex for mathematics in its present state," he told me. In trying to gain some understanding of how biological landscapes operate, he suggested, if you simply take static snapshots of single entities you will only get a frozen kaleidoscope; you need to study interrelationships, and to do this you need to decide how to measure moving processes.

The Golden Gate at sunset, before the bridge. The San Francisco Peninsula is on the left.
DETAIL OF OIL ON PANEL, 6 X 10 INCHES, 1999

Methods of Historical Ecology

I can recommend no better place to learn the state of the art of historical ecology than the website of the San Francisco Estuary Institute (SFEI), at www.sfei.org. Here you can peruse digital maps reconstructing, in great detail, the bay as it may have looked in the year 1800. Hundreds of estuarine plants and animal species are discussed, habitats are reconstructed, and goals for sustaining the ecological health of the bay are presented.

The information used to reconstruct these landscapes includes:

NATURAL ARCHIVES:

- pollen, spore, phytolith, algae, and invertebrate records buried in sediments
- tree rings, fire scars
- forest stand age plots (made in the 1930s, for example)
- charcoal layers in sediments
- lake levels
- coral growth rings
- soil and dune sediment layers
- travertine deposit layers around mineral-rich water
- geomorphological features, such as old meander bends in rivers
- packrat midden fossils
- glacier extents and moraines
- ice cores with layers
- relict distributions of species
- relict habitats
- contemporary analogs—the biology of living species

DOCUMENTARY ARCHIVES:

- old maps
- early sketches and paintings
- old photographs and repeat photography, including aerial photos
- explorers' journals
- missionary texts
- engineering reports
- land surveys
- toponymy—place names
- hunting magazines
- weather records
- oral histories, anecdotal reports, interviews with people who have lived in a place for a long time, elders
- ethnographic accounts and archaeological records

Using these sources, SFEI's Robin Grossinger is directing the development of maps and time lines to show the diversity of habitats and species of the San Francisco Bay Area at different times in the past. Thousands of documents are used to calibrate the accuracy of data sources by redundancy. As they explained in their "Historical Landscape Ecology of an Urbanized California Valley" (2007), Grossinger's team has specialized in using "overlapping sources of varying origin." The resulting databases beautifully reveal likely native vegetation, for example, around the bay in different pre-European periods. This detailed information can be used by local land managers, habitat restorationists, flood control workers, climate scientists, fishery biologists, endangered species recovery teams, contemporary Native people, and anyone else wanting to know the stories of the land they live on.

"Biology is best described in stories," Richardson would often say, stories lifted out and clarified from the complex matrix of changing ecosystems. So in this book, as I attempt to tell some stories about Old California's changing lands and waters, perhaps we will begin to see not just a single sardine or marsh, but some of the web of moving interrelationships that create the landscape we live in.

"Forgotten Landscapes Reappear"

I strolled through the exhibit hall, studying the colorful maps, old photographs, and text as crowds of people sipped wine and chatted. Not the usual art show, this 2004 exhibition at Berkeley's Lawrence Hall of Science about the BayBoards project opened up a view of the Bay Area as it might have been before European settlement, with cartographic artwork created by the San Francisco Estuary Institute's Elise Brewster, Robin Grossinger, and Susan Schwartzenberg.

"How do we gain the ability to see the subtle world?" a sign read. "How do we recognize the seemingly static places we inhabit as the dynamic products of nature and history—when the clues are hidden and most of us moved here in recent decades?"

On billboards at three locations around the bay, BayBoards had depicted the sites as they looked in the past. Passersby could contemplate the hidden story of a place revealed by "tapping into the land below." The billboard for San Francisco's Fifth Street, for example, told the story of a land of sand hills, scrub oak, and wildflowers merging with seasonally flooded grasslands, tidal salt marshes, and mudflats next to the open bay. Rather quickly, the topography here was scraped down and massive amounts of debris were piled into the marshes, resulting in the present cityscape, a "thin, freshly-constructed veneer over the native land," reminded the project artists. The billboards stood as "ghosts of the former landscape."

I admired the SFEI project for the impact of their serene landscapes juxtaposed with today's cluttered reality, and also for the depth of their research. As I had discovered trying to imagine grizzly bears in El Cerrito Plaza's past, detecting the underlying legacy of the land is not an easy task. The clues are hidden well, here in the Bay Area. And looking deeper into time, the landscape is almost unimaginable. During the Ice Age the bay did not exist. So much of the world's water was tied up in the huge continental glaciers that sea levels were lower, and the coast at this time was well outside the Golden Gate—at 15,000 B.P. a person could walk to the Farallon Islands.[1] The bay was a wide valley with ancient bison, horses, and Columbian mammoths roaming over its grasslands and oak-conifer forests. The Sacramento and San Joaquin Rivers met and combined into a single large river, which flowed through what we now know as Carquinez Strait, then between today's Angel Island and Tiburon, and out to the sea. By 10,000 B.P., as glaciers melted at the beginning of the Holocene and sea levels rose, the ocean began to flood this valley. The waters swept higher, across one hundred new horizontal feet of landscape annually; by 8,000 B.P., narrow tidal mudflats and marshes had formed. By 6,000 B.P., more cordgrass had grown and tidal marshes had become extensive.[2] San Francisco Bay waters are still rising at one foot per century.[3]

The Abundant Bay

About four thousand years ago, people began to build mysterious shellmounds around the bay, including a few within miles of El Cerrito Plaza. Some were large, one hundred feet across. Others were small. People picked mussels off rocky areas, scooped oysters at low tide from gravel flats, and dug clams from mud and sand. They shucked these shellfish for food and discarded the shells in

ELLIS LANDING SHELLMOUND, RICHMOND.
EAST BAY SALT MARSH AT HIGH TIDE - PICKLEWEED AND
CORDGRASS. CORMORANTS FLYING.

Reconstructed from photographs in N. C. Nelson's "The Ellis Landing Shellmound" (1910)

mounds, and also apparently left much fishing debris and some from hunting as well. Whether the shellmounds were the sites of fishing villages, temporary kitchen middens, ceremonial centers, burial grounds, or some combination is not known. There are multiple human burials in many of them, standing high and dry above the surrounding tidal marshes. Over time some of the mounds were flooded, as bay waters continued to rise slowly in the late Holocene, and building tapered off around A.D. 900.

Development destroyed most of the shellmounds, but in 1908 there were still 427 located around the bay and along the Pacific Coast.[4] In a small park downtown, the city of Emeryville has placed a memorial to one of the largest in the Bay Area, destroyed in 1924. It was thirty feet tall, towering over the mudflats, as archaeologist Brian Fagan describes it, long before the present city filled the skyline. Charcoal from the lower levels dated to 850 B.C., and in these early times people apparently ate more oysters; later people preferred bent-nosed clams. More than seven hundred burials were found here. Some of these mounds must have been used for centuries.[5]

In those centuries before European arrival, the Bay Area was home to as many as fifty thousand people living in villages on the flatlands around the marshes, in the hills, and in the oak-shaded valleys. Fray Francisco Palóu, traveling up the San Francisco peninsula in November 1774, came over a ridge to see the estuary thick with large villages. People came here to seek mussels and fish. Many marshes lined the beaches on the plain in what is today Belmont.[6] Evidence suggests Native people modified the wetlands in certain areas: in the North Bay, some Miwok groups may have helped to create large tidal marsh ponds to enhance waterfowl habitat and hunting. Above Petaluma, earthen dams may have held runoff water emerging from the hills, to create small lakes. And fire management was ubiquitous (see chapter eight).[7]

Records of commercial fishing and hunting from the 1800s give clues as to the natural resources that were available to the many groups living around the bay. As early as 1800, San Francisco became a trading center for sea otter and fur seal pelts, and by 1840 whaling was prominent. The first commercial fishery began in 1848 to 1850.[8]

By 1870 Chinese fishermen were netting thousands of tons of the bay shrimp that drifted back and forth with the tides in the shallow waters and mudflats. This increased to more than five million tons annually until about 1910. When the bay waters were "shrimped out," the fishery moved outside the bay into the ocean. Go to China Camp State Park, in Marin County on the bayshore, to see some of this history.

San Pablo Bay was the major fishery in the state for green and white sturgeons. The former preferred brackish or salt water, while the latter migrated up the Sacramento River yearly to breed. White sturgeons are impressive beasts that can grow to eighteen hundred pounds (in the Columbia River) and live to be one hundred years old or more. Before the fishery bottomed out in 1917, white sturgeons weighing three hundred pounds were regularly caught in California, and during the 1870s six- to twelve-footers flooded the markets.[9] A sport-only season reopened in 1954 as the sturgeons recovered from overfishing and damming of their spawning rivers. In the fall, possibly while feeding on herring and anchovy, they sometimes jump out of the water in a forward leap, coming down with a huge splash—perhaps this was a common sight once in San Pablo Bay. Otherwise they are principally bottom-feeders, on clams, crabs, shrimp, and herring eggs.

From 1870 to 1915, San Francisco Bay was considered one of the leading fishing centers in the U.S. In an 1893-94 report, Fish and Game commissioners wrote, "So extensive is the supply of fish from all sources that in the matter of market prices there is never any cause for complaint from the consumers."[10] The fish stalls in the city were brimming: annual clam production reached 2.5 million pounds, oysters 15 million pounds. In 1899 Dungeness crabs reached 3.6 million pounds; in 1885 sturgeon reached 1.65 million pounds; and the salmon catch twice hit 10 million pounds.

Most fisheries declined steadily through the twentieth century. The fishing take was not the only problem. A series of introductions ensured that native species had plenty of competition for limited habitats: in 1872 carp came, in 1874 the first of many catfish were introduced, in 1879 striped bass; eastern oysters and softshell clams followed, as well as crayfish, in 1925.[11] Pollution levels became so high in the bay in my lifetime that clams and oysters were banned for human consumption.

WHITE STURGEON

Exploring the Mudflats

Although I did not have a boat to explore aquatic bay habitats, in my own wanderings I have searched the bayshore for hints of ecological history. In the area by San Pablo Avenue in El Cerrito,

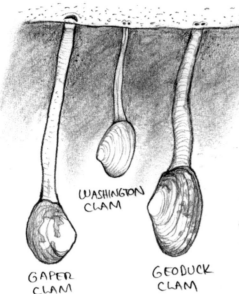

WASHINGTON
CLAM

GAPER
CLAM

GEODUCK
CLAM

remnants of mudflats and tidal marsh exist, but most of the natural areas had been filled, extending the shoreline out into former bay water. In earlier times, as the tides swept back toward the ocean each day, thousands of acres of bare mudflats were exposed; fifty thousand acres of such habitat once existed in the San Francisco Bay, especially around the shallow South Bay.

The 880 freeway lies atop the ancient marshlands, but there are still clues: crushed oyster shells litter the dirt between sidewalk and street in certain sites—remnants of Indian shellmounds long since dredged away and built upon. Further north are the Albany mudflats, alive with shorebirds, surrounded by a horse-racing track, houses, and more freeways. I have watched the birds gather at low tide on the broad mudsheet, which reflected the bright golden sun at day's end. The bay waters rolled back, and thousands of western sandpipers, dunlins, and least sandpipers landed in tight groups to peck at the mud. Giant flocks of them rose over the inlet as the tide came back in at dusk, a compact white and buff blur of wings searching out a bit of land to loaf on. Marbled godwits, larger, plunged their long bills into the mud after deeper invertebrates, and Forster's terns flew gracefully over the water farther out, with smooth, even wingbeats but harsh, noisy calls. A flash of intense white might catch my eye as a great egret flew in. Surf scoters stretched their wings in the open bay waters, flashing piebald patterns. Not just an expanse of blackish mud, this place was always alive with the colors of feathers.

Native Olympia oysters grew here as well, in rocky areas and stream mouths. Extensive beds of oysters once grew around the western part of San Francisco Bay, and high winds would wash up dead shells to form glistening beaches and bars around San Mateo and other places. These deposits were so abundant that cement was made from them.[12] Since the 1870s other oysters have been introduced: plantings of Virginia oysters, Japanese oysters, and European flat oysters in Tomales Bay and Drake's Estero.

The mudflats were most famous for clams, however. The bent-nosed clam was common in mud and sand in bays and sloughs, and below surf along the coast. It was a great source of food for Native people but was not much harvested commercially. Washington clams were fairly common in California, especially in Humboldt Bay, Crescent City, Bodega Bay, Tomales Bay, Bolinas Bay, and Morro Bay. Native people camped annually at Tomales Bay to clam, and they used the shells for money. Gaper clams were the largest California clam, weighing in at four pounds if you were a lucky clammer in Tomales and Bodega Bays. Introduced species, such as softshell clams in 1870 from the Atlantic Coast and the Japanese littleneck

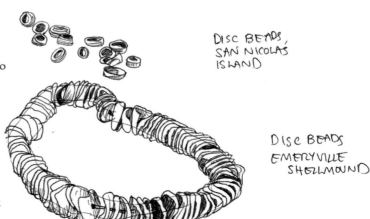

DISC BEADS,
SAN NICOLAS
ISLAND

DISC BEADS
EMERYVILLE
SHELLMOUND

clam in 1931, soon displaced many native clam beds. Clam numbers have declined since 1919 from excessive harvest by sport-diggers.[13]

I went clam digging with friends Juliet and Mariette once at Tomales Bay, but we spent more time running after the minute holes made by the clam's mouth tube on the mudflat surface, and madly shoveling mud and sand after them, than we did actually finding clams to eat. The "sport" takes some know-how.

The native Pismo clam, also called quahog (a name lifted from a type of Atlantic clam), grew from Half Moon Bay south, preferring sandy ocean beaches. Excessive digging and pollution have led to very low numbers. In 1861 Pismo clams were dug at Santa Cruz beaches, but they are now gone. In 1922 at Oceano, a single mile of beach yielded 5.27 million clams, but these were quickly depleted by commercial and tourist harvesting—in 1925 thousands of cars and campers lined Pismo, Oceano, and Morro Beaches to dig clams.

Farther south, the Port of Los Angeles, dredged into a massively busy deepwater harbor in the early 1900s, was in earlier times a mudflat of some thirteen hundred acres at low tide. It was a lagoon with shallow channels and a large sandbar on the seaward side, and it had "numerous rattlesnakes" (undoubtedly the western rattlesnake) in its drier salt marshes.[14]

Local resident Herbert Minshall recalled that in 1917, the shore of San Diego Bay was a quiet area with a few piers and wharfs and some salt evaporation ponds at the south end. The waterfront by India Street was a mudbank. Off the northeast shore was a long sandbar deposited by the San Diego River, and people went there to collect clams. Boys scooped up sardines with tin cans. Porpoises were commonly seen blowing in the bay, and halibut, sharks, and skates swarmed over the mudflats on the incoming tides. The water was so clean you could swim by the Broadway Pier. On moonlit nights fishermen threw their lures into the water, causing tracers of phosphorescence to shimmer as they caught "sea trout" (white sea bass). There was no limit back then.

Distichlis spicata
SALTGRASS

BULRUSH

Tidal Marshes

Moving shoreward from the mudflats, I have encountered relict salt marshes, special places where unique plants and animals thrive, where nurseries of young fish feed and rest, and where shorebirds and waterfowl rest during migration. Rivers actually form these marshes, bringing mud and sand down from the land and carrying it out to sea to be dumped on shore edges. Marsh plants quickly colonize these sediments and add their own organic detritus.

Vegetative zones are often divided into lower marsh, with cordgrass and pickleweed; middle marsh, with pickleweed, sea-blite, alkali heath, saltwort, arrowgrass, saltgrass, fleshy jaumea, and sea lavender; and upper marsh, on the upper areas flooded less regularly, with saltgrass, shoregrass, and saltbush. (There is considerable overlap in these categories—we humans try to classify nature to understand it, but natural systems are rarely so tidy.)

Dams on the rivers have slowed sediment deposition and marsh formation. On the other hand, dirt from hydraulic mining in the Sierra foothills during the gold rush is still washing down through

An ancient bay marsh near present Hayward, in the southern San Francisco Bay. Greater white-fronted geese fly in a winter sky over a tidal marsh pan with water. Black-necked stilts, a great egret, willets, a whimbrel, and a lesser yellowlegs feed and loaf in the mud. A tule elk herd looks on as a coyote hunts in the saltgrass, creeping wildrye, and dry bulrushes. Willow sausals at right in the distance indicate a freshwater creek emptying into the marsh. Cordgrass grows in salty waters in the distance on the left. OIL ON PAPERBOARD, 9 ½ X 15 INCHES, 2006

the rivers into San Francisco Bay, only now gradually declining in amount. Whole bays became mudflats from mining sediments. The San Francisco Bay's tidal marshes declined 80 percent in the last hundred and fifty years, due to these processes and the ever growing development that eats away at the bayshores.[15]

A few early visitors recorded their observations of the extensive tidal marshes, botanist William Brewer for one. In the 1860s he climbed a hill near present San Jose, looked out over the South Bay, and exclaimed at the view of "swamps intersected and cut up with winding streams and bayous crossing and winding in every direction, [making] by far the prettiest arabesque picture of the kind I have ever seen."[16]

At Long Beach, the Los Angeles River, before 1825, spread out into lakes, ponds, and marshes over a wide area with no single channel. Sand beaches were interspersed with fresh and salt marshes. In some places, extensive cottonwood forests also spread over the mesic flats. The Tongva (or Gabrielino) people made atole from tule seeds and baskets from rushes and willow stems. From shallow bay waters, people fished for such species as California halibut, leopard shark, gray smoothhound, and spotted sand bass. In winter edible shellfish were collected: cockles, abalone, oysters, limpets, and clams, as well as octopus.[17]

The dense coastal Indian population on the lower marine terraces and bay edges created midden soils, dark and enriched with crumbling shells, that may have held a distinctive plant community of amaranth and goosefoot, as well as plots of planted tobacco.

Los Angeles County originally had an estimated sixty-eight hundred acres of wetlands. By 1971 that number was reduced by 96 percent.[18] Long Beach is now the third busiest port in the world.[19] Despite this, support is strong at places like Newport Bay for restoration projects (see www. newportbay.org).

I heard a woman call a green marsh near where I live a useless "swamp." "Why can't we get rid of that thing?" she asked, wanting a lawn park put in. Fortunately that did not happen, and as urban people have looked more closely at their marshes in recent years, they have found out how incredibly diverse and useful they actually are. Recently, I was pleased to hear, the owner of this marsh, a businessman developing truck stops, has agreed to let land managers do controlled burns in the old cattails and bulrushes to help restore its health.

Marsh Habitats

I have tried to search out the remnants of once various marsh habitats to see them firsthand. For example, there are the small, shallow pools of salt water or freshwater, called *pans* (or *pannes*), that existed by the hundreds of thousands along the sinuous channels and within marshes. They filled with water from high tidal input, spring sources, runoff from the hills, or rainfall. Some were only a few dozen feet long, others almost a mile, and most were only a foot deep. Often lying in back of salt marshes next to the uplands, they provided fantastic bird feeding and loafing grounds.[20]

Some of these remain, at Suisun Marsh and Point Pinole Regional Shoreline. I traveled to Point Pinole to look for them, and my sister and her husband accompanied me, as they often do on my ramblings around the bay. After trudging about in the grassy flats along the shore, I finally found a marsh pan in the pickleweed. It was full of water from November rains and rich with green algae. Pierre did not look impressed with the little shallow pool, but I defended the habitat, saying it was a great indicator of an "old growth" marsh. Over time, once colonizing plants have established vegetative beds and a new marsh has begun to form, the number of pans increases and the channels become deeper and more complex in their winding. This was a fantastic relict.

Natural *salt ponds* existed along the east side of the southern end of San Francisco Bay; the largest complex was at Crystal Ponds, covering one thousand acres but probably fluctuating in size. Brine flies and brine shrimp thrived here, and Native people collected salt for use and trade: the Yrgin Ohlone may have placed willow sticks in the water for a period of time to harvest the clinging salt that built up. Salt crusts eight inches thick were described in these lakes.[21] American avocets, snowy plovers, black-necked stilts, and many terns gathered in these unique pools. Artificial salt collection and diking began in the 1800s.[22]

Upland transition zones, farther away from the water, are increasingly rare because of urbanization and agricultural development. Many endemic plants were once found in these low beds of pickleweed and saltgrass that gradually meld into moist grasslands of creeping wildrye. Sedge swales, wirerush, and rush stands mixed in with other seasonal wetlands: areas of freshwater marsh with bulrushes and cattails; creeks; backshore springs and seeps; and perennial ponds. Early botanists exploring San Francisco reported colorful wildflower displays (especially downingia) around vernal pools in grasslands in back of salt marshes; some temporary pools were fresh and others were alkaline.[23] Drier sites on shell beds, natural marsh berms created by wave action, natural levees of coarse sediments deposited on slough channels, and alluvial fans emerging out of nearby hills allowed high marsh specialists to grow: gumplant, spearscale, salt marsh bird's beak, and salt marsh owl's clover in the San Francisco Bay region, for example. These microhabitats were commonly found on U.S. coastal survey maps of the 1800s but are today very rare.[24]

The original transition vegetation for southern California salt marshes is even more difficult to reconstruct, as most of these lands are developed. At Tijuana Estuary, in Baja California, coastal sage plants abruptly meet the high marsh: boxthorn, California sagebrush, jojoba, laurel sumac, lemonadeberry, goldenbush, and Palmer's frankenia.

Similar scrub as well as grassland probably met the marsh in many areas around San Diego in the past.[25]

Historical ecologist Robin Grossinger speaks of "forgotten habitats," mostly destroyed before today's local biologists began their careers, and only discovered with diligent research.[26] One such habitat was the *sausal*—Spanish for willow grove— small thickets where creeks fanned out into low wet ground. Remnants can still be seen around San Francisco Bay in back of historic salt marsh areas. If I walked a half-mile from the bayshore towards El Cerrito Plaza, I would soon arrive at a remnant willow copse, a quarter-acre of arroyo willow near San Pablo Avenue in Richmond (visible in the distance of the grizzly painting on page 18). It is still there, in a state of benign neglect, its relict green, rounded canopy contrasting sharply with cars rushing along paved streets.

"Laguna" was the local term for ponds, lakes, or "sea swamps" formed in back of sandbars that

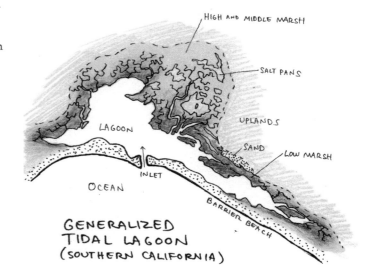

GENERALIZED
TIDAL LAGOON
(SOUTHERN CALIFORNIA)

blocked coastal streams during times of low flow, or in areas subject to periodic inundation by hide tides. These made great waterfowl habitat, according to hunter Charles Holder. A long series of lagunas ran from San Pedro to Long Beach, and geese, ducks, and cranes wintered there. In 1906 Holder wrote, "No more beautiful sight than this can be seen in southern California when these vast flocks pass up and down, silhouetted against the chaparral of the mountain slopes."[27] The "sprig" (northern pintail) was the first duck to arrive in winter. "In the old days, or twenty years ago," Holder wrote, "...I have seen the waters of the lagoons covered with them, while the adjacent lands and mounds would be white with cranes and geese."[28]

Historical ecologists work to track changing landscape features—eroding hills, moving water channels, or disappearing ponds, for example. The lagoon at Point Mugu, in Ventura County, protected by a naval base, gives a glimpse of a more pristine condition. Normally sandbars would enclose these southern California lagoons, and the ephemeral flow of feeder creeks would allow the trapped seawater to become hypersaline. Only big storms freshened their waters, sometimes temporarily killing off the oceanic starfish and mollusks inhabiting them. Other lagoons were seasonally freshened, and still others experienced tidal action twice a day through inlets opened by storms. Mugu Lagoon probably formed within the last three thousand years, as bay waters became trapped behind a long sand spit formed by longshore currents and wave action. Old maps show that this sand ridge has been fairly stable over the last hundred years, continually supplied by ocean current sand transport. In 1939 Port Hueneme jetty was built, cutting off some of this sand supply, and six kilometers of beach eroded away, undermining some buildings by 1948. At any given moment an estimated half-million to one million cubic meters of sand are passing by the point, heading southeast, partly from the Santa Clara and Ventura Rivers.[29]

The history of Mugu Lagoon shows how variable the community has been, continuously recreating itself—researchers like to use the term "nonequilibrium." Storms may rip out the eelgrass beds, thus reducing the fish fauna that use them as nurseries, but storms may also deposit new sediments that pickleweeds can colonize. Or waves may wash over the sand ridge into the lagoon, adding salt water. The inlet may migrate, algal mats may grow and smother shellfish, the sea level may rise, or increased rainfall may add freshwater. Change is the nature of the game.

Habitat Loss and Restoration

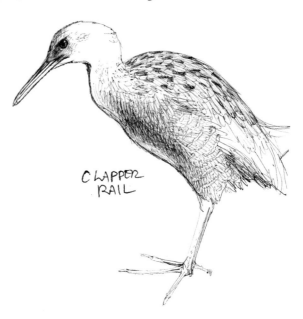

CLAPPER RAIL

At Tijuana Estuary since the 1850s, as fill has crept seaward, 80 percent of the tidal prism (the area covered by the tides sweeping in and out) has been lost, according to old maps. A pollen record from the estuary at Torrey Pines State Reserve, in San Diego County, shows that pickleweed dominated there for thousands of years, and the sediment deposits of a local stream kept pace, more or less, with the rise in sea level. But with Euro-American settlement, a tenfold increase in the sedimentation rate occurred.[30] Fires, overgrazing of nearby uplands, and erosion from development all contribute to increased sedimentation of marshes.

Some denizens of the salt marsh are now very rare due to habitat loss: the California clapper rail, for example. They used to be common enough to be hunted and served in restaurants in San Francisco.[31] It is normal for species in a community to change, expanding and shrinking their area. Even if a marsh appears to stay the same over the years, small-scale dynamics are varying. When extreme events coincide, local extinctions may happen naturally. Before 1900, estuaries were apparently more resilient because they were larger and more connected. In our fragmented landscape, an area may be cut off from the seeds needed for recolonization. Active restoration efforts are needed to make up for this.

I looked for the salt marsh harvest mouse at its last stronghold, in San Pablo Bay National Wildlife Refuge, during the Flyway Festival one January with my sister and her husband. On that cool and clear morning, the acres of flat, brown pickleweed stretched past the old Navy shipyards at Mare Island out to the bay, which was barely visible in the distance. Harriers , kestrels, and white-tailed kites hunted over the tidal marsh as killdeer and willets waded in ebbing water on nearby mudflats.

Salt marsh harvest mouse in pickleweed

As we walked around old naval buildings, memories came to Pierre, who worked at Mare Island on nuclear submarines in the 1980s. I asked him what he thought about the place now, this vast, flat, russet marsh meeting blue sky at the horizon.

"Well, not much has changed with the land. It's still here, and all the people and a lot of the buildings are gone. I'd say the land is the same."

I took his observation to heart, as this was one of the few places in the Bay Area megalopolis that had been protected from massive development, albeit by a military base. And after the base closed, the area was opened to the public, allowing us to see a huge chunk of original bay salt marsh.

We did not see any harvest mice that day, but we learned from a naturalist that these rodents nest in and dine on pickleweed and can swim easily if overtaken by high tides; they can even drink salt water. They have lost 80 percent of their habitat to development, and in 1970 the little rodents were placed on the federal list of endangered species.

Some plants, such as California sea-blite, are now regionally extinct from San Francisco and Oakland tidal marshes. Chilean cordgrass and other exotics are spreading, taking ground from natives. But many efforts at restoration have been successful. The goal is to restore not only native species, but the natural processes, such as tidal action and sediment accumulation, that will allow these marshes to maintain themselves. Biologists have come to admit that the best goal is to have self-sustaining habitats, not managed ones; to have habitats that slowly evolve towards complexity as they mature.

Another goal is to link the low-lying marshes with upland transitions, once highly diverse in plant life. Uplands also provide dryland refugia for marsh animals, such as the salt marsh wandering shrew. When restoring marshes, biologists and volunteers are also trying to avoid

PIGEON
GUILLEMOTS

COMMON
MURRES
WITH EGGS
& CHICKS

TUFTED
PUFFIN

DOUBLE-
CRESTED
CORMORANT

GULLS
FLYING

Brown pelican

excessive homogenization—too many marshes of the same age and stage of development; diversity is the key. Disturbance should be worked into the picture, as some rare plants are adapted to long-term cycles of extreme tides, wave-driven debris, and erosion.[32]

Beyond the Bay: Seabirds

Our family once took a boat trip out from the San Francisco Bay to the "Islands of the Dead"—the name people gave the distant, rocky peaks hundreds of years ago. In 1603 the Spanish explorer Sebastián Vizcaíno named them Los Farallones de los Frayles—"the promontories of the friars." The seas around these islands roughly fifty miles west of the Golden Gate are very productive when the cold upwelling currents dominate and nutrients are churned up from the seafloor. As the Golden Gate grew smaller and we headed out into the open Pacific, I realized how connected life in the bay is to life out here. The seemingly desolate waves were in fact rich feeding grounds, fueling a myriad of fish, seabirds, and marine mammals that often visit the bays, or used to.

Our boat arrived at the cold granitic islands—even in July the sea temperature was 52 degrees Fahrenheit. Common murres were everywhere, flying in single file or alone, fast, direct, and low over the waves. They nested all over the rocky heights, and the noise was incredible, the murres calling their name loudly. Little black pigeon guillemots whistled, and Brandt's cormorants dried their wings in groups on the cliffs. A single tufted puffin floated by our boat, eyeing us with a flip of its yellow head tuft and orange bill.

Hundreds of thousands of common murres once occupied the cold waters of the Gulf of the Farallones, catching anchovies, smelt, and rockfish. Perhaps four hundred and fifty thousand bred on those rocky island peaks in the mid-1800s.[33] Their numbers went down in the late 1800s as ships reached the islands to collect eggs for market. From 1854 to 1879, commerce took twelve million eggs from the Farallones. In 1880 domestic chicken farms became more lucrative,[34] but nonetheless, by 1900 fewer than one hundred murres were seen on the islands. In the twentieth century oil spills killed many seabirds, as well as the use of highly toxic pesticides like DDT. These concentrated in the fatty tissues of the birds, causing calcium deficiencies and eggshell failure (DDT was banned in 1972). Happily, by 2002 the number of murres counted on the Farallones reached one hundred thousand.[35]

El Niños severely affect fish-eating seabirds, such as brown pelicans, cormorants, western gulls, murres, Cassin's auklets, and tufted puffins. Brandt's and pelagic cormorants may entirely forego breeding during these warming events, as they did during the 1982-83 El Niño. Similar warm-water events apparently affected the birds in the 1800s. Biologists say that seabirds were then able to "prey-switch": if one fish population plummeted due to warming sea temperatures, the birds could switch to another species: rockfish, sardines, herring, anchovies, or squid. But in the late twentieth and early twenty-first centuries, people have harvested all fish heavily. Since about 1976 sea temperatures have been warmer and more variable annually than at any other time since measurements have been taken, and this climatic stress combines with intense fishing to keep seabirds (and pinnipeds) at lower than historic numbers.[36]

Other, more bizarre seabirds were once found in California, many not since the 1800s. Around Monterey Bay, floating whale blubber from the early whaling operations attracted the Antarctic giant petrel, or "gong" (so named for its unique call). This robust bird with an eight-foot wingspan is

Left: Short-tailed albatross

Below: The extinct diving goose

WING BONES:
Chendytes

SCOTER

currently a Southern Hemisphere breeder, but it was once reported along the Pacific Coast as far north as the mouth of the Columbia River. In 1871 the ornithologist William Cooper described the scene at Monterey Bay:

> The enormous petrel...could often be seen swimming lazily near the try-works to pick up scraps of blubber, sometimes accompanied by the dusky young of the short-tailed albatross....The Pacific fulmars...called by the whalers "tager" or "haglet," were common offshore, feeding also on whale meat, but oftener observed chasing the gulls to make them disgorge.[37]

In the nineteenth century short-tailed albatrosses were a fairly common sight inshore at San Pedro, Monterey, San Francisco Bay, and around the Channel Islands, and bones from these seafaring birds have been found in shellmounds at Point Mugu and other locations.[38] In the early 1900s millions were slaughtered for their feathers on their breeding ground on Torishima Island, near Japan. A count of over one hundred thousand breeding birds fell to two hundred and fifty, and this albatross was considered nearly extinct in the 1940s. With protection they have slowly increased.[39]

One truly unique seabird went extinct during the Holocene prior to the arrival of Europeans: the flightless diving duck. The wings of this bird were small and too weak to allow fight. The size of a Canada goose, but apparently most closely related to scoters (sea ducks), it had bones denser and heavier than those of flying birds, to aid in diving. The skull of this flightless "diving goose" was large and robust, with a strong beak, giving it the ability to wrench off mussels and other invertebrates as it dove down to the rocky sea-bottom.[40] The bones of flightless diving ducks have been found in late Pleistocene deposits from San Nicolas and Anacapa Islands, various sites on the mainland around Orange County, Los Angeles, and Ventura, and at Port Orford, on the southern Oregon coast. Bones dating to about thirty-seven hundred years ago have been found in shell middens at Laguna Creek, in Santa Cruz County, and perhaps the Año Nuevo midden south of that.[41] They were the most common bird bones found in the Laguna Creek midden.[42]

These diving ducks are absent from the last two thousand years.[43] People may have been hunting these birds, as they did cormorants, for their feathers, as well as for food. The diving ducks probably bred on rocky isles and sea stacks, and some researchers suggest the adults were overharvested by people boating to these sites—eggs the size of goose eggs must also have been a draw. I wonder, however, if environmental factors affecting their habitat and prey could have played a more important role: as the Xerothermic climate phase ended and the Pacific Coast became moister, more stream sediment was transported oceanward, and sea level rose more slowly. Many shallow, rocky, shellfish-producing shorelines became stretches of sandy beach.

The giant petrel was a scavenger with a formidable bill. It spit stinking stomach oil at intruders, wobbling about on land with an awkward gait but gliding gracefully for hours.

MOTIONS VERY
FLUID & ROLLING,
LIKE A SLINKY
TOY. CLUMSY MOVING
ON ROCKS.
RUBS HIS BACK
& PAWS, RUBS
FUR AGAINST ROCKS.

Sea otter sketches

Fur Bearers

On the barren slopes of the Farallones our tour group marveled at the groups of Steller's sea lions hauled up onto the rocks, sometimes climbing quite high. Cows and pups made warbling sounds when greeting each other, and bulls mixed in like great brown slugs amid the white breaker-spray. A group of elephant seals lazily slept on a small sandy beach.

Northern elephant seals may have crowded the beaches and coves from Drake's Bay to Baja California two hundred years ago. But they were hunted for their oil-rich fat, which burned in lamps and streetlights. It was also used as a lubricant, in soap making, and in hide tanning. One bull eighteen feet long, taken at Santa Barbara Island in 1852, produced two hundred and ten gallons of oil; usually they yielded three barrels.[44] The population dwindled until none were found anywhere by the 1880s. Then a relict group of perhaps one hundred showed up on Isla de Guadalupe, off Mexico, in 1892. With protection, by the 1930s the great seals had begun to repopulate areas to the north, and by 1972 they were again breeding on the Farallon Islands. By 1984 the population had zoomed to eighty thousand, and it is still growing.[45]

Another marine mammal, small and easily overlooked along the coast, ranks high in the history of California. The sea otter is the most valuable furbearer ever known, and Europeans were quick to hunt it for its luxuriant pelt. "They were so abundant in 1812 that they were killed by boatmen with their oars in passing through the kelp," said General Vallejo.[46] That year at Fort Ross the Russian American Company was founded to trap the region, bringing one hundred hunters from the Aleutian Islands to hunt sea otters and fur seals from skin kayaks. Within a decade of intense hunting the population became scarce. By 1914 they were almost extinct—only fifty were found along the whole coast. An international treaty was signed in 1911 to protect them,[47] and the otters are now extending their range again.

Not a fur bearer but another creature that once swam in California nearshore seawaters, the Steller's sea cow was a denizen of North Pacific waters. A skull was trawled out of Monterey Bay and radiocarbon dated to about eighteen thousand years ago. Related to the manatee and Florida dugong, this marine beast grew to thirty-five feet or more in length and weighed ten tons. With small head and forelimbs, a flattened tail, and a barrel-shaped body with barklike hide covering its blubber, this peaceful floating mammal entirely lacked teeth and used horny plates on its palate and mandibles to tear kelp and other algae to eat. At some unknown time, possibly during the Holocene, sea cows shrank back to a relictual range in the cold Bering Sea. But they were easy prey even there for hunters. In 1768, twenty-seven years after their discovery to science, they went extinct from the world.[48]

The greatest overall commercial wealth from the ocean came from the once "countless" fur seals, robust with fat at the beginning of the pupping season that took place off California from May to August. They preferred remote, rocky islands and delighted to play in the surf, feeding on fish. "When a great number are collected on shore their barking and howling is almost deafening; and when passing to leeward of a seal island, the odor arising from it is anything but pleasant," said one early seaman.[49] Many used to congregate on beaches blocked from the mainland by steep gullies, but sealers coming from the ocean side drove them back and clubbed whole herds.

Guadalupe fur seals once flippered from the Farallon Islands south to Islas San Benito, off Baja California. Their rookeries there were ancient, the lava rocks worn smooth from their bodies. At least four hundred thousand were taken along the California coast from 1806 to 1820. A single vessel took one hundred and thirty thousand fur seals in two years. The seals were extirpated on the Farallones by 1834.[50] In fact, the entire species was nearly slaughtered before scientists recorded it. Zoologist C. Hart Merriam realized he had found an unknown fur seal when he saw some skulls, but scientific expeditions through the first half of the twentieth century failed to find any live seals at their last stronghold, on the San Benito Islands. Then in 1954, fourteen Guadalupe fur seals were found there: a few loudly roaring

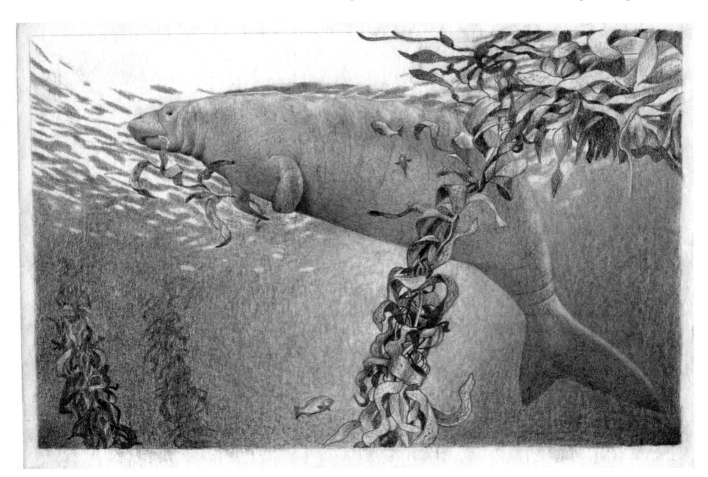

Steller's sea cow munching on giant kelp

GUADALUPE FUR SEALS

bulls, bleating cows, and most importantly, several pups on the rocks and "disporting in the surf."[51] The species came back from the brink of extinction. By 1968 the population had climbed to perhaps five hundred, and by 1980 to two thousand.[52] They are occasionally seen on the Channel Islands, but in the past they must have been much more common. Their bones are found more frequently in San Miguel Island archaeological sites than those of any other pinniped.[53]

The anchovy-eating northern fur seal was also harvested off the Farallones, by the Russians, before 1833.[54] Their decreasing numbers on the Pribilof Islands, in the Bering Sea, reveal the extent of hunting pressure on them: perhaps 2.5 million were found there in the late 1700s, but by 1911 the count had dropped to two hundred thousand. Fortunately the number has increased since then, and a colony has developed on San Miguel Island.[55] In the 1990s northern fur seals returned to the Farallones.[56]

A debate has raged concerning the human impact on seal populations in California before European contact. Archaeologist William Hildebrandt argues that Native people in sophisticated watercraft caused seals, through intensified hunting pressure, to keep to remote, protected, offshore locations. Archaeologist R. Lee Lyman counters that the present-day restriction of seals to offshore rookeries is a product of overexploitation by Euro-American hunters, and that before this seals could be found along the mainland.[57] Neither argument assumes significant predation by grizzlies and wolves.[58]

Seaworthy craft may have been developed in the Channel Islands as early as seven thousand years ago. Intensive sea-mammal hunting may have begun as early as 5000 B.C., on Santa Catalina Island, as people clubbed seals and sea lions at their rookeries and haul-outs, or speared them from watercraft. But archaeologist Michael Glassow notes that many of the sites he has studied were occupied for two thousand years with no significant changes in faunal remains, which indicates that the seal population was not depleted.[59]

The impact of climatic factors should not be underestimated, as seawater temperatures increased beginning about A.D. 1300 (the Medieval Warm Period), possibly creating crises for both cold-water marine fauna and local human hunters. The development of the pelagic plank canoe (some forty feet long and able to go sixty-five miles from the coast) in about A.D. 650 corresponds with cooler sea surface temperatures and increased marine fisheries, as if the Chumash and Tongva were taking advantage of good times.[60]

Lyman found that Indians did hunt the pinnipeds' rookeries, as evidenced by the presence in middens of juvenile seal bones, but they did not exploit them into oblivion, as Euro-American hunters did. Lyman also suggests that precontact seal and sea lion behavior and migratory patterns might have been quite different from what we see today. Fur seals, sea lions, and elephant seals may be more abundant today on the Channel Islands than prehistorically; Holocene hunters probably pushed breeding off the island shores to rocky islets in the ocean nearby.[61] And some species that are now only seasonal may have stayed year-round on the California coast before the pressures of Euro-American hunting.

Though far from conclusive, this study of the history of California seals and sea lions is also a case study in the ways that historical ecology can be crucial to recovering seal populations today: we must understand their past if they are to prosper in the future.

Great Whales

Perhaps California's greatest, and most tragic, display of industrial hunting techniques was seen during the age of whalers. Shore whaling began as early as 1851 in Monterey Bay and 1852 in San Francisco.[62]

In 1874 over one thousand gray whales were observed passing daily, from December 15 to February 1, off San Francisco—as many as thirty thousand to forty thousand per season, according to whaler Charles Scammon. The grays often entered shallow lagoons and bays and swam through the once abundant kelp forests, and they were seen tossing in the breakers by Monterey. Men with lances in hand lay in wait for them in small boats in the kelp beds, although the whales could be "sagacious," sometimes chasing and upsetting the boats. By 1884 the number of migrating gray whales was as low as forty, and boats had to cruise out ten miles into the ocean to kill them with handheld harpoons, then drag them back to shore for processing—boiling their blubber in great vats, accompanied by screaming gulls. More than seventy-five thousand barrels of gray whale oil were produced from whaling sites in the San Francisco Bay Area, Monterey Bay, Half Moon Bay, and San Diego.[63] Today's gray whale population is perhaps half what it was before the commercial whaling era.[64]

Blue whales were once abundant along the California coast, found at all seasons. Large numbers of these so-called sulphur-bottoms "at times play[ed] about the ships at anchor near capes or islands," according to Scammon in 1874. They were attracted to the swarms of sardines and prawns enlivening the waters off Baja California; in July 1858, by Cerros Island, Scammon saw that "the sea, as far as the eye could discern, was marked with their huge forms and towering spouts."[65] At first they were rarely taken, as they were considered the "swiftest whale afloat." In 1862 whalemen at Monterey caught a monster ninety-two feet long, so large it broke the capstan used to lift whales onto the beach. But eventually, with more modern equipment, the blue whales too were hunted to near-extinction, and by the 1960s the world population was only one thousand animals. Since the 1980s they have increased in the Gulf of the Farallones.[66]

Natural historian Jules Evens imagined seasonal pods of blue whales and humpbacks wandering nearshore in central California, as orcas and great white sharks patrolled for seals.[67] Humpback whales tended to travel close to shore and therefore were subject to heavy whaling pressure. Scammon described them as "moving about in large numbers, scattered over the sea as far as the eye can discern from the masthead."[68]

Even the whaling industry itself noticed declines in their catches, and the *Handbook to Monterey and Vicinity* of 1875 predicted that "the whale fishery, which for the last twenty-five years has constituted one of the most important of our local industries, is likely soon to become a thing of

FUR SEALS
HEADING FOR
SARDINE GROUP

MASSIVE SHOAL OF
SARDINES BY SHORE
— AERIAL VIEW —

WHALE
SWALLING
THOUSANDS OF
SARDINES AT
ONE GULP

the past." (The last whaling company in California, in Eureka, closed in the 1940s.[69]) The invention of the factory ship in 1925 and explosive harpoons proved disastrous to whales worldwide, and the gray whale and right whale went economically extinct until international treaties were signed in 1938 to regulate the take of the marine giants. Fortunately, many species are making a comeback in California waters.

The sea has always been mysterious to me; I never owned a boat, did not dive, and could not easily access the ocean secrets. But sometimes the Pacific lets us glimpse her hidden wonders. While at the illustration program at UC Santa Cruz, a few of my student friends and I visited Long Marine Lab to see what we could sketch for an assignment. We were in luck that day, for a very rare deep ocean predator was revealed to us. A baby sperm whale had washed up on Capitola Beach, and marine biologists at the lab were dissecting it to learn more about this amazing animal. We were invited to watch—and draw.

Sperm whales must be one of the most bizarre creatures I have encountered. This "baby" was car-sized, still suckling at six months old, its skull more cartilage than bone. As an adult it might have reached sixty-eight feet and weighed seventy tons. Sperm whales are usually black in color, but old males may turn white. The smaller females and calves stay closer to the Tropics, but the males may travel sixteen hundred miles in a year, wandering to the polar seas. What was this calf doing in Monterey Bay? The sperm whales occasionally congregate into giant herds of one thousand, following a lunar cycle: migrating during the waxing moon and grouping at the full moon. They communicate with clicks and low roars.

These whales are specialists in deep diving. They descend, at 550 feet per minute, into the inky darkness of the deep sea with power-strokes of their huge tail flukes, using echolocation to find prey as they dive. They can hold their breath for hours. They do not suffer from the bends like humans do, because their superefficient hemoglobin keeps as much air out of the bloodstream as possible; the muscles absorb 50 percent of the total oxygen store during this time. Squid makes up as much as 80 percent of their diet, and they also eat fish, shrimp, crabs, and octopus. A whale can swallow a forty-foot, 440-pound giant squid—whole. Sucker marks on whales' heads attest to the battles that occur in the deep—some are reported to be eight inches in diameter, making for a squid one hundred and fifty feet long!

Sperm whales are believed to dive to the bottom of incredibly deep trenches at 10,500 feet, where they shovel up the seabed, swallowing bottom-dwelling sharks. After a particularly deep dive, the whale may ascend with a rush and jump completely out of the water, falling back with a great splash.

The most incredible part of the sperm whale's story is its head. One-third of the total body length, it contains the largest brain of any animal. We tried to sketch the complicated anatomy of the baby's head, which was stripped of its two-inch-thick skin and blubber. Tubes in the snout may fill with cold water to alter the temperature of organs containing a waxy solid, spermaceti, that changes the buoyancy of the whale for diving. The whale breathes air in from a blowhole on the left side of its head, sending it through a long nasal passage to the lungs, and apparently then back out through the right nasal passage to the tip of the spermaceti organ. This organ, a long sac, is so large in adults that whalers have been known to fall in and drown. At the tip are "monkey lips" of hard tissue, hidden under the skin of the snout—normally you can't see them. Air pressure vibrates the lips, and the vibrations move back through the spermaceti organ, which bounces this sound through a solid fat body below. The sonar vibrations are focused and amplified in concentric circles of fat and connective tissue, out through the snout and into the water, and they are of such magnitude that they can stun fish and blast their swim bladders. Divers who have placed their hands in front of sperm whales' heads have felt themselves silently pushed away by these strong vibrations.

We left late in the day, after the impromptu class. I was humbled by this small hint of the ocean's treasure, and I wondered how we could ever understand whole ecosystems, let alone single organisms. Some stories of nature are stranger than we can imagine.

FOUR

THE INLAND MARSHES

Living Locally

As we move inland from the mysterious sea, we encounter transitional places, summer-green swards of freshwater plant growth and associated faunas. These marshes are not places we now usually think of as homes, but people have lived alongside them for ages because of the all-important presence of freshwater.

Moving away from the broad methods of historical ecology, in this chapter I'd like to talk about the local place; how people related in the past to their land, and how we can again learn to live locally. Lately, marsh conservation and restoration projects have become common because of the rich biodiversity found in these habitats. Historical ecology should not be some abstract theory you simply read about, but part of a way of life—a perfect fit with restoration. In this chapter we will see how the inland marshes of California have changed over time, what animals used to live in these jeweled havens, and how we can help bring these places to health. Think of it as cultural historical ecology.

Getting Your Hands Dirty

The morning was hot already, but we persisted in cutting tall bulrush and cattail stems from the shallow pool. After testing different kinds of cutting tools, we found that curved sickles worked best. Holding the plants in one hand and swinging the blade with the other, I began to realize how medieval peasants felt harvesting wheat.

I live near a small desert wetland full of cattails, tules, and bulrushes along the Amargosa River. A linear oasis full of endemic fish, amphibians, and rare birds, it cuts across artificial political boundaries from western Nevada into eastern California. Quite a few of my jobs and volunteer activities have taken place along this river and other desert streams, the Owens and Mojave Rivers, and much of the work involved clearing "excess" marsh vegetation to make open water for various rare pupfish, tui chub, speckled dace, and even isolated toad populations. The little artificial refugium pond where we were working held colorful blue pupfish. It was crammed full of old, dead cattail stems, years of growth piled higher and higher, leaving only slits of water for the fish to swim through. I often wondered how they survived before we came along to cut the marsh growth. What was pupfish habitat like a thousand years ago?

Back home, more marsh vegetation awaited. The Nature Conservancy (TNC) had been working hard to restore Amargosa toad habitat in the local spring system, an area impacted by livestock grazing, alfalfa irrigation waterworks, and invasive mosquitofish, bullfrogs, and crayfish that were devouring the toads' eggs and tadpoles. In addition, the cattails, tules, and bulrushes were, as usual, spreading densely and filling all the open water that the toads used to breed in. TNC constructed new pools and channels with tractor-hoe machines. Plastic liners were spread over the bottoms of some waterways to prevent new growth of marsh vegetation. The restoration project was designed to reshape the former irrigation ditch system into a more natural form. But after a few years the bulrushes began poking through and shredding the liner.

Light, fluffy, floating cattail seeds quickly colonized the other open-water channels and pools, and within one season a green, dense, hip-high thicket of their stems and leaves had grown up.

Again, we went out to parts of the shallow marsh edge with shovels and hand clippers and dug small, open pools a few inches deep. The toads did not need much to be happy—that night they discovered the newly open water and began calling their soft, piping songs; the next morning the pool glittered with strings of tiny black eggs encased in clear "jelly." The toads seemed to favor disturbance, and I wondered what natural processes created such disturbances before we came along with our shovels and metal blades to dig new pools every year.

Clues came when TNC began to manipulate the habitat in different ways, based on historical ecological studies of what the valley might have been like before Euro-American development. The local Paiute and Shoshone elders told biologists that their people had regularly burned the marshes to open up waterfowl habitat and renew useful plants. After a long permit process and careful planning, TNC carried out a controlled burn on a selected part of the marsh. As the low, orange flames singed the tall, dry grass, rush, and bulrush, a big patch of blackened charcoal ground became visible. No longer hidden, sinuous water channels and pools suddenly appeared from underneath the vegetation mat. The spot had not seen toad breeding in years, but within a week toads found the open water and laid their eggs. Six months later, in spring, luxuriant green grasses, rushes, and bulrushes grew over the burned ground, and a new generation of toads hopped about the underbrush (see more on fire in chapter eight).

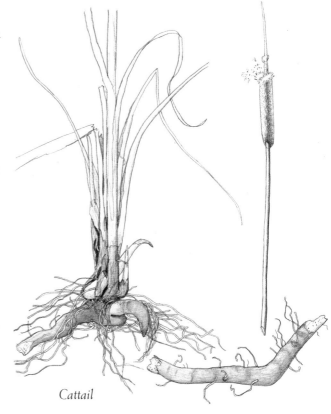

Cattail

One winter, on another part of their property, TNC tried grazing: cowboys herded eighty head of cattle onto a pasture where spring-flow spread out into a wide marsh. The cattle grazed down the old dead vegetation, which had grown up for more than a decade after the property was purchased, and then after a few months the herd was moved off. That spring the toads exploded in a breeding frenzy in the newly opened shallow water, only a few inches deep in saltgrass and rushes. By April the waters were swarming with little jet-black tadpoles feeding on bits of green algae and leaf detritus.

Within a month most metamorphosed into "toadlets," miniature, adult-shaped toads that gradually grew larger and moved out into the surrounding rabbitbrush to feed on insects. The next spring the toads bred again in the previously grazed meadow. Living nearby, we watched as the vegetation began to grow back again, and the toad breeding lessened. A new disturbance would have to open up breeding waters in the future, in a cyclic way.

The question of the past again came up: disturbance must have been a regular part of this valley ecosystem. The Indians here regularly set fires. They dug marsh plants with digging sticks, they trimmed willows to encourage long shoots for basketry, and they trimmed mesquites to increase the yield of their edible beans. Native grazing animals, although not present in large numbers in these desert river valleys, did graze marsh plants and trample open water in spots—elk in the Central Valley, and bison in northeastern California. Deer, antelope, bighorn sheep, and rabbits added minor grazing effects in other parts of the state (see chapter six for more on grazing).

In addition, the rivers flooded periodically, scouring away areas of vegetation, flattening dead plant material, and even transporting fish and toads into new areas. When I lived in Bishop (in Inyo County along the Owens River) and worked for the California Department of Fish and Game, I used to talk about prehistoric pupfish with Steve Parmenter, fishery biologist and expert at ridding fish habitat of weedy cattails. The Owens River today is heavily controlled for water storage and transport via pipeline to Los Angeles, and for sport trout angling. But trout are not native here, and hundreds of years ago the river probably held thousands of Owens pupfish, thriving in its shifting channels and overflow pools. Floods would form new marshes that later dried up, stranding some of the fish, but other new habitats formed: a shifting disturbance mosaic of marsh destruction and re-creation.

Now the pupfish must be carefully tended in pools away from the river, to keep them from the hungry mouths of the introduced trout, and to reproduce the habitats they desire—not the cold, fast-flowing, deep river channel, but warm, shallow marsh edges and pools of open water. Excess tules and cattails must be removed by hand. Steve developed various cutting tools, such as the rice knives he attached to long poles to reach into deeper ponds. From him I learned that the best conservation biology involves getting mud on your hands, and the willingness to try different methods and see what works.

"I've found that the cattails don't grow back if you cut them below the water surface," he told me as he rubbed his reddish beard and looked out over the fish lake. "Bulrushes are trickier, though."

The Department of Fish and Game carries out other methods as well for optimizing the desert fish communities, like controlled burns at Fish Lake Slough. "Managed disturbance" has replaced the natural disturbance of flood and fire.

But as I pulled cattails for toads at my home, I realized that we humans have always been a part of the landscape. For thousands of years people have been changing, caring for, and manipulating marshes and other habitats. And I do not think it is a bad thing. It may be the idea of "wilderness" that is artificial. At her residence in Furnace Creek, in Death Valley National Park, discussing how Western science and traditional knowledge could mutually work to benefit the natural world that is our home, Timbisha Shoshone elder Pauline Esteves explained to me one day that people need to take care of the springs. "We are related to the springs, to the water," she said. "If we don't take care of them, they won't take care of us."

Land management agencies and organizations have not reached that depth of connection to the land, but locals like me are beginning to develop more personal relations with our springs and marshes and willow groves; we are learning to live with them in an ongoing way. Quick fixes are not going to work—working with the land must be a part of our daily life. Nature includes humans, and the ways in which we make our homes on the land.

Marsh Foods and Fibers

As I dug out extra cattails from the toad marsh by my house, I sometimes washed a few root-rhizomes and ate pieces of them—the cream-colored marsh food tasted slightly sweet and starchy. Marshes have been storehouses of raw materials, foods, and medicines for thousands of years. The traditonal native diet here includes cattail roots roasted on hot coals or dried and ground into meal, the fluff-covered seeds, and new stems peeled and eaten raw, like bamboo shoots. Native people sewed the tall stems and flat leaves together as floor mats, bundled them for roof thatch, made them into cordage, used them in duck decoys, lined storage pits and roasting pits with them, dried them for kindling, and wove the young stems into baskets: all parts of the cattail plant were dried and stored for year-round use.

The tall, round stems of tules could be twisted into rope or woven into floor mats for sitting and sleeping on, and for covering willow-pole houses; bundles were tied together to make boats; women pounded tule strips soft to make skirts; and rope was fashioned from tule stems. The roots were edible.

Basket makers still visit the marshes to collect plant fibers, although today these storehouses are rarer. They search out and tend the long rhizomes—horizontal roots—of sedges that stretch through the marsh mud. Traditionally, mud was cleared away from the four- to five-foot-long rhizomes with a digging stick, and a clamshell was used to cut them. Then they were coiled up and taken home in a burden basket. Once home, basket makers split, dry, and store the rhizomes and are rewarded with strands of white, yellow, tan, and brown from which they make baskets of all kinds.

Tulare

Overcast skies and cold air blew on my cheeks, and round, tan-colored tules rose against the silver-gray clouds—November in a freshwater marsh, far inland from the sea. A song sparrow chirped loudly from the depths of the tule stems, and red-winged blackbirds flew about, calling, gathering

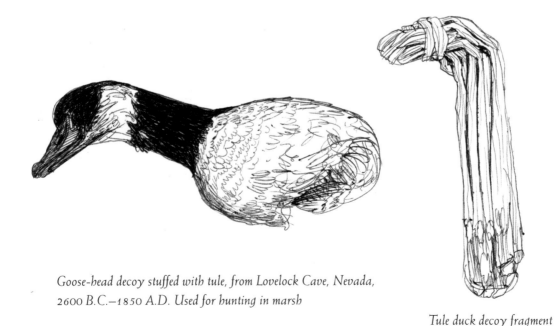

Goose-head decoy stuffed with tule, from Lovelock Cave, Nevada, 2600 B.C.—1850 A.D. Used for hunting in marsh

Tule duck decoy fragment

SEDGE
Carex obnupta TUFT SHOWING ROOTS,
Carex tumulicola SEEDHEAD STEM

for the night. As I turned a bend in my raft, a group of ring-necked ducks and mallards exploded out of the water with gurgling splashes, some rising powerfully, others running along the surface, feet pattering, wings flapping loudly. Silhouettes of ducks in lines and groups smoothly flowed overhead. Three hundred years ago, there might have been enough to block the light of the sun.

This was hugely different from the minute desert springs and ribbons of river-fringe I had been working in. The Sacramento–San Joaquin River Delta and low parts of the Central Valley that receive flooding from the great rivers were once a vast, freshwater marsh. The Delta was a thousand square miles of wetlands, and at high tide some six hundred square miles went underwater.[1] Dominated by tules, it was a world of summer-green stems standing taller than people, where masses of rhizomatous roots decayed into rich, organic soils and where, in the winter, river waters rolled over the dead, graying stems to create an enormous feeding ground for waterfowl.

The Spanish called it "tulare," the land of tules. Pedro Font, traveling east from San Francisco in April 1775, looked over a low hill and saw an immense plain, "immeasurable," with few trees and a confusion of water and tules, islands and rivers. He saw large elk herds near the water and an Indian village by a river, with the great Sierra Nevada on the other side. A few days later, Font's party followed the numerous well-beaten elk trails down to the water and found they led into boggy mires. The party came to the track of a man leading to a little village, but the trail got marshy. Font noticed piles of snail and turtle shells left in the silt by floods. The party finally gave up trying to reach the Sierra after meeting a man who had spent the whole day getting around a tule marsh, only to see many more marshes ahead of him.[2]

Tule

What an amazing world this must have been. From my own explorations of the marsh remnants, I could tell that tules and cattails probably dominated deepwater fresh marshes, while shallower marshes were a riot of American threesquare, alkali bulrush, Baltic rush, spikerush, sedges, and bur-reed. Common reed, called *carrizo* (cane) in Spanish, choked wet places, especially along the margins of rivers, and helped to prevent the banks from washing away in floods.[3]

Natural levees, built up by sediments carried by the river, blocked many streams emptying into the Sacramento Valley from the surrounding hills—some levees were as large as twenty feet high and one was ten miles wide. The stream waters pooled up into "sinks" full of tule marshes. Putah, Cache, and Butte Creeks are examples.[4]

The Spanish explorers gave way to American farmers. In 1861 members of the San Joaquin Agricultural Society boated around the muddy sloughs of the Delta, noting reclamation efforts, diking, grazing livestock, hay making, grain crops, and orchards. They saw an Indian rancheria by Bear Creek after leaving Stockton and passed by camps of Chinese fishermen on the banks who were netting perch, trout, salmon, and "slough-fish" to salt and send to the gold mines, and also catching beavers, otters, and muskrat. They met "Whisky Bill" and other hermits living in the

THE STREAM WATERS POOLED UP INTO "SINKS" FULL OF TULE MARSHES.

The Delta one thousand years ago, a maze of tule marsh islands merging with a valley grassland.
The Sierra Nevada rises in the distance. PASTEL ON GRAY BOARD, 6 X 8 INCHES, 2006

depths of the quiet riparian woodland, and workers stripping the bark off trees. It would be shipped to San Francisco for use in tanning. They noted the "millions of blackbirds" (possibly tricolored blackbirds) that nested in the tules and sang overhead. Mount Diablo rose in the dim distance, above the broad, level landscape. Seeing the flags of levee builders, the Agricultural Society boaters happily commented on the "improvement" of thousands of acres of tule lands, albeit with a fleeting recognition of the disappearing "charms of solitude" and the strange beauty of the freshwater marsh. As they drifted down Georgia Slough from the Calaveras River, they wrote about the "wide expanse of sky and land" that "carried the weary eye away into the hazy limits of the tule world, where the mingled tints of green and blue formed rainbow galaxies of Earth's creation."[5]

Before contact, the Central Valley as a whole may have had five million acres of marshes,[6] and in some places the marsh may have been fifty miles across.[7] Today only 10 percent of California's wetlands remain.[8] Two million acres of overflow land were "reclaimed," starting with the Swamp Land Act of 1850.[9] Dikes and levees were built, canals were dug, and waters were drained or redirected out of the fertile bottomlands for agriculture.

Some inkling of the ancient and vast tulare may be gained by traveling to Malheur National Wildlife Refuge in eastern Oregon. Although the climate and some species differ from those of central California, and the whole wetland region is artificially managed by dikes and channels for controlled flooding and drying, some semblance of a natural order can be seen. It is common for lightning to cause fires there. A complex mosaic of lakes, pools, bands of marsh, islands, and interfingering upland vegetation presents itself to the viewer, and the birds are abundant in any season.

Vanished Lakes

It takes study to imagine, with any accuracy, a completely vanished landscape. Driving Highway 5 from the Bay Area into the San Joaquin Valley I passed such a landscape. What I saw was a flatland covered with thousands of acres of cotton and wheat, especially visible as the road leaves the low hills out of Kettleman City, in Kern County. There it was—the old Tulare Lake bed, an ecosystem gone. Before draining, it was a fabulous system of sloughs, a maze of channels, a sea of tall, waving sedges, grasses, and cattails, and a vast, open-water inland sea. Now lost in time, it had been a home to people for ages.

The southern San Joaquin Valley is a closed basin formed by a ring of tall mountains and the merged alluvial fans of the Kings River in the east and Los Gatos Creek in the west. The Kings and Kaweah Rivers drained snowmelt off the Sierra in spring, and each divided into multiple channels that spread out to "a perfect swamp," according to early travelers.[10] Large inland seas formed here: Tulare, Buena Vista, Kern, and Goose Lakes. These were shallow, and sometimes they dried up altogether. In wet years they joined into one large lake that emptied through Fresno Slough into the San Joaquin River, and thence to the Pacific.[11] When Tulare Lake joined with the smaller lakes, twenty-one hundred miles of shoreline were created, one of the largest freshwater lakes west of the Mississippi River, and the largest single wetland in California.[12] In the wet year of 1978, the old Tulare Lake suddenly appeared again, spreading over seventy square miles to a depth of forty feet.[13]

In the highly recommended book *Indian Summer: Traditional Life among the Choinumne Indians of California's San Joaquin Valley*, Thomas Jefferson Mayfield describes the amazing Tulare Lake as he first saw it, in 1871: great growths of tules twenty feet high and more than two inches thick, clouds of blackbirds, and mile-long swarms of wild geese flying over. He was greeted by tule stands and mudflats that took days to travel through, and rivers lined with beautiful willows, blackberries, and grapevines. Choinumne Yokuts Indians set basket traps in the shallow waters to catch hundreds of trout, steelhead, salmon, suckers, and eels. Some families built fifty-foot-long tule balsas and floated on the spring meltwaters coming off the Sierran streams, spearing fish near shore next to drifting mats of decaying tules.

Then came the cattle barons, and next the wheat barons, and as early as the mid-1850s, people began to divert the Tule River.[14] Agriculture led to the total draining of the lakes in the twentieth century.

A fragment of Tulare Lake can still be seen at Creighton Ranch Preserve, in Kern County. Here remnants of the extensive freshwater marshes can be found, including the endemic goldenbush.[15]

"How can you take all these sad stories?" a friend asked me. I answered that maybe, if we collectively remembered these events in California's unfolding history, we could use what we learned when we had to face large environmental problems, such as droughts.

"The Sky Was Blackened"

Explorer-naturalist John Xantus, collecting specimens during the mid-1800s out of Fort Tejon, in Kern County, found waterbirds abundant in the tulares of the southern San Joaquin Valley, for example Buena Vista Lake, into which the Kern River flowed. In May he found breeding birds:

Old Tulare Lake under the Sierra. Snow geese fly over a Yokuts tule balsa. OIL ON TONED COTTON RAG PAPER, 9 X 8 INCHES, 2006

Little green heron   *Snowy egret*   *Coot*

fulvous whistling ducks, cinnamon teal, black-necked stilts, and white-faced ibis. By January he described Tulare Lake as "literally covered" with waterfowl.[16]

A survey party exploring the San Joaquin Valley in 1853 found wood ducks, as well as grizzlies, to be plentiful by the Kaweah River. Across an alkaline desert they approached Tulare Lake, where they found elk, long-billed curlews, common snipe, and an Indian village:[17]

> Your ears are confused with the many sounds—the quacking of the mallard, the soft and delicate whistle of the baldpate [widgeon] and teal, the underground-like notes of the rail or marsh-hen [coot], the flute-like notes of the wild goose and brant, the wild ranting of the heron, not to forget the bugle-like notes of the whooping crane and swan and a thousand other birds mingling their songs together—creates that indescribable sensation of pleasure that can only be felt by one fond of nature in its wildest and most beautiful form.[18]

Nearly forty years later, A. K. Fisher, ornithologist on the Death Valley Expedition, stopped at Buena Vista and Tulare Lakes and noticed abundant coots, western grebes, eared grebes, California gulls, white pelicans, American avocets, mallards, green-winged teal, and Canada geese. Northern harriers (marsh hawks) were said to abound in the San Joaquin Valley around the extensive marshlands.[19]

North of the Delta, Sacramento Valley residents in the mid-1800s complained of the "almost deafening, tumultuous, and confusing noises of the innumerable flocks of geese and ducks which are continually flying to and fro and at times blackening the very heavens with their increasing numbers."[20]

Lesser sandhill cranes (called "little brown cranes") were once common: "thousands" were seen feeding in open grasslands near marshes, wintering in the San Joaquin Valley and San Francisco Bay transitional marsh grasslands, and at least once in the Los Angeles region. They may have bred in the Central Valley at one time as well.[21] Greater sandhill cranes were common in interior California, but their breeding range has been greatly reduced; they no longer nest in the Central Valley marshes. Hearing the rattling and cooing of a siege of cranes approaching a wildlife refuge at dusk, and

Sora   *Black-necked stilts*

(HEAD SMALLER, NECK LONGER)

HEAD VERY SMALL

HEAD FROM BACK

Whooping crane

then watching them land—their huge wingspans, their eerily dangling legs—I try to imagine how powerful their presence must have been when their numbers were larger.

The rare, large, white-colored whooping crane was also once a California bird: John J. Audubon reported it from "upper California northward"; ornithologist Lyman Belding saw a flock in 1884 over the tules on Butte Creek, in Sutter County, and another flock in April 1841 near Gridley, in Butte County.[22] Today the range of this endangered crane has shrunk down to a narrow belt in central North America. At Yellowstone National Park one spring I watched two of them feeding in a wet meadow at dusk, picking up grasshoppers and frogs.

It is thanks to the conservation efforts of sport hunters that geese—Canada geese, greater white-fronted geese, snow geese, and Ross's geese—have rebounded from the lows they suffered by the early twentieth century. Two diminutive subspecies of Canada geese, the Aleutian Canada goose and cackling Canada goose, are still at low numbers. (The San Joaquin National Wildlife Refuge is helping the Aleutian Canada goose to rebound.) Bird illustrator John Cassin called the Aleutian goose "one of the most abundant of the species of geese" on the West Coast.[23] Snow geese he described as extremely common and widespread all over California marshlands—flocks of white birds must have looked like snow patches covering the ground as they fed in grasslands or loafed on marsh edges. By 1913 there was one goose left for every one hundred to one thousand geese that had been present in the late 1800s—.1 to 1 percent—due to habitat loss.[24] The endemic "tule goose," a large form of the white-fronted goose, now winters only at certain marshes in the Sacramento Valley and Suisun area and may be in danger of going extinct.[25]

Common goldeneye male

In the 1870s and 1880s, market hunters specializing in waterfowl hunted the Central Valley in fourteen-foot cedar scull boats called "tule splitters," using 10-gauge shotguns to bring down "bluebills" (scaup), "whistlers" (goldeneyes), "spooneys" (shoveler ducks), "speckled breasts" (white-fronted geese), and many others. Since waterfowl were considered "vermin" by farmers, there was no limit in the early days on the number of birds hunters could take—sometimes ten thousand ducks a day were shipped to San Francisco.[26] In game stalls in the city, restaurant buyers could choose from among offerings arranged on hooks.[27] This commercial hunting tapered off by 1910,[28] but droughts across the Canadian and American prairies in the 1930s helped fuel a plunge to thirty million—from an estimated four hundred million ducks in the 1850s. So in 1937 a group in New York formed Ducks Unlimited, dedicated to restoring waterfowl populations. Oakland's Lake Merritt had officially been a wildlife refuge since 1870. Gray Lodge came about in 1931, under a federal program to acquire wildlife refuges. By 1934 the Duck Stamp program had put hunting fees back into conservation.[29]

Green-winged teal

Pied-billed grebe

Furred Gold

Not just feathered creatures, but inland furbearers as well, brought the British Hudson's Bay Company into the Central Valley from 1826 to 1845. The main attraction was the golden beaver, a special California beaver that dug burrows into the banks of marshes and rivers. They thrived in high numbers in the Delta, around the hundreds of small, rush-covered islands and sluggish streams there, and were not found above 1,000 feet in elevation.[30] In 1840 Thomas Farnham exclaimed, "There is probably no spot of equal extent in the whole continent of America which contains so many of these much-sought animals."[31] The beavers also made their homes in fresh and brackish marshes in San Francisco Bay and along the Napa River. Hunting sent the beaver population into a steady decline, although a great many fur trappers abandoned the pursuit in favor of gold digging after 1848. Restrictions were enacted in 1917, although open seasons on beavers continued into the 1950s.[32]

River otters and mink also had a center of abundance in the Delta and lower Sacramento River marshes, and they also abounded in the Tulare Lake region. In 1927–28, there were 5,854 mink trapped in California.[33] Muskrat, native in California in the northeastern marshes, were introduced into central California in 1943.

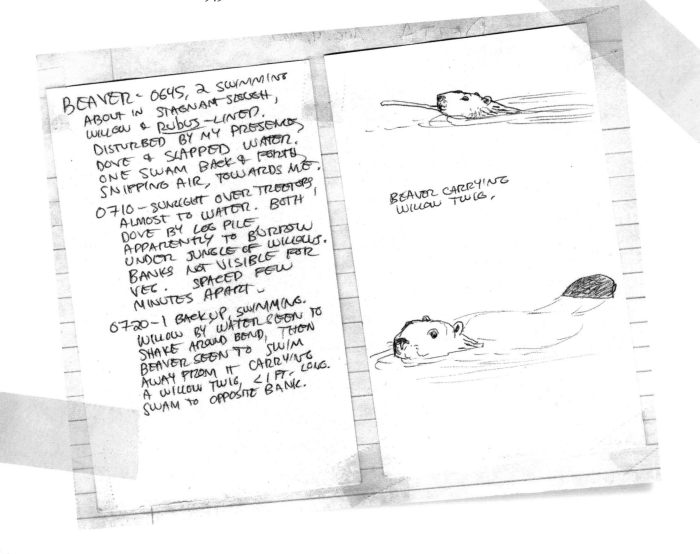

Cultural Landscapes

Not everyone lives next to a marsh today, but you can still get an idea of what these communities are like, and a hint of the grandness of the watery inland realms, by visiting places like Grizzly Island Wildlife Area, in Solano County, managed by the California Department of Fish and Game. This refuge encompasses more than ten thousand acres of freshwater, brackish, and salt marsh on the edge of Suisun Bay, where the Delta meets the San Francisco Estuary. I watched two river otters play and splash in the sunset-colored waters of a slough channel one evening, the tall silhouettes of cane waving their feathery, flaglike seed heads in the breezes. Mink and golden beavers swim here too, and tule elk roam the uplands (see www.suisunwildlife.org/grizzly).

Today the signs of human culture are obvious at Suisun Marsh, with roads and built levees of dirt to hold back the tides, and as you hike the trails you often pass pumps, gates, and valves controlling where water goes—which areas are flooded and which are dried out. Agriculture surrounds the area.

But as ethnobotanist M. Kat Anderson points out, these habitats have always been cultural landscapes, managed by people long before Europeans arrived (and, I would add, impacted by grazing elk herds, digging grizzly bears, and Ice Age megafaunas in the more distant past). Indians have always selectively burned, transplanted, dispersed, and harvested plants, creating "small-scale human disturbance regimes" that helped shape the very genetics of the species they used.[34]

The Owens Valley Paiute practiced a form of irrigation agriculture, by damming Bishop Creek and constructing ditches miles long to deliver water to wet meadows and marshes, increasing the supply of such foods as blue dicks bulbs (called "grass nut"), and the seed-bearing species lovegrass, wildrye, sunflower, water cress, and pigweed. Women got together to communally harvest the bulbs with digging sticks and collect the ripe seed with seed beaters. The Paiute also irrigated other parts of the Owens Valley, and Shoshone groups built ditch systems in various valleys of Nevada.[35]

Back in my home valley east of Bishop, in the local spring marshes, I can see down through the different layers of land use. Signs of historic irrigation on the old cattle ranch that used to operate here are visible: ditches, stock ponds fringed with cattails, old fields of weedy alfalfa, rusty antique water pumps. An older layer shows up as white flint knives, scrapers, and other stone tools of Native people scattered over the marsh edges, and possible remnants of small ditches spreading out over the meadows. These would have benefited the toads by creating new wetland habitats.

I am learning that I too can interact with the landscape, in its present use, as a wildlife refuge, by acts of habitat restoration. Anderson, in discussing how to move beyond modern society's separation of nature and culture and develop a "culture of place," reminds us:

> For California Indians, nature was not an abstract concept relegated to the remote fringes of human communities but was intimately intertwined with daily living. Indigenous peoples' lifeways show us that intimacy comes from interacting with plants and animals *where they live* and establishing relationships with them.[36]

EE DOWN THROUGH THE DIFFERENT LAYERS OF LAND USE.

FIVE

RIVER WORLD

The river canyons, where the old bars were located, were romantic places previous to being disturbed and torn up by the gold-digger. The water was as clear as crystal, and above each ripple or rapid place was a long, deep pool, with water blue as turquoise, swarming with fish. Salmon at that time ran up all the streams as far as they could get, until some perpendicular barrier which they could not leap prevented further progress. Before the falls at Murderer's Bar was cut down, during spawning time the salmon would accumulate so thickly in a large pool just below that they were taken in great numbers by merely attaching large iron hooks to a pole, running it down in the water, and suddenly jerking it up through the mass.

—*Myron Angel, 1882*[1]

What caused the stunning richness of California's Delta marshes and the great tulares of the valleys? A gigantic delivery system of moving water: eons of floods bringing nutrient-laden silt from the mountains. Humans manipulate and change their homelands, but water processes change the environment in big ways, ways that are often beyond the control of people. They can be massively obvious, like floods, or they can be subtle and hidden. Besides learning to live with our landscapes and waterscapes, we also might learn to live with the natural processes that shape them.

The great rivers of California are amazing forces: starting as snowpack in the Sierra Nevada and Cascades, descending through gorges and over waterfalls into deep canyons, carving ever deeper as the mountains uplift. For two years I lived along the Merced River in a steep, V-shaped canyon where I could watch the flow rise with the snowmelt, then run low and quiet in the sultry summer. Hiking about, I noticed everywhere the workings of the past: diggings, old ditches, mine shafts, and ghost mills. The busy times of the gold rush still echo in these now wild and lonely canyons. Wild? Perhaps, but as I dug deeper into historical accounts, I found that the changes wrought by mining and settlement were lasting, and that the rivers ran differently in early times than they do today. Many of the animals dwelling along the rivers and creeks have been affected by these changes to the landscape, which are now often invisible to the local observer. The gold rush account of journalist Myron Angel recalls this time vividly:

Upon every little bend or plot of land bordering the stream, grew the white ash, alder, maple, laurel, honeysuckle and rank ferns and mosses....Tussocks of rank bunch-grass covered the bottoms, and wild grapevines clambered over every convenient tree. The water ousel [dipper], a little dark-colored bird, flitted from place to place in search of food, and the vigilant kingfisher darted from his perch on overhanging limb into the clearwater and rose again with some finny victim in his beak. Deer wandered

Harlequin ducks nested along the Merced River before the gold rush.
OIL ON CANVAS, 10 x 7 INCHES, 2003

unscared amid these beauteous scenes, for there were none to do them harm. When first dug over, the old river bars were simply beds of clean-washed gravel, containing gold—natural ground-sluices—where nature had been for untold ages at work, and the innumerable fierce floods had so thoroughly washed away the finer alluvium and abraded material that what remained, after getting below the surface soil, would scarcely roil the element in which the miner washed it.

Such was the condition of the California streams when the gold-seeker first approached them—things of rare beauty, joyous to behold, inconceivable to those who only know them as they are found to-day—treeless, mud-laden, turgid, filthy, and fishless.[2]

Vanishing Frogs

My own in-depth acquaintance with the river world began on Merced River tributaries after the spring snowmelt floods receded, leaving sparkling ripples and long, mirroring glides of cold mountain water. I saw big, bronze-scaled Sacramento suckers hiding among cobbles, little minnows—the California roach—and trout, but an animal I had great difficulty finding was the foothill yellow-legged frog. And my job was to find it. At the time I worked for the National Biological Survey and was stationed along the Merced. What a wonderful name for a Department of the Interior agency, I thought. It reminded me of the exploratory survey parties of the 1800s, outfitted by the government to catalog the nation's wealth of biodiversity.

Our team, led by Gary Fellers of the United States Geological Survey, searched every creek, stream, lake, and wet meadow for amphibians. This was one of numerous studies undertaken to find the reasons for mysterious and catastrophic declines of amphibians worldwide. And frogs had

Gold nugget and California roach. OIL ON COTTON RAG PAPER, 3 ½ X 7 ½ INCHES, 2003

been hit hard. Our target, a beautifully colored little frog with lemon yellow on the undersides of its jumping legs, was found abundantly in foothill streams of the Sierra during surveys in the first decades of the twentieth century. Since then it had vanished from all but a few isolated creeks.[3]

My work partner, Jenny, and I waded along stream margins hour after hour, scanning the banks with binoculars, dipping our nets into the sedges, hoping to see a frog. We found Pacific treefrogs and plenty of introduced bullfrogs, but no yellow-legs. These seemingly pristine streams held no more of the native *Ranas*, frogs adapted to holding onto slippery rocks in riffles and splash zones, able to dart from a perch into the water and under a river cobble with barely a noise.

But then we struck gold: an egg mass in the creekside shaded by oaks and gray pines, a round, melon-sized conglomeration of eggs, fixed by the yellow-legged frog with glue-like jelly to the rocks to keep it from washing away in the current.

Returning to the same spot in a few weeks, we saw an "explosion" of tadpoles, the egg mass disintegrated. As the tadpoles grew in the low water during the heat of summer, feeding on algae and diatoms, speckling camouflaged their bodies against the submerged mud and pebbles.

In spring, we watched the adult frogs cling to high, wet banks or hide in side seeps and little tributaries, away from the raging floodwaters pouring down the mountainsides. After the white water subsided, the frogs bred again, in quiet pools and pocket waters.

Yellow-legged frog

We felt lucky to see these things.

What caused this frog to disappear from much of the foothill region, and altogether from the San Gabriel Mountains and Transverse Ranges, in southern California? They still can be found along coastal streams, especially in northern California. Urbanization has affected their habitat in some streams, but so many Sierra streams seemed untouched. Hungry bullfrogs and some predatory exotic fish contribute to the disappearance of some eggs and adults, but an even more insidious factor, a silent agent, may be affecting California's waters.

Knocking on the door of a ranch house in the low foothills, we were greeted by a woman in a calico dress. Jenny and I explained our purpose and asked permission to survey the stream that crossed her property.

"Sure, I don't mind," she said. "We moved up here ten years ago to get away from the pesticides. We had a sow that kept having stillborns, and heck, we didn't want that to happen to us. It was almost a macho thing, how much pesticides you pumped onto your farm."

We thanked her but walked away looking at each other with raised eyebrows. The stream was beautiful, and perfect frog habitat. But no frogs.

Growing evidence indicates that pesticides and herbicides applied to agricultural areas, such as the Central Valley, are borne on winds and deposited in snow and stream waters hundreds of miles distant. Organophosphate pesticide residues can be found in air, water, snow, and even pine needle samples at Sequoia National Park and Lake Tahoe.[4] Fellers and Donald Sparling, a USGS research biologist and contaminants specialist, found pesticides in the bodies of Pacific treefrogs in Yosemite National Park: the pesticides bound with the enzyme cholinesterase, which is essential for proper nervous system functioning. Fifty percent of frogs and tadpoles at Yosemite had measurable levels of pesticides in their bodies and lowered cholinesterase activity, which is potentially fatal.[5]

More research is needed, but patterns are emerging. Foothill yellow-legged frogs have disappeared east—downwind—of the big agricultural areas of the San Joaquin Valley. They are still fairly common along the north coast, which is swept clean by ocean winds. Is there a link? Perhaps these frogs are "canaries in the coal mine," alerting us to hidden toxic effects of agrochemicals deposited by the rains and flowing down meltwaters into every river, creek, and pool downwind. During the lazy, hot days of summer, the frog collapse mystery continues, as cobbles and bedrock channels remain quiet.

Jenny later moved to live and work on an organic farm.

The Sacramento River: curtains of wild grape hang among valley oaks and sycamores. Blackberry and blue elderberry occupy the middle foreground, and swaths of creeping wildrye grow on the woodland floor.
Oil on toned cotton rag paper, 4 ¼ x 10 ½ inches, 2003

Riparian Jungle, Moving Water

Living in the tiny town of El Portal during our amphibian surveys, deep in the Merced River Canyon just below Yosemite Valley, we experienced an unusual spring: a sudden warm rain soaked the already melting snowpack, causing an enormous conversion of ice into liquid. Bridalveil Fall that year was a monster of rushing water, pouring off the sheer cliff face, roaring and misting; the river below became churning white water from bank to bank and began to flood the town precariously perched on a low terrace beside it. The dams below us had to release water as the reservoirs filled to capacity. I imagined these waters hundreds of years ago, before the great dams, broiling downwards to flow out over their banks in the Central Valley, delivering fertile silt to the woodlands and marshes along their channels.

Edward Belcher, traveling up the Sacramento River in 1843, wrote that the banks were:

> well wooded, with oak, planes [sycamores], ash, willow, walnut, poplar [cottonwoods],
> and brushwood. Wild grapes in great abundance overh[u]ng the lower trees, clustering
> to the river, at times completely overpowering the trees on which they climbed, and
> producing beautiful varieties of tint....Within, and at the very edge of the banks, oaks
> of immense size were plentiful. These appeared to form a band on each side, about 300
> yards in depth.

Floodwaters played a large part in creating and sustaining the great riparian jungles of vines, shrubs,
and trees that once lined the rivers. It seems we are now in an age of dams and dikes. But as we shall
see, the rivers can be made static only with great difficulty. They are always moving their curving
courses, changing their beds, leaving gravel and silt piles, cutting new banks. Only by completely
cementing their channels in, as has been done with the Los Angeles River, can the wild streams be
trained to flow straight in one direction.

John Work, a fur trapper from Fort Vancouver, visited the Sacramento Valley below Red Bluff
in 1832: "All the way along the river," he wrote, "there is a belt of woods (principally oak) which is
surrounded by a plain with tufts of wood here and there which extend to the foot of the mountain,
where the hills are again wooded."[6]

Maps from the gold rush era show a two-mile-wide belt of woodland on either side of the
Feather River. The American River had a wooded riparian belt four miles wide. Butte Creek, the
Yuba River, and the Bear River had two-mile-wide riverine woodlands. The widest belt was along
the Sacramento River—four to five miles wide.[7] This oak-cottonwood-willow-sycamore woodland,
estimated to have covered nine hundred thousand acres in the Sacramento Valley, is now less than
10 percent of that size.[8] Woodcutting became an industry in the 1850s through the 1870s to supply
steamboat fuel—by the early 1900s, most trees in the Delta had been cut. The foothill riparian zones
were stripped of trees for mining purposes.[9] Later, more riparian woodland was cleared to make way
for orchards and crops, then housing. Flood control projects stripped away vegetation and replaced it
with barren riprap and concrete banks.[10]

IDEALIZED SACRAMENTO VALLEY RIVER RIPARIAN VEGETATION

(modified from "Riparian Vegetation and Flora of the Sacramento Valley" by S. G. Conard et al., 1977)

The Merced is still scarred by gold mining. By 1850 miners were applying high-pressure jets of water to mountainsides—hydraulic mining, which sluiced away more sediment from California's riverbanks than was created by the digging of the Panama Canal, an estimated 1.7 billion cubic yards. All this debris was carried down the rivers and into San Francisco Bay.[11] By 1854 four thousand miles of ditches and flumes had been built to deliver water to the mining operations.[12]

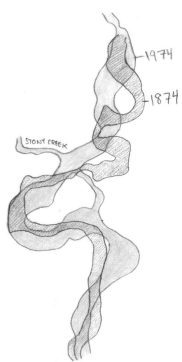

THE SAME STRETCH OF THE SACRAMENTO RIVER, SHOWING SHIFTING MEANDERS FROM 1874 TO 1974.

(adapted from James Brice's "Lateral Migration of the Middle Sacramento River, California," 1977)

Today, after recovering somewhat from gold rush chopping, cutting, and silt, the valley river scenes look unchanging: winding ribbons of green trees among the cities and farmlands. But they are actually in a state of flux. Rivers are constantly, slowly meandering, shifting their channels, wiping out old forests and creating fresh gravel beds for new growth. Cycles of floods shape the riverlands and life-forms that cling to them. Historical ecologist Robin Grossinger tells of the unrelenting natural processes of floods and landslides, of tree roots splitting sidewalks, salmon swimming through city rivers, trying to spawn—urban dwellers expend a tremendous nonstop effort to try to hold all this back, to maintain levees and dams, dredge silt from shipping channels, and fix potholes caused by water erosion.[13]

In May of 1995, as I watched the normal splashing rapids of the Merced River change into a roaring fury of white water, boulders lurched downriver under the torrent-waves. Yosemite Valley was partially flooded. This had happened regularly in the past, sometimes associated with El Niño cycles. Repeated floods in Sacramento in the 1850s and 1860s caused its citizens to build levees to hold back the floodwaters of the American and Sacramento Rivers. William Brewer described how, in 1862, six feet of rain fell at Sonora, in the foothills, causing the river to overflow its banks. The channel had already flooded twice during December 1861, but this was the worst yet. At Folsom the water rose sixty feet above the low-water mark, and the force of the flood destroyed every bridge but one along the American River.[14] Soon a vast lake formed in the Central Valley, the size of Lake Michigan.[15] In February the lake of "ice cold muddy" waters was still three hundred miles long and sixty miles wide.[16] For three months Sacramento lay underwater, and into March townspeople still had to use boats to get around. Reminiscing about the "Flood of '61," which he had watched from a ranch five miles south of Sacramento, Paschal Coggins said:

> When we retired one quiet night, it was with the bright moonlight gilding the hilltops and deepening the shadows in the meadows all about us. When we awoke, we were upon an island with the astonished sun darting his rays across a sea of turbid mountain water that was swirling on every hand.[17]

These floodwaters gradually soaked into the giant "sponge" of tule marshes, giving rich silt to the fertile low valley lands, as they had for millennia.[18]

We can get an idea of the frequency of floods from the great Colorado River, which flows along the southeastern edge of the California desert, draining an immense area of the mountain West.

Before the many dams were built that now regulate its flow, you could stand on the bank and watch a huge swell of spring snowmelt move past, lasting for weeks. If you came back each year, you would find that in eighty out of a hundred years, a flood greater than 50,000 cubic feet per second (cfs) would gush by you down-canyon. In one-third of those hundred years, the flood would top 100,000 cfs. Gargantuan floods, occurring less often, sometimes corresponded with El Niños. The largest flood ever recorded on the Colorado, in Utah in 1884, was estimated at 225,000 cfs. An even larger one may have raged through the Needles area of California in 1862, possibly 400,000 cfs. Evidence of immense Holocene floods of 500,000 cfs awes the imagination. Floods decreased somewhat in intensity after the 1930s, perhaps due to the changeover from the Little Ice Age to global warming. In the late twentieth century these scouring flows stopped completely: Glen Canyon Dam allows only 3,000 to 31,500 cfs to move through the Grand Canyon.[19]

Many trees were adapted to these floodwaters. Cottonwoods especially were prime pioneers on scoured river edges and in freshly deposited gravel bars. Where floods were frequent, alder, cottonwood, and various willows dominated in a mix of low thickets, sapling stands, and old, tall patches. Farther from the river, where flooding was less frequent and the groundwater level was lower, valley oak and sycamore were more common.[20] But even in the mature, open valley oak woodlands miles from the river, there may have been an annual overflow in places.[21] Belcher, in his 1843 travels along the Sacramento, noticed the roots of immense sycamores, willows, ashes, and oaks

Sacramento Valley underwater in a flood. OIL ON PAPER, 4 X 7 ½ INCHES, 2003

scoured along the riverbanks by the force of floodwaters. He would have also noticed a mosaic of woodland ages and heights: young willows and cottonwoods, their seeds quick to colonize bare areas, growing into dense thickets, while in old, deep river bends, cut off and isolated as oxbow lakes, trees would grow old and tall.

Historical ecology informs us that a certain type of vegetation does not necessarily represent the same history wherever it occurs. At Coyote Creek, flowing through what is now known as the Silicon Valley, in Santa Clara County, careful study of Mexican land grant maps, early American journal descriptions, scientific surveys, and old photos and paintings showed a picture at odds with what conservationists had thought was the "original" vegetation. Current remnants are of dense cottonwood forest crowding the banks and floodplain. But the early sources revealed that this was a result of Coyote Dam, built in 1936 and resulting in flood control and summer water releases. The former riparian community had been what ecologists called "sycamore alluvial woodland," a now rare type that was until recently thought to be a degraded habitat. In fact it is a habitat of gravel bars with scattered trees adapted to big winter floods and little or no summer flow: another forgotten habitat revealed.[22]

Flood Birds

One bird was specially adapted to Old California's ever-changing riverine environment: the yellow-billed cuckoo. It favored dense, new willow copses and broad expanses of cottonwood-willow woodland along rivers and streams. Sitting motionless, waiting to spy movement, it hunted caterpillars, moth larvae, katydids, and other insects. This cuckoo was wonderfully adapted to take advantage of short-term booms in food supply.[23] Its nesting was synchronized with the hatching of the most common insect in the area. Chicks fledged very quickly. And when food was abundant, the cuckoos could increase their clutch size. Living near Berkeley, I used to try to imagine cuckoos feasting on the tent caterpillars that would break out in huge numbers in the live oaks every few years, stripping the leaves. But no cuckoos have been seen here, nesting and feasting, for over sixty years.

Originally the yellow-billed cuckoo nested in most Coast Range valleys from San Diego to Sebastopol, throughout the Central Valley, and in many desert riparian areas.[24] Widespread along rivers in the Los Angeles and San Bernardino areas in the past, they are now rare.[25] In the 1920s one observer found twenty-four cuckoo nests in cottonwoods and willows along the Santa Ana River. But in the 1930s he wrote:

> In contrast with those good old days, we now have very little water in Warm Creek
> and seldom any surface water in the Santa Ana River, the large thickets have been
> replaced by farms and pastures, the trees cut down, and the evergrowing population
> has crowded in the old haunts of the cuckoo to such an extent that if they come here
> now at all they must be exceedingly rare.[26]

Ornithologist Stephen Laymon estimates the original population of California yellow-billed cuckoos could have been seventy thousand to one hundred thousand breeding pairs. In a 1977 census only one hundred and ninety pairs could be found in the entire state, and by 1994 this was down to fifty to seventy-five pairs.[27]

The dawn chorus rings through flooded creeping wildrye meadows along a creek lined with dense willows and cottonwood. This is nesting habitat for willow flycatchers. OIL ON TONED COTTON RAG PAPER, 4 ¼ X 8 INCHES, 2003

Birds in the Glade

Early ornithologist Lyman Belding called the willow flycatcher "a very common summer resident in willows of the Central Valley, most so along the valley rivers."[28] Robert Ridgway, an artist-naturalist who accompanied many government survey parties out West, called it "the most abundant and generally distributed" of the small flycatchers. But it is now a rare event to hear the loud, sneezy song of the willow flycatcher in an early morning thicket, mixing with the songs of innumerable other birds during the dawn chorus. I must travel long distances to see them in their few remaining colonies.

Riparian habitat destruction and cattle browsing—especially the lower branches of willows, where these flycatchers prefer to nest—have helped to reduce their population. But one threat stands out especially: the brown-headed cowbird. After mating, the female cowbird watches for nest building activity among flycatchers, vireos, wood-warblers, and finches. Detecting a clutch, she slips in before dawn and deposits her own egg within seconds, then flies off. Later that day or the following, she

WILLOW FLYCATCHER

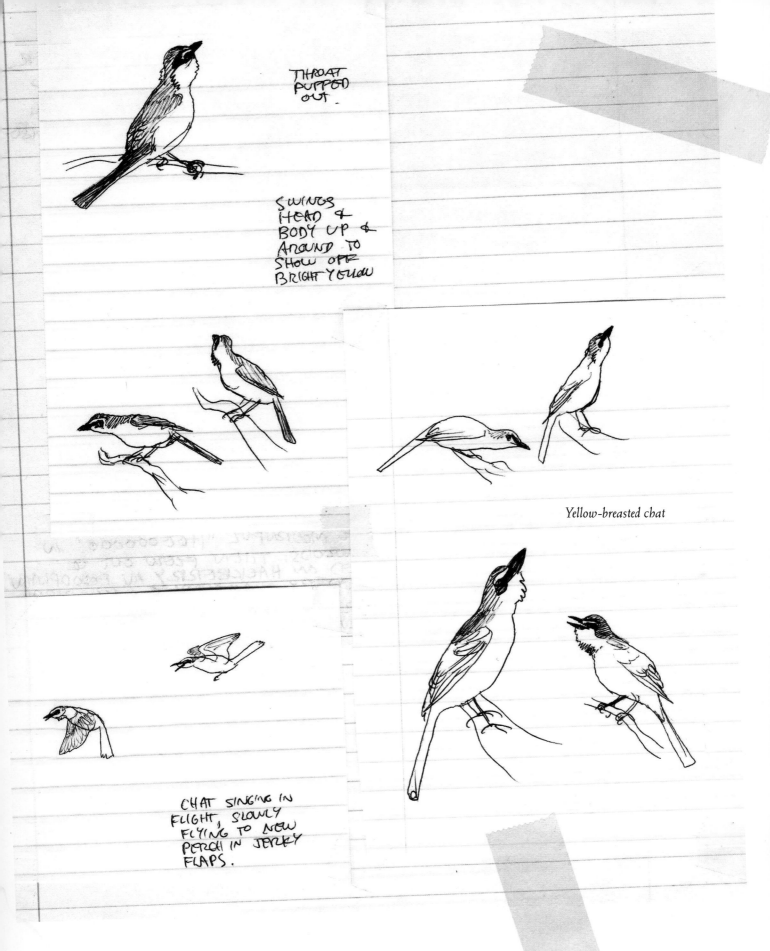

THROAT
PUFFED
OUT.

SWINGS
HEAD &
BODY UP &
AROUND TO
SHOW OFF
BRIGHT YELLOW

Yellow-breasted chat

CHAT SINGING IN
FLIGHT, SLOWLY
FLYING TO NEW
PERCH IN JERKY
FLAPS.

returns to remove one of the host's eggs. Then she goes on to find another nest to parasitize—perhaps as many as six. Other cowbird females may find the same nest; one researcher found eight cowbird eggs in a single nest alone. About half of the host parents accept the changeling as their own and rear it. Some abandon the nest or build another on top of it. The cowbird chick grows large and often consumes most of the food brought by the parents, starving out its smaller "siblings." Ornithologist John Harris found that the central California bird that cowbirds parasitize most is the willow flycatcher.[29]

Before 1900 brown-headed cowbirds were rare in California, mostly found along the Colorado River and in the Great Basin. But with the increase in their favorite foraging grounds: stubble fields, irrigated lands, orchards, feedlots, overgrazed pastures, suburbs, and golf courses—they underwent an explosive expansion. Since about 1915 they have been increasing in southern California; by 1922 they were invading the San Francisco Bay region; and by 1927 they had reached the Sacramento Valley. They are now abundant over much of California and by 1960 they had colonized Oregon.[30]

Bell's Vireo

The breeding ranges and numbers of other denizens of the warm riparian valleys have also been reduced. Cowbird parasitism, agricultural development, brush removal, and riparian destruction are to blame. Fewer yellow warblers are singing "sweet-sweet-sweet-I'm so sweet" amid green cottonwood and willow leaves, and fewer yellow-breasted chats are squawking, clucking, and rattling their songs in swampy thickets. I only occasionally see blue grosbeaks in the Central Valley, and warbling vireos no longer breed there either.

The least Bell's vireo, California's own endemic subspecies, nested in riparian locales from Baja California to Tehama County.[31] Declines were noticed by about 1930, and by 1970 only a few isolated streams in southern California supported breeding pairs.[32] In the Central Valley, formerly 60 to 80 percent of the bird's range, a few were recently found nesting at San Joaquin National Wildlife Refuge, the first in over fifty years.[33]

Flooding scours away older vegetation, and in five to ten years new, dense willow thickets form, perfect habitat for nesting and foraging vireos.[34] By rebuilding riparian habitat and reducing cowbird populations, we can restore the boisterous, musical songs of the Bell's vireos to the willows.

Feather Colonies

Scenes like this one must have been common in precontact times: showy and white great egrets and snowy egrets, leggy great blue herons, hunched black-crowned night-herons, and shiny, black double-crested cormorants all feeding together and nesting in colonies, their rookeries made of stick nests in river trees. Chicks chattered and called for food, and "whitewash," the liquid excreta of generations of birds, coated the low branches. These rookeries were once large and conspicuous along Central Valley rivers. At Putah Creek herons nested "by the hundreds"—today there are none. A rookery west of Gridley had six hundred great blue heron and great egret nests, but it was completely cut down in the 1950s. The largest colony was discovered in 1937 along the Sacramento River, in Butte County: a thousand nests filled the cottonwood trees, with four hundred pairs of great egrets, two hundred pairs of great blue herons, one hundred and fifty pairs of cormorants, and eighty pairs of night-herons. Hundreds of birds could be seen flying to and from their nesting trees.[35]

Egrets were nearly killed out in the 1880s and 1890s by the feather trade, a rather bizarre phase of commercial hunting devoted to providing stuffed waterbirds and their feathers to milliners for women's fancy hats. Egret plumes were much in demand, and by the first decade of the 1900s, snowy and great egrets were a rare sight in California.[36] So grave was the situation that in 1883 the American Ornithologists' Union was founded, and then in 1886 the Audubon Society formed, both to promote laws against the slaughter of American birds.[37] Egret numbers began to increase after 1910, and they are now once again common.[38]

A great place to observe a major rookery is the Bolinas Lagoon Preserve, along Highway 1 in Marin County. Here great blue herons, snowy egrets, and great egrets nest from March to July, unmolested by modern development, thanks to the efforts of the nonprofit Audubon Canyon Ranch.

A winding valley river lined with willows in the past. With no dams, the river swells after a spring rain. As the floodwaters recede, egrets and cormorants gather to feed on fish killed by the surging waters. OIL ON COTTON RAG PAPER, 7 X 8 ½ INCHES, 2003

Although the nests are not in cottonwoods but in tall redwoods, and the birds feed not in big rivers but in nearby coastal salt marshes, this wondrous place allows close observation, with binoculars or spotting scope, of a rookery as it would have looked in the Central Valley hundreds of years ago.

California was once a land of dry, summer-baked uplands contrasting with the lush water gardens of the lowlands: winding rivers, tule wetlands, springs flowing out of the ground, green jungles. Much of this water has been moved from wild areas to urban spreads and agribusiness fields, but there are still spots where a glimpse of Old California can be caught and the river world imagined. Another of my favorite places to sketch wildlife and bird-watch is along the green bands of river forest at the Audubon Society's Kern River Preserve, located in a broad valley of the Tehachapi Range in Kern County. Here dense, extensive cottonwood-willow forests harbor southwestern willow flycatchers, summer tanagers, yellow warblers, red-shouldered hawks, and other birds, in a place where the dawn chorus sounds primeval.

♀ YELLOW WARBLER
~1000–1100h

STRETCHING

INSPECTED
BLOSSOMS OFTEN.
? DRINKING NECTAR

CAUGHT A LARGE
CATERPILLAR – 'PLAYED'
WITH IT FOR WHILE IN
BILL TURNING ABOUT
HOLDING TIP. FINALLY
SWALLOWED IT IN ONE GULP.

The Cosumnes River Preserve, in the Central Valley southeast of Sacramento, was purchased by The Nature Conservancy in 1987 and is now run by several partners, including the Bureau of Land Management, California Department of Fish and Game, and California Department of Water Resources. They have my gratitude too for preserving a pristine piece of California. Go here to see the only undammed river coming off the west slope of the Sierra, and watch it flood its banks regularly to create new riparian forests. This is a great place to visit an Old California habitat that is now very rare: it is the largest remaining riparian valley oak woodland, along the largest free-flowing river, in the state.

I have spent much time at the beautiful California State Parks campground at Woodson Bridge State Recreation Area, along the Sacramento River in Tehama County, hunting for yellow-billed cuckoos at oxbow lake jungles and exploring the acres of woodlands: the same oaks, walnuts, ash, willows, cottonwoods, and wild grapes described by Myron Angel, Edward Belcher, and other travelers in nineteenth-century California.

People today are working hard to restore riparian woodlands and flood-adapted birds, and to create opportunities for rivers to naturally flood without damaging human property. The Napa River Flood Control Project, for example, resulted when folks grew tired of fighting the annual river flood and decided to work with the moving water. Recognizing that rivers are always changing and not static, the "Living River Strategy" combined habitat

Valley oaks flooded in a temporary shallow lake, before the dams and levees.
OIL ON TONED COTTON RAG PAPER, 4 3/4 X 11 INCHES, 2003

restoration, recreation, and pollution cleanup with the usual flood protection projects. Local people started the Napa River Watershed Historical Ecology Project to figure out what the river looked like in 1820, to provide a blueprint and map to inform restoration work. Old valley oaks were mapped; residents were interviewed about where the good salmon fishing and spawning spots were; 1920s mosquito control marsh maps were consulted; and early photos were gathered.

Engineers recognized that in the long run, levees do not work: rivers gradually get higher than the surrounding land, as waterborne sediments are deposited in the confined channel instead of spreading out over a lush wetland. This is a recipe for disaster when a levee breaks during a big storm. So some levees were removed, to create fertile estuarine marshes that could absorb floodwaters. This incidentally created excellent salmon-rearing habitat, as we shall see later. Some bridges that impeded water flow were taken down, and buildings too close to riverbanks were removed. The land was terraced to reconnect it with the historic floodplain. This way the dreaded "hundred-year floods" could be allowed to pass through. After so many years of trying to hem in floodwaters in order to stave off damage to poorly designed housing developments, it may seem like back-paddling to accommodate the river. But sometimes it is necessary to reverse direction. We may begin to see the rivers in all their moods of movement—shifting, silting, eroding, flooding, changing.

Red-shouldered hawk

SIX

CALIFORNIA GRASSLANDS

"You ought to cut those weeds down!" someone snarled, walking along the sidewalk.

I stood in my sister Margot's front yard in an urban Richmond neighborhood, delighting in the native plants she had cultivated over the years: long, interwoven, coarsely textured, straw-colored stems of purple needlegrass bent over the asphalt and cement, along with compact, brown-ochre junegrass spikes, fine fescues, bright orange poppies, tall masses of pink-blooming farewell-to-spring clarkias, and a newly planted local native, Point Molate silver lupine. Butterflies flitted by, bumblebees visited white buckwheat flowers and fragrant, purple coyote mint. Towhees picked up fallen needlegrass seeds.

A time machine couldn't have given me a better idea of how this very slope looked a thousand years ago. "I suppose we have to learn a new aesthetic about gardening," I commented to Margot as we stood in the yard, discussing people's reactions to her restored plant community.

Instead of keeping the tidy, cut green lawn and square hedges that came with the house, Margot had gradually pulled out the hedges and planted native grasses and flowers. It was a work in progress: "I'm going to pull up that hedge next and plant coyote brush," she explained.

To encourage acceptance by her neighbors, Margot had put up a "Certified Wildlife Habitat" sign she got from a National Wildlife Federation program to help rewild yards. Other signs were playful: "Rattlesnake Crossing" and "Mountain Lion Crossing."

Pierre, Margot's husband, had added to the ambience by placing statues of various animals within the tall grass: lizards, little metal wrens and sparrows, a coyote confronting a fake rattlesnake, even a small grizzly bear. Kids loved it, pointing out the hidden critters with glee.

I asked Pierre if the wildlife models had won any naysayers over.

He looked thoughtful. "Half the people who come to look at the yard come to see the animals. Viewing plants is more complex—you need more knowledge to really appreciate them."

But the aesthetic caught on slowly. A few neighbors pulled out their lawns and replaced them with natives. One enthusiast from a nearby block often gave impromptu talks about Margot's little prairie patch. Soon both he and Margot planned on joining a local native garden tour. I consider the yard beautiful, and I was happy to learn that more and more people are educating themselves about this special California habitat.

The Golden Hills of California

The fabled golden hills—perhaps no other plant community here was changed as much by the arrival of Europeans. Now mostly composed of annual grasses from the Mediterranean region, such as wild oats, soft chess, and ripgut brome, in the past these prairies were dominated by perennial bunchgrasses, spreading swards of rhizomatous natives, and sheets of colorful wildflowers.

I have a special interest in native grasses that began when I learned that the site of my childhood home, now crowded with stucco walls and covered by asphalt streets, was once open, treeless, and grassy; an undulating, windswept emptiness of ridges and swales, a rolling, rippling sea of grass once burned by Huchiun Ohlone people, grazed by elk, and inhabited by burrowing owls and abundant summer grasshoppers. Interior grasslands once covered more than thirteen million acres of California, and another nine to ten million acres of grass existed in oak savanna—altogether, almost one-quarter of the state.[1]

Signs of this older layer of the place where I grew up were still visible in black-and-white photographs from the 1930s, but today they are only found in unused lots and sidewalk cracks. I became fascinated with reconstructing the lost landscape. Grasses are such an essential component of it that I have spent a great deal of time hunting out remnant populations among the sea of introduced European grasses all over California—now a bigger challenge than ever, as prime flatlands are developed, weeds mount new invasions, and poor range management eliminates further remnants. The good news is that while our grasslands have been greatly disturbed, more and more people—from home gardeners to biologists to cowboys—are becoming interested in restoring them. The relatively new field of restoration science has emerged as a result.

One vanished community, the Los Angeles coastal prairie, has been reconstructed from anecdotal history, photographs, voucher specimens, and biological field notes.[2] Covering extensive dune sand deposited along the coast by the Los Angeles River, this wildflower-rich habitat mixed with California sagebrush on sandstone outcrops, wetlands, and vernal pools. On mesas and plains rolling toward the sea, travelers were greeted by showy poppies, dove lupines, verbenas, phacelias, lotus, dwarf plantain, California sun cup, purple owl's clover, and tidy-tips. Specimens of native grasses collected before 1940 indicate a typical California grassland with nodding needlegrass and prairie junegrass, creeping wildrye in low areas, saltgrass, and the native annual foxtail grass. San Diego coast horned lizards were said to be the most common reptile on this prairie. The vernal pools contained fairy shrimp when wet, as well as the tadpoles of breeding spadefoot toads. The vernal pool endemic California Orcutt grass was recorded here. Attempts are being made to restore this interesting community.

Clues in the Field and the Lab

To restore the native grasslands, the first step is to try to look into the past. What is the basis of our efforts, our ground plan? Most of my clues for reconstructing early grassland come from my own observations of the relictual patches of native plants and animals that still dwell across California. I have shelves of sketchbooks filled with notes on grass habitats and locations, maps, drawings, and photographs from my travels around the state. A surprising number of native grasses and wildflowers can still be found lurking in the weedy places in my own neighborhood, and more hide in regional parks and rangelands.

Instead of blindly trusting other people's books on the original grasslands, I preferred to strap on my hiking boots and go out to find the native relicts myself. Taking a lead from historical ecologists in the Mediterranean region, I explored cliffs as natural refugia from the pressures of livestock grazing and agriculture,[3] as well as other little-used places, like pasture corners, roadside and railway buffers, and the like.

With knowledge from the source—nature—I then compared my notes with old botanical collections and surveys, historical accounts, and modern floras to piece together the composition and look of California's primeval prairies. What was it like, I asked, to walk through delicately waving seed panicles, stepping over ground squirrel mounds, noticing the variety of wildflowers between grass bunches? Old photographs and paintings gave clues as well, and recent literature in the fields of botany and restoration science.

During studies at college I became interested in the use of pollen analysis to identify past grassland composition, so I enrolled in a class taught by Roger Byrne at UC Berkeley. Pollen grains have proven useful in reconstructing plant communities worldwide, although they have a limitation: they are only recoverable from moist sediments, such as lakes or bogs. When so deposited, however, these minute, male fertilizing bodies are almost unbelievably persistent. Pollen grains have been recovered from lake and ocean sediments a hundred thousand years old, and they can even be extracted from rocks from a hundred million years ago, when dinosaurs roamed the planet.

Taking pond mud cores from lakes back to the lab, we looked at a dazzling array of spheres, bubbles, octahedrons, and other shapes on a microscope slide, the collective windfall from the plant community in the vicinity of a lakeshore. The pollen of many plant families and some species has distinctive morphology, so types can be catalogued and counted by using a microgrid on the slide, producing a diagram that shows the changing relative percentages of each type over time—often many thousands of years. But unfortunately, grass pollen shows no such distinct features and the method is not useful for distinguishing between native California grasses and European invasives.

I turned to another method of paleovegetation study that was beginning to show promise in the early 1980s: phytolith analysis. The leaves and stems of plants, and especially grasses and sedges, contain a "skeleton" of microscopic opal silica bodies within their tissues to aid in structural strength. Grasses, being tough and coarse, contain many thousands in their leaves, stems, and flower parts, which may also serve as an antiherbivory strategy—horses have had to evolve large, high-crowned teeth to grind grass up. Unlike pollen, these phytoliths showed many differences between grasses. Another advantage was that phytoliths did not require moist sediments to preserve them; they could be found in many soil types, dry or moist, and could potentially preserve a record of a grassland in situ. Archaeologists had discovered distinctive maize phytoliths in some North American Indian sites. But no one had systematically looked at grass phytoliths in California.

I began to collect various native and introduced grasses, chemically extracting the opal phytoliths and examining them under the microscope. I soon found that the variability of phytolith shapes was too great to neatly distinguish purple needlegrass from, say, wild oats. There were numerous phytolith shapes in each grass. Some seemed to be distinctive, but the complexity and overlap overwhelmed me. I left that endeavor for future workers, who could use computing power, scanning electron microscopes, and statistical methods for separating out groups according to taxon.

Despite these concerns and limitations, I was convinced that enough evidence existed to develop a reasonably accurate picture of the old grasslands that formed so much of California's scenery. I agreed with the Solomeshch approach (named after Ayzik Solomeshch of UC Davis): the assumption that native plants have not significantly changed their ecological requirements since European colonization, so we can still see community patterns of the natives, even as they grow amid the new invasives.[4]

The present: city of San Bernardino on the I-15 freeway

The past: San Bernardino five hundred years ago. The Santa Ana River flows through the valley, lined with Fremont cottonwoods, willows, and sycamores. Giant Los Angeles sunflowers grow fifteen feet tall around a marsh of green sedge and brownish rush. These sunflowers were thought extinct by 1937, but botanists recently made an exciting discovery of a surviving population near Los Angeles. Gray bunches of alkali sacaton grass occupy the left. This is kingbird heaven: a western kingbird flies into the sky; a Cassin's kingbird glides over the water; and a rare tropical kingbird perches on a giant sunflower. OIL ON PANEL, 7 ½ X 21 INCHES, 2006

Clues in the Library

Spanish and American explorers provided a few tantalizing but hazy glimpses of the grasslands, seldom specific enough to determine species composition, but interesting in a general way.

In May 1770 Juan Crespí described Point Arguello, north of Santa Barbara, "a very grassy level land" with "not a bush" for miles:

> At once after setting out, we commenced to find the fields all abloom with different kinds of wildflowers of all colors so that, as many as were the flowers we had been meeting all along the way on the channel, it was not in such plenty as here, for it is all one mass of blossom, great quantities of white, yellow, red, purple, and blue ones; many yellow violets or gilly-flowers of the sort that are planted in gardens, a great deal of larkspur, poppy and sage in bloom, and what graced the fields most of all was the sight of all the different sorts and colors together."[5]

The "sage" Crespí described may have been chia, and the yellow violet could be *Viola pedunculata* or *V. douglasii*. The purple and blue flowers might be various annual lupines, so common in California to this day, and perhaps he also saw California poppies. The description may also tell us about the community itself, that Indian burning kept these grasslands very open and prevented south coastal sage scrub from invading. Fires every one to three years would accomplish this (more on this in chapter eight). The description also gave hints at the patchiness of the California grasslands, the unevenness of wildflower abundance and distribution—native grazers, such as elk, would have to stay on the move to find the lushest patches in the mosaic.

In August 1775 Don José Canizares, sailing master of the *San Carlos*, entered San Francisco Bay and gave us a hint at the dry grasslands that surrounded the waters. He described the East Bay as "broken hill country with very little woodland, bay trees and live oaks here and there making up what there is." San Pablo Bay, he continued, "is bordered by rough hill country without trees except for woodlands in two coves to the southwest; the rest is barren, irregular, and of melancholy aspect." They sailed on into Suisun Bay: "All the eastern shore is wooded, and all the western shore is barren, filled with grasshoppers, and unfit at any time for settlement."[6]

Rare hints of the grassland composition during the early 1900s are afforded by brief mentions, such as that of R. A. Thompson, describing the Sacramento Valley pastures of Yolo County near the town of Woodland: "The indigenous forage plants, some of great value, notably alfilerilla, burr and redtop clover, bunchgrass and wild oats, are thoroughly cured standing as they grow."[7]

The bunchgrasses may have been natives, while the others were introduced. He indicated that even in the summer months this dried, standing "hay" was excellent forage, and it greened up again in winter.

Later descriptions also give clues to earlier conditions. The owner of the San Lucas Rancho, in Monterey County, recalled a stand of needlegrass so heavy that six yoke of oxen were needed to plow the field when it went into cultivation for the first time.[8] This was probably purple needlegrass, still found relictually all over the county.

Livestock Comes to California

The Spanish brought longhorn cattle to the California grasslands. At six to seven hundred pounds, they were smaller than the thousand-pound cattle of today. They were hardy and easily became feral. Sheep of the era, the "churros," were small and leggy.[9] Because fences were rare before the 1860s,

Spanish livestock roamed over huge areas. Vaqueros on well-trained horses rounded them up and separated them out by brand. These wide-ranging cattle may have had less impact on the grasslands than those kept on smaller, fenced ranges year-round, grazing down the best bunchgrasses without rest.

From 1824 onwards, livestock grazing was widespread well inland.[10] In 1848 approximately one million cattle grazed the ranchos of California.[11] In 1860 there were one hundred thousand head in Salinas Valley alone.[12] Overall, there have often been as many as four million head of cattle in California, and since 1970 the number has reached five million.[13]

As far back as 1820, big problems began in the livestock industry during severe droughts. During the eleven years of very low rainfall from 1853-54 to 1864-65, christened "the great drought,"[14] huge numbers of cattle were lost.[15] In May of 1864 William Brewer found the hills at Gilroy, in the Coast Range in Santa Clara County, parched and brown, "totally bare of foliage" below the scattered live oaks. The scene grew worse inland. Looking over the San Joaquin Plain, he saw the horizon fade, the Sierra invisible: "Dirt, dirt, dirt—eyes full, face dirty, whole person feeling dirty and gritty," he exclaimed. "Where there were green pastures when we camped here two years ago, now all is dry, dusty, bare ground. Three hundred cattle have died by the miserable water hole back of the house." Whole sheep ranches disappeared. Thousands of cattle retreated to the marsh edges, where some greenery could still be found: "fine rushes, called wire grass [possibly *Juncus*], and some alkali grass [*Distichlis*]," and they "gnawed it almost into the earth."[16]

This combination of factors may have broken the dominance of the native grasses, allowing Mediterranean annuals to gain a big foothold in barren and highly disturbed areas. Droughts of even a few months can severely affect grass productivity, and may be a limiting factor in California.[17] Agriculture and tillage also left a long-lasting legacy of destroyed native grasses that have not recolonized the fields, even after they lay fallow for decades;[18] new communities of introduced plants grabbed hold and remain today.

The Takeover

The spread of different species of introduced annual grasses and weeds can be traced through the decades of colonial expansion. The Mediterranean forb filaree may have preceded overland Spanish arrival, as the seeds floated to shore from ship ballast in the seventeenth century. Others arrived with the first Spanish livestock and quickly gained a foothold around settlements.

A snapshot in time was preserved in the adobe bricks of the Spanish missions, with weeds and local grasses incorporated into the clay. Native creeping wildrye seeds were found in mission bricks from Soledad (built in 1791) and Salinas (1837). But most of the species found were introduced: Italian ryegrass, wild oats, wild annual barleys, rabbitsfoot grass, curly dock, black mustard, filaree, prickly sow thistle, and tocalote thistle.[19]

Even the exact origin points of these weeds can sometimes be traced: an abundant exotic, slender wild oat shows genetic links to plants from southwestern Spain, a trade center during the colonization era.[20]

Wild oats spread far and wide over the rich soils. Reports from 1833 have them already covering large parts of the central San Joaquin Valley and the hills around Fort Ross, in Mendocino County.[21] Wild oats tolerate light grazing, which may indicate that overgrazing was not yet a large-scale problem. By the 1840s and 1850s European black mustard had swept into the valleys of Los Angeles and Santa Clara and up the coast to Fort Ross, in places so thick that horses could barely penetrate the stands.

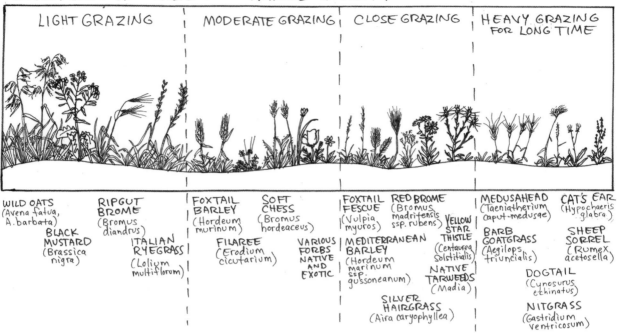

EUROPEAN ANNUALS AND RANGE QUALITY

LIGHT GRAZING	MODERATE GRAZING	CLOSE GRAZING	HEAVY GRAZING FOR LONG TIME
WILD OATS (Avena fatua, A. barbata)	FOXTAIL BARLEY (Hordeum murinum)	FOXTAIL FESCUE (Vulpia myuros)	MEDUSAHEAD (Taeniatherium caput-medusae)
BLACK MUSTARD (Brassica nigra)	SOFT CHESS (Bromus hordeaceus)	RED BROME (Bromus madritensis ssp. rubens)	CAT'S EAR (Hypochaeris glabra)
RIPGUT BROME (Bromus diandrus)	FILAREE (Erodium cicutarium)	MEDITERRANEAN BARLEY (Hordeum marinum ssp. gussoneanum)	BARB GOATGRASS (Aegilops triuncialis)
ITALIAN RYEGRASS (Lolium multiflorum)	VARIOUS FORBS NATIVE AND EXOTIC	YELLOW STAR THISTLE (Centaurea solstitialis)	SHEEP SORREL (Rumex acetosella)
		NATIVE TARWEEDS (Madia)	DOGTAIL (Cynosurus echinatus)
		SILVER HAIRGRASS (Aira caryophyllea)	NITGRASS (Gastridium ventricosum)

A second invasion of annual weeds began in the 1860s and 1870s, with range deterioration: nitgrass, hare barley, soft chess, and ripgut brome. In the 1880s a third stage occurred in southern California and the Central Valley: red brome, Mediterranean barley, European hairgrass, and Mediterranean mustard. In southern California, Saharan mustard invaded by 1927, and splitgrass had arrived from the deserts of the Middle East by 1950.[22] By then the worst species—medusahead grass, goatgrass, and hedgehog dogtail grass—were obvious indicators of heavy grazing.

The aggressiveness of Mediterranean grasses and forbs, evolved with the disturbance of European livestock and adapted to the similar, summer-dry climate of California, allowed these plants to jump into gaps between bunchgrasses (prior to this occupied by wildflowers) and other bare areas: trails, animal wallows, rodent burrow diggings, water hole edges, and other locally disturbed habitats. The annual grasses took over.

In the twentieth century many perennial grasses from Europe and Asia were brought to California as forage and hay grasses. In the East Bay several are now common in regional parks, some tricky to separate from the natives: velvetgrass, common in moist sites; meadow fescue, in mesic rangelands; and orchardgrass, to name a few.

A new grassland habitat has been created. Restoration practices can increase the native grassland species, as we shall see, but the annuals from Europe, Asia, and Africa are here to stay. Despite this the natives are still a vital part of the prairies, so let us look at some of the more important ones.

A Perennial Favorite: Purple Needlegrass

I collected needlegrass seeds in 1995 and gave a bag of them to Margot, who then planted them in a narrow strip along her walkway. They took off and then spread to the adjacent brick patio, and later, after she removed some nonnative bushes, to bare dirt in the parking strip by the street. This

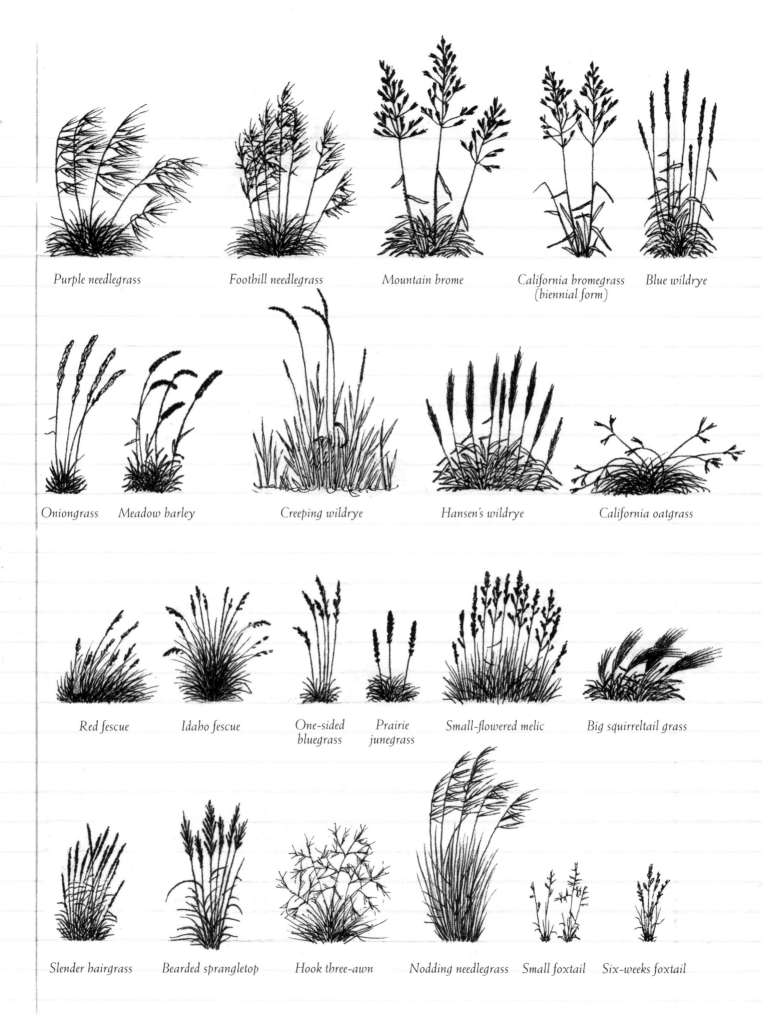

Purple needlegrass

Foothill needlegrass

Mountain brome

California bromegrass
(biennial form)

Blue wildrye

Oniongrass   Meadow barley

Creeping wildrye

Hansen's wildrye

California oatgrass

Red fescue

Idaho fescue

One-sided
bluegrass

Prairie
junegrass

Small-flowered melic

Big squirreltail grass

Slender hairgrass

Bearded sprangletop

Hook three-awn

Nodding needlegrass

Small foxtail

Six-weeks foxtail

grass became so successful here that Margot occasionally had to weed it back to make room for the junegrasses and red fescues she had planted. Wildlfowers seemed to thrive in the company of these native bunchgrasses.

The state grass of California, purple needlegrass was called "beargrass" in the past, apparently due to the appetite of grizzlies for its green blades. It can still be found below 5,000 feet from northern Baja California to Humboldt County, and in all rangelands except the driest parts of the San Joaquin Valley. In my travels I found it to be dominant in many of the state's native open landscapes, and often appearing as well in exotic annual grasslands that have not been completely degraded.

Field notes: "Lazuli bunting male alternately singing and reaching down to pick seeds of purple needlegrass and eat them— hull drops from bill."

The California grassland was one of the few in North America dominated by needlegrasses, and purple needlegrass and its relatives foothill needlegrass and nodding needlegrass are endemic to this region. Purple needlegrass reached the coast in much of the state, but in the arid inner South Coast Ranges, nodding needlegrass generally replaced it. Showing a preference for full sun, purple needlegrass was also found in oak savanna where woody cover did not exceed 80 percent.[23]

On a west-facing slope in the East Bay's Wildcat Canyon Regional Park some twenty years ago, I pondered the potential for lush wildflower growth where bunchgrasses thrive. Purple needlegrasses clothed this slope in January, the bunches one to three feet apart. Forming thick little blankets of green around them were dove lupine rosettes a few inches high, waiting to flower in spring. The lupines were dense only where the ground was bare—along trails, on old gopher mounds—or around the needlegrass bunches; they did not grow where introduced annual grasses or old leaf litter crowded them out of light and water. The lupines grew right up to the bases of the needlegrass if the ground was bare, and wild pea and lotus grew there as well.

That spring, in the same park, I found that blue-eyed "grass," a wildflower, mingled well with purple needlegrass when the bunches were spaced about a foot apart, but dropped out if annual grasses filled in the spaces and grew higher than six inches. Wild pea and American vetch did well in a wide range of situations because they could stretch taller, to one and a half feet, to get the sunlight. California poppies favor disturbed ground, so they do well in grazed ranges but not among tall annual grasses. Poppies were fairly common here, between open needlegrass bunches. White yarrows were one of the few natives that could compete with tall, exotic grasses, as they could reach two feet. They often formed their own perennial patches within the grassland and they grew well with needlegrass too. Yellowcarrot did all right with shorter annuals and was conspicuous among purple needlegrasses. Mules ears fared well among annual grasses but seemed most common in needlegrass fields.

There were also stable, ungrazed patches of pure purple needlegrass nearby with nearly 100 percent cover—no ground visible in between the bunches, so that only a few other plants could grow with them.

Inland, at Lake Berryessa Recreation Area, in the dry interior North Coast Ranges, the scene was similar. In spring I found purple needlegrass abundant all over the flats and gentle slopes near the picnic areas, which were mowed periodically but not grazed except by deer herds. Sometimes the individual bunches were scattered, one about every three square feet, interspersed with fiddleneck, popcorn flower, and chia. But a couple of acres were covered uniformly by large, old bunches, about one bunch per square foot, with plenty of gray leaf litter built up. Standing in the pure needlegrass was like being back in time, the culms reaching thigh-high and so dense as to mostly obscure the bunches beneath them. The wind blew the stems, making a loud, rustling noise. A few trails of California ground squirrels and Audubon cottontails ran through the bunches. Western bluebirds softly chirped in the blue oaks nearby.

In southern California, I have often come across purple needlegrass in open areas in the Santa Monica Mountains National Recreation Area, where it grows with scattered prickly pear, California buckwheat, Whipple yucca, black sage, and small-flowered oniongrass.

I imagine the life cycle of this noble bunchgrass repeating itself through layers of time in Old California. Purple needlegrass would produce new green leaves with the first quarter-inch of rain in the fall, after the long, dry summer. A flush of green would tint the tan-colored hills. Leaf growth was slowest during the cold of December and January but picked up in February with warming weather. By early spring new shoots would appear—vegetative tillering—and expand the bunch outward. The plants would need enough good top growth to be able to store carbohydrate food reserves in stem bases and roots so that they could survive the five-month summer dry period. Growth reached its maximum in April and May[24] and might continue to mid-July. Flowering culms appeared in early April, with spikelets that opened in May to reveal the flowers for pollination. The seeds set in May and early June, then fell from the stems or were caught on the fur of passing animals to be dispersed. Leaves were usually 3 mm wide or less, flat or rolled (involute). The roots extended three feet underground, densest in the upper six inches of soil.[25] Soil in perennial grasslands is sometimes more moist than in annual grasslands, as the perennials do not suck up surface soil water as much as the shallow-rooted annuals. Oak savannas may be significantly affected by this as annual grasses compete with oak seedlings for soil moisture (see chapter seven).

Western bluebird

Needlegrasses' strong awns function in several ways to disperse seeds: they act as hairy, "sticky" hooks to catch on the fur of passing animals (or my socks). When the seeds fall to the ground, the rains wet the awn and cause it to straighten out; when dry it bends back. This process continues until the floret drills itself into a crack or loose spot on the ground—perhaps dirt left by a burrowing rodent. The scabrous (rough) seed body, covered with stiff, unidirectional hairs, can work itself into the fur of an animal or into the ground. Margot's yard showed this specialty quite clearly when needlegrass seeds happily bored into all the crevices between the bricks of her patio, producing a pure stand free of competition.

Seeds can germinate three weeks after a good rain but may be killed by competition with rapidly growing annual grass seedlings; high levels of mulch suppress germination, and thus fire, grazing, or disturbance may actually aid the seeds in getting established.[26] Centuries ago, a man or woman with long experience might have walked through the dry tufts of grass in a valley and lit a late summer fire. Crackling through the dried, dead leaves and stems from the previous growing season, the fire would stimulate new stem and seed production, regenerating the population.

A large herd of tule elk grazing through in early summer might prolong the green growth of the needlegrasses. After being clipped by grazing animals or burned by fire, the needlegrasses could produce new blades within two days. But they would use much of their food reserves to put out new leaves, delaying the start of growth in the following rainy season.

Western meadowlark

A flock of western meadowlarks flies over recently burned purple needlegrass bunches on the Berkeley–El Cerrito Hills. Albany Hill and the spot where El Cerrito Plaza will be are on the left. Marin County and the Golden Gate occupy the distance—Mount Tamalpais is on the upper right. Oil on panel, 7 ¼ x 21 ½, 1998

Purple needlegrass, in my opinion, can survive moderate grazing better than most native bunchgrasses, one exception being California oatgrass (see below). Cattle relish needlegrass, and on heavily grazed ranges the bunches thin out and become quite small compared to those on ungrazed ranges—down to one inch in basal diameter, I noticed. Cattle also eat the dry "hay" of September needlegrasses. By November they favor the new green blades.

Recently a few botanists and restorationists have suggested that purple needlegrass was never dominant, and that some areas had no cover of perennial grass; there are theories of a coastal annual wildflower community on the Los Angeles plain, and tarweed-lupine dominance in central California. Glen Holstein, for instance, argues against the "bunchgrass paradigm" of dominant purple needlegrass lands in the Sacramento Valley and instead sees pre-agricultural communities of creeping wildrye or tarweed.[27] I agree that creeping wildrye (see below) must have formed luxuriant communities along the rivers and in flatland oak savannas. But I disagree that the bunchgrasses were insignificant: I have found purple needlegrass on well-drained areas of the valley, where it probably formed a complex patch mosaic with creeping wildrye.

An unfortunate byproduct of this attempt at a "paradigm shift" is that the work of early ecologist Frederick Clements has been attacked. Clements developed a method he called "relict analysis" to find evidence of former native grasses along relatively undisturbed sites—railroad right-of-ways, some roadsides, fenced-out areas, rocky slopes—where competition is reduced. He thought these could indicate lost habitats when backed up by diverse evidence, such as old botanical surveys and historical accounts. At Banning, in Riverside County, for instance, he found relict purple needlegrass that had survived in an overgrazed pasture by growing within the protection of a prickly pear patch.[28] Because some of Clements's theories on ecology, such as that of a "climax" state of vegetation, have fallen into disfavor, a few contemporary researchers have questioned all his methods. They ask whether the stands he analyzed are actually relict, or rather invasive themselves. But Clements began his searches early enough to witness changes that we, a century later, have all but collectively forgotten:

> The search for bunch-grass relicts in 1917-18 was first directed to [railroad] trackways, not merely because such relicts were often remarkable in purity and extent, but also because they were rapidly being destroyed as a war-time measure to produce a great crop of wheat. Many hundred miles of a nearly continuous consociation of *Stipa pulchra* [purple needlegrass, now called *Nasella pulchra*] were obliterated in the Great Valley, leaving sparse fragments where plough and fire had taken lighter toll....It was especial good fortune to record these extensive relicts and then to have them reduced to patches here and there, as it not only confirms the other evidence to the effect grassland was the original great climax of California, but it throws needed light upon other regions known only by the mosaic of relicts.[29]

Clements photographed large purple needlegrass bunches growing along a railway near Fresno, and I have explored these same areas and found similar relicts, beautiful stands inside the fences that lined the tracks. Outside the fences I saw well-tended vineyards, wheat fields, houses, and weedy pastures with cattle, goats, and sheep grazing so heavily that not much remained. Much of the moister eastern edge of the primordial San Joaquin Valley might have been covered by such bunchgrasses. Similar relict methods are used today by historical ecologists in the Mediterranean region to reconstruct old layers of vegetation.[30]

Other positive evidence comes from opal phytolith analysis. Grass ecologist James Bartolome and his colleagues found a significant presence of panicoid-type phytoliths, which match purple needlegrass types, several inches below the soil surface in what are presently introduced annual grasslands. They suggest this indicates that purple needlegrass once grew more densely in places where today only isolated bunches remain.[31]

We might think of California's past grasslands as inherently disturbance-oriented ecosystems. "Highly variable nonequilibrium systems," say ecologists: whole communities adapted to the regular disturbances of droughts, El Niños, fires, people gathering seeds for food, elk grazing, and rodent burrowing.[32] Purple needlegrass may have been dominant in many areas because it was so well evolved to this kind of unstable regime. Margot's yard is certainly a good example.

Foothill Needlegrass

Foothill needlegrass has short, delicate, straight awns, bronze, green, or purple in spring. The dense blades look finer than those of purple needlegrass. In May the bunches are a slightly different shade of green than purple needlegrass. By October the bunches turn light yellowish.

Foothill needlegrass often mixes with purple needlegrass. It forms small, pure stands on the open ridge grasslands of Tilden and Wildcat Canyon Regional Parks, and it also grows in the shade of live oaks. Inland, at Mount Diablo State Park for example, it is fairly common in the shade of chaparral.

I discussed native grassland ecology with restorationist Tim Gordon in 1984, while we gazed on the beautiful slopes of El Cerrito's Albany Hill, covered with foothill needlegrass—not far from the plaza where I had imagined grizzly bears feeding on acorns. At the time, he was helping to restore the "little hill," an urban island of open land. An Ohlone acorn mortar lay under live oaks by a creek at the base of the hill, and shellmounds lined the bayshore nearby. He told of watching pools of water form between the grass bunches during rains. Little grass dams between the plants held the water in, allowing much more to seep into the soil than in annual grasslands. The extensive root systems of the bunchgrasses help stabilize the soil, and perhaps in the past aided in preventing extensive landslides. Tim thought that this water seeping downhill in the bunchgrasslands might take a year to reach the bottom slopes and might have produced many springs. With this increased water storage capacity in the uplands, some local creeks may have flowed longer into the dry season and may have been perennial instead of intermittent, positively affecting salmon and steelhead (see chapter thirteen).

Cattle eat foothill needlegrass with relish, and in moderately to heavily grazed ranges it will "retreat" to the cover of coyote brush and other hiding places.

Field notes: "Grasshopper sparrow—three in nodding needlegrass field on hill, feeding on seeds on ground in open patches among tall bunches. Much calling."

Nodding Needlegrass

I have heard nodding needlegrass called "feathergrass," a fitting name for one of the most beautiful of our grasses. Its bunches are tall and sturdy, yet the flower panicles, tinged with purple, are graceful and delicate. The long awns curve sinuously in May and June. On a windy day a field of feathergrass waves like fine hair or the mane of a blonde horse, glinting in the sunlight quietly. The blades are narrower than those of purple needlegrass (usually 1.5 mm wide) and are often glaucous (light green tinged with bluish white). Very drought-tolerant, it never gets as lush as purple needlegrass can.

I have found feathergrass growing in a grassland mosaic of one-sided bluegrass, small-flowered and California melic, and big squirreltail along Mines Road, in the arid inland part of Alameda County, with blue oak, gray pine, and chaparral. In Solano County I have seen it growing down to the edges of the tule marshes of Suisun Bay. In one section fenced off from cattle, the nodding needlegrass was dense and abundant on the gentle slopes—this grass must have originally covered the hills and plains away from the marshes. One of the best places to see acres of nodding needlegrass is at Basalt Camp, in Merced County's San Luis Reservoir State Recreation Area: on a February visit to this inner Coast Range locale I found abundant large and small patches, the blades greened up but the culms old and gray from last season. In June I returned and found wildflowers in the needlegrass prairie: tarweed, doveweed, milkweed, milkvetch, a pink-flowered buckwheat, a yellow-flowered gumplant, and vinegar weed with deep-blue flowers. In the Sierra foothills I found relicts in blue oak savanna growing with one-sided bluegrass, California melic, soap plant, doveweed, yarrow, and phacelia. One year the rains fell just right to produce large patches of waving, straw-purple panicles of needlegrass above the introduced annuals along Tehachapi Pass roads in May—the awns glinted in the setting sun like threads of white gold. The next year a wet spring made the wild oats and ripgut brome grow tall, and I could barely detect the bunchgrasses.

I found feathergrasses scattered on a mowed divider of Highway 65 just north of Porterville, in Tulare County. The mowing seemed to benefit the natives, eliminating much of the exotic competition. At Carrizo Plain National Monument, in San Luis Obispo County, nodding needlegrasses were recovering from historic agriculture and drought: on steeps too dense to plow, they grew dense; elsewhere they dotted rolling flats and saltbush barrens, often along fenced-out roadsides and parking lot edges, away from cattle overgrazing. In June 2004 I drove from El Cajon to Ramona, inland and north of San Diego, inspecting hills once covered with chaparral, now burned off by devastating wildfires. But I noticed long nodding needlegrass stems waving in the breezes on the burnt hills, ready to regrow into a grassland.

Little Tufts with Wildflowers: One-Sided Bluegrass

One-sided bluegrass is a small, tufted bunchgrass that probably grew abundantly in between the needlegrasses and in pure stands. Sometimes the culms grow no taller than a foot, in moister spots to two feet. This bunchgrass is an obligate dormant plant: by the June dry season, it turns dry-tan and yellow ochre. In the wet season its little green (not particularly blue) tufts form waving fields of foot-high seed heads among thousands of orange California poppies. (This can be seen at the Antelope Valley California Poppy State Reserve, in the transitional desert grassland of northeastern Los Angeles County). Bluegrasses allow the wildflowers full rein to bloom, as there is plenty of bare ground between the grasses. Today these spaces are usually filled with introduced annual grasses.

Black-tailed jackrabbit

Also called malpais bluegrass, steppe bluegrass, or pine bluegrass, this is a very widespread species in the western United States, common in the Great Basin, the Mojave Desert, and into the sagebrush steppes of Idaho, Montana, and Wyoming. Sereno Watson, in his *Botany of California*, called it frequent throughout the state from San Diego to Oregon, a "most valuable bunchgrass." He said the Indians collected its purplish grain for food. I have seen bluegrasses put out their slender seed heads earlier than most other native grasses, in March—a good early food plant, perhaps.[33]

In the Palouse Prairie of eastern Washington, I found these bluegrasses growing with the bunchgrass needle-and-thread, a species reminiscent of the needlegrasses that replace it in much of California. Here, even though the climate differs from that of western California, the grassland observer can gain a clue as to the pristine habit of a bluegrass-needlegrass association free of the hordes of introduced annuals. The little bluegrass tufts mix evenly with the larger needlegrass bunches over hills and flats.

In very arid areas, such as the saltbush flats of the western San Joaquin Valley and the Kern County oil fields, on the edges of the hills, I have found bluegrasses. In the North Coast Ranges I found them growing on rocky or thin soils, while purple needlegrass and California oatgrass dominated the heavier, deeper soils. At Vina Plains, on the east side of the Sacramento Valley south of Red Bluff, I found scattered, small, purplish tufts of bluegrass fairly plentiful on the flats in and around dry vernal pools in April; wildflowers, such as goldfields, grew abundantly around them.

What the community was like before the weedy invasions cannot now be known with certainty, but I suspect that much native bluegrass has been eliminated by livestock grazing, especially by sheep, who find its small, tender tufts particularly palatable. In unfenced elk and bison ranges bluegrass can take heavy grazing. Aboriginally it was probably widespread in open, well-drained grasslands of many topographic types, as well as in blue oak savannas and woodlands, up into the pine belts, and out into the deserts.

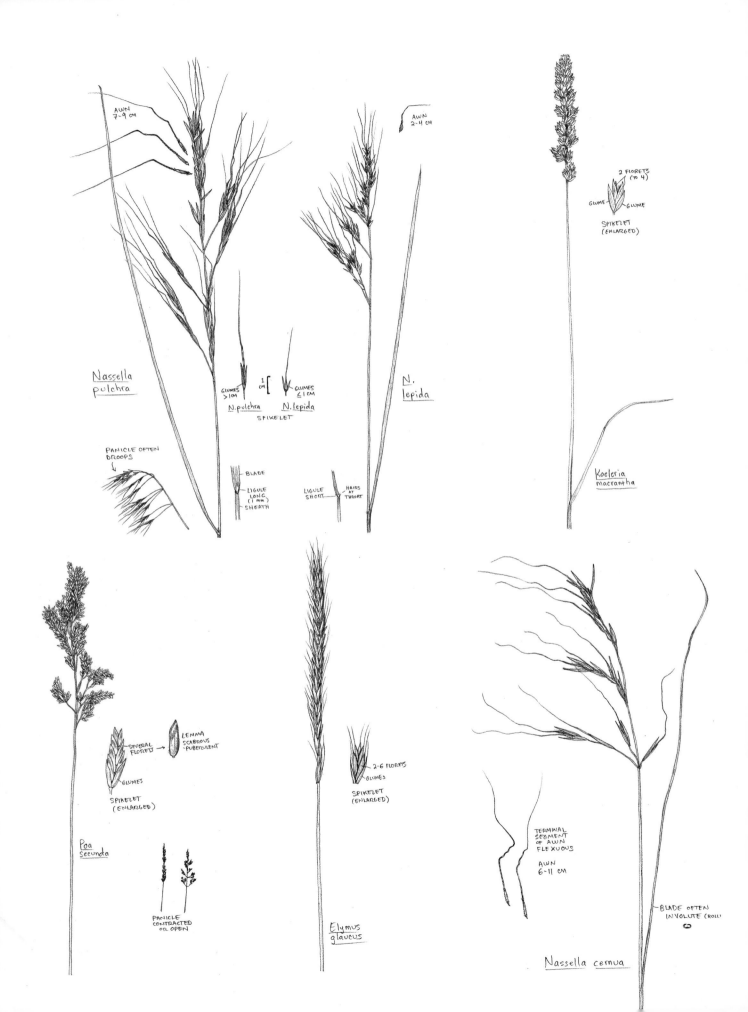

AWN
7-9 CM

Nassella
pulchra

PANICLE OFTEN
DROOPS

GLUMES
>1CM

1 CM

GLUMES
≤1CM

N. pulchra   N. lepida
SPIKELET

BLADE

LIGULE
LONG
(1 MM)
SHEATH

LIGULE
SHORT

HAIRS
AT
THROAT

AWN
2-4 CM

N.
lepida

2 FLORETS
(TO 4)

GLUME   GLUME

SPIKELET
(ENLARGED)

Koeleria
macrantha

SEVERAL
FLORETS

LEMMA
SCABROUS
- PUBERULENT

GLUMES

SPIKELET
(ENLARGED)

Poa
secunda

PANICLE
CONTRACTED
OR OPEN

2-6 FLORETS

GLUMES

SPIKELET
(ENLARGED)

Elymus
glaucus

TERMINAL
SEGMENT
OF AWN
FLEXUOUS

AWN
6-11 CM

BLADE OFTEN
INVOLUTE (ROLL'

Nassella cernua

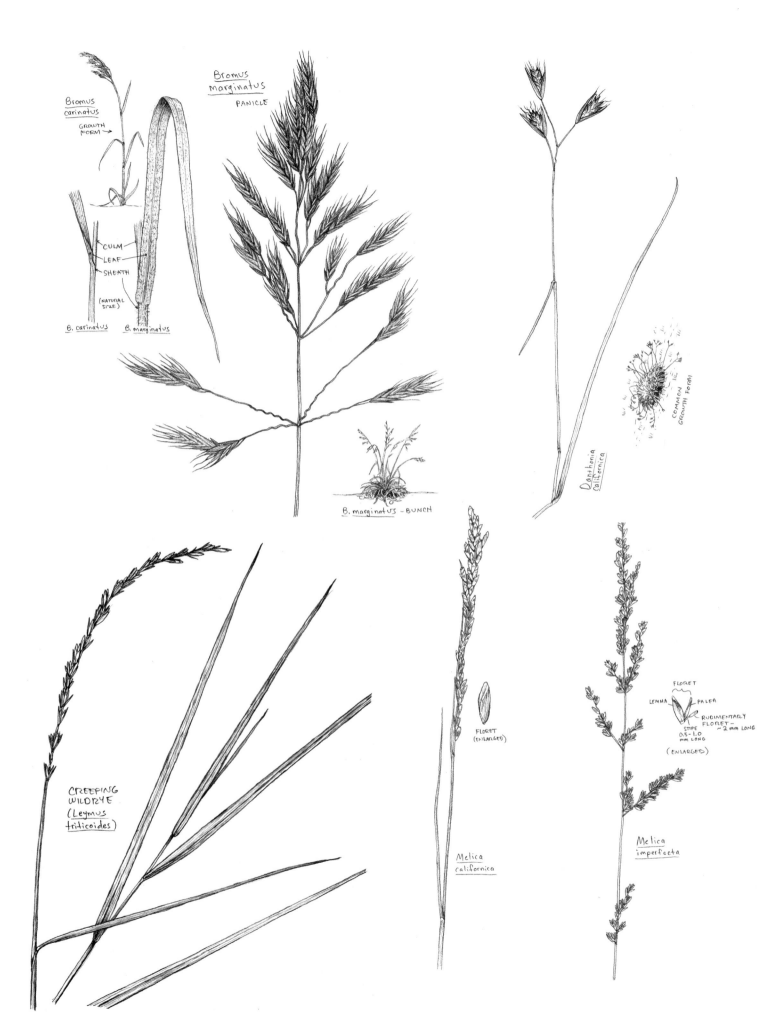

Bromus
carinatus

GROWTH
FORM

CULM
LEAF
SHEATH

(NATURAL
SIZE)

B. carinatus   B. marginatus

Bromus
marginatus
PANICLE

B. marginatus - BUNCH

Danthonia
californica

COMMON
GROWTH FORM

CREEPING
WILDRYE
(Leymus
triticoides)

Melica
californica

FLORET
(ENLARGED)

Melica
imperfecta

FLORET

LEMMA   PALEA

RUDIMENTARY
FLORET ~ 2 mm LONG
STIPE
0.5 - 1.0
mm LONG

(ENLARGED)

SOME EAST BAY WILDFLOWER BLOOM TIMES
CONTRA COSTA AND ALAMEDA COUNTIES

	FEB	MAR	APR	MAY	JUN	JUL	AUG	SEP	OCT	NOV	
PEPPERGRASS											Lepidium spp.
CALIFORNIA BUTTERCUPS											Ranunculus californicus
ARROYO LUPINE											Lupinus succulentus
BLUE DICKS											Dichelostemma capitatum
BLUE-EYED GRASS											Sisyrinchium bellum
RED MAIDS											Calandrinia ciliata
CHECKER											Sidalcea malvaeflora
DOVE LUPINE											Lupinus bicolor
HEDGE NETTLE											Stachys rigida
POPCORN FLOWER											Plagiobothrys nothofulvus
YELLOW CARROT											Lomatium utriculatum
TOMCAT CLOVER											Trifolium willdenovii
BABY BLUE-EYES											Nemophila menziesii
FIDDLENECK											Amsinckia menziesii
WHITE YARROW											Achillea millefolium
CREAM CUPS											Platystemon californicus
MICROSERIS											Microseris elegans
BUTTER-&-EGGS											Triphysaria eriantha
PURPLE OWL'S CLOVER											Castilleja exserta
OOKOW											Dichelostemma congestum
RANCHERIA CLOVER											Trifolium albopurpureum
GRASS NUT											Triteleia laxa
FAREWELL-TO-SPRING											Clarkia amoena
YELLOW MARIPOSA LILY											Calochortus luteus
SOAP PLANT											Chlorogalum pomeridianum
CHIA											Salvia columbariae
GUM PLANT											Grindelia camporum
GOLDENROD											Solidago californica
BUCKWHEAT											Eriogonum nudum
CHILEAN ASTER											Aster chilensis
TARWEEDS											Madia elegans, M. gracilis
CALIFORNIA FUSCHIA											Epilobium canum
CALIFORNIA POPPY											Eschscholzia californica
SUMMER LUPINE											Lupinus formosus

Grassroots Movement: Creeping Wildrye

One of the most important native grasses, creeping wildrye once covered many of the valley floors, floodplains, marsh edges, basins, and hill-swales in the state. Before European arrival it probably covered hundreds of thousands of acres of bottomlands, while the needlegrass-bluegrass community interfingered with it on drier flats and slopes. It is not a bunchgrass, but rhizomatous, spreading out vegetative runners and roots to form wide patches sometimes an acre or more in extent—thus the "creeping" growth form. The blades are flat, to 6 mm wide. Though rhizomatous, the plants do put out seed spikes, often curving or drooping. Continuous swards were made up of many plants that covered whole valleys (see page 164 for such a scene in the Tulare Plains). At Point Pinole Regional Shoreline, in Contra Costa County, large, leafy patches about two feet tall can cover almost a quarter-acre each. Wildrye patches are widely scattered among grassland flats of purple needlegrass and California oatgrass. Four-foot-tall stands full of robust, nodding culms grow above cliffs, creating a beautiful silhouette against smooth, pastel blue, pink, and orange bay waters shimmering at sunset.

Creeping wildrye needs fairly deep soil but is tolerant of alkaline and saline conditions. On the coastal fog belt it grows on hillslopes and ridgetops in large, round patches. It will also line creeks, form an understory in riparian woodlands, grow around quiet backwater sloughs, and fringe both saltwater and freshwater marshes. One could call it "friend of the valley oak, friend of the cottonwood." Go to Cosumnes River Preserve, in Sacramento County, to see acres of this grass next to valley oaks. It is also the dominant grass in the open floodplain and oak woodland understory at Ancil Hoffman Park, along the American River in Sacramento.

In southern California, early botanists described this spreading grass filling bottomlands and alkaline places.[34] Patches grew on valley floors around western sycamore. I searched under spreading valley oaks and shrubby native walnuts in Woodland Hills, on the edge of the San Fernando Valley, and found a remnant of creeping wildrye growing on an open flat; Highway 101 roared noisily nearby.

This is another plant that ignores geographic and climatic regions. I detected little difference in its growth pattern between the Great Basin, where it is still extensive and not hidden from view by a crush of alien weeds, and the oak savannas of west-central California. The tall, green or bluish wildrye "lawns" filled most creekbottoms around willows and formed abundant large patches in wide valleys.

I have watched tule elk graze lightly on green creeping wildrye in April at San Luis National Wildlife Refuge, in the San Joaquin Valley marsh edges. I have seen it respond well to mowing along roadsides in May, producing juicy, new, green growth by June. I have also seen it survive an episode of plowing, the rhizomes able to continue growth. It seems to have adapted to moderate grazing by elk as they gathered in the summer-green, moist lowlands that were dominated by this plant. Although it is somewhat coarse, cattle and horses will dine on it—in July, when it is green on swales, slopes, and around springs, I have noticed all the tops "mowed off" by cattle. Creeping wildrye can remain lush into September, when the upland bunchgrasslands are dry. By the end of the dry season in October, cattle will have grazed it down heavily. In the southern part of Mount Diablo State Park, on Stone Valley Road, this grass is dominant on ungrazed valley floors, fills ravines, and extends three-quarters or more of the way up to low ridgetops. But it is absent on overgrazed parts just outside the fences, which appear to be 99 percent nonnative plants.

More Native Grasses: A Catalog

Alongside the needlegrasses, bluegrasses, and wildrye, California prairies have many native grass species. Those that follow are but a few of the more common ones I have encountered.

Mountain bromegrass: leaves, sheaths, and culms are pilose (covered with soft hairs). The wide blades (usually to 5 to 9 mm) combine with the narrower leaves of the needlegrasses to form a rich, varied texture. In moist areas in good years I have occasionally seen mountain brome culms growing to five and six feet tall. In April the seed panicles are rich green or tinged purple. The spikelets shatter when dry, and their multiple awned, scabrous florets catch easily on animal fur for transport. On the open prairies of the Coast Range I have often seen bromes growing in pure patches, several yards square. Inland of the fog belt they occur on deep, rich, moist soils or in the shade of oak savannas and foothill woodlands. Watch out for the similar *Bromus stamineus*, an exotic from Chile, which has wider lemmas (2.5 to 3 mm) with winglike margins, and Eurasian *B. japonicus*, which has more cylindrical spikelets. Bromes can withstand moderate grazing and will easily colonize bare areas with a horde of new seedlings. Out of all the native grasses, I have noted mountain brome leaves to be the most favored by hungry black-tailed deer. In May I have watched sparrows land on the panicles to pluck the seeds.

California brome is a biennial or sometimes perennial form, although it often takes on an annual habit; I have seen all forms growing on Bay Area ridges and flats. Its leaves and culms are scabrous, or with a few scattered long hairs, or sometimes even glabrous. This grass often looks "stemmy," with fewer leaves at the base, growing in tufts that are thin at best. The sheaths are smooth. California brome can handle drier habitats than its perennial relative mountain brome. I have seen tall, weeping panicles of California brome growing under valley oaks in warm Coast Range valleys, and in the Central Valley at places like Natomas Oaks Park, in Sacramento by the American River. It was fairly common in southern California before cities overran the grasslands.[35]

A pure stand of mountain brome in the shadowed foreground of the hills above Richmond. San Pablo Bay and Mount Tamalpais are in the distance. OIL ON PANEL, 8 X 21 INCHES, 1998

California melic, or oniongrass: You can pull out a stem of this important tufted grass and find a small, onionlike bulge at the base. The spikelets are large, 7 to 10 mm long. When the patches start to dry out in late May, their papery glumes turn silvery white. Found from Ventura County north, throughout the Coast Ranges, the Central Valley, and the Sierra foothills,[36] this oniongrass is endemic to California and the southeast corner of Oregon. In the East Bay this beautiful plant is common on hills and open slopes. Around Mount Diablo's Rock City, for example, I found this grass abundant on open hills and flats, with nearby groves of live oak, gray pine, and buckeye; large bunches grew along the Summit Trail. I have watched mule deer nip off the seed heads of oniongrass in spring, and even in grazed cattle ranges I can often manage to find California melic "hiding" next to boulders or on steep slopes. In moderately grazed areas, it holds its own.

Small-flowered melic: This arid-adapted oniongrass is found from Baja to central California; it may have been one of the most common native grasses in southern California.[37] Its blades are relatively wide. As early as March, on warm slopes, the bunches become full of narrow but often branching panicles with dense, shiny, purplish spikelets. By May the seeds begin to dry and turn brown. The spikelets are half the size of those of California melic. In Tilden Regional Park I have found this dry-adapted grass keeping to the poorer soils of chert, basalt, and shale, and not on the more mesic substrates of sandstone-based clays and loams dominated by the other natives. At Ronald W. Caspers Regional Park, in Orange County, I saw lush fields of small-flowered melic taking over recently burned coastal sage scrub hills—acres of panicles waving in the sea breezes. And I have found remnant plants elsewhere, on the edges of the town of Rancho Palos Verdes, as well as in Griffith Park and the Santa Monica Mountains, just north of Los Angeles—relicts hanging on to scraps of open space. I have watched cattle pick out green bunches of small-flowered melic in winter, apparently preferring them to exotic annual grass. Oniongrasses will not stand heavy grazing and have been eliminated from many overused ranges.

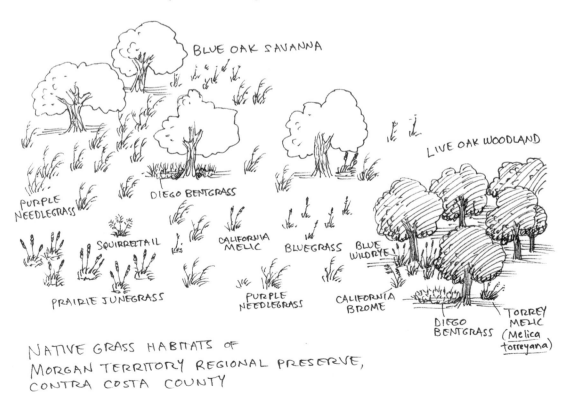

NATIVE GRASS HABITATS OF
MORGAN TERRITORY REGIONAL PRESERVE,
CONTRA COSTA COUNTY

Prairie junegrass grows in a beautiful, neat bunch with compact spikes of seeds. The long, crowded basal leaves are around 2 to 3 mm wide. The spikelets and seeds are scaberulous—covered with hairs, but fine, short ones, and so are not well adapted for transport by animal or wind. Therefore they may only distribute themselves in small patches, which makes plenty of room for wildflowers to thrive. This grass knows no maps and is equally at home across Eurasia, on the Great Plains, across the West on desert mountain ranges, and into California, where it grows on open grasslands, savannas, conifer forests, and mountain meadows up to 11,500 feet.[38] At Las Trampas Regional Park, in Contra Costa County, I found junegrass bunches in grassy openings, on open hilltops and ridges, on northeast-facing slopes in oak savanna, and on drier, southwest-facing slopes in open, blue oak savanna. Livestock eagerly seek out this grass for forage. It can withstand heavy grazing, but not long-term in fenced pastures; thus it may have been more widespread in Old California than the relict evidence indicates.

Blue wildrye bunches contain dense, fairly wide blades (often 6 to 8 mm), varying in color from deep green to glaucous. The numerous spike-culms stretch up and survive well into winter as they turn gray with the cold. Blue wildrye is abundant in western North America below 7,500 feet.[39] It occurs in conifer forests, oak woodlands, riparian groves, chaparral, and in grasslands on rich loamy soil. In the East Bay it forms dense, tall stands on slopes that face west and receive the fog-carrying winds. It is less common in the interior Coast Ranges, Sierra foothills, and southern California, often retreating to mesic spots under oaks and along streambanks, springs, and flood margins. In the Central Valley it was apparently not common. Visit Fort Tejon State Historic Park, Kern County, and look under the oak edges and hillslopes for this grass. Cattle will graze the wildryes, even when the blades are dry. But anything more than light grazing will eliminate them or reduce them to locations under the cover of brush. The plants will, however, quickly invade bare areas with fast-growing, vigorous seedlings that mature in one season.

Meadow barley is a common, moist-soil bunchgrass of lowlands, mountain meadows, swales, seeps, streamside flats, and open bogs. Its narrow, spiky seed heads make dark, brown-purple textures in wet meadows. It tolerates subalkaline areas of drying pools with intermittent flooding. In the East Bay I have seen it on moist flats, meeting purple needlegrasses that grew on drier flats. One May, walking through sloping grasslands east of the Berkeley-Richmond hills, I found it growing especially thick in dry mud; California buttercup, blue-eyed grass, grass nut, harvest brodiaea, and wild onion grew with it. In the dry inner Coast Ranges I have found it on moist flats and in vernal pools. In the Delta I discovered dense bunches along the road, on a bank next to a willow slough in San Joaquin County, a probable relict of former abundance. It seems to be better adapted to grazing than many natives, and cattle will take the green blades in winter and early spring; they avoid the prickly flowering spikes, but I watched cattle return in August to crop off the dry stems after the spikes had shattered and dropped their seeds. No doubt elk fed on meadow barley as they searched for moist, green grass patches in the dry summer months.

Field notes: *"California ground squirrel reaching up and pulling off green seed spikes of meadow barley and eating them."*

Diego bentgrass, or *thingrass,* is fairly common in coastal areas in open grassland, mixing with both purple needlegrass and coastal prairie species. It is a rhizomatous native, forming small, loose patches that are usually no more than six to ten feet across. Its leaves are around six to eight inches high, and it sends up only small seed heads: the patches are perfect nesting spots for deer to curl up and sleep on. Along the Wildcat Peak Trail, in Tilden Regional Park, I found Diego bentgrass in large patches, filling swales and growing on slopes and ridgetops in the summer fog zone. In March it formed beautifully soft, green, meadow-like patches of uniform blades, contrasting with the surrounding taller, uneven purple needlegrass. Inland, away from the fog belt, it recedes to the cover of thickets and woodlands. In southern California it was reported occasionally along streams on the plains, and in dry grasslands of the mountain foothills.[40] Constant grazing eliminates it quickly, and relicts can be found only under the cover of low shrubs, on steep banks, and in other protected places.

Big squirreltail grass is common in dry, open grasslands, often on gravelly, sandy sites. Its blades can be green or glaucous. Its unique, wide spikes add textural quality to a grassland: in spring, the bunches look like heads of green-blonde hair, and the long, unopened awns look like miniature horse tails; in summer the awns dry and open up into "bottlebrushes" with a fine, light bronze or silver sheen in the hot sun. When ripe, the rachis (seed-head stem) breaks off and, with long awns spread out laterally, the seed heads roll about in the wind, an apparent adaptation to ensure seed dispersal on the bare soil that would have been common before the invasion of the dense, European annual grasses that now clog even xeric grasslands. This suggests that on drier sites, the native grasslands were often noncontinuous in cover, allowing coast horned lizards, Heerman's kangaroo rats, pocket mice, and other small animals to move about freely: useful information for restorationists. The low bunches of big squirreltail grass are common in Big Springs Canyon, in Tilden Regional Park. At Los Trancos Open Space Preserve, in San Mateo County, I found this species covering large areas of some slopes in pure stands. Along the American River in Ancil Hoffman Park, near Sacramento, I found big squirreltail bunches on dry, cobbly, and gravelly floodplains.

Squirreltail, the shorter-awned relative of big squirreltail grass, is in the Coast Ranges, the Sierra foothills, and other higher elevation locations. At Burma Ridge, in Mount Diablo State Park, for example, I saw abundant squirreltail in arid, rocky grasslands with one-sided bluegrass, prairie junegrass, small-flowered melic, native foxtails, and buckwheat. I also found some on a serpentine outcrop in Alameda County's Ohlone Wilderness, and on basalt barrens in the Sierra foothills. I have found plentiful squirreltail bunches on the arid edges of the Mojave Desert, and covering 20 to 30 percent of some areas along Highway 58, in the Tehachapi Mountains.

King needlegrass, or *giant needlegrass,* is a robust bunchgrass found in the South Coast Ranges, south coastal California, and the deserts to Baja California. Its name must derive from its spearlike seed-spikes, eleven inches long, and its shoulder-high stems. The blades are coarse and wide (to 7 mm). Plant ecologist W. James Barry speculates it was present on upper slopes of the Central Valley.[41] I believe it was once more common in open southern grasslands, but cattle will graze it out and now it is principally found on rocky cliffs and in brushy areas protected from grazing and development. (See page 22 for a painting of hills by the San Fernando Valley as they may have once looked.) At Eaton Canyon Park, in the low foothills of the San Gabriel Mountains, I discovered bunches of this grass on a cliff a mere hundred feet above arroyo beds and flats on the Los Angeles Basin, growing with small-flowered oniongrass. Nearby, a curious, treelike prickly pear or "Indian fig" stood, a remnant of Spanish days when "tuna" cactus from Mexico were introduced. As I looked over my shoulder, the bustle of Pasadena brought me back to the twenty-first century.

California oatgrass is not a true oat, but its seeds have a slight resemblance. The culms arch outward and down. Each node on the culm puts out flowering spikes. In ungrazed parts of Wildcat Canyon I have often seen bunches growing to ten inches in basal diameter, many with more erect culms that knit together to form a continuous, dense grass layer. In grazed areas, the bunches are four to five inches in diameter. Even in ungrazed areas, oatgrass forms a flatter grassland than other bunchgrasses, but I have also seen ecotypes of the grass that are tall and erect. California oatgrass used to grow in coastal regions from the vicinity of Los Angeles north to British Columbia. Needing soil moisture, it is quite rare in the inner Coast Ranges, Central Valley, and Sierra foothills. At Point Pinole Regional Shoreline, oatgrass bunches mix evenly with purple needlegrass over the flats in back of the bay marshes overlooking San Pablo Bay. You can also see this grass along Nimitz Way, in Tilden and Wildcat Canyon Regional Parks, where cattle graze the ridges. Oatgrass's prostrate, "pre-trampled" growth form helps it to resist grazing. The arching culms can spread flat out sideways along the ground, away from hungry cow mouths. The culms fall off easily, perhaps so that hoofed animals will kick them away and spread the seeds. Sheep can chew the low nodes off with their small incisors, sometimes killing the plants if allowed to graze year-long. See page 138 for a painting with this grass.

Idaho fescue, an important northern coastal prairie bunchgrass, forms fountainlike, bluish bunches with dense, fine blades. The spikelets are less than 1.5 cm long and the lemmas have an awn 4 mm long. This distinguishes Idaho fescue from bromes, which have spikelets longer than 1.5 cm, and from bluegrasses, which are awnless or very weakly awned. Like red fescue, Idaho fescue can have reddish culm bases, but the culms are only slightly bent at the base. In February the bunches are dark green in color, and walking among these large, almost shrublike forms—sometimes mounded into mushroom shapes—is a far cry from walking though an annual grassland. When the bunches flower, in spring, they put out two-foot-high seed panicles that vary in color with each plant—some glaucous-green, others yellowish, and some pastel-brown. As the panicles open, they begin to look feathery. Idaho fescue can be found continuously from San Mateo County northward. It is abundant in the open forests of the North Coast Ranges, and also on the Modoc Plateau and in the interior West. Go to San Bruno Mountain south of San Francisco, in San Mateo County, to find good stands of this grass. Surprises are always in store for the seeker, as I was reminded one day along the back roads of southern interior Monterey County: I happened upon a large stand of Idaho fescue growing in a blue oak savanna in a dry valley—unusual habitat for this bunchgrass in California.

Red fescue is a sod grass that grows by short rhizomes into small patches—I have seen them growing, tuftlike, as much as a yard across and spreading. The plants have red at the culm bases—a good way to identify this grass—and unlike those of Idaho fescue, the culm bases are very bent (decumbent). In some locations I have seen red fescue with no awns, or awns only 1 mm long; in other areas the awns grow to 4 mm. Unlike the many native grasses that have scabrous leaves that you can feel when you run your hand along them, red fescue has smooth blades that are usually rolled up. It is found in the summer-cool areas of the Coast Ranges from Monterey County northward. Hike in Mount Tamalpais State Park, in Marin County, and look on open slopes and potrero meadows for red fescue.

Tufted hairgrass is a large, northern coastal prairie bunchgrass found in moist or marshy soils, and also in ecotones with drier soils. Some forms are salt-tolerant. According to botanist Sereno Watson, this robust bunchgrass furnished good yields of hay in moist meadows of Oakland and San Francisco[42]—this must be a lost habitat, dug up and now covered with concrete and asphalt. At Point Reyes National Seashore, in Marin County, large bunches of this grass dominate the coastal prairie behind the dunes, in dry areas as well as moist puddles. It is also common in Sierran meadows.

CALIFORNIA'S NATIVE ANNUAL GRASSES ARE SMALL PLANTS, EASILY OVERLOOKED, IN MAN

Hook three-awn, an arid-adapted bunchgrass, is named for its tripartite awn, which facilitates windborne travel along open ground. This is a grass of the xeric regions of the Central Valley, shallow soils of desert grasslands, and open or rocky slopes. It was apparently common in southern California but is now spotty in distribution.[43] Its most northern locality may be at Salt Creek, draining into the Sacramento Valley in Colusa County, as well as on the Sutter Buttes, where I have seen it on steep, xeric, south-facing slopes with shallow soils. Drive along Bear Mountain Road (Highway 223) up from Arvin, in the San Joaquin Valley, and look on roadcuts and slopes in the open hills for these tufts. When I found them they were growing with one-sided bluegrass and nodding needlegrass, and in March the three-awns were surrounded by purple owl's clover. In southern California I saw this grass at Rancho Mission Viejo Conservancy, in Orange County, growing in coastal sage scrub with Diego bentgrass and bearded canegrass. I also found it common with purple needlegrass in a valley along Highway 79 near Santa Ysabel, in San Diego County. Three-awn has a high fiber content; cattle leave it alone unless other forage is scarce.

Native Annual Grasses

California's native annual grasses are small plants, easily overlooked, and in many places they have no doubt been crowded out by exotic grasses. The original California grasslands may have had more native annuals than is supposed. Small foxtail was probably one of the most common, although I do not think it was ever as abundant as exotic annual grasses are today. It was very common the whole length of the state, and abundant on dry hills.[44] It was one of the few native grasses that survived in the desert-like bottom of the San Joaquin Valley. Twisselman called it "often abundant" there, up into the blue oak zone.[45] Similarly, it was found in open, gravelly areas and foothills across southern California.[46] Twisselman described small foxtail as an important late winter and early spring forage plant for stock.[47]

In my own explorations I have found these little *Vulpias*—from six to eighteen inches high—to be most common in the drier interior, from the oak belt to the lowest valley floors. At Lake Berryessa, tiny foxtail grasses were abundant in June of 1989, in the open and under blue oaks in the picnic areas on the rolling flats of the valley. This is one of the few places where I have found this species common on flats; elsewhere it is confined to relict places on cliffs or rocky sites, due to competition with the introduced annual grasses that normally fill the ground. The picnic area at Lake Berryessa is regularly mowed, and this may be why the exotic grasses do not thrive—wild oats and soft chess were uncommon. In addition, the bare ground of the receding reservoir shoreline offered competition-free habitat: where bare ground is widespread and leaf litter is minimal, *Vulpia* thrives.

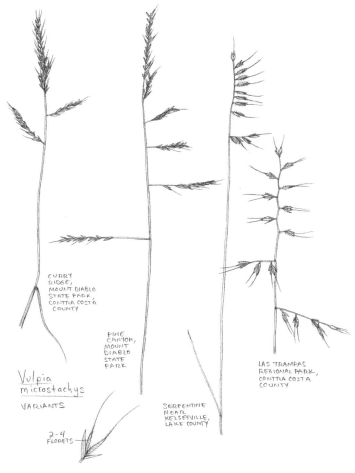

Vulpia microstachys VARIANTS

CURRY RIDGE, MOUNT DIABLO STATE PARK, CONTRA COSTA COUNTY

PINE CANYON, MOUNT DIABLO STATE PARK

2–4 FLORETS

SERPENTINE NEAR KELSEYVILLE, LAKE COUNTY

LAS TRAMPAS REGIONAL PARK, CONTRA COSTA COUNTY

In pristine times I believe small foxtail was able to grow in better soils in many areas, between the bunchgrasses and sharing the open spaces with wildflowers. At Morgan Territory Regional Preserve, in Contra Costa County, I was delighted to find abundant native annual foxtails growing densely in the open and under blue oaks, on all exposures, with goldfields and by themselves. They were small and green and did not block the flowers; variable in character, some were pubescent (hairy), others scabrous.

The variety of habitats that this grass once inhabited became more apparent when I found them in dry hog wallows on open, basaltic terrace grassland on the upper Sacramento Valley floor near Rocklin. At Vina Plains, in Tehama County, small foxtail was abundant, but not in the vernal pools; instead it grew around them, forming a matrix for wildflowers such as goldfields, meadow foam, mariposa lilies, tidy-tips, and blue dicks. At Byron, in the desertlike alkaline flats of the San Joaquin Valley, I found a small patch of this grass on a flat by an alkali scald, with Parish brittlescale and iodine bush.

Six-weeks foxtail, or six-weeks fescue, an annual similar to small foxtail, is found in dry, open places throughout the state and much of North America.[48] It occurs on gravelly soil, but I have also found it hiding on sandstone banks along a hillslope trail, and occupying bare dirt left by gophers in an otherwise dense grassland in Wildcat Canyon Regional Park. On grassland burns I have seen it spreading out in large numbers. Hiking Garin–Dry Creek Pioneer Regional Park in Alameda County in July of 1997, I came upon this little grass growing abundantly on the grazed sandstone hills and ridges, sometimes mixing with rancheria clover and tarweeds, as well as bunches of nodding needlegrass that were spaced six inches apart. The foxtails were dry and tangled at this time of year, six inches high or less on windy ridgetops.

Today their niche has been filled, I think, by closely related Mediterranean species, sometimes difficult to distinguish from the natives. The spikes of native foxtails usually have strongly reflexed branchlets (bent at right angles to the main stem).

Special Habitats

Besides the basic grassland matrix, many other types of grassland communities persist in the California, varying with soil type, water availability, climate, and topography. Here are a few examples.

Vernal Pools: At Vina Plains, in the upper Sacramento Valley, it was April and I had missed the wildflower peak by about a week—the foothills to the east were already turning tan-brown. But the larger vernal pools on this terrace still held water. Brilliant, glowing goldfields ringed the edges of the water, filled small pools of drying mud, and lined drainages in unexpectedly geometric configurations. Tiny, white popcorn flowers ringed other pools. Small native grasses—annual hairgrass and annual foxtail—filled the centers of many of the pools.

Sometimes called hog wallows, vernal pools fill with rainwater in the winter, then dry up in the summer heat. Hardpan, claypan, or volcanic mudflow substrates trap the water in these little basins. At one time, there may have been about four million acres of vernal pools in the state—in central

---

Seasons of a vernal pool. Oil on toned cotton rag paper, 11 x 9 inches, 2007

Winter: purple needlegrass bunches are green, as the pool is full of water. Ducks, black-necked stilts, and spadefoot toad tadpoles inhabit it.

April: the pool is ringed by wildflowers: goldfields, downingia, lupine, meadow foam, blennosperma.

Summer: heat has parched the pool, but a new plant greens up—little Orcutt grass. Pronghorn antelope come to dine on it.

WINTER

SPRING

SUMMER

California, the Coast Ranges, the Delta, the Sierra foothills, along the coast from San Luis Obispo to Santa Barbara, in the Transverse Ranges, and over to the eastern Sierra and the Modoc Plateau. Whole communities of plants and animals developed to fill this habitat, and in spring colorful rings of wildflowers would form in the pools as they slowly dried out, each new ring taking advantage of a particular soil moisture content.

Often associated with the pools are mima mounds, little hills a few to several feet high, sometimes clothed with relict natives such as purple needlegrass, one-sided bluegrass, white yarrow, and lupine. Various theories exist to explain their origin, for instance soil patterning due to expansion and contraction during frost and heat cycles, or soil movement caused by pocket gophers digging over long periods of time, each in its own territory.

A UC Davis survey team found as many as fifty types of vernal pool vegetation associations. Bright yellow Fremont goldfields were widespread and common in the pools. Purple-and-white downingias were also common. Whole genera of unusual, endemic vernal pool annual grasses exist in upper and lower California. California Orcutt grass was found in vernal pools and drying mudflats on the grassy plains of Los Angeles, western Riverside County, San Diego County, and northern Baja California—it is today in danger of extinction.[49] Several other species found in vernal pools and seasonal lakes in the Sacramento and San Joaquin Valleys are endangered.[50]

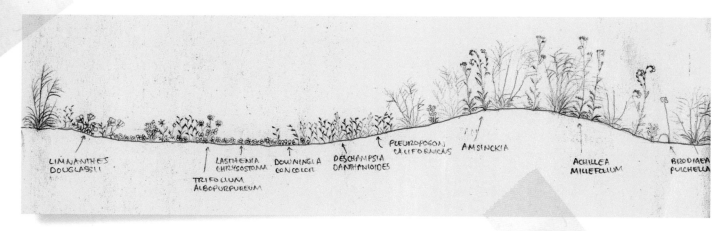

Mima mounds and vernal pools

Crampton's tuctoria often grew on alkali soils, and botanist Beecher Crampton himself speculated that this odd grass might have evolved around the edges of the shallow Tertiary sea that covered much of the San Joaquin Valley some fifteen million years ago.[51] In October 1985 I traveled to Jepson Prairie, in Solano County, to find tuctoria. The large vernal pool named Olcott Lake was dry, the ground cracked with mud chips. I found the little tuctoria grasses on the east side, very small and inconspicuous on the dry ground—I might have mistaken them for a layer of windblown dust. They had greened up in July, August, and September and were now brown.

A surprisingly wide array of invertebrates and vertebrates make the seasonal pools their home. I have good memories of a chorus of continuously trilling spadefoot toads breeding in rain pools one night on the eastern floor of the San Joaquin Valley, on still out-of-the-way ranchland. The night rain soaked us but brought the buried toads out from their sealed mud cocoons in the seemingly barren grasslands. Predatory larvae of the rare California tiger salamander also live in vernal pools; the large adults (some males to nine inches in length) spend 90 to 95 percent of their lives in the burrows of ground squirrels and pocket gophers in grasslands and oak savannas.[52]

Because grazing livestock can increase the richness and cover of native annual wildflowers around vernal pools, as well as the number of aquatic invertebrates, range ecologists Randall Jackson and James Bartolome think these green habitats might have been especially adapted to the large herds of tule elk they attracted.[53]

A great diversity of small crustaceans, such as ostracods, copepods, and fairy shrimp (anostracans) inhabit these temporary pools. Millions of individuals might swim about a single pool when the rains filled it. As the pool evaporates they enter a "cyst" stage of eggs buried in the dried sediment. In this phase of life they could, like dormant seeds, survive for decades—possibly centuries—until the next pool formed.[54]

Massive steam combines, pulled by as many as three dozen draft animals, leveled many San Joaquin Valley many hog wallows and mima mounds during the wheat boom of the 1880s.[55] Statewide, from 60 to 90 percent have been lost.[56] Development continues the damage (see www.biologicaldiversity.org for more information), but preservation and restoration efforts are yielding hopeful results. Ecologists are realizing that vernal pools are not isolated bits of habitat, but rather embedded within complex landscapes and connected to other habitats, such as upland grasslands, marshes, and riverine communities. Bees in the family Adrenidae, for example, specialize in pollinating only downingia, blennosperma, meadow foam, and other showy vernal pool wildflowers. These bees are the dominant pollinators, and thus a key to the wildflowers' reproduction, and because they nest in small holes in the ground in grasslands sometimes a mile away from a vernal pool, they link these habitats.[57]

Moist Grassland Marsh Edge: Several native grasses adapted to the semiaquatic edges of marshes that were flooded in winter but dried out most summers. These neglected ecotones between freshwater marsh and upland are increasingly rare: agricultural demands push them out, dams stop natural flooding cycles, and hordes of introduced meadow grasses crowd the pastures. But I discovered what an interior valley marsh-edge grassland would look like while walking along the edge of an artificial lake, San Pablo Reservoir (East Bay Municipal Water District land—obtain a hiking permit to enter). Full during most winters, the lake fluctuates regularly from water use by the surrounding cities. The cycle may imitate the riverine flooding over wide plains that occurred in the Central Valley before the water projects and still happens along the Cosumnes River.

Here in this little window back in time, the winter valley flats were covered with water. During a storm, brown water gushed out of the creeks, submerging the lower parts of the bare willows and spreading silt over the plain. Wood ducks flew among the riparian trees. Ring-necked ducks, pintails, and Canada geese swam in the shallows.

But by summer, a whole new ecosystem seemed to come into being: freshwater mudflats and drying valley floors with a complex of native grasses and marsh plants (see sketch next page). Buckeye butterflies and mourning doves fed on the ground among meadow barley bunches. Turkey vultures wheeled in the sultry air overhead. A doe emerged from the dense willows to graze on a lime-green mat of lovegrass on the drying mud. Knotgrass, which in winter forms rhizomatous colonies in standing water, now formed green, leafy, oval-shaped patches on dry ground near the

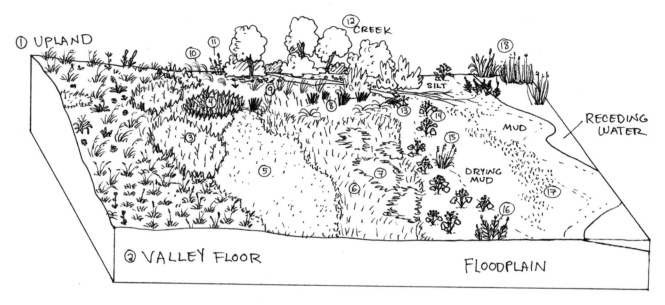

EDGE OF SAN PABLO RESEVOIR, CONTRA COSTA COUNTY, JULY 1997

← SHALLOW WATER FLOODING — DECEMBER.

← BIG RAIN EVENT IN JANUARY — MUDDY WATER FLOODING INTO WILLOWS.

① UPLAND:
PURPLE NEEDLEGRASS (*Nassella pulchra*)
CALIFORNIA BROME (*Bromus carinatus*)
DIEGO BENTGRASS (*Agrostis pallens*)
SLENDER TARWEED (*Madia gracilis*)
SOAP PLANT (*Chlorogalum pomeridianum*)
NATIVE DANDELION (*Agoseris heterophylla*)
CHIA (*Salvia columbariae*)
GOLDENROD (*Solidago californica*)

② VALLEY FLOOR:
MEADOW BARLEY (*Hordeum brachyantherum*)
TARWEED (*Hemizonia* sp.)

③ CREEPING WILDRYE (*Leymus triticoides*)

④ SEDGE (*Carex tumulicola*)

⑤ ANNUAL HAIRGRASS (*Deschampsia danthonioides*)

⑥ SPIKERUSHES (*Eleocharis* spp.)

⑦ KNOTGRASS (*Papsalum distichum*)

⑧ RUSH (*Juncus patens*)

⑨ BENTGRASS (*Agrostis exarata*)

⑩ SLENDER HAIRGRASS (*Deschampsia elongata*)

⑪ STINGING NETTLE (*Urtica dioica*)

⑫ CREEK RIPARIAN:
YELLOW WILLOW (*Salix lutea*)
ARROYO WILLOW (*S. lasiolepis*)
NARROW-LEAF WILLOW (*S. exigua*)

CALIFORNIA BLACKBERRY (*Rubus ursinus*)
SNEEZEWEED (*Helenium puberulum*)

⑬ UMBRELLA SEDGE (*Cyperus* sp.)

⑭ COCKLEBUR (*Xanthium strumarium*)

⑮ SPRANGLETOP (*Leptochloa fascicularis*)

⑯ WATER SMARTWEED (*Polygonum amphibium*)

⑰ LOVEGRASSES (*Eragrostis hynoides* and *pectinacea*)
LEMMON CANARYGRASS (*Phalaris lemmonii*)

⑱ TULES (*Soirpus*)
CATTAILS (*Typha*)

cattails and tules. I imagined tule elk herds flocking to these lush oases next to the marshes. On the way they might pick up the hitchhiking seeds of cockleburs, a native marsh-edge plant with sticky burs that catch in fur, feathers, and clothing—I had to remove many of them from my socks after walking through a patch.

San Joaquin Valley Flower Fields: Surely one of the strangest California landscapes before Euro-American settlement was the San Joaquin Valley. From south of the Merced River and west of Fresno and extending northward along the western valley to the Delta, this was an arid complex of sand desert, alkali flat, and saltbush scrub; lying behind the rain shadow of the Coast Ranges, the plains receive only six inches of rain annually. Fragments of these habitats linger today outside of the vast agricultural fields.

In olden times, during much of the year the arid San Joaquin Valley appeared to be lifeless. Having climbed a peak to overlook it in the summer of 1860, William Brewer called it "wide and dreary." He saw a plain "without trees, save a green belt along the river—all the rest dry and brown." In places, through the veil of dust that hung in the air, he could see the snows of the Sierra Nevada glittering in the sun. The alkaline plains left behind from the expansion and contraction of Tulare, Buena Vista, and Kern Lakes were probably the source of the dust. Brewer came upon thirty or forty antelope at Del Puerto Canyon, galloping leisurely away. The tracks of grizzlies, wolves, and coyotes were common. He saw a deer and a mountain lion up a canyon, and ground squirrels and reptiles everywhere. Heat mirages flitted about. Brewer watched a rodeo, vaqueros herding several thousand head of wild cattle down from the hills—the women of the house rode superbly, he noted.[58]

Brewer encountered the region during a bad drought, but I have ground-checked relict areas around the plains and bordering hills and found much to match his descriptions. His accounts of the San Joaquin Valley before agriculture have great value and stimulate the imagination besides.

But still more difficult to contemplate today is the fact that during early spring, the valley transformed from a barren desert into an amazing landscape of blooms and greenery, a wildflower garden perhaps unrivaled by any other spot in the state.

John Muir in 1844 saw the plain in spring as "one smooth, continuous bed" of flowers crowded together.[59] Thomas Jefferson Mayfield in the 1860s described the San Joaquin Valley covered with "great patches of rose, yellow, scarlet, orange, and blue. The colors did not seem to mix to any great extent. Each kind of flower liked a certain kind of soil best and some of the patches of one color were a mile or more across." He saw what must have been hundreds of acres of coyote melon, or calabazilla, a small, round gourd, growing on sandy soil near the rivers.[60]

The greatest wildflower shows, according to botanist Robert Hoover, were on the sandy loams of the more elevated parts of the valley.[61] Here grew spectacular spring fields of California poppy, baby blue-eyes, fiddleneck, cream cups, dove lupine, chick lupine, owl's clover, gilia, tidy-tips, goldfields, and evening primrose. Perennials shared the plains with these annuals: silver lupine, wild cucumber, milkvetch, woolly milkweed, and jimsonweed.

By July, the fields of flowers turned into tarweeds. Hoover thought the summer-flowering species occurring on the plains included the pungent yellow tarweed, gumplant, occasional buckwheats, vinegar weed, San Joaquin bluecurls, fireweed, lagophylla, and dove weed.

As for the grasses, Hoover reported that bluegrass and native foxtail were common in some spots on the plains, although never abundant over large areas.[62] The native annual Arizona brome was said to be common on the valley floor in disturbed places.[63] Creeping wildrye filled marshy wet spots and the upland edges of freshwater marshes. Saltgrass, which still grew abundantly on the floodplains of the San Joaquin River in Kings County around 1900, was said to be the principal forage of cattle year-round. Much of it was replaced by irrigated alfalfa.[64]

I explored the western edge of the hyper-arid San Joaquin Valley for native vegetation remnants in the summer of 1986. In the oil fields of Maricopa, Taft, and McKittrick, side-blotched lizards darted around the dry flats where no cattle or agriculture had disrupted their habitats. The blue tails of skittering western whiptail lizards were also visible in numbers. Old, slowly moving oil pumps, like black beasts, surrounded me. Sage sparrows called from their saltbush hideouts, and LeConte's thrashers whistled at me. Amid the drying red brome, ripgut, and cheatgrass, I found some native bluegrass and native foxtails on the low hills. As hard as I searched the plains, I could find the larger bunchgrasses only up in the canyons: nodding needlegrass (some with huge basal diameters, nearly a foot) and squirreltail. Botta's pocket gophers and California ground squirrels were legion, and at night I watched a juvenile kangaroo rat sit in the dry grass eating exotic cheatgrass seeds. Along my westward transect, above 4,000 feet in the inner Coast Range, I came into a more luxurious grassland with common relicts of purple needlegrass, pine bluegrass, California melic, prairie junegrass, and mountain brome. I could see that the floor of the San Joaquin Valley below me was just too dry to support a dense perennial grassland and most likely had been dominated by native annuals in the past.

On those plains the Yokuts Indians had organized rabbit drives, catching as many as two hundred in a morning. William Saroyan, traveling in the 1930s, described the basin as "overrun with prairie dogs, squirrels, horned toads, snakes, and a variety of smaller forms of life."[65] His "prairie dogs" were probably small, endemic San Joaquin antelope squirrels.

Several other unique species inhabit the southern Central Valley and surrounding grasslands. The blunt-nosed leopard lizard is endemic to the San Joaquin Valley and nearby foothills, in arid sparse grassland. Agriculture and development have eliminated it from all but a few areas, such as Carrizo Plain National Monument. The San Joaquin kit fox can still be seen lurking in arid grasslands and saltbush scrub.

California ground squirrel

Prairie Fauna

A medical doctor and naturalist, H. H. Behr, saw the San Francisco Bay Area develop rapidly during the latter half of the 1800s. He spoke of the "wild and only half-explored mountain at our doors...the range of hills back of Oakland and Berkeley" full of rattlesnakes; the "uninhabited upland abounding in gopher and squirrel holes."[66] Reading this, I was reminded again of the changes that have swept over the hills I grew up hiking on: not once have I seen a rattlesnake here, and only on one remote swale at the north end of San Pablo Ridge could I find a California ground squirrel colony. Many changes have happened to the fauna of the grasslands; some are recovering, others are not.

The California ground squirrel was (and is) a key species whose grassland burrows provided habitat for numerous animals unable to dig their own: burrowing owls, tiger salamanders, rattlesnakes, and others. Pedro Font, accompanying the Anza expedition in 1775, commented that the plains adjacent to the great tulares of the Delta region looked "mined" by ground squirrels.[67] The activities of ground squirrels, pocket gophers, and kangaroo rats were probably an important source of soil disturbance in precontact grasslands, making way for wildflowers—and today, for exotic weeds as well.[68]

In the early 1900s farmers plowed under much Sacramento Valley grassland and planted wheat, to be shipped by rail to Port Costa and then on ocean steamers to European markets. California ground squirrels benefited from the excess grain, but farmers began to reduce their numbers, using carbon disulfide gas. An organized campaign developed against the squirrels in the 1920s.[69] Two million pounds of poisoned grain were strewn out to lure them each year. Most successful of all was the deadly Compound 1080, used to rid large areas of ground squirrels completely. Biologist Tracy Storer recalled seeing "dozens and hundreds" when driving on back roads but, by the 1960s, not a one in former haunts.[70]

Kit fox

But ground squirrels are survivors. They are still tilling and digging our grasslands, providing homes for other animals. At the north end of San Pablo Ridge, in Wildcat Canyon Regional Park, I watched a small colony at work, trimming the California oatgrass in the center of their burrow town; smaller trimmed patches and little paths radiated out through the taller grass. Purple needlegrass bunches grew in scattered groups around the burrows, and the squirrels had not destroyed them, only eating the leaves around the peripheries. After a wildfire burned through the grassland one September, I found the low grass "lawns" and dirt burrow entrances that had protected the animals from the passing flames that engulfed the taller grass.

California vole

Gophers can turn over most of the soil in their habitat every three to fifteen years.[71] Sometimes reaching a population density of forty per acre in grasslands, they create a micro-mosaic of disturbed ground with their diggings and little earth mounds. Certain plants will colonize these gopher mounds, such as lotus, fiddleneck, and lomatium.[72] I have seen gophers till the ground in a circular patch fifteen feet in diameter, digging out dead, dried-up California oatgrass bunches—bare ground for wildflowers to colonize. I have found gopher mounds in pure purple needlegrass stands, oniongrass patches, and Idaho fescue prairies. A passing grass fire bothered them not—new gopher holes appeared with a flush of new, green needlegrass on the bare ground. In a creeping wildrye swale, I watched a gopher on the surface chew the tough rhizomes of the grass by digging a little depression down into the ground. I have also found evidence that they eat small rootlets of foothill needlegrass, mountain brome, and Diego bentgrass. They will devour grass leaves, soap plant leaves, and the roots and leaves of many other forbs.

California voles, still common today, are miniature grazers of grass. From November to May, each female gives birth to five to seven young every twenty-two days. They undergo population crashes, however, when their numbers build up to levels that outstrip the food supply, or when droughts hit. There have been years when no voles scurried underfoot when I was hiking across a grassy slope. And I have seen wet years when voles ran through grass tunnels everywhere, and kestrels and red-tailed hawks gathered, soared, and dove into the grass in a feast of prey. In the past grizzlies and wolves must have enjoyed the cyclical boon as well.

One day in May I sat in a purple needlegrass prairie and heard two voles frenetically squeaking while running about irregularly in their tunnels through the dense blades of the bunchgrasses. I did not know what was disturbing them until I spied, a few feet away, a western terrestrial garter snake; it slipped silently away. The voles disappeared and I studied their tunnels, which are often hidden by dry, old leaf litter. Sometimes the tunnels dove underground for a few feet, with two- to four-inch openings. Along the tunnels the voles grazed the green needlegrass, stretching their little bodies to six inches high. They had apparently eaten the seeds as well, for I found none anywhere on the ground under the flowering panicles. Nearby, green leaves of mountain brome, California melic, and blue wildrye had been cropped. Little vole teeth had neatly cut all the blades of one brome into a tiny green pompom.

Kangaroo rats are still common in places, harvesting and hoarding seeds and digging their burrows. Sometimes their mounds can dominate the landscape, as on the Carrizo Plain, in Kern County. There, giant kangaroo rats each build burrow mounds many feet across, spaced closely over the landscape and covering as much as 32 percent of the ground.[73] (The giants are about six inches long, not counting their tails.) "K-rats" like bare dirt to hop around on, and before the Mediterranean grass invasion this was probably more available, and they were probably more widespread. I have found only one Heerman's kangaroo rat mound in all my years of hiking in Tilden and Wildcat Canyon Regional Parks.

Coast horned lizards have a similar problem. They declined drastically all over their California range, perhaps due to overcollecting, but also probably because of habitat changes. They need at least some open ground where they can forage for insects and dig into loose, sandy or loamy soil, and this would have been available in bunchgrass prairies. I have found them on open roadsides, sand-gravel washes through grasslands, and desert transition shrublands with plenty of open ground. The dense, continuous cover of introduced annual grasslands may not be favorable to these lizards, yet they hold on, visiting anthills to lap up the bitter morsels, impervious to their bites.

Tribal Management

Grass seeds provided much food to people in California during the early and middle Holocene, according to archaeologists. A mainland Milling Stone culture lasted from 11,500 to 4,500 years ago.[74] Women continued through recent times to gather seeds of various grasses and forbs, such as chia, using shallow baskets to tap the seed heads into woven trays and then transferring them to large burden baskets. They charred the seeds, tossed them with hot coals to singe off unpalatable awns and hairs, and then ground them into flour.

Even after acorns became a staple in the diet of people in California a few thousand years ago, seeds still held significance. The Chumash, for instance, used chia as a staple food, stored in baskets and eaten throughout the year, ground into dry flour or mixed with water. They toasted tarweed seeds and pounded them into pinole. Huge quantities of the seeds of the beautiful little red maids flower were stored in baskets for food; some have been found placed in graves.[75] All these forbs increased on burns. I have noticed that red maids increased after wet years in the Bay Area, and during the rainy phase of the Little Ice Age this plant may have been more available for harvest.

Many tribes collected wildrye seeds. The Pomo beat or brushed the stalks with a round, flat basket and caught the seeds in a second basket.[76] A Chumash woman, Lucrecia Garcia, reported that thirteen types of seeds were collected, including three wildryes (perhaps blue wildrye, creeping wildrye, and giant wildrye). Wild oats and brome grasses were pounded and baked into bread in earthen ovens. Needlegrass seeds were also edible.

Wild food, I discovered, requires a lot of processing, but it is satisfying to know that every spring thousands of acres of free edible seeds grow over the hills and plains of the land. Once I collected seeds from the waist-high spike-stems of blue wildrye, knocking them into a basket as the Native people had done, and then attempted to grind the cured seeds into flour. I was not expert at separating the grain from the chaff—grinding on a rock metate and throwing the mess up into the breezes, allowing the heavier, edible parts to fall back down. My resulting pinole was delicious but quite fibrous! Singeing off the glumes, awns, and lemmas with hot coals in a vigorously shaken pan can produce more "professional" results. I collected a basketful of purple needlegrass seeds one May when the seeds easily fell from the panicles, knocked off the hard awns, and tossed the seeds with hot coals in a pan to singe off the hairs that covered the lemmas. Then I ground them on a stone and ate them—delicious and rather like wheat.

Native people used pointed digging sticks of fire-hardened wood, such as manzanita or mountain mahogany, to dig up bulbs and tubers of many plants. Brodiaeas, wild onions, camas, lilies, mariposa lily bulbs, and soap plant roots were gathered in large quantities, and this tilling of the soil and breaking up of the rootlets helped the plant colonies to increase.

Fire was a tool for increasing the yield of grass seeds, chia and other forbs, and bulbs, as will be seen in chapter eight. Grass enthusiast Judith Larner Lowry argues that Indians maintained many California grasslands in a quasi-agricultural condition by burning, harvesting, and other activities: a form of permaculture of "wild" plants.[77]

Power in Numbers

Arguably the grasslands are more affected, changed, built, and managed by insects than any other animal, including us, and California's early prairies were undoubtedly swarming with interesting interactions.

"Ant management" of grasslands takes the form of seed collection. Harvester ants favor the seeds of native dandelions and the related tiny, yellow-flowered "mini-dandelions (*Microseris*)." I sat and watched some black harvester ants one day on a grassy ridge as they carried various seeds and bits of grass leaf into their small hole. The ants discarded inedible chaff around their nest openings, creating fertile spots in the grassland that many forbs colonize—tidy-tips and calycadenia, for instance.[78] And one day on a grassy ridge I watched as numerous large, winged, male ants crawled up grass blades and flew off one by one; cliff swallows swarmed above them to snap them up, and a lazuli bunting stuffed its bill with them.

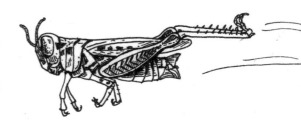

Melanoplus devastator—*grasshopper*

Probably the most abundant grazers were neither elk nor voles, but grasshoppers. With their rugged, "toothy" mandibles, they can graze down tough grass leaves and wildflowers. We have had our own plagues of locusts in the past, outbreaks of tremendous numbers of the innocent-looking *Melanoplus devastator*—"devastating grasshopper." At Black Diamond Mines Regional Park, near Antioch, I watched this grasshopper graze the purple needlegrasses. Many blades on each bunch had been munched down to an inch by the hungry grasshoppers, which sought out the green blades. In Tilden Park, the summer of 1983 was a boom time for grasshoppers, perhaps related to the huge rainfall from the El Niño winter of 1982-83. I found roasted grasshoppers one day in a grassland burn—not all animals survive the fires that sweep through their haunts. Others were still lively, however, on islands of unburned grass within the blackened charcoal stems.

Hiking in the East Bay hills, I began to go grasshopper-watching; identifying them required catch-and-release tactics. Pallid-winged grasshoppers flew up in "stridulation flights," snapping loudly and showing off the bright yellow of their wings. Clear-winged grasshoppers used a different tactic in courtship, walking toward one another, each tipping a yellow femur (the long jumping leg) to the other. Flightless and robust valley grasshoppers with vestigial wings hopped about. Rose-winged grasshoppers and orange-winged grasshoppers were rarer. These insects I found to be common in the short-grazed grass of cattle ranges, but in ungrazed areas with tall grass they were confined to bare ground. The short-horned grasshopper was common in tall, ungrazed needlegrass prairies, meadows with mountain brome and Chilean aster, and short-grazed California oatgrass fields. In September, desert grasshoppers were common in an ungrazed needlegrass prairie, calling a soft "dzi-dzi-dzi-dzi..."

Ice Age Grazing Ecology

For the painting "40,000 Years Ago on the Franciscan Valley" (page 138), I attempted to reconstruct a community from a more distant past than I had been working with: the Ice Age. First I located relict native sites in East Bay flatland areas, and then I looked at some of the old botanical surveys for the area. An estimated two-hundred-mile shift south occurred in many species during the full glacial phase twenty thousand years ago, so I consulted my notes on floras I have encountered in northern coastal California, where plants similar to Ice Age fossils now live. Reconstruction was not so simple, though. Glacial-age climates and communities have no real modern counterpart: in many parts of North America summers were cooler than they are now and winters slightly milder, allowing animals and plants to commingle that today we consider "northern" and "southern." The grasslands of southern and central California may have been more suitable to grazing animals in the Ice Age, due to moister conditions. The green growing season may have been longer. Paleontologist R. Dale Guthrie theorizes that the incredible diversity of giant grazing mammals seen during the Pleistocene might have been due to a "plaid" pattern of vegetation, versus a "stripe" pattern seen during the Holocene; in other words, plant communities grew in a finer-grained mosaic during the Ice Age, rather than the simpler regional biome zonations we see today. The big game animals could dine on a buffet of diverse plant foods.[79]

Unfortunately, almost no remains of fossil grasses have been found in Pleistocene deposits in California. In the High Plains of Kansas, Miocene and Pliocene fossils of several ancestral grasses occur, from some twenty million to two million years ago, and they include genera of the tribe Stipeae, the group to which our needlegrasses belong.[80] I know of no studies specifically addressing this connection, but other studies have hypothesized that purple needlegrass and its relatives are North American endemics.[81] Other grasses may also have a Tertiary (from sixty-five million to two million years ago) record in North America, according to genetic evidence: meadow barley, the Bromus sections Bromopsis and Ceratochloa (which include our mountain bromegrass and California brome grass), the one-sided bluegrass lineage, and California oatgrass, for example. Other lineages may be more recent arrivals from Eurasia across the Bering Land Bridge during the Pleistocene: for instance, blue wildrye may have evolved from a Siberian ancestor, and such species as prairie junegrass and red fescue are common across the boreal-temperate Northern Hemisphere and probably reached California during the Ice Age.[82] Each grass species has a separate history, and many are still undergoing rapid evolution and hybridization today.

My hypothetical Franciscan Valley floor communities developed in several stages. In glacial times, a mixed evergreen forest grew over the valley, as we know from fossil ʳ of Douglas fir. Purple needlegrass and other grasses probably found pockets of dry, rocky soil, open plains, and inland hills to grow on. A mosaic of forests mixed with grassland meadows that may have been dominated by California oatgrass. In addition, low wet areas may have contained mannagrass, California semaphoregrass, and bentgrass. Then, during the pluvial phase eight thousand to eleven thousand years ago, the climate moistened and a rich mesic grassland probably grew over the Franciscan Valley. Four thousand to six thousand years ago, the arid conditions of the Xerothermic phase prevailed. The ranges of moister grassland types may have been restricted, and dry-adapted species may have spread: small-flowered melic and big squirreltail grass, for example. The adaptable purple needlegrass still probably dominated.

Relicts and neighboring areas indicate that in the recent past, but before European intrusion, the East Bay flatlands may have been a grassland dominated by purple needlegrass and California oatgrass on the drier plains, with lesser amounts of prairie junegrass, one-sided bluegrass, brome grass, blue wildrye, and oniongrass in a mosaic. In mesic spots, thingrass may have formed small patches. Creeping wildrye must have been common in the deep soils along willow creeks and low sites. On the lower plains, next to bay marshes, creeping wildrye, meadow barley, and sedges probably dominated. Jepson found meadow foxtail, a native annual grass, with vernal pools in the Berkeley area.[83]

Some of the only direct evidence of grass species from the Pleistocene comes from plant remains caught in the molars of herbivores at the Rancho La Brea tar pits in Los Angeles—teeth of the extinct Ice Age bison, extinct camel, and extinct horse. Brome, fescue, grama grass, galleta, and dropseed are among the types identified.

Interestingly, several of the plants listed are Mojave Desert–Great Basin species. This could indicate two different scenarios for the late glacial grassland ecology of southern California. Paleontologist George Jefferson theorizes that ancient bison herds may have migrated out of the Los Angeles Basin in the summers, into surrounding high-desert montane edges, and eaten these Mojave plant species.[84] Palynologist Roger Byrne disagrees, believing that what this plant list suggests is that the climate in coastal southern California was drastically different during glacial times: summer-rain dependent species of the desert, such as grama grass and galleta grass, grew closer to the coast during parts of the Pleistocene, allowing ancient bison to graze them locally.[85]

The dental boluses from the La Brea tar pits contained a much higher proportion of dicot plant matter to monocot (including grass) species than is usually expected in modern bison and horses: plants such as composites, mallow, buckwheat, legumes, cactus, junipers, and winterfat. This throws into question the assumption that the grazing habits of fossil ungulates were similar to those of their contemporary relatives.[86]

These are a few examples of the pitfalls of trying to guess what the past looked like. Pitfalls notwithstanding, my assumption here is that most of the present native California grasses are roughly similar to those back in time to at least the Sangamonian Interglacial, one hundred and twenty thousand year ago, and including the last glacial cycle, during which they coexisted with Pleistocene megafauna.

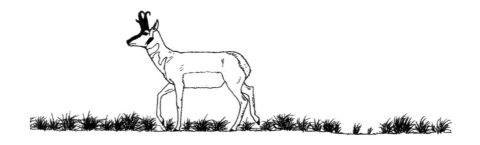

The San Francisco Bay Area forty thousand years ago, during the Pleistocene, when the bay was a broad valley covered with meadows and live oak–Douglas fir forests; during glacial times sea levels were lowered and the coast was miles to the west of the Golden Gate. Extinct megafauna— ancient bison and western horse—graze on purple needlegrass, California oatgrass, sedges, and tarweed. ACRYLIC ON PAPER, 18 X 26 INCHES, 1991

As I strolled through bunchgrass stems waving in the breezes, I began to speculate about how these megafauna might have interacted with the grasses. Western California had an amazing array of big game animals that for the most part went extinct by ten thousand years ago, during the start of the Holocene. Large mammals that probably inhabited grasslands and grass-woodland mosaics in the Pleistocene include Columbian mammoths, which were equipped with large grazing molars; giant ground sloths; at least four and perhaps five species of equid; a llama; a camel; a giant peccary that may have rooted for bulbs; the pronghorn antelope (still extant in California); a small antelope; a giant musk ox; a "shrub ox"; three bison species; and the still-living elk.

Reconstructing the prehistoric grazing regime in California is speculative, to say the least. "Browsing by prehistoric wild animals is one of the hardest factors to quantify in ecological history," observe A. T. Grove and Oliver Rackham.[87] The carrying capacity of a given landscape, usually defined as the maximum number of animals that can be sustained on a range, cannot be easily figured. Is the year of measurement an average one, or one of the worst droughts in a hundred years? The ecologic carrying capacity may be self-limiting: animals grazing heavily produce less milk, or none at all; if they graze too little, vegetation accumulates, leading to wildfire.[88] Studies of the age distribution of savanna trees indicate phases of "excessive" and "insufficient" browsing in the past. Overbrowsing may only be harmful if it goes on too long, as it often does today in our industrialized farming era.

Some indirect evidence of heavy grazing by Pleistocene megafauna comes from Eurasian studies of the "mammoth steppe" habitat, a huge, cold, dry grassland that extended from Europe across Asia and Beringia into northern North America. The last meals of numerous mammoths, reindeer, horses, and other creatures are contained in their frozen carcasses. Grasses dominate much of this refrigerated stomach content. The frozen remains of the Jarkov Mammoth, from the Taimyr Peninsula in Siberia, contained pollen of steppe plants, including moss microfossils from species particularly adapted to ground disturbed by trampling and grazing. Abundant spores were also found of specialized dung-living fungi (*Sporormiella*) that thrive where there is a high population density of herbivores.[89]

After the Melt

How do we start to reconstruct the Holocene grazing ecology of ten thousand years ago, up to European contact? Considering, first, the fine-grained pattern of species present—what ecologists call alpha-diversity—we might speculate that grass species grew not evenly over the ground, but in patches and clumps. Floodplains might have had the lowest diversity of species, while slopes had the highest. Grazing animals would exploit these, walking from one patch of a favored species to the next. I have seen this type of diversity in California native grasslands: prairie junegrass and brome grass often grow in pure patches or dense clusters, while purple needlegrass dominates nearby sites. Creeping wildrye forms great swaths on low areas that have deep soils. And different wildflower species often grow together in groups.

Beta-diversity, one step up in the ecologist's view of the landscape, involves environmental gradients, such as local topography or varying soil, that produce continuous variation in plant cover. Grazers concentrate in favorable areas, following the green grass. California elk may have moved upslope with the winter green-up in the foothills and Coastal Ranges, then down into valleys, where moist grasslands and marshes greened up in the summer. Vernal pools and rings of marsh plants left when floodwaters retreated would have offered good food patches as well. Grazers always search out the greenest, lushest vegetation containing the highest levels of protein and other nutrients (see chapter ten for more on elk ecology). Competing with this desire, however, is the need of elk herds to seek windy ridges in order to avoid biting flies!

An even larger scale of diversity occurs on the regional landscape level, where rainfall gradients or large geomorphological effects cause long-distance migrations of grazing mammals in search of green grass. Perhaps some north-south or east-west migrations of big game took place in California during droughts.

From Green to Brown and Back Again

The state of the grass has important effects on tule elk and other grazing animals. Young herbage has a high moisture content (70 to 87 percent), as does grass just after a rain or in the morning. Animals sometimes become bloated with water, unable to extract enough nutrients. As the grasses mature and flower, the moisture content decreases. Mature green foliage has the highest amount of protein, though curing vegetation still holds some; when dry, the herbage contains a lot of carbohydrates but fewer nutrients. Winter rains gradually leach the last cured nutrients out of the leaves, turning them from yellow-brown to gray. Thus season has everything to do with reconstructing a grazing landscape.

In Tilden and Wildcat Canyon Regional Parks, the warmer south slopes green up a full month before the north slopes. The ridgetops green up first and then dry sooner than the lower slopes. The valley and canyon floors stay green the longest. Following the rainy green season in 1985 and 1986, I made special notice of when the native grasses completely dried out: one-sided bluegrass lost its green first, by May; thingrass and brome grasses became dry in June, and prairie junegrass by June and July; by July blue wildrye and purple needlegrass dried out; meadow barley still had green blades in August, and last, in September, California oatgrass and creeping wildrye finally turned tan-brown.

An oft-quoted passage by Edwin Bryant about the Livermore hills in September 1846 is of interest here. From the plain, he commented, "We entered a hilly country, covered to the summits of the elevations with wild oats and tufts or bunches of grass, which remains green through the whole season."[90]

Perhaps this was an observation of purple needlegrass stands that had been burned, or grazed by the abundant cattle Bryant noted, which would allow the bunches to produce new green growth. In a vacant lot, mowed annually, next to the Kensington Library, I have noticed purple needlegrass and mountain bromegrass growing deep green, leafy blades in July—looking like rainy season plants while the uncut bunches next to them were a dry, yellow-gray. Fire once added a diversifying factor, producing green-up within days, even during the dry season. Elk, antelope, deer, and grizzlies probably searched for grassland burns where they could feed on succulent new growth.

In the past, grazing elk and pronghorn might have turned to forbs, well past flowering but still green even in the driest years, during times of drought. During the drought year of 1987 I looked for grassland plants in Tilden Regional Park that retained green foliage. In September the gumplants had green leaves, as well as the Chilean asters, California poppies, willow herbs, California fuchsias, tarweeds, buckwheats, phacelias, peppergrasses, chias, and summer lupines—green bits in a sea of dry grass. I also noticed that the ridgetops, sometimes immersed in moist air from ocean fog, provided some green grass.

Our present grassland is but a slice in time of one particular mix of species, a mix that has been undergoing changes due to climate fluctuations, migrations, and coevolution with insect and vertebrate herbivores for millions of years. Grasses are still evolving, changing, and adapting to

California climates and geology. Squirreltail grasses, for example, often hybridize with each other and with blue wildrye. One hybrid I often see in the East Bay is Hansen squirreltail, an unusually large bunch growing singly or in small groups with tall spikes and seed heads that combine characteristics of both its parents.

Species that make up a community might each have had radically different tolerances to climate and grazing, and the abundance of each plant type varies over time with the continually shifting processes at work in the world. On the Mongolian steppes at Hustai National Park, for example, despite a very different continental climate, the mix of grass species is reminiscent of early California prairies. *Stipa krylovii*, related to our needlegrasses, is dominant with light to moderate grazing, but under increasing pressure (largely by native horses) *Leymus chinensis*, similar to our creeping wildrye, took over in abundance. The latter grass, more dependent on a moist climate, declined during droughts and dry phases.[91] Perhaps similar dynamics happened long ago in California: purple needlegrass took over in drier climatic phases, and creeping wildrye increased during wetter phases. Perhaps elk grazing shifted the abundance locally, depending on soil moisture.

Indeed, grassland ecologists in California are realizing that our native plant communities may be more weather-driven than herbivore-driven; climate here may have an overriding effect no matter what grazing management scheme is used.[92]

Managing Grazing Pressure

Can California native grasses withstand grazing pressure? This question is at the heart of a roaring controversy among ecologists. Botanist and ecologist Steve Edwards asserts that California native grasses were well adapted to the diverse array of Ice Age grazers and that during the Holocene, although megafauna populations were reduced and simplified, grass species did not lose the genetic capability of readapting to heavier grazing pressures.[93] Other ecologists disagree; many believe that California's natives are not well adapted to grazing.[94] The question is vital when considering how best to restore and maintain the health of native grasslands.

At the base of this discussion are the growth needs of grasses. All grasses grow by tillers—vegetative buds—that start at or below the ground surface. During the growing season, the tillers continually produce leaves. When reproduction is triggered they stop producing leaves and elongate to produce seed heads. A grass plant needs its tillers intact if it is to nourish itself and reproduce before going dormant. In California, grasses go dormant during the dry summers in the main grasslands, or during cold-season flood times in the lowland marshes, or during snow season in the mountains.

If the growing point on a tiller is eaten but the plant still has other leafy tillers, the plant can continue to develop carbohydrate reserves, enabling itself to put out new leaves in the next growing season. If all tillers are grazed off, the plant must use its root reserves to initiate new ones. Many grasses are able to do this and vigorously recover. The problem occurs with repeated, heavy defoliation during the growing season—the grass uses up all its root reserves and may die.[95]

Many grasses keep their growing points close to the ground and away from the hungry mouths of grazing cattle and elk. Other species, however, elongate their growing points upwards on the tillers rather early in the growing season and are thus susceptible to damage by grazing. California oatgrass can withstand heavy grazing: much of the plant's current growth can be removed without damaging the plant.[96] Other grasses, such as prairie junegrass, bluegrasses, melicgrasses, bentgrasses, hairgrasses, needlegrasses, and fescues, can withstand less grazing, but still a fair amount. More susceptible to grazing harm are creeping wildrye and bromes. Blue wildrye is one of the least able to sustain heavy grazing.

I have found purple needlegrass in Tilden Regional Park under continual cattle grazing pressure to respond by becoming smaller, with more bunches; grass ecologists also found this on Hastings Reserve, in the Monterey County Coast Range.[97] Going out to ungrazed parts of the East Bay Coast Range and comparing these grasslands to areas with year-long cattle stocking, I found some plants that could be labeled "increasers," some "decreasers," and some that were little changed. California oatgrass and some forbs, such as tarweed, chick lupine, microseris, and rancheria clover, increased with heavy grazing. Sensitive species, such as California melicgrass and blue wildrye and the forbs blue dicks, wild pea, soap plant, and dove lupine, decreased or were eliminated by heavy grazing.

Local conditions can be crucial. My observations of purple needlegrass on the Tilden Park hills, a moist region, indicate it could withstand fairly heavy grazing here, although it would need time to recover from prolonged grazing or spring grazing. In arid southern California ranges, native grasses may not do so well.

To complicate matters, different stands may show different reactions to grazing;[98] at Jepson Prairie, the emergence and survival of needlegrass seedlings were more strongly linked to their position on the land—whether they grew on or between mima mounds—than to grazing.[99]

Studying photos showing changes over time in various habitats of Yellowstone National Park, biologists Mary Meagher and John Houston noticed that bunchgrass steppe under moderate or heavy grazing by elk and bison showed few signs of change—herbivory was difficult to detect through time, except in wallows, on trails, and on ridgetops where herds concentrated to rest.[100] The researchers believe fire and drought to be more important than grazing in these Yellowstone communities, and this probably applied to precontact California grasslands as well.

Shifts in species dominance occur with different patterns of rainfall. In the spring after an El Niño winter in Tilden Park, I found a normally small patch of meadow barley grown greatly by the wet conditions, to several acres on the mesic saddle of a ridgetop. Waving, dense culms of perennial barley filled the ground to the exclusion of all other species—the sight was beautiful and evoked the long-ago past. The next year, after a drier winter, the same spot held almost no meadow barley.

But there is also stability in these communities: I staked out a plot of ungrazed purple needlegrass on an open slope in the Coast Ranges, the bunches covering 90 percent of the ground. Fifteen years later I went back to check on the plot, after droughts and El Niños, and found no change in ground cover whatsoever.

During a 1988 workshop on grass ecology, we discussed "rotation grazing" methods, including the Savory system of grazing management, topics which have inflamed controversy among ecologists in California in recent decades. The Savory method, termed "holistic management" by biologist Allan Savory, advocates "rotating," or herding high numbers of livestock around several separately fenced pastures. He developed this method after watching the behavior of large native game herds on African grasslands.[101] We toured some of the dairy ranches in the Point Reyes National Seashore area, in Marin County, and saw that several were working well with their coastal prairie lands, especially those cow-calf operations that moved their animals around. Native grasses did well when pastures were grazed after the grass seeds had matured, a form of deferred rotation. Burning was only occasionally needed on these ranges, letting the grasses knit together before cattle were allowed to graze again, which helped stop weeds and invasive coyote brush. The fenced areas should not be arbitrarily rectangular, but should follow the natural lines of the watershed, the workshop organizer told us. This system of management favors bringing back the cowboy and keeping the herds on the move, not letting them hang around waterholes, overgrazing and picking out the "ice cream plants."

Many ranchers using holistic management seek to use livestock to mimic the disturbance and accompanying ecological processes caused by native ungulate herds in wild grasslands. In the past, fire, burrowing animals, and grazing would remove the dead, dry grass material that inhibited certain plant species—tarweeds and other "disturbance-loving" annual wildflowers.[102] Joe Morris's T.O. Cattle Company, in the South Coast Ranges near San Juan Bautista, manages livestock to mimic wild herds, moving them often, even daily, based on close observations of grass growth stages. Sometimes they herd cattle with dogs, to mimic wolf predation pressure. Trampling breaks up dung and hard crusts, allowing seeds to penetrate the soil; hoof tracks act as small pits to capture seeds and water, creating a good microclimate for germination.[103]

I witnessed the benefits of disturbance firsthand in the East Bay hills in spots where fewer wildflowers grew on the ungrazed grassy slopes than in the cattle pastures. In an ungrazed, unburned area, I found many patches of purple needlegrass smothered in old gray leaves and stems. I took some clippers one year and cut the bunches, in imitation of a passing grazing animal, down to a few inches above ground level. A month later I watched the bunches grow a new, bright green bouquet of blades, quite a contrast to the surrounding gray, uncut needlegrass. Interestingly, the bunches began putting out new leaves in the summer dry season; after a good rainy winter I returned to view a beautiful, lush patch of green with waving purple seed heads. The neighboring bunches remained much grayer and less vigorous. These bunchgrasses appeared to benefit from some disturbance, I thought—a good fire or a pass by a grazing herd, whether native elk or domestic cattle.

A balance has to be struck, however. The purple needlegrasses in nearby grazed pastures were small and feeble, a result of the year-round grazing scheme then in action. Fortunately, East Bay Regional Parks changed its grazing plan here, and farsighted managers realized that everything is interconnected. The new grazing management plan benefits Wildcat Creek and its new steelhead population by reducing erosion, in part with the help of native perennial grasses. To increase their presence, park managers changed from continuous to rotation grazing. Rest periods were scheduled for the times when native grasses set seed. Fences divide the 312 acres of grazing land into four pastures. Healthy grasslands benefit fish as well as grazers.[104] See chapter thirteen for more on this.

Despite these results, holistic management and other such grazing schemes are not universally accepted. Critics argue that high-intensity, short-duration rotation is unproven in California.[105] California grasses, they assert, are unlike those of the African savannas where Allan Savory developed his management scheme; they did not evolve under intense grazing pressures, and so would be harmed by repeated cropping of leafage in the same growing season. In addition, heavy trampling could destroy delicate algal soil mats, compact soils too much, and cause erosion.

Certainly most of the arid desert grasslands in California, the Southwest, and the Great Basin should not be used as livestock ranges at all, whether holistically managed or not, as they are quickly destroyed (see George Wuerthner and Mollie Matteson's *Welfare Ranching* for some sad photographs of "cow-bombed" ranges).

But what of the moister, lowland grasslands in western California that were once grazed by large herds of elk? How can these be kept in health today? Recreating the conditions that these native grasslands evolved under might be tricky. In precontact grasslands the herds of tule elk were unrestrained by fences and probably wandered long distances erratically in search of the greenest pastures, traveling to water sources and mineral licks, herded by wolves. Local grass ranges were given rest periods—a natural form of complex deferred rotation grazing.

Perhaps in an ecosystem with a simplified ungulate grazing system such as Old California, with elk as the primary grazer, forage exceeded demand. Under this regime, a "patch grazing" pattern might have developed: a herd ate down favored patches of grass, perhaps in areas with more minerals in the soil or a moister microclimate. The regrowth on these patches became higher in quality than on the surrounding grassland. The elk continued to eat these patches, making them diverge even more in quality and growth form than other areas, and this may have persisted for several years. Use of these patches gradually fell away and new patches were grazed down, forming a mosaic that shifted over time. Some patches may have been used so heavily that barren "scalds" appeared. During droughts, ungrazed patches provided emergency forage. Grass fires could bring the whole pasture back to an even, unpatterned state.[106]

The key here is the spatial component: the large size of original rangelands over which native ungulates roamed and grazed. Disturbance was regular in the grasslands (and other habitats)—the process of adjusting to change was fundamental in the life of the grasses, wildflowers, elk, and people who lived on the prairie. Many alternate "stable" communities might have been possible in a given locale, over time.[107]

I hesitate to say whether humans can imitate this dynamic complexity, and on many small ranches this may be a problem. Whether holistic management or other types of grazing systems will work on California's grasslands today is a question on which I will defer to future naturalists with notepad in hand, practicing keen powers of observation, walking among the swaying grass stems.

Cowboy Joe Morris says, "My ranching time is spent managing *relationships* to produce healthy animals, people and land."[108] (emphasis added) Anyone who takes the time to consider ecological processes and the relationships of plants, animals, and people must be on the right path.

Restoration: Welcome Back the Natives

> "Restoration of California grasslands, once thought to be nearly impossible...is now under way at many sites, although usually with less ambitious goals than the complete eradication of exotics or complete ecological restoration."
>
> —*Mark Stromberg*[109]

We may not own vast ranches with large wandering elk herds, but even city people can learn to start and care for a pocket of native grassland. Margot's yard is barely the length of two parked cars along the street, yet it is a flourishing world of beauty and interest. How did she do it?

Restoration is defined as assisting the recovery of a natural community that has been destroyed, damaged, or altered back to a state of "reference ecosystems," where native plants, fungi, and animals form all or most of the species present, in a self-sustaining way. Ideally, native ecological processes, such as fire, herbivory, rodent burrowing, and migration and recolonization by native species would also be included.

Horned larks

BARN
SWALLOW

Gaining strength in 1991 with the formation of the California Native Grasslands Association,[110] biologists, ranchers, landowners, and seed growers are sharing knowledge in the emerging science of restoration, working on everything from small home gardens to huge landscape architecture and reclamation projects in parks, ranches, and construction areas.

No site is too small to plant natives in: I was delighted to discover the beautiful wildflowers, needlegrasses, oaks, and California sagebrush in a few feet of strip along Berkeley's Ohlone Bike Path, paralleling the BART train tracks at Gilman Avenue.

In restoring any plot of land, the following steps can be followed. This information is based on "California Grassland Restoration," by Mark Stromberg and colleagues, published in *California Grasslands: Ecology and Management.*

Select a reference site to use as a goal, so you can gauge progress on the degraded site. With the methods of historical ecology, you can find nearby relict grasslands, and past information about the site you are working on. What plants would have been here? What animals? Make sure you consider annual variation when comparing your work with your reference site, as a single year of observation may not take into account rainfall differences that will affect species composition.

Survey the land to be restored, inventorying what is already there: plants, animals, soil types, seeds (are there native seeds in the seedbank waiting for a chance to sprout?), topography, drainage (will the site flood at times?), and local climate. Also consider the landowner's wishes: Is this a garden to maximize wildflower beauty? Or a working cattle ranch that must have healthy grasses? Or is it a highway right-of-way, where vegetation should be low for visibility? The California Department of Transportation has been active in restoration, using native plants along road edges (search "native grass database" at http://www.dot.ca.gov for details).

In most places this will be the single greatest challenge: the dominance of invasive weeds. The historical legacy of the place is also important to examine. Did farming eradicate native perennials and disrupt the soil microbial community? Has the lack of fire converted a grassland into a woodland? Has good, nutrient-rich soil been scraped away to build a house?

Site preparation is the next step. Weed control may be most pressing, and there are several ways to go about this. For small areas, hand weeding can be effective. Use gloves and simply pull exotics, or use shovels, clippers, sickles, hoes, mattocks, and other tools to get deep-rooted plants. Volunteer stewardship programs can efficiently organize labor in larger areas. The California Native Plant Society has organized annual workdays to pull out invasive weeds, such as pampas grass (from South America), at parks (see www.cnps.org).

Mowing, disking, or tilling with tractors have worked to initially reduce weeds on larger sites. Herbicide application, from aircraft spraying to backpack spotting, has controlled the painfully spiny yellow star-thistle, a Mediterranean import, at least for the short term. But care must be taken not to kill off native forbs as well, and I am always suspicious about the negative long-term side effects of chemical methods. Goats and cattle have also proved useful, nibbling star-thistles—cattle will graze the young plants, and goats will even browse the spiny mature plants. Cattle or sheep, in numbers large enough to make them less choosy about what they eat, can be effective on areas infested with medusahead grass. Prescribed fires in spring will kill weeds before they have time to seed, and repeated summer burns have wiped out yellow star-thistle populations.[111] Park managers carry out prescribed burns in late summer or fall every two to three years at Skyline Serpentine Prairie to help control weeds.

Growing cover crops, such as clover, to swamp out noxious weeds is a temporary method until more natives can grow to cover the land surface. I used this technique successfully in my garden,

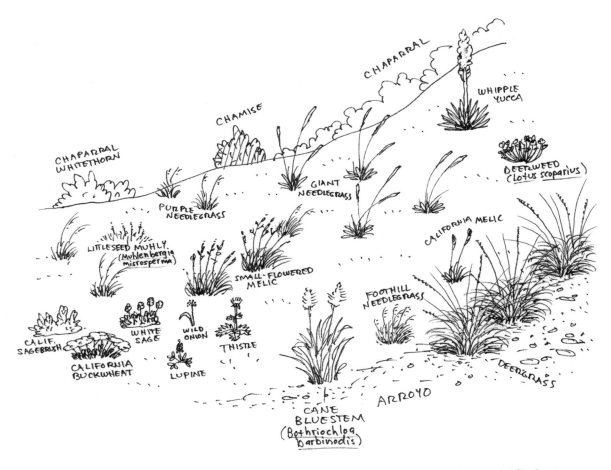

NATIVE GRASS RELICTS IN THE EL CAPITAN AREA, SAN DIEGO COUNTY, ~ 3,000 FEET, 1987.

where previous owners had planted crabgrass in their horse pasture. I determined that a hundred years ago, the flat was part of a riverine marsh edge. I seeded the plot with store-bought clover seed, and over a few summers of irrigation the clover gradually shaded out much of the crabgrass. It was easier to plant native rushes, sedges, and goldenrods into clover than crabgrass. I had to actively "help" the clover, digging out swaths of crabgrass by hand, and the battle continues—every restoration project needs to integrate several methods of weed management, as one alone may fail.

One day I accompanied my sister to her job as a suburban garden restorationist. She had finished digging out a lawn along a street in Albany, using hand tools—the owner was not in a hurry, and she had plenty of time to work at her own pace. She spread out clear plastic sheets over the dirt, and I asked her why. "Solarization," she answered. Clear plastic sheets will raise the temperature of a weed bed by trapping the sun's rays, killing the remaining weed roots and their seeds as intense heat builds up on the ground surface. A year later, when I stopped by the yard I found it filled with glowing orange California poppies, blue-eyed grass, prairie junegrass bunches, and purple needlegrasses. Over the years, Margot has shifted the balance to natives by slowly hand pulling weeds. Lately the needlegrasses have taken over, and she must pull some of them to keep room for the poppies. I joked with her that she needed an elk herd. In her own parking strip restoration garden, Margot depleted the weed-seed bank by watering the dirt, then pulling up the sprouting weeds over the next few months.

Other site preparations may involve loosening compacted soil on former construction sites, or inoculating sterile ground with cultures of soil fungi to increase fertility. Bare areas may need to be covered with clean straw (free of weed seeds!) to control erosion.

Native seed and plant gathering come next, now that your site is relatively free of weeds and fertile enough to encourage native growth. Ideally, you can collect seed from areas near the restoration site, which will match local ecotypes. (This match is less important in more urban areas, but if your project is next to wildlands there may be pollination between your plants and wild plants, and seed dispersal from your plants to wild areas.) Sometimes whole plants can be salvaged, with permission, from lots that are slated for development. Or you can purchase seeds and plants from commercial or government native seed farms (check out the Natural Resource Conservation Service, http://plant-materials.nrcs.usda.gov/capmc). Botanic gardens often have native plant sales. Go to the California Native Plant Society website (www.cnps.org) to find a list of native plant nurseries for the whole state. Also, check out plantnative.org to see a nationwide list of good nurseries.

At the Native Here Nursery (www.ebcnps.org, a project of the California Native Plant Society), located next to the East Bay's Tilden Regional Park, staff and volunteers meticulously collect native seeds from grasses, wildflowers, shrubs, and trees in surrounding areas, then grow potted plants for sale, labeling each with the locale of collection. I was amazed, while volunteering there recently, at the surge of native gardeners storming the place during a weekend plant fair. A man from Walnut Creek who had just bought a house next to a stream and wanted to plant a native meadow asked, "Which native grasses should we plant? And flowers?"

"Maybe a few native shrubs, too!" the wife added, as she scanned the racks of potted plants.

I asked them how much shade the place received, was it a cold, north-facing slope, a sunny west slope, or flat? Was the soil rocky or silty or clay-mud? I recommended some creeping wildrye and rushes, as well as various perennial flowers in the Walnut Creek section of the nursery. They rushed off with a wheelbarrow to select their plants. Another woman wanted to know which native bunchgrasses would grow on her dry, south-facing hillside in Orinda. I directed her to the Orinda section to get purple needlegrass, foothill needlegrass, and squirreltail.

In the last decade people from all over have been getting to know their indigenous flora and involving themselves in restoration projects, whether on public land or in their own little private home preserves.

Now to plant. On sites under two acres you can seed by hand or transplant potted plants or small "plugs." For larger areas, restorationists sometimes use a rotary seed spreader towed by an all-terrain vehicle, or a tractor-towed seed drill. A tractor-hydroseeder sprays water, seed, and compost over hillsides.

A nifty method of planting is to harvest native hay, such as purple needlegrass stems with seed, bale them up, and then spread the native straw over a site. This works well for rocky areas and provides instant mulch to protect the seeds from ravenous bird bills.

See David Amme's guidelines, which detail some of the mechanics of planting native grasses and sedges, in "Creating a Native California Meadow," available online at www.cnga.org.

Long-term site management will be needed to keep weeds from re-invading, and to aid the natives in growing and reproducing. Grazing, mowing, burning, mulching, or irrigation may be called for.

Nodding needlegrass, one-sided bluegrass, and six-weeks fescue on hills overlooking what will be San Jose. OIL ON COTTON RAG PAPER, 8 X 10 INCHES, 1997

In a small garden you can lightly clip or rake your bunchgrasses and rhizomatous natives to remove old matter, imitating grazing. Monitor the responses of each plant over the years and share your observations. The field of restoration ecology is wide open for finding out what works and what doesn't.

A Backyard Prairie

Anyone can learn more about restoration, even a kid. In 1984, as a teenager, I obtained the permission of my patient parents to dig up the lawn in the backyard of their house in the Berkeley-Richmond hills. The goal was to restore a native California grassland, and I think abandoning the lawnmower appealed to my father. I told my mother that colorful wildflowers would turn the boring square into a garden of high interest. She played along with my experiment.

After shoveling the lawn out and tilling the soil in the forty-foot-long yard, in early October I planted different batches of native grass seeds that I had collected locally: Idaho fescue, small-flowered melic, mountain brome, big squirreltail, prairie junegrass, purple needlegrass, blue wildrye, and meadow barley. By December the blue wildrye and brome were sprouting, and a single junegrass seedling grew in the dirt.

After extensive weeding of introduced annual hare barley and Australian brome, which seemed to come out of nowhere, the lush blue wildryes attained bunch form and were already putting out spikes. The mountain bromes also matured early, growing panicles from small tufts. Coming from behind, however, the meadow barleys had shot up, grown fast into several large tufts, and were also seeding. The junegrass seedling had disappeared and none of the other species sprouted, except for a few purple needlegrass seedlings. The fog-drenched, rich soil of this location no doubt influenced which grasses responded, as well as the "early successional" nature of the wildrye, brome, and meadow barley.

That spring a local landowner allowed me to dig up some native bunchgrasses from an empty hillside lot slated for the bulldozer. I moved two purple needlegrass bunches by backpack into the backyard (I didn't own a car yet). I watered them, and by June they seemed to take a firm foothold in their new home. Finding blue wildrye and mountain brome bunches in other empty lots destined for construction, I transplanted them to the new prairie experiment.

By July most of the little purple needlegrass seedlings had died—they were slow to grow and had high mortality in the summer heat.

Piles of fallen seeds gathered around the transplanted bunches in September, and a few California towhees came to dine. After two heavy rainstorms in November, I discovered two- to three-inch meadow barley seedlings sprouting from the piles. The needlegrass transplants greened up. The wildrye and brome transplants were not doing as well as the bunches grown from seed, which were now lush and green, growing quickly.

After some showers I planted wildflower seeds I had collected: California poppy, buttercups, blue dicks, grass nut, lomatium, yarrow, fiddleneck, and various lupines. I also threw out seeds of more grasses, namely bluegrass, bentgrass, and oniongrass.

By January and February of 1986, leafy rosettes of poppies had appeared, but also a surprise, a strange wildflower that I did not plant. A native bitter-cress, *Cardamine oligosperma*, became abundant on the bare ground, with a few early flowers. I had never seen it before—had it waited out the decades in the seedbank of the yard for a chance to bloom?

In April and May I had great patches of California poppies, some blue-eyed grass, and dove lupine. Mom looked pleased. The bunchgrasses from seed were doing well, especially the meadow barley, which was spreading new tufts from the original seed pile. The transplanted blue wildrye, however, died. Some outlaw wild oats grew up among a needlegrass bunch, and I pulled them. In June tall fiddlenecks came up, but also two seedlings of coyote brush, which had apparently wafted in on the winds to colonize bare ground. I pulled them out too, as I did not want my grassland to convert to a shrubland.

In July I noticed a dozen new young needlegrass plants that had finally taken from the seed dropped by the transplants. For some reason the seed I had collected never sprouted (a different ecotype?). The seeded blue wildrye spread well into a larger patch. A Diego bentgrass surprised me by leafing out and sending up thin panicles next to the needlegrasses and poppies. The leaves and stems of the bunches, which I no longer watered, even in summer, had colored the meadow straw-yellow and buff-ochre. Some people might not like having a dry garden for part of the year, but I reveled in the natural tones and subtle shades of the curing hay (and Dad enjoyed the lower water bill).

A year later the blue wildrye had almost completely taken over the yard, squeezing out the brome and barley. The needlegrasses held on, and the poppies grew only in the last open areas. The bitter-cress continued. In October 1987 I cut the grass with shears to half-height. In the next two years the wildrye maintained dominance, remaining dense and tall, perhaps favored by the partial shade from trees on the yard edges. By trial and error I had discovered which native grasses were best suited to this little plot of land facing the bay. Wildrye liked this partially shaded yard, while Margot's open sunny yard favors needlegrass.

But as I took jobs farther away and visited home less often, a wave of introduced plants crept in and took over: it was like a miniature history of the California flora. In the 1990s I found wild oats and soft chess dominant, as well as some curly dock. The wildrye was still fairly common, and I could find a few meadow barleys, mountain bromes, and needlegrasses mixing in. Poppies and checker remained on the edges.

Visiting deer brought weed seeds in on their fur, scrub jays planted live oaks into the grass, and flying finches dropped the seeds of Himalayan blackberry in the yard. The latter, a thick, tenacious vine, slowly formed great thickets over the grasses, shading them out in places. The food web had won, although I had learned a lot in the process. I dug out the yard again, back to bare dirt, and gave it back to my parents.

But the landscape constantly changes. My folks passed on and the house sold. By the year 2008, my old neighbors told me, the new owners had planted a neat, shiny lawn in the yard that was once my native prairie experiment. I like to think that under the turf where children play, a few native forb and grass seeds remain buried in the soil seedbank, waiting their chance to pop up one day.

As disturbed and changed as California's grasslands are, the native plants still grow over hills and valleys, sometimes hidden in a sea of Mediterranean grasses, sometimes holding their own. The opportunities for restoring these native prairies are endless. Despite the arguments volleyed back and forth about what our original golden hills were like, anyone can get started and plant a few bunchgrasses in a garden, or get together and protect a relict grassland community. We have much to learn and many secrets to uncover.

Purple needlegrass at sunset, East Bay hills. OIL ON COTTON RAG PAPER, 4 ½ x 10 ½, 1998

SEVEN

THE OAK

A Lifetime That Spans Centuries

Acorn Bread

Before I owned a car, I took a backpack and bicycled along the inland Bay Area routes, searching for plentiful acorn trees in October. For many California tribal people the acorn of the coast live oak was a staple food, due to its abundance and flavor. Acorns of blue oaks and valley oaks were said to be inferior in taste. But the gem of the acorns, said to be of the highest quality in taste, came from the California black oak. When I learned this, I searched out the nearest black oak grove but learned that this oak produces a crop only every two years. The trees were barren. So I turned to coast live oaks and soon found a grove that had a huge crop—acorns were dripping off the branches and littering the ground. Collecting bagfuls, I took them home and cracked them open with a rock while sitting out on the patio, arranging the yellowish nutmeats to dry hard in the sun.

I sorted the wormy ones from the good, and soon a pair of flashy blue and white scrub jays noticed my refuse pile. One flew down, hastily grabbed an acorn in its bill, and flapped off. The second jay then did the same, and I watched, amused, as the whole pile disappeared. The jays stored them for later use, hiding them in the ground, hammering them deep and sometimes placing a leaf over the spot, perhaps to make sure a marauding squirrel would not steal them. The jays worked to place acorns in the crevices of tree trunks, the gutters of my house, and potted plants. A

Acorn meats

Scrub jay

particularly greedy jay stuffed two to three acorns at a time into its bill at each visit to the pile. The jays had an excellent memory for these varied caches, and through the following winter I watched them eat an occasional acorn from their stores. Some, however, were missed. Nineteen years later there were five sapling oak trees in my yard, sprouted from a few forgotten acorns planted by jays. The birds were spreading woodlands.

At a local museum I had studied an old Indian mortar and pestle, the original acorn processing tools. The wondrously elegant stone bowl was slightly larger than a bowling ball, with a deep cup polished from use. The accompanying pestle was made from rougher basalt, giving it a tooth for breaking up the acorns. I wondered about the hands that made it, the history that it had seen. The rhythmic hollow thuds of women pounding acorns must have been a pleasing sound in California oak groves for thousands of years.

Having dried and sorted my acorns, I now used a small coffee grinder—less efficient than the stone tool—to make flour from the dried acorn halves. The jays sat in a tree and watched me.

To make the bitter meal edible, its tannic acid had to be leached out with many soakings of fresh water. Native women did this near creeks, in shallow sand hollows where they could spread the meal out and pour water over it. Ground finely enough, it would stick together like gelatin and could be picked up in chunks. My method involved laying a bed of pine needles out in my backyard and placing cheesecloth over this. I spread the meal out on the cloth and poured cold water over the bed, allowing the water to soak through. This phase took several hours.

The resulting acorn mush had a subtle flavor, oily and slightly nutty. Next I wrapped cakes of mush in the leaves of sword fern, but unable to bury these, as was traditional, in hot coals in a ground pit to bake, I covered them in aluminum foil and baked them in my oven, slowly, into bread unlike any made from wheat flour. The cakes were dark brown and crunchy, delicious with a hint of tannic flavor like spent tea leaves.

I now had more respect for the work of making acorns into food for humans, however imperfect my experiments had been. And I gained a deeper understanding of the acorn itself, abundant, flavorful, seasonal, locked with secrets.

Old Growth

Through the early and middle Holocene, Native people apparently relied upon grass and wildflower seeds for food, grinding them into meal with flat milling stones and handstone cobbles (also known as metates and manos). Archaeological evidence indicates that a major switch to acorns pounded in rounded mortars with pestles happened about 4000 B.P. in the San Francisco Bay Area, by 2800 B.P. in the Central Valley, and at 1000 B.P. in the Sierra Nevada.[1] The oiliness of the acorns inhibited the sliding action of manos in metates—pounding in a deep mortar worked much better.

When the acorn crops failed, Indians often turned to the California buckeye, mashing and leaching its bitter fruit as a poor substitute for the oak's bounty and letting the leftover stores sprout into trees. The buckeye's distribution has been influenced by people for perhaps thousands of years—it often grows in "orchards" at archaeological sites and old Indian camps. Also associated with midden sites are California black walnuts such as those as at Walnut Creek, in Contra Costa County, and Round Valley, in Mendocino County.[2]

This is useful information for those who want to restore California's grassy hills and oak-studded

Clockwise from top left, coast live oak acorns, valley oak acorns, interior live oak acorns, a single buckeye and a bay fruit, blue oak acorns, California black oak acorns OIL ON PAPERBOARD, 15 x 16 INCHES, 2004

valleys to health, and it is a pleasure to contemplate the slow and steady nature of the changes that indigenous people—and even scrub jays—have made to the landscape. But are there other factors from centuries ago, factors we are entirely unaware of, that affect the arrangement and pattern of the trees on the land? For restoration of these old oak communities to be successful, these past causes and effects must be understood.

"Old" is a key word here. In the study of beings that live for centuries, how do scientists and observers begin to unravel the tangle of clues present in their own snapshots of time, and where do they lead? We try to comprehend the situation, over time, of an oak savanna or woodland, but the lives of the trees go on beyond our own generations and we often miss their births, reproductive years, and deaths. But as we shall see, botanical "detectives" have begun to piece together a story from the slice of evidence we can find today.

Learning the Landscape

Having lived most of my life next to coast live oak woodlands, I have a large store of memories of hiking through them, fascinated by the changes that happened from season to season: in the dead of winter during a light rain, I heard the eerie calls of varied thrushes hiding in the oaks—long, thin, organlike notes—and the tinkling calls of spritely golden-crowned kinglets. Early in the spring the trilliums and milkmaids bloomed on the woodland floor, and pink currant bushes burst into flower, attracting Allen's hummingbird migrants. Later, the oaks burst with the songs of Wilson's and orange-crowned warblers, dogwoods showed large white blooms, and the oaks themselves produced small strings of wind-pollinated flowers. By June I looked forward to picking thimbleberry fruits. September, October, and November marked the season of acorns.

After walking these trails for twenty years or so, I had seen cyclical events that happened only once or twice a decade. An El Niño storm caused a landslide one day in the oak woodland, opening up the dense canopy and revealing a huge barren scoop of mud. I watched the pioneer plants gradually colonize this bare area, then sapling trees and shrubs grew, and after ten years a new woodland had developed. Another year, the California oakworms had a natural outbreak. This moth larva is usually inconspicuous, but in rare years its population densities increase terrifically, and it nearly defoliates the oaks. Walking the oak trails that summer was different than any other—sunlight poured through the normally closed evergreen canopy, and masses of partly eaten leaves littered the woodland floor. Next year the worms virtually disappeared and new leaves sprouted.

Some changes to the oak woodland were quick and unexpected. One afternoon, while waiting for an evening class in an open space park in the town of Pleasant Hill, I strolled through grassy openings of coast live oak and blue oak woodland, enjoying the slight fall display of the deciduous blue oak leaves turning yellow ocher and tan. I suddenly felt dizzy as I stood observing the scenery, and I wondered if I was about to faint. But then the very earth beneath me began to roll and jolt, back and forth, the first heave nearly throwing me off my feet. An earthquake! I realized, and rode it out. This one seemed to go on for several seconds, shaking many leaves off the blue oaks and startling a pair of ducks off a nearby pond. To my amazement Mount Diablo in the distance moved as well, as if sitting in a giant rocking chair. I then noticed a gray fox that had been curled up in a ball in the oak leaf litter, completely hidden; it quietly stood up, looked around, and nestled back into its bed, unconcerned. The rolling stopped, and all was quiet. A few birds called, but I continued my hike as if all were normal. Not until I returned to my car and switched the radio on did I realize that this was the "Big One." It was October 1989, and away from the peace of the oak woodland, sirens blared, traffic lights went out, and horrendous news came of parts of San Francisco burning. How different my serene and curious experience of the earthquake among the oaks was, compared to that of the urbanized world. The oaks seemed not to change much at all.

More recently I have seen changes to the live oak woodlands that were not naturally cyclic, but wrought by modern humans. While walking one day to one of my favorite trails, I was stopped by an orange warning fence and a sign prohibiting entry. This was to prevent the spread of sudden oak death, a disease first reported in 1995 that has been killing coast live oaks in the San Francisco Bay Area and from central coastal counties north to Oregon. It is attributed to the funguslike pathogen *Phytophthora*, introduced from nursery plants. These organisms apparently enter the bark of susceptible trees, causing girdling and rapid death. Marin County was a hotspot for the tree kills;

coast live oaks, California black oaks, and tan oaks were affected. Other species of *Phytophthora* have been a serious problem for trees and agricultural crops in various parts of the world.[3]

Finally, I became aware of changes to oak communities that have taken course over time periods longer than my lifespan, changes from factors that occurred a century or more ago: European settlement practices, introduced plant and animal species, and altered fire ecology. An examination of several species—coast live oaks, interior live oaks, valley oaks, Engelmann oaks, and blue oaks—with a look at some of the early recorded observations and an eye to their present condition reveals the significance of these factors.

Live Oak Woodlands and Savannas

Today coast live oaks grow in two basic vegetation types: woodlands and savannas. Dense oak woodland, which favors north-facing canyon slopes of the coastal hills, features a closed canopy and a highly diverse shrub and forb layer. The "southern oak woodland" of the central Coast Range south to Baja California often contains toyon, California coffeeberry, California sagebrush, black sage, and laurel sumac. In drier areas the woodlands break up into oak "parklands" consisting of a mosaic of small, closed groves and open grasslands.

Coast live oak leaf

Oak savannas, more open than woodlands, are essentially communities of grasses and shrubs with scattered lone trees.

On his march up the coast of California in 1769, Pedro Fages found "great forests of oak" one league (approximately 2.64 miles) from San Gabriel Mission (around Pasadena). Many Indians lived there, as well as deer. In the canyons surrounding San Luis Obispo, Fages and his party found dense oak forests—these can still be seen. The site of the future city of Oakland must have been a prime example of coast live oak woodland when Fages arrived there on his visit to the San Francisco Bay in 1772.[4] Father Juan Crespí labeled it "Llanura de Robles" (plain of oaks) on the map he made at the time. Gigantic old oaks grew for miles along parts of the bayshore and its inlets.

The young sailor Richard Dana, who in 1835 rode into San Francisco aboard a hide-and-tallow ship, called Angel Island "Wood Island" because it was covered with oaks, bays, buckeyes, and madrones down to the water's edge, and ships in harbor could cut enough wood to last them a year out at sea. By the 1850s the island was almost stripped bare. Eucalyptus from Australia was planted to supplement the wood supply, a legacy that lasts today in many coastal areas of California.[5]

Interior live oaks, a different species from coast live oaks, usually grow in mixed oak woodlands in the northern and central Coast Ranges and the Sierra foothills above the blue oak zone. They were once dominant along rivers and streams flowing from the Sierra into the Central Valley, but dam building and clearing for agriculture in this zone have reduced them to remnants.[6]

The open, scattered savanna form of the coast live oak community is less common than the denser woodland type, and judging by early written accounts, it has experienced more changes to its species diversity. It may have dotted valleys and coastal flats from northern California to Baja. At one time there were large live oaks scattered between Salinas and Castroville, two to three and a half feet in diameter. They were cleared for strawberries, artichokes, and rangeland.[7] In the mid-1800s William Brewer, at Nipomo Ranch, exclaimed at the coast live oaks "with great spreading branches, gnarled and knotted trunks," beautiful with dark green foliage.[8]

From Founders' Rock in Berkeley, the view in 1860 was of a vast meadow dotted with ancient oaks.[9] The Hanging Oak where a horse thief met his end used to grow on Allston Way. It was cut

A scene from the past along a quiet inlet of the San Francisco Bay where Oakland exists today. Coast live oaks grow
down to the water's edge and blue wildrye grows in the understory. A black-tailed deer watches an Ohlone hunter.

OIL ON PANEL, 6 X 11 INCHES, 2004

The same scene in 2003

down in 1980. This oak savanna, though it has been urbanized and cleared away, remains in memory: a few old trees are scattered among houses and city streets. A grand live oak dominated one small Berkeley street for years, taking up a small island and shading the asphalt around it—cars drove around it on the narrow hillslope avenue. Out-of-town folks laughed when I showed them this relict tree allowed to stay in the middle of a road, but locals planted a new oak at the same spot when the ancient sentinel finally died.

Seeking Out the Savannas

Father Crespí's description of Santa Barbara in August 1769 yields a clue to the species present in a coastal southern California savanna:

> We went over land that was all of it level, dark and friable, well covered with fine grasses, and very large clumps of very tall, broad grass, burnt in some spots and not in others. The unburned grass was so tall that it topped us on horseback by a yard. All about are large tablelands with big tall live oaks (I have never seen larger), and many sycamores as well. We have come across rose-patches in such great amounts that the plains here were full of them in many spots.[10]

Giant wildrye, as Jan Timbrook and her colleagues have suggested, may be the grass he speaks of. It could well be described as "very large clumps of very tall, broad grass"—patches of this coarse rhizomatous grass can grow higher than my head. In January 2004 I traveled to the Santa Barbara region to gather information for a painting reconstructing the city's natural setting, using Crespí's description as a starting point and my own field notes of relict vegetation to fill out the picture. Sure enough, as I drove down Highway 101 from the north and entered the narrow coastal terraces below the Santa Ynez Mountains, I was immediately struck by the abundance of giant wildrye growing on open grassy slopes and flats, at the edges of sage scrub patches, and amidst scattered live oaks—just as Crespí had described. I stopped in several areas to sketch the patterns of vegetation and take notes of my observations. I noticed a few purple needlegrass bunches in open areas as well, probably indicating the matrix of grassland that the tall wildrye grew in during past centuries.

Remarkably, despite areas of cattle grazing, shrub invasion, roads, and houses, the area north of Santa Barbara shows a good relict landscape. I wondered if this survivor was a unique "lost habitat," a giant wildrye and coast live oak savanna of a type that once occurred on other areas along the coast. I have seen a few giant wildrye patches in open spaces near Berkeley, so perhaps centuries ago a similar community grew on East Bay flats.

Seeking out the oak savannas that have not been engulfed by urbanization, I found most of them with weedy understories of introduced European grasses and forbs under the shade of their spreading boughs. But relict natives can be found under them in some places as well.

Growing near the oaks of San Luis Obispo, San Diego, and Orange Counties I found remnants of purple needlegrass, nodding needlegrass, California melicgrass, bluegrass, foxtail grass, California oatgrass, and other natives typical of the original open grasslands of California. Directly under the oak canopies grew grasses that required slightly more moisture: mountain brome, blue wildrye, Torrey melic, and Diego bentgrass. Scattered shrubs were also present, such as toyon, blue elderberry, and California sagebrush.

Valuable mosaics of oaks, grass, and shrubs must have attracted many kinds of wildlife. Lark sparrows, for instance, preferred edge habitats in live oak parklands and savannas, where they nested on the ground and perched in trees and shrubs. Biologists speculate that the lark sparrow population in California oak lands may have declined since the 1960s as habitats were removed or degraded, and they advocate using this bird a a "focal species" for monitoring conservation efforts—when the lark sparrow's ecological requirements are met and it appears to be breeding successfully, then other species, including the oaks themselves, will also benefit.[11]

Lark sparrows

At Hastings Reserve, in Monterey County, where oaks abound in both woodland and savanna habitat, scrub jays each cache about five thousand acorns every fall. It is estimated that the birds relocate and eat a full 95 percent of them. The rest are often germinated.[12] Steller's jays and yellow-billed magpies also cache acorns. Considering this highly effective distribution system, one wonders what kept these savannas so open. Wildfires played a large role, as we shall see. Grazing may also be an important process in keeping the oak communities open. In northern Baja California, ecologists found that coast live oaks grew from acorn to tree poorly under even slight grazing pressure by cattle. Without cattle present, stands were dense and of mixed age.[13] Speculation: did elk in precontact times help to maintain the live oak savannas that used to be common along the coast?

Valley Oaks

The towering valley oaks that dot California's grasslands were an impressive sight for early visitors. William Brewer noted the great curves of their limbs, thirty to fifty feet long, some almost touching the ground. There was one close to his camp that had a crown over a hundred feet in diameter, a trunk fifteen feet in circumference, and lichen hanging from every branch. At Carmel he found the "roble" very fine, one specimen attaining more than twenty-six feet in trunk circumference, one with branches spreading seventy-five feet each way. Two deer wandered through the scene.[14]

The valley oak is the largest North American oak, reaching 120 to 150 feet in height[15] and living as long as five hundred years. These oaks send deep taproots down to permanent groundwater under the dry plains, as well as extensive lateral roots that can be as long as seventy feet just under the ground.

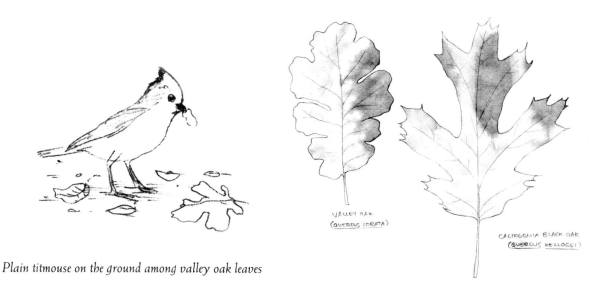

Plain titmouse on the ground among valley oak leaves

Early settlers called the valley oak "swamp oak" or "water oak," a name indicative of the habitat it favored: floodplains and valley floors that were sometimes subject to winter overflows of their rivers or streams.

Flooding of the great Sierran rivers in the past, as they emptied their waters out onto the valley lowlands, may have given valley oak seedlings the chance to put on growth spurts. Researchers at the Cosumnes River Preserve in Sacramento County have found that oak seedlings need soil moisture in order to grow well—irrigation of planted seedlings in fields allows them to surge up fast. The age structure of oaks in the riparian woodland also correlates seedling establishment to floods.[16] Water is ever important in summer-dry California.

The parklike nature of the valley oak savannas across the state was noticed over and over by European visitors. On the Santa Clara Valley plains, along the southern edge of San Francisco Bay, Captain George Vancouver in 1798 observed:

> We arrived at a very pleasant and enchanting lawn, situated amid a grove of trees....For almost twenty miles it could be compared to a park which had originally been planted with the true old English oak; the underwood that had probably attained its early growth, had the appearance of having been cleared away and had left the stately forest in complete possession of the soil.[17]

Indeed, the local tribes had probably been setting low ground fires for thousands of years here to keep the savanna open. Botanist Willis Linn Jepson noted in 1923 that:

> These oak orchards, of great food importance to the native tribes, indicate plainly the influence on the trees of Indian occupancy of the country. The extent and nature of the relations of Indian tribal culture and the habitat of the oaks cannot yet, if ever, be completely defined, although it is clear that the regular spacing of the trees is a result of the annual firing of the country.[18]

The British ship HMS *Sulphur* in 1837 traveled one hundred and fifty miles up the Sacramento River to explore. Her captain described the scene:

> Oaks of immense size were plentiful. These appeared to form a band on each side, about three hundred yards in depth, and within (in the immense park-like extent, which we generally explored when landing for positions) they were seen to be disposed in clumps which served to relieve the eye wandering over what might be described as one level plain or sea of grass.

Seeing fires in some stands of trees and brush along the river, the crew noted that the Native people set fire to the bases of large oak trees to help in gathering acorns.[19]

One of the most famous valley oak savannas was the Kaweah Oaks of the southeastern San Joaquin Valley. Jepson had a correspondent who remembered "four hundred square miles of Valley Oaks" on the alluvial soils along the Kaweah River.[20] The immense oaks of these wide rich plains east of Tulare Lake at times grew so densely as to form closed canopy woodlands that hindered the passage of settlers' wagons.[21] On other spots the oaks formed "most lovely groups, masses, and single specimens."[22]

Out West magazine could not say enough about the wonders of this place. By the Kings River delta, on rich valley soil, was the Laguna de Tache grant, having a "scattering growth of magnificent oak trees, giving it the appearance of an English park." Wildflowers were abundant. What may have

*Santa Barbara five hundred years ago: coast live oak savanna with giant wildrye, purple needlegrass,
California sagebrush, and prickly pear.*

OIL ON TONED COTTON RAG PAPER, 6 ½ X 16 ½ INCHES, 2004

The same scene in 2003

The Kaweah Oaks: stately valley oaks with a lush understory of creeping wildrye.
OIL ON CANVAS, 24 X 36 INCHES, 2004

been creeping wildrye growing in rhizomatous fields with the valley oaks, as it does commonly today, is described as a "perennial growth of green grass" in "broad park-like stretches of green pasture land." So good was the grass here that thousands of cattle were grazed on the grant, brought in from as far as Nevada, Arizona, and New Mexico. By 1899 the old rancho had been subdivided and planted with corn, alfalfa, hay, grapes, and orchards.[23] Immense relict trees in Fresno and Tulare Counties hint at the grandeur of these fields of oaks.

Trying to reconstruct the original valley oak savanna community complete with its native understory species is a tough prospect, but relicts can still be found. In Walnut Creek, for example, I saw enormous old valley oaks on flatlands with remnants of creeping wildrye under them. This grass must have been the dominant understory species in valley bottomlands in the Coast Ranges, on floodplains in the Central Valley, on flats around and under valley oaks, and up onto low hillslopes. Sedges grew in wetter spots. On drier hills, various bunchgrasses can be found next to the oaks. At Sebastopol, I found a hint of what parts of the Sacramento Valley may have looked like hundreds of years ago: plains of large valley oaks had a grassy understory that flooded in winter and dried out in the summer heat. Lush green stands of four-foot-high reedgrass grew on short-grass flats of meadow barley. Creeping wildrye, bentgrass, sedges, rushes, spikerushes, and nutsedges also grew in the valley wetland.

Researchers have noticed evidence of limited regeneration by valley oaks since the early 1900s in parts of California. What grows under the oaks today may be quite important: greedy annual grasses induce severe water stress on valley oak seedlings, enough to kill them. Soil moisture is often lower in introduced annual grasslands than in native perennial grasslands. Valley oak seedlings grow most rapidly in February and March, in direct competition with annuals such as wild oats.[24]

I mention the gray and white Swainson's hawk here because it used to nest abundantly in tall valley oaks and cottonwoods. The Central Valley historically had 1,000 to 2,000 pairs, but in 1984 only 280 pairs were found from Fresno to Chico. California has had an estimated 90 percent decline in nesting pairs since 1900.

In fall, gatherings of hundreds of these summer hawks once circled about over the plains, then sailed south of the border, forming columns of migrants past the southern California peaks. What a sight that must have been. Today I treasure a glimpse of even one of these hawks. Fortunately, The Nature Conservancy's Cosumnes River Preserve and other places are now harboring excellent valley oak habitat for these raptors, and their future looks better.

Little Oaks of Southern California

A true California endemic, the Engelmann oak used to grow between Claremont, Pasadena, and Pomona on deep valley clay soils, and on the foothills of the San Gabriel Mountains. The rounded crowns of these small, bluish oaks look like those of blue oaks, but these trees are more closely related to several Mexican oaks of arid summer-rain climates.[25] A few still grace the Huntington Gardens and the Los Angeles Arboretum, but to see their natural community one must now head south.[26]

Engelmann oaks once grew in a wide band through the south coastal counties. Some lived on the Perris Plain, but most occupied the rolling hilltops and foothills, sometimes in pure stands, of San Diego and southwestern Riverside Counties. In precolonial times an estimated 80,500 acres of open oak woodlands dotted the interior. Recently many of these woodlands have been invaded by housing tracts or cut to make way for avocado orchards.[27]

The Blue Oak Savanna

The stars of the black night sky outlined the barely visible crowns of blue oaks. As poorwills, hidden, called their name softly, the dawn light washed over the eastern horizon. Then the morning chorus started up: a clamor of birds calling and singing to greet the sun. California thrashers, towhees, goldfinches, and acorn woodpeckers sang simultaneously among the oaks. The dusky blanket of night gradually lifted, and the landscape awakened to warm air and soft pink morning light.

My hike through a blue oak savanna in the early morning of a summer day at Mount Diablo State Park was a delight to the eyes. The rounded leaf canopies,

Field notes: "Swainson's hawks: two calling over valley oaks and grass."

a subdued gray-blue, dotted the yellow grasslands. I saw western fence lizards and later a southern alligator lizard climb up the gray-furrowed oak trunks, and I spotted a single blue oak seedling less than a foot high in the dry grass.

No one knows what the precontact blue oak habitats looked like. Constructing a picture of the structure and composition of these woodlands and savannas before European contact was ever on my mind as I hiked through the oak ridges and valleys, looking for clues and taking notes on the plant and animal associations I found.

Although the spread of European annual grasses during the eighteenth and nineteenth centuries changed the grass component of the blue oak savanna drastically, I have been able to discover clues as to the original makeup of the native ground cover by examining hundreds of blue oak habitats and searching for native remnants. These habitats are in fact fairly common, and I think a good idea of the original matrix for the oaks and wildflowers of the savannas can be reconstructed.

I noticed that the grass species growing under the canopies of blue oak trees were often different from those growing out in the open. Some of the bunchgrasses that especially favor the shade of blue oaks are blue wildrye, which I often saw forming dense patches under the oaks, as well as California melic, mountain brome, and Diego bentgrass. In rare instances I found Idaho fescue growing under blue oaks: near Redding, in northern California, and near San Miguel, in the South Coast Range. California fescue, a mesic shade species, prefers the cover of the various oaks. Studies on Hastings

Pasadena a thousand years ago: Engelmann oak savanna on the edges of the San Gabriel Mountains at dusk. Lupines, purple needlegrass, and one-sided bluegrass grow on the plains in spring. OIL ON PANEL, 5 X 10 INCHES, 2004

Blue oak savanna in the Sierra foothills with larkspur and California melic,
or oniongrass, a bunchgrass. OIL ON PANEL, 14 ½ X 12 INCHES, 2004

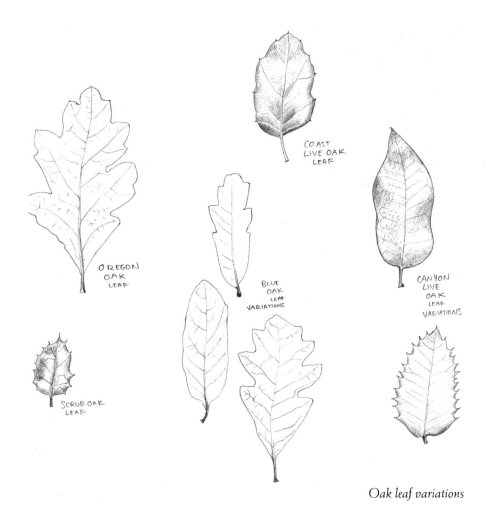

Oak leaf variations

Reserve have shown that vegetation under the oak crowns grows faster and produces almost twice the biomass of vegetation in the open. Herbs also mature later and, because of the oak leaf litter, have a higher nutrient content.[28]

Open grassland species that I observed growing around but also freely under the oak canopies included prairie junegrass, one-sided bluegrass, the native annual small fescue grass, big squirreltail, and small-flowered melic.

Purple needlegrass is mainly an open-grassland species, but occasionally I have seen bunches under canopies, and even right next to the trunk. I found nodding needlegrass almost wholly growing in the open between oaks. Creeping wildrye can be found in patches on open flats with deep soils or in low areas. I also occasionally met with the dryland bunch rush *Juncus tenuis* in the oak savannas.

The Ever Changing Wildlands

Many observers have noticed subtle hints at changes in seemingly pristine blue oak wildlands: what ecologists call the "age structure" of the woodland is skewed. On my hikes I often saw only seedlings and old trees, but no middle-age saplings; in some woodlands there were no seedlings either. If this pattern continues, the old trees will not be replaced as they die.

At the huge Tejon Ranch, in the Tehachapi Mountains in Kern County, ecologist Scott Mensing did a stand age analysis, taking small cores from trees and comparing their annual ring counts. From 1570 to 1850, he found, recruitment (young trees making it to maturity) was fairly regular. A dramatic increase occurred in the 1850s and 1860s, but only 9 percent of the trees now present grew since 1864. After 1900, no new trees grew to adulthood. The oldest tree was found to be 412 years old, and even small stems (less than nine inches in diameter) were over a hundred years of age.[29]

What is the cause of this pattern? That is still a mystery. The lack of recruitment may be due to a natural cycle or it may be a response to environmental changes from European settlement, but the picture is unclear.

Numerous range ecologists, paleoecologists, and botanists have been traipsing out into the field to study the situation, adding pieces that help to fill in the picture. Proposed explanations for the lack of young trees include cattle grazing, herbivory by deer and rodents, insect predation, fire suppression, competition from introduced annual grasses, and climate change. This is a typical example of the complexity that confronts the historical ecologist, and the difficulties humans face when trying to understand such a long-lived entity as an oak tree.

"Seed-caching corvids"—scrub jays for instance—may be largely responsible for increasing or maintaining woody plant populations, and they apparently are doing their job well. Something is happening after the acorns reach the ground and sprout. Some researchers have tried to solve the mystery by looking at the early stages of the young oaks. One group observed that blue oak seedling populations may be large but are ephemeral, with high mortality rates. If a seedling reaches the sapling stage its chance of survival improves as it sends its taproot down deep into the soil.[30] Another group noticed that blue oak seedlings were constantly present in the oak understory of their Sierra foothill study site, and that fire and sheep grazing had little effect on their survival, but they found no saplings.[31]

Acorn woodpecker

Rodents were found to be the most important predators of acorns and seedlings—mostly pocket gophers, as well as mice and voles.[32] But could these small mammals cause wholesale population changes in a woody species? Probably not. Cattle and deer leave a browse line at roughly four feet on small trees. They can retard the growth of oaks and have been observed to keep them shrubby for thirty years. In some studies the trees that were protected from browsing grew tallest.[33]

Perhaps competition is the key. One of the most picturesque blue oak savannas is found around Lake Berryessa, in the dry inner North Coast Range of Napa County, a relatively pristine place despite the reservoir that exists there. At a quiet picnic ground I saw deer, house finches, Nuttall's woodpeckers, and bushtits, and western wood-pewees sang in the oak branches over a layer of dry yellow grass. I noticed many blue oak seedlings on the bare ground along the receding lakeshore, along with the diminutive native annual foxtail. Here, few introduced annual grasses grew, although they were common nearby in the main oak savanna: wild oats and soft chess. Perhaps the low level of competition on this scoured reservoir edge allows both native annual grasses and blue oak seedlings to thrive.

White-throated nuthatch on oak

Other "plant detectives" have found that dry winters kill many oak seedlings just after they sprout from their acorns, but that if the surrounding cover of ripgut brome and other introduced

BLUE OAKS.

SWALLOW ENTERING NEST.

PEERING OUT BEFORE FLYING OUT.

Field notes: "Violet-green swallow nest in hole in knot of large, horizontal blue oak limb. Chirps. Parent flew into hole."

annual grasses is pulled out, the oak seedlings sprout in larger numbers and their roots grow longer.[34] In Mediterranean Spain and Portugal, periods of severe grazing were found to benefit the oak savanna, reducing the competitive and thirsty annual grasses and thus allowing trees to grow upwards. At other times, decades of "undergrazing" allowed the grass understory to grow dense, gulping up rainwater and stunting the oak saplings or preventing seedlings from growing at all. Thus, through the centuries the oak woodland had a range of variation of its age structure: in some centuries mature trees dominated; in other times young saplings abounded. The researchers offered the suggestion that neither state was abnormal for the woodland. Short-lived humans were expecting a static picture, but oak life cycles vary over longer stretches of time. Variation is normal.[35]

Competition from mature trees themselves can inhibit sapling growth: in Mediterranean Europe, ecologists found that large trees growing in a savanna with space between them could monopolize the underground soil space, filling the soil with their roots.[36] Young trees had a difficult time getting at the water supply.

A Longer View

The role of competition in oak woodland life cycles is complicated by another factor: climate. Short-term climate changes have a definite impact on blue oaks: during drought, seedlings often die back and few germinate. But during a following moist period, many seedlings will germinate and older sprouts will regrow. Long-term climate cycles may also play an important role. Not surprisingly, it has been proposed that a favorable climate is a prerequisite for successful recruitment: blue oaks and coast live oaks regenerate more successfully in moister geographic areas, at more mesic, shady sites. If it is a cyclic event in any given woodland for oak trees to reach mature stature, then we have information only about the most recent reproductive episode, which was disrupted during the time of European settlement, a time associated with other major disruptions—changes to fire regimes, introduction of new plants and animals, and other factors—that can influence oak establishment.[37] The clues seem hopelessly tangled. But the key to understanding the conditions under which the trees thrive or decline is to reconstruct what has happened to them over a long enough period of time.

Is the savanna a remnant of the Little Ice Age? That dramatic increase in recruitment during the 1850s and 1860s that Mensing found took place just as Sierran glaciers reached their maximum extent, in 1850 to 1855, and just after.[38] Glacier size and oak recruitment have since shown a steady parallel decline.

Long periods of greater rainfall during the last few centuries may have favored oak regeneration. What we are seeing today could be the dry part of a long-term cycle, coming out of the wet period that ended in the last decades of the nineteenth century; poor recruitment could simply be the result of less favorable spring rains. Mensing's data may reflect the disastrous droughts that plagued the early twentieth century.

Extreme climate events may be more important than shifts in averages. Severe droughts in the Southwest have been known to topkill (kill the canopy of) oaks, which later resprout and recover. Pulses of woody plant recruitment have resulted there from brief periods of high soil moisture. Mesquite savannas in Texas grow in clusters. During dry periods, more clusters die; during average and above-average rain years, new clusters form and existing clusters expand.[39] In Mediterranean Iberia, a world strangely parallel to California, oak savannas can look strikingly like those here, with prickly oak, live oak, and cork oak trees scattered in a summer-dry grassland that also has a history of fire and grazing. An area may have trees 90, 210, 240, and 570 years old in clusters, but none of intermediate ages. These trees apparently represent years when circumstances—plentiful late spring rains, a preceding fire, and disease among the browsing goats—conspired to favor their growth. Large areas of oak savanna in Portugal have an age structure that could date the trees to a high rainfall period in the 1880s and 1890s. Ecologists A. T. Grove and Oliver Racham, who have been reading the vegetation and land for clues for decades, admit that the long, episodic nature of ecologic processes makes the historical ecology of Mediterranean areas difficult to study. There is no equilibrium model that land managers can strive for—the same thing does not happen every year.[40]

The Human Factor

In search of more recruitment data back at the Tejon Ranch, Scott Mensing next looked at fire history, dating the scars left by flames on oak trunks. Blue oaks survived fires well. They have thick bark, an adaptation to resist burning. Those that were crown-scorched resprouted leaves as soon as two weeks later. Smaller trees, under about eight inches in diameter, were often topkilled, but they resprouted vigorously from the base to grow a new trunk. In one study 93 percent of blue oaks survived two years after a fire.[41] In Mensing's fire scar research, scars were regular prior to the 1860s, increasing in occurrence about every ten years. From 1843 to 1865 the fire interval was every four to five years. Fires were most numerous in the 1850s. From 1864 to the 1920s there was a complete absence of fire scars.

Prior to European arrival, recruitment was low but regular; the blue oaks were replenishing themselves. Four Mexican land grants were established in the Tejon area in the 1840s, and European settlers began arriving in 1853. Fort Tejon was built by the U.S. Army in 1854. Young oaks were unusually successful during the 1850s. Was this due to a change caused by European land use, or a coincidental change in climate or some other aspect of the environment? In 1865 General Edward Beale bought and consolidated the land grants and moved fourteen thousand sheep onto his new ranch. In the 1880s he exchanged them for cattle, which have been on the Tejon Ranch ever since. Cattle grazing may have decreased the fuels necessary to maintain ground fires, thereby allowing the oak canopy to increase in density. More fires were recorded in the 1930s, but by then the oaks were large enough to withstand ground fires. Mensing could not determine from his study the effects that cattle grazing had on the oak population. James Bartolome, a range ecologist at UC Berkeley, has been studying the problem for years. He believes that the hungry muzzles of browsing deer and cattle can retard fire-stimulated growth on saplings. Perhaps protection from these herbivores would allow small trees to grow large.[42] Could the many fires on the Tejon Ranch during the 1850s have "flooded" browsers with so many sprouts that a large number of trees escaped chewing and grew to maturity?

The historic fire return interval (the number of years between two successive fire events at a site) for blue oak habitats in general in California hasn't been determined; estimates range from an average of every eight to twenty-five years before 1900, and every seventy-eight years afterward.[43] More study of the long ages embedded in the oak landscape itself will be needed to tease out the story of how fire affects oak growth and woodland structure.

I have been thinking a lot about the causes of change in the blue oak lands in order to develop accurate paintings of precontact scenes, or at least best-guess hypotheses presented in visual form, and I cannot escape the conclusion that nature presents us with multifaceted and interconnected processes that often operate simultaneously. There is no one answer.

Blue oak establishment could be episodic. James Bartolome and his colleagues determined that only eighteen new trees might be needed each decade in a favorable rain period to continue a stand of six hundred trees per hectare (2.47 acres).[44] Long-lived trees could afford to wait for the rare combination of a good acorn year coupled with a wet winter and low browsing pressure.[45]

Thus we may be living in a time when oaks are not reproducing, for "natural" reasons or because of a century of altered landscape practices, and our own generations are too short to see the oaks' big picture. The answer to the question of whether the oak woodlands and savannas of California will continue far into the future requires more evidence, gathered by plant detectives looking at the long-term processes of competition, herbivory, climate change, and wildfire. Your observations now could be invaluable a hundred years in the future.

Tejon Ranch

Fantastic blue oak and valley oak habitats can be seen on the Tejon Ranch. The ranch's more than two hundred and seventy thousand acres are still privately owned, but a movement is afoot to purchase the great ranch and preserve the oak woodlands, grasslands, flower fields, and California condor homelands from potential future sprawling developments. The Center for Biological Diversity, Sierra Club, Natural Resources Defense Council, Environment Now, Endangered Habitats League, and Planning and Conservation League are teaming up to try to make this mountain-and-valley chunk of Old California into a state or national park. Go to www.savetejonranch.org, www.tejonpreserve.com, and www.biologicaldiversity.org to learn more, and drive along the public roads to view the area (please do not trespass on private lands and property). Some of my favorite drives are Highway 223 from the agricultural town of Arvin up to Highway 58, and the road to Castaic Lake from Highway 5.

EIGHT

FIRE
Red-Hot Cycles of Renewal

Landscape Patterns

I arrived in Aliso Campground at sunset, in a canyon in Los Padres National "Forest," which is more a shrubland with some oaks, and sat at a picnic table admiring the subtropical diversity of plants in the vicinity. Coast live oaks nestled in the canyon along with sycamores, blue oaks, scrub oaks, poison oak, manzanita, junipers, bay trees, cottonwoods, and a wide assortment of aromatic shrubs. Western bluebirds called softly among the live oaks, oak titmice and scrub jays bounded around camp, and California thrashers sang from the chaparral slopes above. I had the campground to myself in the summer heat. My intent was to study Cuyama Valley below me (the name taken from that of a Chumash Indian band), a broad remote river flat stretching west through the Coast Range from near Carrizo Plain to Santa Maria on the coast, a forgotten area of California that is one of my windows into the past. The imprints of fire are obvious here, the landscape showing multiple episodes of burning and renewal—a pattern that I read like the pages of a book (that is still being written).

Adjacent to the national forest, large cattle spreads with names, like Rancho Rinconada, that recall Mexican California occupy the valley floor. Despite the grazing, native grasses still dot the plains; coastal sage scrub, oak savanna, chaparral, and riparian glades remain undisturbed by subdivision; and most intriguingly, the whole area shows signs of recent burns of various ages, giving the plant communities a more pristine aspect than "protected" parks. Fire is a common event in this valley.

In fact, one was burning as I arrived at camp—way up on the chaparral ridgeline.

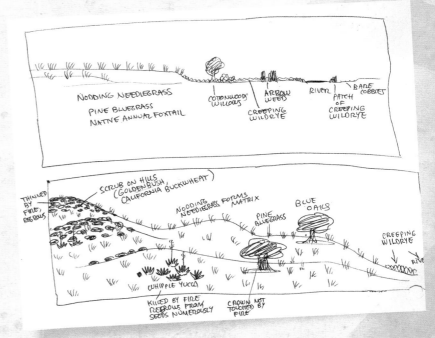

Field notes, Cuyama Valley

I could see at dusk a swath of brown smoke blown eastward. The sun set into the smoke, becoming a bright ruby disc.

At dawn I woke up to poorwills calling in the chaparral above the live oaks. The blaze continued to burn on the mountain slope in the far distance; on the lower foothills it had blackened the grass under an open group of oaks, leaving the trees unscathed. In the higher hills, however, the brush was completely ablaze, leaving only gray ash and bushy shrub skeletons. Some bigcone spruces burned like giant candles.

Hiking up Aliso Canyon, I examined the gray-green chaparral along the trail under a clear, sun-filled blue sky. Whipple yuccas grew more abundantly than I had ever seen, covering many of the steep slopes with a carpet of blue-green spear-rosettes. Some had blackened stems—signs of old burns. Perhaps the yuccas increase in density with regular burning. The scrub where past fires had burned included many bunchgrasses and was more open than the long-unburned patches. A canyon wren called its long, descending crescendo, and an Anna's hummingbird fed on a scarlet-flowered penstemon. Wrentits laughed at me from their hiding places in the sage.

Arriving back at camp in the afternoon, I found my once empty campground strewn with human bodies lying haphazardly on picnic tables and stretched across the ground in the shade of oaks. An exhausted fire crew had arrived from up on the ridge, and firefighters lay resting, too tired to move in their smoked-yellow jackets. They were trying to extinguish the Spanish Fire, named for an old adobe near its start, that had already burned five thousand acres. I never found out the cause, but it was late July and to the south the monsoon season had been giving Los Angeles repeated thunderstorms and flooding. Had lightning started the fire? A few months later, a lightning bolt ignited another fire up on the same ridge, bringing fire suppression crews back again to Los Padres National Forest.

I packed up and headed out to explore the old fire patterns on the valley itself. I sketched the vegetation mosaic of open grassland on the flats and terraces above the Cuyama River, and on parts of the sloping bajadas—accumulations of flood sediment at the bases of the mountains. Old burns were evident, dominated by grass. This was mostly exotics, such as wild oats and red brome, but I also found several acres of native bunchgrass: pure stands of feathergrass or mixes with one-sided bluegrass on the flats and rolling low hills. A section along the road had just been burned off, probably by a cigarette tossed from a passing car. Blackened, charred bases of *Nassella* bunchgrasses remained, forming a dense pattern of dark spots on the bare dirt. Patches of unburned cane cholla and prickly pear darkened the grassland in widely scattered groups, with occasional feathergrasses poking up through their protective spiny arms.

Coastal scrub, here dominated by California buckwheat, was common on low hills around the valley edge, and in gullies and ravines interfingering with grassland. California sagebrush, Whipple yucca, and goldenbush (*Ericameria*) grew in large patches on slopes, mixing with patches of open grassland, perhaps in a burn mosaic. This scrub dominated the bajadas, and on old burns it was less dense, with shrubs more scattered.

Live oaks lined the bottoms of riparian ravines, and blue oak savanna was widespread on mountain bases. Chaparral of chamise, manzanita, and black sage grew in localized patches on lower hillsides with oaks and buckwheat scrub, but the really extensive chaparral areas were higher on the mountain ridges.

The patterning of fire could be read on this land. Indeed, nearly every habitat in California shows adaptations to burning, with renewal emerging from the ashes.

Habitat Conversion

Ecologist P. V. Wells carried out a careful comparative study of the vegetation mosaic around San Luis Obispo, just north of Cuyama Valley, to determine if the seemingly random jumble of grassland, scrubland, and oak woodland patches on the hills and valleys was related to geological substrates—what grew on sandstone, basalt, clay, or volcanic ash? He found certain plant species, such as specific manzanitas and Sargent cypress, limited mostly to just one or two substrates. But this was a function of the fire history of the area, as well as chance dispersal of seeds and nuts—not soil type. To some extent, though, substrate mattered. He theorized that on deep, rich soils, frequent fire in an oak woodland could turn it into grassland; but on thin, rocky soils, coastal sage scrub or chaparral would replace the oaks.[1]

In another study, at Gaviota State Park on the coast south of Santa Maria, researchers looked at aerial photographs taken of the same areas over time—"repeat photography"—to see how the vegetation mosaic had shifted. Over a forty-year period, on unburned and ungrazed plots almost a third of grassland converted to coastal sage scrub; almost a third of coastal sage scrub converted to oak woodland or chaparral; and 5 percent of chaparral converted to oak woodland. Ten percent of oak woodland converted back to grassland, possibly on drier sites where no new trees grew to maturity. On plots that had fires, grassland increased, coastal sage scrub decreased, and the proportions of chaparral and oak woodland remained the same. On thin, rocky soils chaparral appeared to remain unchanged indefinitely as an edaphic climax (soil climax). Areas that were grazed showed slower conversion rates, and in some areas grazing may have prevented coastal sage scrub from invading grassland.

As we have seen, fire, grazing, and soil affect the dynamic shifting mosaic of vegetation patches on the landscape. Aspect and slope are also factors: coast live oak woodland favors shady north slopes, and oak savanna is found on gentler, drier topography. Subtle biotic interactions between plants themselves may also have an impact. And of course climatic fluctuations, which could over time change the transition rates between vegetation types, cannot be left out of the mix.[2]

Studying the Cuyama Valley landcape, I began to understand something of the complexity of its history, a story of fire and other disturbances combined with cycles of succession and the accompanying renewal of plant communities. I think everything we have learned so far is just a hint at solving this mystery of change in nature.

We do not know what the historic fire regimes—duration, ground pattern, intensity, and season—were in the plant communities of precontact California, although guesses can be made using early accounts and current studies of fire ecology. We do know that quite a few native habitats—we'll be looking at wetlands and grasslands, oak forests, chaparral, and the Sierran forests—were adapted to burning by both wildfire and Indian-managed fire.

Marsh Fires in Old California

In 1859 James Hutchings, travel writer, publisher, and promoter, described the San Joaquin Valley in his journal. He later published this material with other accounts of his travels in *Scenes of Wonder and Curiosity in California*:

> An apparently interminable sea of tules extends nearly one hundred and fifty miles south, up the valley of the San Joaquin; and when these are on fire, as they not infrequently are, during the fall and early winter months, the broad sheet of licking

and leaping flame, and the vast volumes of smoke that rise, and eddy, and surge, hither and thither, present a scene of fearful grandeur at night, that is suggestive of some earthly pandemonium.[3]

What might have caused these marsh fires? Chuck Striplen, a biologist with the San Francisco Bay Institute and also a descendant of the Bay Area's Mutsun Ohlone people, advised me on a painting reconstructing the bay marshes. He emphasized that an updated version of aboriginal life would show that the Indians burned the grasslands, the marshes, "they burned everything." I got the distinct impression that to him, no more beautiful scene could be painted than an orange blaze engulfing a tidal marsh edge centuries ago.

Native people used burning as a tool in rabbit drives, to flush deer, to increase the number and quality of basketry plants, to clear the ground under oaks and pines, to encourage new growth of grasses and forbs for food, to keep wildfires from damaging villages, and to create the varied mosaic of habitats that favor game animals.[4]

Fires favor herbaceous plants over woody ones, and so repeated marsh fires in the past probably got rid of a lot of trees. The only exception to this rule would be willow (an important basketry plant in much of California), which will increase after a fire and stump-sprout readily. Fires also stimulate plant productivity, releasing minerals into the soil; burns encourage the growth of marsh plants, their size, and their seed production, especially three to five years after a fire; after that, productivity diminishes as old, dead matter builds up again.[5]

In a surface fire, only above-ground or above-water vegetation burns, leaving the roots and rhizomes intact. Marsh plants like common spikerush and common reed are fire-adapted: the top of the plant may be killed but it will resprout from its underground rhizomes. The rhizomes of threesquare are buried six inches deep and so are well protected from fire—it starts to regrow a week after a burn.

During long droughts, a second type of fire burns through the marsh, a "peat fire," in which the substrate is so dry that the burn reaches the deep root layer and accumulates organic mat. These root fires can reduce productivity, change the composition of plant species, and even make way for open water within the marsh. Open water spots create habitat for fish, as well as places for geese and ducks to feed and rest in. Dense climax stands of marsh vegetation are removed in spots, allowing colonizers like ditch-grass and goosefoot—valuable bird foods—to come in. The marsh is renewed.

In southern California, the areas of marshy vegetation with small spring-fed lakes scattered about the Los Angeles and San Gabriel plains were called cienegas ("hundred waters") in the Spanish period. Other cienegas were created from the seasonal overflow of rivers.[6] Rushes, spikerushes, sedges, and creeping wildrye and other grasses grew around these waterholes, grading into surrounding meadows. O. K. Davies at the University of Arizona studied pollen cores from several of these habitats and found a similar pattern of change had taken place at all of them following European settlement: a drastic decrease in fire frequency that allowed willows and cottonwoods to invade the wetlands. Frequent burning prior to European arrival had kept the marshes open and herb-dominated.[7]

Fire probably benefited western toads, opening up shallow pools that otherwise would be matted with old vegetation, thus renewing the wetlands the toads needed for breeding. Toad populations may actually be declining due to fire exclusion in the northern Rocky Mountain wetlands, according to a USGS study initiated by Blake Hossack and P. S. Corn.[8]

A Miwok man burns a bay tidal marsh. Oil on cotton rag paper, 4 ½ x 6 inches, 2005

Grassfire

Ethnobotanist M. Kat Anderson, in her wonderfully detailed book *Tending the Wild*, makes the point that early California was a cultural landscape, not the so-called wilderness found in so many European descriptions. Burning, digging, transplanting, clipping, and other small-scale disturbances helped shape the California we inherited.[9] So regular and common was fire in the grasslands, mostly from Indian land management, that ecologist James Barry called these communities "pyric" (of, related to, or a result of burning).[10] Interior grasslands may have burned every one to about five years, according to botanists.[11]

Like the marsh fires, the burns in the grasslands were often the subject of Spanish explorers' accounts. Father Crespí's party camped near a village on the coast just north of Santa Barbara in August 1769, and he recorded that the place was "well covered with very fine grasses that nearly everywhere had been burnt off by the heathens."[12]

The governor of California from 1774 to 1777, Fernando Rivera y Moncada, wrote that between San Gabriel and the Santa Clara River on the broad plains there was no fodder for the horses and mules because of the "great fires of the Gentiles [unbaptized Indians], who burn the fields as soon as they gather up the seeds." He said that burning "is universal although on some occasions it happens that it may be greater or less, according to the winds or calm."[13] Another Spanish governor, José Joaquín de Arrillaga, issued a proclamation about burning and urged the missionaries to warn the "Christian Indians, and particularly the old women" not to set fire to the pastures.[14]

The Kumeyaay and Cahuilla of inland southern California burned grasslands from summer into fall. In what sounds like a carefully planned rotational burn, the Kumeyaay torched some of the coastal sage scrub and chaparral slopes every five to ten or fifteen years but left others for twenty to thirty years, to keep some sage available.[15] In the north, the Wintu caught grasshoppers for food by burning patches of grassland.[16] The Pomo women of Ukiah Valley set fire to the grasslands after collecting seeds for pinole: "The grass was burned every year. The fires were started and allowed to burn in every place. Burning was to make the weeds grow better and to keep down the brush."[17] Sometimes the seeds of mules ears and clarkias were sown into recent burns.[18] Like the native people in Australia, where the term was coined, Californians practiced a form of "fire-stick farming," using patch-burning techniques instead of the plow to stimulate edible plant growth.

Visit Point Pinole Regional Shoreline, by the San Francisco Bay, to explore a good native grassland relict that has been regularly control-burned for decades. The purple needlegrasses, California oatgrasses, and swards of creeping wildrye are lush and dense and attest to the power of fire to renew the land.

Cactus was common on the grasslands of old southern California, giving them a southwestern character. Large, low-growing thickets of prickly pear grew on grassy plains and foothills. Chollas also mixed into the grass and shrubland communities, increasing in abundance around San

Fire sweeps through dry bunchgrass.
Coast live oaks line the distance.
Alkyd on panel, 13 ½ x 30 inches, 1998

Diego and southward. J. M. Bigelow, botanist on the Whipple expedition in 1852 to 1854, described "immense patches as large as half an acre" east of Los Angeles in the valley of what is now Rancho Cucamonga, in western San Bernardino County.[19] The cactus "swarms" often grew on canyon mouths, where they received floodwater outwash, as well as on the drier shallow soils of plains and south-facing slopes. Grassfires apparently played a large role in the adaptations of these cacti. Fires sweeping through the grass killed the small ones outright, but larger cacti were able to resprout from underground roots or lone pads that survived the burn. Frequent grassfires caused the prickly pears to form large, sprawling, clonal plants, dense patches which, aided by seed-eating rodents living among the spiny pads, eventually excluded grasses within their thickets. These "nopaleras" were fire-resistant, their piles of joints protecting the interior of the patch, and their edges grew vigorously outwards after each grassfire.[20]

Grassland or Shrubland? A Moving Boundary

While hiking in Wildcat Canyon Regional Park I often see grassy hillslopes thick with dark-green coyote brush patches where cattle are fenced out, while the grazed pastures are largely free of it. Old photos of the park from 1935 and 1965 show that the amount of brush on the ungrazed ridges and valleys has increased. One August I watched several cows munch on the green leaves of coyote brush, jerking at the twigs, muzzling the bushes, and sometimes rubbing their heads on them, creating stunted forms. University of California range managers Joe McBride and Harold Heady have confirmed that coyote brush seedlings are sensitive to grazing by cattle and rodents, trampling, and fire.

In the past wildfire kept brush thickets from invading the open grasslands of the East Bay hills, but early park policy eliminated burning and, in places, large-mammal grazing.[21] The results are there to see for anyone who walks along a barbed wire fence separating grazed grasslands from protected grasslands.

Down south, similar stories can be told: grazing, flood, and fire kept the boundary between shrub and grassland on the move. Green-gray, silvery, and russet masses of low aromatic shrubs clothed the hills and mesas south of Santa Barbara County. California sagebrush, sages, silver lupine, brittlebushes, bush buckwheat, and deerweed were low in stature and often went dormant during the summer dry season, losing their leaves. Evergreens such as lemonadeberry, sugar bush, Whipple yucca, and various cacti mixed in the pungent community.

In some years torrential rains in the mountains let loose massive flash floods down the dry washes and river channels, often overtopping their banks to spread out onto alluvial fans and lowlands. These disturbances created new habitats, such as open matchweed communities on the arid, stony fans. Alluvial scrub types such as blue elderberry, scale-broom, and cottonthorn often grew on dry washes. Early botanists described white sage as very common on dry plains toward the foothills, again probably in a fluctuating grass-shrub boundary depending on disturbance from fire and floods. Elsewhere the San Gabriel Valley was said to be "pure llano"—prairie—with groves of oaks.[22]

On dry, rocky, steep sites, on river bluffs, on beach dunes, and on hillslopes, patches of low scrubland mixed with grassland. Whether it was more widespread on hills and plains in the past has been a topic of debate, as the complex interactions of wildfire, climate, grazing, and competition with introduced annual grasses are difficult to tease apart, as is usual for California's changing habitats. Repeat aerial photogarphs around Riverside have shown a decrease in many coastal sage shrubs in the last sixty years, yet around San Diego coastal sage scrub has apparently taken over many historic grasslands.

The fast-changing coastal sage scrub boundary illuminates the varied processes that ecologists must address in trying to reconstruct precontact communities. Let us take a closer look at some of the causes and effects of change. Has long-term climate change been a factor? Probably— paleobotanist Daniel Axelrod theorizes that south coastal scrub species expanded in their distribution during the arid Xerothermic interval eight thousand to four thousand years ago, as semidesert and desert plants moved coastward.[23] With global warming we may see the most arid-adapted shrubs, such as brittlebushes, return to dominance.

Smaller climatic cycles also affect the sage scrub. Whole stands of California sagebrush and sage have died off during multi-year droughts, although they recovered again during subsequent wet El Niños. Bush buckwheat and Whipple yucca, however, sometimes expand during droughts, according to the long-term observations of Don Mullally in the Los Angeles area.[24]

Did fire play a role? Most definitely. But how great a role is still debated. South coastal scrub species were mostly killed by fire, but quick to recolonize newly burned areas: sages from seed banks in the soil; and California sagebrush, bush buckwheat, and brittlebushes from small, wind-transported seeds drifting in. Some shrubs resprouted, especially closer to the coast, where moisture levels were higher. Fire intervals of less than three to ten years have apparently led to grass domination because the shrubs were not able to get established before the next burn.[25] Periods of ten to twenty-five years fire-free are needed for coastal sage scrub to mature.[26] So today's fire suppression policies may have led shrubs to increase over grassland in places.

But complicating the picture, coastal scrub has lost acreage to introduced annual grassland, which apparently differs from the open bunchgrassland and native wildflower fields typical of prehistoric southern California. The dense, crowded growth of European annual grasses outcompetes many coastal sage shrub seedlings for soil moisture, light, and nutrients.[27] The native forbs that in the past pioneered burns contain less hard silica in their leaves than do annual grasses such as red brome, and so may decompose more quickly, posing less of a repeat-fire danger than today's weedpatches.[28]

In old southern California the boundaries between wildflower/bunchgrassland and aromatic coastal sage scrub probably fluctuated continually, depending on drought and rainfall, the frequency of Indian burning and rare summer thunderstorms, soil type, and slope aspect. But restoration is even more complicated than this would indicate. As researchers have pointed out, waves of invading plants will tip the balance away from natives.[29] Simply protecting a piece of surviving coastal sage scrub from development will not necessarily save it, as it is not a stable community. A "dynamic one-way process of conversion" is taking place, they point out, due to the newly arrived waves of introduced bromes and mustards that have changed the face of the state.

Fire-Adapted Oaks

In the Tehachapi Mountains I came upon a recent accidental burn next to a highway. Hills of blue oak and gray pine had been swept by a fire, which singed the lower branches of the mature oaks; two or three saplings were already resprouting on their small, torched crowns. The gray pines, with their low, long-needled twigs, were scorched brown, apparently topkilled. On the open ground between oaks, which was blackened with burnt grass, I found many purple needlegrass bunches, some unburned, others burned down to their roots and already growing new, green blades. Most of the acorns I saw lying on the ground unharmed. Some tall, silvery milkvetches and low little mats of rattlesnake weed had greened up on the burn and were flowering. Plants responded quickly to the nutrients released by fire and the reduced competition on these fired grounds—amazingly, even at the end of the long dry season.

Four years later I went back to examine the scene and could not distinguish the old burn from the surrounding areas. Renewal was quick.

Indians regularly burned oak groves to make acorn gathering easier, increase green fodder for game animals such as deer, and encourage the growth of new straight shoots of hazelnut, sourberry, redbud, and buckbrush for basketry. They set individual plants on fire, or sometimes patches or large areas.

Keeping the oak groves "clean" by burning regularly probably removed pest insects, such as the California acorn weevil. The larvae of this weevil feed on acorns, then drop out of the trees to the leaf litter below to pupate in the soil. Burning woody debris, fallen bark, and layers of leaf litter may have kept their populations down.[30]

Near San Luis Obispo I walked through an oak woodland that had recently been charred. The formerly closed woodland was now an open forest of black trunks. But the coast live oak is very resistant to fire, and despite the destruction all around, small new green leaves were appearing on some twigs. Blackberry leaves had begun to unfurl along vines remaining on the barren ground. It was a scene of green specks in a charcoal world—new life was evident.

ILL NOT NECESSARILY SAVE IT, AS IT IS NOT A STABLE COMMUNITY.

Top: A blue oak savanna fully regrown from a burn. Purple needlegrass cloaks the ground, and large, gray deergrass bunches grow in a low, moist area. OIL ON COTTON RAG PAPER, 4 X 10 INCHES, 2003

Middle: Tongues of flame move across a dry blue oak landscape, burning slowly. OIL ON COTTON RAG PAPER, 4 ½ X 5 ¼ INCHES, 2003

Bottom: A month after a burn, the blue oaks look scorched but they are not dead. Late summer forbs such as milkvetch and dove weed grow in the newly opened ash. New leaves also appear on bunchgrasses. OIL ON COTTON RAG PAPER, 4 ½ X 10 INCHES, 2003

As I hiked among the oak hills and valleys, I had difficulty imagining the scene three hundred years ago. What we can know is that fire played a much more important role than it is allowed to do now. These charred landscapes were common in California, undoubtedly, for millions of years.

Fire Forest

Traveling up into the higher ranges of California, I was not surprised to see signs, in the emerald evergreen forests of the Sierra Nevada, of adaptation to fire. Foresters early in the twentieth century noticed that "The virgin forest is uneven-aged, or at best even-aged in small groups, and it is patchy and broken, hence it is fairly immune from extensive, devastating crown fires."[31] This was soon to change. The primeval forest was well adapted to fire, a different kind of fire than we are used to today.

John Muir watched a fire in a sequoia grove along the Kaweah River in the fall of 1875. It was coming upslope from the lower chaparral belt like an "ungovernable flood." But as it reached the old forest the flames calmed, "creeping and spreading beneath the trees." It left most of the thick, orange bark of the old giants alone, merely adding black scorch marks. Occasionally branches on the ground flared up into bonfires, and in other spots the flames managed to climb up young tree trunks and ignite the leaves with a roar. Sometimes fire crawled high up a giant sequoia and lit its top into a fiery lamp that burned for days.[32] But the forest as a whole was unharmed.

Here, from 1894, is Muir's description of the look of these Sierran forests:

> The giant pines, and firs, and Sequoias hold their arms open to the sunlight, rising
> above one another on the mountain benches....The inviting openness of the Sierra
> woods is one of their most distinguishing characteristics. The trees of all the species
> stand more or less apart in groves, or in small, irregular groups, enabling one to find
> a way nearly everywhere, along sunny colonnades and through openings that have a
> smooth, park-like surface, strewn with brown needles and burs.[33]

Forester George Sudworth in 1900 described a similar openness in the forests he had examined: "The single big trees, or groups of three to six, stand far apart, forming a characteristically open forest."[34]

Among the hundred-foot-tall giant ponderosa and sugar pines, spaced singly and in groups, were open areas of bare pine-needle duff, montane bunchgrasses such as western needlegrass, shrubs such as snowbrush and kit-kit-dizze, and on the east slope, bitterbrush. Small, moist meadows also interfingered with the forest groves in low spots. Some giant ponderosas reached 260 feet in height, with nine-foot diameters at their bases, and explorer John Frémont, crossing the Sierra, saw one titanic sugar pine with a ten-foot diameter.[35] The forest canopy was not continuous; it probably shaded only 50 percent of the ground.[36]

For untold millennia, low-intensity ground fires crackled through these "mixed coniferous forests" at intervals of two to thirty years, some apparently set by Native people and some caused by lightning. "These were creeping surface fires that licked a few feet up the sides of large trees, and then only briefly," says Thomas Bonnicksen, forest scientist at Texas A&M University.[37] George Sudworth found fire scars on the lower trunks of 50 to 75 percent of the trees and concluded that "the fires of the present time [1900] are peculiarly of a surface nature, and with rare exception there is no reason to believe that any other type of fire has occurred here."[38]

FIRE-RESISTANT BARK

FREQUENT REGULAR GROUND FIRES

PONDEROSA PINE

SUGAR PINE

LESS FIRE-RESISTANT BARK

FREQUENT BUT MORE VARIABLE GROUND FIRES

DOUG FIR

WHITE FIR

INCENSE CEDAR

FIRE-SENSITIVE BARK

LESS FREQUENT FIRES, FIRE INTENSITY MORE VARIABLE

(AFTER SKINNER 1996)

Precontact Sierran burn regime in the mixed coniferous forest

Keeping the Forest "Fruitful"

Mormon militiaman Henry Bigler, in August 1848 on the West Fork of the Carson River in Alpine County, reported that "The mountains seem to be all on fire and the valley full of smoke. At night we could see as it were a hundred fires in the California mountains made no doubt by Indians."[39]

In the Yosemite Valley, archaeological remains suggest Native Americans resided there permanently at about A.D. 1200, and they may have begun a burning regime. Before this, people visited the valley seasonally to hunt and gather, but now an intensive acorn economy developed. In 1865 H. W. Baxley observed that "a fire-glow in the distance, and then the wavy line of burning grass, gave notice that Indians were in the valley clearing the ground, the more readily to obtain their winter supply of acorns and wild sweet potato root—'huckhau.'"[40] Joaquin Miller described elderly Native women in the spring looking about for the "little dry spots of headland and sunny valley, and as fast as dry spots appeared, they would be burned." Miller noted that this kept the forest "fruitful" and open.[41]

Indian-set fires were most common in lower west-slope and eastside forests. Ron Goode, a North Fork Mono man, told ethnobotanist M. Kat Anderson in 1989 that he recalled people setting fires in a particular area in a five-to-ten-year rotation, from 1,500 to 6,000 feet elevation in the San Joaquin River drainage. In other areas people lit fires annually or every two years when they saw that the brush was getting too high in the forest along their travel routes. "They'd burn areas when they would see it's in need," said a Mono woman.[42]

Visiting Yosemite Valley in June 1860, William Brewer described a green and grassy plain dotted with trees, the Merced River winding through, a product of Indian fire management and the climate of the time.[43] But resurveying the meadows in Yosemite National Park from 1864 to 1943 showed that invading conifers had reduced meadowlands from 745 acres to 327 in about eighty years, most probably because of the lack of periodic Indian burning.[44]

Lightning Strikes

Lightning from summer and fall thunderstorms sets many of the high-country fires that burn through forests and meadows. In Yosemite National Park alone, over a period of thirty years in the late twentieth century, lightning started an average of fifty-five wildland fires each year. In some years, tens of thousand of acres burned, in other years only a few acres; on average an estimated sixteen thousand acres per year burned naturally.[45] In August 1987 a single storm threw more than fifteen hundred lightning strikes in the Sierra foothills above Visalia and the conifer forests near Fresno and Merced, causing 325 wildfires.[46]

Examining the impact of lightning fires in the past, researchers have determined that drier, open ponderosa forests burned often, every two to fourteen years. (Reconstructions based on fire scar studies vary widely, so these ranges are only estimates.) To escape the next fire, ponderosa seedlings shot up into pole-sized saplings quickly (in tree terms)—in fourteen years, on good sites. Flames seared their lower branches off, giving them fuel-free trunks. But the less fire-resistant white fir and Douglas fir seedlings were killed by passing fire.

Higher mixed conifer forest may have burned about every ten to twenty years. Fire intervals in giant sequoia groves ranged from three to sixty years, most commonly every three to eight years. Fires in the more arid eastside Jeffrey pine forests may have been less common, perhaps every sixty years, and on steep, moist, cool, north-facing slopes dominated by white fir, the fire interval may have ranged from sixteen to eighty years.[47]

The periodic presence of fire in the forests created uneven-aged mosaics in open, parklike stands. There were mixes of young saplings and huge old-growth trees, as well as old standing dead snags that made superb habitat for owls, woodpeckers, and bats. Dominance shifted through time between the major tree species. Ponderosa pines and California black oaks were favored when frequent low-intensity ground fires opened up the forest (their seedlings needed sunlight to grow), while white fir and incense cedar were fire-sensitive, with thin bark, and they required more shade.[48] Less frequent, more variable fires favored a mix of white fir, incense cedar, Douglas fir, and sugar pine.[49]

The old-growth patches of large trees produced more cones that chickaree squirrels ate, and more prey for goshawks, which favor these large trees and old forests. California spotted owls also need large tree patches, and black-backed woodpeckers depend on freshly killed fire snags.

Deer and elk roamed about searching for the latest succulent regrowth on burns—their populations rose for ten or twenty years on a fire-patch, then declined as the animals moved on when the vegetation grew older.[50] Mule deer on the west slope preferred to nibble on the newer growth of such shrubs as deerbrush, while on the eastside they took the new leader twigs of bitterbrush—both plants become old and less palatable without the regenerating effect of fire. In the 1950s, as more shrubs displaced young conifers, people began to notice that deer populations were lower.[51]

Climate Change in the Forest

Fire scars within the tree-ring samples of sequoias illustrate how fire frequency fluctuated with climate change in the past. From A.D. 500 to 800, there were thirteen to twenty-nine fires per century in the sequoia groves. This increased, in A.D. 800 to 1300, to twenty-seven to forty-six fires per century. This latter period marked an extended drought punctuated by a very wet period.[52] The extreme droughts that broke out in the mid-1200s lasted several decades, part of the Medieval Warm Period. A decrease in fire occurred after this, in conjunction with the Little Ice Age, although restricted tree-ring growth indicates that several more extreme droughts took place in the 1500s.[53] After about 1860 fires suddenly became far less frequent, as Native American burning decreased and American fire suppression policies took hold.

Pollen, leaf fossils, and charcoal from Woski Pond, in Yosemite Valley, show that from 1,550 to 650 years ago, the valley had a forest of ponderosa pine, Douglas fir, incense cedar, and some white fir. Lodgepole pine and mountain hemlock, which do not grow in the valley today, were also found. Meadows blanketed nearby areas. Charcoal indicates there were regular fires. Pollen indicates that at A.D. 1300, the start of the Medieval Warm Period, there was a shift to a more open mix of ponderosa pine, incense cedar, and California black oak, with increased shrubs. A temporary jump in charcoal levels accompanies the pollen change, indicating that a large fire disturbance swept through the area, reducing the conifers. After the wetter climate took over during the Little Ice Age, moisture-loving Douglas fir and incense cedar increased, and charcoal levels decreased.[54]

Above the mixed conifer forests, one finds red fir and lodgepole pine. The repeat photographs of George Gruell show more gaps and clearings among the red firs and lodgepole pines in the late 1800s than now.[55] The boundary between the two forest types must have constantly and slowly shifted in a mosaic of patches, due to influences from fire and climate change. Moister climate phases and low-intensity ground fires favored red firs, while drier times and the occasional hot crown fire favored lodgepoles, as high-intensity burns opened up new areas for the pines to colonize.

Geographer Thomas Vale and writer Geraldine Vale deduced from repeat photographs of the Yosemite high country that over the last century a huge invasion of lodgepole pines has taken place in open places like Tuolumne Meadows and Dana Meadows. Photo pairs also show that the lodgepole forest itself has increased in density.[56] Gruell believes that fire is the single most important factor in the changes.[57]

John Muir in 1894 described creeping ground fires burning for weeks in strips across the lodgepole forest, killing the thin-barked trees. Strong winds sometimes drove the flames into the crowns, "forming one continuous belt of roaring fire that goes surging and racing onward above the bending woods, like the grass-fires of a prairie."[58] Fires in these subalpine forests were "stand-replacing," that is, they killed the forest outright, unlike in the lower pine forest regime. Even though lodgepoles are fire-sensitive, the gaps in the forest allowed them to regenerate quickly by seeds, which sprouted within a year. Lodgepole stands were often a patchwork of different ages, each associated with a specific fire event.

I watched a lightning-caused fire burn slowly through a red fir–lodgepole pine forest in Yosemite's high country. The park staff let the fire burn while keeping crews nearby to monitor it. At a distance, I saw a small, white plume of smoke emerge from the dark forest. Upon closer inspection I saw only a low line of flickering orange tongues creeping along the fir-needle floor, crackling and popping as it hit a resin-filled cone or fallen twig, breathing out blue smoke among the trunks. The fire blackened some lower bark but did not climb the trees—the forest looked well. I

TUOLUMNE MEADOWS : INVASION BY
LODGEPOLE PINES.   AUGUST 18, 2003.

have seen many living red fir forests with blackened trunks and lush green carpets of newly grown bracken ferns under them, sprung up after a fire.

Because vegetation lags behind climate change, the condition of the forest at any given point in time is a legacy of the preceding decades or centuries. During low fire-frequency periods more fuels accumulate, producing more widespread and intense burns; this in turn tends to homogenize the vegetation pattern. Fuels and vegetation became patchy during high fire-frequency phases. This matches Richard Minnich's findings for chaparral. In the sequoia groves, researchers realized that through time, fire frequencies and sizes constantly change—there exists no steady-state, no "normal" scene. Change is paramount in the forest ecosystem in what ecologists called a "nonequilibrium" condition.[59] Fire in the forest, as elsewhere in California, has been called a "keystone process," a part of nature that deeply affects every living thing.[60]

Chaparral: Burning Like a Torch of Fat

Local naturalists had taught me long ago about the "hard chaparral": dense thickets of woody growth more difficult to move through than the soft sage scrub, unless of course you followed an old grizzly trail. They had said that chaparral was prone to fire, and now I realized the emphatic truth of this as I watched quick yellow tongues crackling upward, dry branches exploding with sizzling sap, flames roaring, and gray ashy smoke billowing skyward, building cloud columns and carrying the smell of charcoal on hot winds. Swirls of sparks jumped the fire ahead.

Wildfires like the one I was witnessing have occurred regularly in California's brushlands for hundreds of thousands of years, as charcoal deposits in ancient sediments show, yet investigations into the secrets of fire ecology have proceeded slowly and have led to great controversy.

Pedro Fages, during his journey up California during 1769 and 1770, noticed Indians making a sort of native sugar from the fruit of "a very leafy, tufted shrub six feet high with a stem of reddish color and leaves like those of the mangrove." The ripe fruit was gathered and its pulp separated, pressed into cakes, and dried.[61] This was manzanita, a shapely, colorful, and varied shrub typical of the chaparral. What Spanish explorers often called "romero," or rosemary, may have been chamise, with its diminutive linear leaves. Their word "chamiso" meant "thicket."

William Brewer complained about the difficulty of traveling through chaparral on his explorations to see the different parts of California in 1860 and 1861. Ascending the Santa Ana Mountains he encountered very dense chaparral that tore his pants into ribbons. He followed deer trails to avoid the hard shrubs and saw the tracks of many deer, wildcats, and coyotes. The chaparral was so dense on the higher granitic crags that it had to be chopped with a hatchet. Near San Luis Obispo he finally bought buckskins and smoked them to harden them against the branches and rattlesnakes, creating a pair of the "chaps" that vaqueros used when riding through dense, brushy country.

Fire-adapted shrubs such as chamise seem to invite burning on a regular basis: their dead branches (called "dead aerial fuels"), resinous leaves, and highly flammable overlapping canopy of dense twigs "burn like a torch of fat," as observer Francis Furtz said in 1923.

Many of the chaparral shrubs, herbs, and grasses have special adaptations to the process of wildfire, and indeed, the whole community shows a regular succession as different groups of plants fill changing niches of soil quality and shade. The spectacular herbland phase often dominates the first wet season after a fire, springing from seeds waiting in the duff layer. There are so-called "pyrophyte endemics," fire followers, that can be found only on burn sites. The fire poppy is abundant in the first year after a fire and usually disappears in the second year. Wild cucumbers are sometimes the first to sprout on the blackened ground, growing during the winter to drape across the skeletons of shrubs. Wildflower displays start in March and different species appear in waves, one group growing and

Fire poppy in fresh ash, chamise resprouting. OIL ON COTTON RAG PAPER, 4 X 7 ½ INCHES, 2004

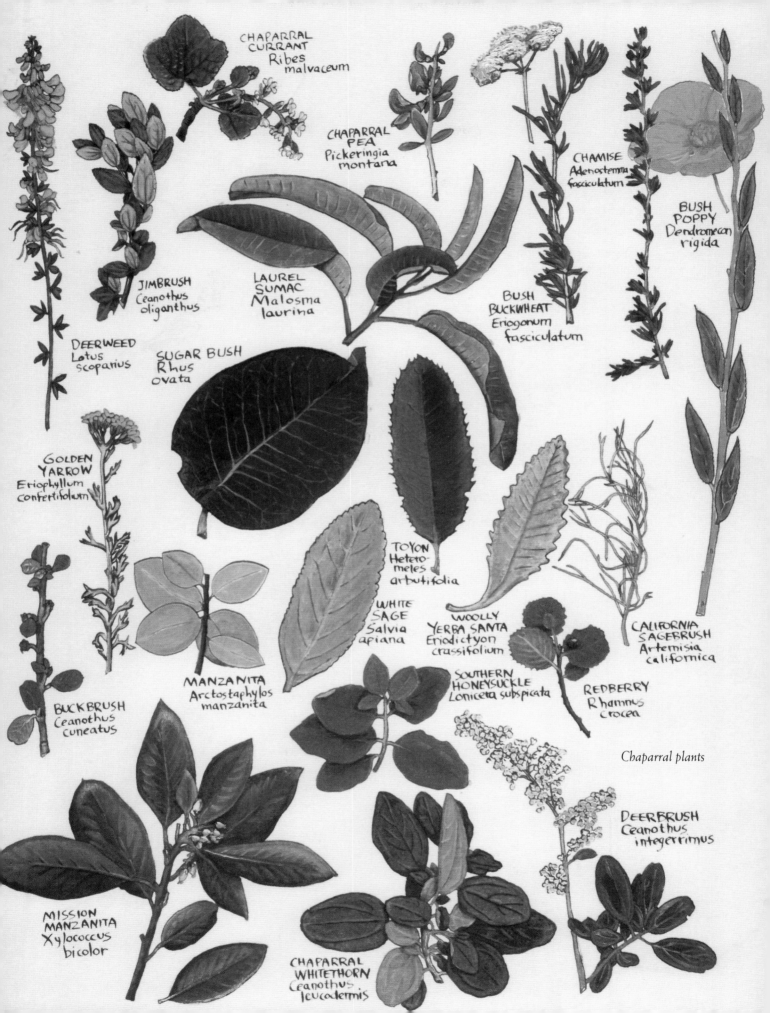

CHAPARRAL
CURRANT
Ribes
malvaceum

CHAPARRAL
PEA
Pickeringia
montana

CHAMISE
Adenostema
fasciculatum

BUSH
POPPY
Dendromecon
rigida

JIMBRUSH
Ceanothus
oliganthus

LAUREL
SUMAC
Malosma
laurina

BUSH
BUCKWHEAT
Eriogonum
fasciculatum

DEERWEED
Lotus
scoparius

SUGAR BUSH
Rhus
ovata

GOLDEN
YARROW
Eriophyllum
confertifolium

TOYON
Hetero-
meles
arbutifolia

WHITE
SAGE
Salvia
apiana

WOOLLY
YERBA SANTA
Eriodictyon
crassifolium

CALIFORNIA
SAGEBRUSH
Artemisia
californica

BUCKBRUSH
Ceanothus
cuneatus

MANZANITA
Arctostaphylos
manzanita

SOUTHERN
HONEYSUCKLE
Lonicera subspicata

REDBERRY
Rhamnus
crocea

Chaparral plants

MISSION
MANZANITA
Xylococcus
bicolor

CHAPARRAL
WHITETHORN
Ceanothus
leucodermis

DEERBRUSH
Ceanothus
integerrimus

peaking, then another, late into summer. The wildflowers decline after a few years as the shrubs take over, remaining in small numbers in openings in mature chaparral or in the seed bank of the soil.[62]

Next come short-lived pioneer shrubs, often with nitrogen-fixing roots that help restore lost nutrients to the soil. They can be abundant on burns: deerweed, chaparral whitethorn, wavyleaf ceanothus, yerba santa, golden yarrow, and rush-rose. In other areas, bush poppy pioneers new burns, its seedlings becoming dominant and then declining as other shrubs, such as bigpod ceanothus, grow large.[63] After seven to nine years the original chaparral overstory begins to develop.

Gradually the pre-burn shrubs regain their dominance, about half of the species from seed and half resprouting from roots. Scrub oaks, manzanitas, and some ceanothus species, such as chaparral whitethorn and greenbark ceanothus, develop a woody platform at ground level as wide as twelve feet. After each fire, the platform sends out sprouts at its periphery, putting on further growth—these root burls can reach two hundred and fifty years of age or more and apparently store reserves of water and nutrients for fast growth during the summer. Chamise can also sprout from such a lignotuber. Other shrubs have deep taproots.

Plants that are obligate seeders—will not resprout after a fire and depend on seeds for regeneration—include many ceanothus (*Ceanothus crassifolius, C. cuneatus, C. greggii, C. megacarpus, C. oliganthus, C. papillosus, C. parryi, C. thyrsiflorus*), several manzanitas (*Arctostaphylos canescens, A. glauca, A. manzanita, A. mariposa, A. nevadensis, A. obispoensis, A. parryana, A. pilosula, A. pungens, A. stanfordiana,* and *A. viscida*), California juniper, and saw-toothed goldenbush. Chaparral seeders often have special requirements for germination and will lie dormant for long periods. Chamise produces two kinds of seeds, those that germinate readily, and those that germinate after exposure to high temperature—exposure to 280 to 300 degrees Fahrenheit for only five minutes induces germination.[64] The temperatures in burning leaf litter during a fire reach 1,000 degrees, but soils one and a half inches deep reach only 300 degrees. A passing wildfire opens up the closed canopy and can produce a flush of chamise seedlings as dense as three thousand in one square meter.

Ecologists have also found that certain seeds depend on chemicals leached from charred wood to penetrate through their seed coats with the winter rains and stimulate sprouting. Whispering bells, many *Phacelia* species, yerba santa, and *Penstemon spectabilis* have this response.[65]

Smoke, too, stimulates many wildflowers to grow after a burn. I have seen hundreds of acres of wild tobacco spring up after burns in the Great Basin. The seeds of native tobaccos may have a permeable membrane that allows smoke to penetrate directly. Thus, slow, smoldering fires under moister conditions bring out a whole set of fire annuals that a hot, fast blaze would not.[66]

Whole communities of dormant seeds lie in the soil awaiting a fire to wake them; a chaparral hillside in any one year may hide several layers of time-released plant communities. (For more information on chaparral and fire, visit the website of the California Chaparral Institute, offering "accurate information about California's most extensive ecosystem" at www.californiachaparral.org.)

Fire Suppression and Forest Fires

As early as the late nineteenth century, chaparral was often cleared around urban areas. In 1872 a state law was enacted forbidding fires on state or federal lands but it was rarely enforced. In 1905, in an attempt to regulate burning by ranchers, the government initiated a permit process. By 1930 the state Board of Forestry had decided the best policy would be to suppress fires in chamise lands, to keep them for recreation (hunting) and watershed use. The board adopted a strict fire suppression policy on timber and watershed lands, state parks, and monuments.[67] Notwithstanding attempts at regulation, sheep and cattle ranchers in the northern counties—Sonoma, Mendocino, Colusa, Tehama, and Shasta—practiced "broadcast" burning into the 1930s and 1940s, torching brush on their rangelands to increase forage temporarily for their stock. No controls were attempted except around buildings, and the fires often spread. Range manager Arthur Sampson thought that most of the ninety-six thousand acres of chaparral he surveyed had burned at one time or another under this practice, in some ways continuing the former fire regime used by Native people.[68]

In regard to the forests, the turn of the century saw heated discussions about fire, as economics drove management. Foresters knew about the old fire regime but did not like it. An early-twentieth-century federal forester disdainfully described Indian burning as "Ancient notions of 'Piute forestry' whose deep fire-scars remain upon so many of our giant landmark pines and sequoias."[69] He disparaged this "unscientific" old way of setting "light surface fires" aimed at "producing a smooth forest floor." Unwittingly, the new crop of forest managers held the key to managing fire in the forests in their hands but they arrogantly threw it away:

> The Forest Service is solidly opposed to every sort of "light burning" because they have seen it in practice many times, under all sorts of conditions; so are the foresters of all civilized nations....The underlying principles of all scientific forestry, however, are these: Save the young growth as well as the mature trees; protect the soil; encourage reproduction; fill up all possible gaps in the forest cover—do not make more by surface fires—fight all fires to a finish."[70]

In 1905 complete fire suppression became U.S. Forest Service policy.[71] This increased density of trees everywhere, and for the foresters the profits seemed to increase as well, for a time. White fir density tripled in many areas and the trees invaded open areas. Meanwhile, leaf litter levels built up and "ladder fuels" developed—old twiggy matter along tree trunks—that would allow fires to climb from the ground into the treetops.[72]

Wildlife biologist George Gruell's collected and rephotographed images of the Sierra, past and present, dramatically show the changes: in the 1800s ponderosa habitats at lower elevations were open, with only herbs, patchy shrubs such as manzanita, and live oaks and black oaks in the understory. The pines grew in groves with many gaps. Shrubs were prone to stick to rocky areas. Logging began with the gold rush in 1848 to supply wood for mining operations, and mills were opened beginning in 1855. First the high-grade sugar and ponderosa pines were cut, further tipping

1859

1977
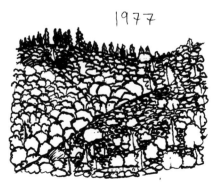

Oak and chaparral increase in pine forest, Spanish Bar Mountain, Middle Fork of American River, 600 ft. elevation. Drawn from repeat photography studies in George Gruell's Fire in Sierra Nevada Forests

the balance towards white firs, which were logged later.[73] A century later, the once open vistas had become blocked by a dense growth of chaparral, oaks, and young second-growth conifers. Higher up, the pines, incense cedars, and Douglas firs had similarly closed in.[74]

Surrounded by saplings that sucked up water, the old trees became increasingly stressed and, as a result, more susceptible to attacks by bark beetles and other insects during droughts. A record amount of beetle infestation was reported in 2004 in ponderosas in the Sierra and southern California mountains (and indeed throughout the West), due to the lack of fires that had normally cleaned the forests and kept beetle numbers lower. UC Berkeley forest ecologist Scott Stephens compared the forests on either side of the California-Mexico border, in the San Bernardino Mountains and the Sierra San Pedro Martir, in recent years. On the California side, there were about three hundred trees per acre; on the Baja side, where ground fires continue to burn, only sixty trees per acre were found. The trees in Mexico remained healthy, even during the drought, because there was less competition for water. In contrast, tree mortality in the San Bernardino National Forest was the highest seen in a century, according to Stephens, who called it "absolutely stunning."[75]

Giant sequoias nearly ceased reproducing, as they needed fire to release seeds from the cones, expose ashy mineral soils, and open gaps in the forest for the seeds to germinate in. The best results came when the fire was hot and flashy, burning a pile of downed branches or a fallen log—clusters of sequoia seedlings would be found on these spots. But now the small cones hung on the trees for years, waiting for the heat of a fire passing below to open the cone scales and release a seed rain as great as eight million per acre.[76]

As fire intervals lengthened (they are now one hundred to three hundred years), fuels built up and the intensity of fires increased; more stand-destroying crown fires occurred. Before fire suppression became standard, surface fuels of pine needles, fallen branches, and small shrubs amounted to fewer than ten tons per acre; today they are forty to fifty tons per acre.[77] Severe, hot crown fires now ravage the Sierra. I remember seeing the Fountain Fire in 1992 as I drove over Highway 120, a gigantic cloud of smoke billowing upwards like a nuclear explosion in the clear blue sky.

Fire ecologists point out that today's fast-moving, catastrophic forest fires are associated with vegetation characteristics that may be outside the natural range of variability: the homogeneous forests that now spring up (or are planted, more usually) were probably very rare before the twentieth century.[78]

Fire suppression does not seem to be working. In 2002 firefighters contained 99 percent of U.S. wildfires before they got out of control, yet in terms of acreage burned, that was the second worst season on record: 7.2 million acres flamed to charcoal.[79] (In 2000, 7.3 million acres had burned.) In the western U.S. in the last twenty years a new phenomenon has erupted: "megafires," wildfires well over forty thousand and even to one hundred thousand acres. Fast, intense, incredibly high flames shoot into the air, so energetic and devastating that firefighters often cannot get close enough to fight them. Since the year 2000 Colorado and Utah have seen the largest wildfires in their recorded histories. The incredible heat creates a "hydrophobic" soil which blocks water penetration, creating conditions that these ecosystems have not seen before.[80]

UC Berkeley forestry professor Harold Biswell suggested in the 1940s that small controlled burns would remove the built-up fuels in forests, restore them to health, and lessen the danger of conflagrations. His economically minded colleagues thought this talk was insane at the time, and the dean of the School of Forestry tried to have him fired, unsuccessfully.[81]

A CLOGGED THICKET OF WHITE FIR AND
INCENSE CEDAR AFTER DECADES OF FIRE
SUPPRESSION. LEAF LITTER AND TWIG BUILD-UP
IS THICK. "LADDERS" OF DEAD BRANCHES
ARE LOW ON TRUNKS. THE CANOPY IS
NEARLY CLOSED. YOSEMITE NATIONAL PARK
HAS BEEN AT WORK CUTTING SMALL TREES
AND GATHERING THEM IN SLASH PILES.

A DEVASTATING CROWN FIRE FROM
TOO MUCH FUEL BUILD-UP AND AN
ALTERED FIRE REGIME THAT FAVORS
INFREQUENT SEVERE FIRES.
— WHITE FIR, SUGAR PINE WILL REGROW
FROM SEED. SNOWBRUSH NOW
DOMINATES.

Not until the 1960s did government agencies reconsider allowing some wildfire to occur, to help forest health. The National Park Service took the lead, admitting that fire suppression had "led to a disruption of ecological processes."[82] Along roads and near communities, workers at Yosemite National Park began using chainsaws to thin the brush and small trees that were clogging the mixed conifer forest, place the debris in brush piles, and burn them in the cold season. Prescribed fires were later set to restore the forests. And lightning fires were carefully allowed to burn in certain parts of the high country. All this work continues.[83] Using fire alone as a tool, forest researchers believe that the mixed conifer forest can be restored, perhaps within two hundred years.

Fire Suppression in the Lowlands and Foothills

Today, with fire suppression policies in effect, grasslands may burn only once every twenty or thirty years or longer.[84] The increased thatch of dead, dry plant matter that shades the soil after years without fire can impede native forb germination, reducing the spectacular wildflower shows that California has been famous for. When a fire does scorch through a field that is dominated by introduced annual grasses and has not burned for a long time, the flames may be quite hot. Bunchgrass fires probably burned "cool" and the heat did not penetrate far below the soil. In fact, the disturbance adaptations of purple needlegrass may be related to frequent burning—seedlings have been found to grow well after a fire, especially in the second year.[85] But today's fires burn hot enough to damage or kill the deep roots of purple needlegrass if there is thatch accumulated around it. Other species also sprout seedlings after burns, including foothill needlegrass, squirreltail grass, lupines, clovers, milkvetches, and lotus.

I talked with biologist Leslie Backus about her research on Florida prairies. After conducting controlled burns on various plots, she looked at how the fires affected the little grasshopper sparrow. These birds need grass to build their nests in and do not thrive when shrubs invade their open grassland territories. On the burned ground, the grasses began growing back within weeks, and soon the sparrows set up their small, quarter-acre territories. The sparrows were most common on plots burned every three to five years. Shrubs invaded grasslands unburned for five to ten years, and grasshopper sparrow populations declined in density.

In the East Bay ridge grasslands, I found grasshopper sparrows singing their insectlike songs only in open grazed prairies free of invading coyote brush. The cattle here imitated a fire regime, reducing the fuel and eliminating shrub seedlings.

Among the oaks, decades without fire can have effects not immediately visible. Fire not only renews the oak landscapes, it also maintains a certain balance between old and young trees. In many cases the lack of regular burning may have shifted the live oak community structure from open to closed groves.

George Gruell's study of Sierra Nevada photographs showed an increase over time in the density of interior live oaks. In several places in the foothills in Mariposa County, photos from 1860 show a savanna of scattered interior live oaks, ponderosa pines, and gray pines, with chaparral shrubs growing as individuals or in patches. By 1993 the same spots had filled in with chaparral shrubs—manzanita, chamise, ceanothus, and toyon—and interior live oaks and gray pines had increased to form denser woodland on the hills. Similar photos from as early as 1858 in Placerville and photos from Amador, Placer, and Tuolumne Counties show changes in the 600 to 3,000 foot altitudinal zone. The early scenes show ponderosa pines relatively sparse and scattered in open live oak–gray pine savannas, and chaparral shrubs patchy and of small size. After a century or more, a remarkable

FIRE NOT ONLY RENEWS THE OAK LANDSCAP

increase in vegetation occurred, with young ponderosas more common and oak woodlands closing in. Fire suppression may be the single most important cause of this change, Gruell has said.[86]

UC Berkeley forest ecologist Scott Stephens is studying whether sudden oak death, a recent outbreak of disease spread from introduced garden shrubs in northern California, might be the result of decreased burning and lowered immunity to stress in the oak groves.[87]

The Great Chaparral Debate

The managers of California's national forests inherited a mosaic landscape that after 1900 became homogenized with suppression. Then large catastrophic fires broke out in the 1920s, and more in the 1950s. The Laguna/Boulder Fire of 1970 burned 190,000 acres. Three huge wildfires in San Diego County burned 284,000 acres in 2003.

Ironically, these record-breaking wildfires ripped through southern California while I was researching the topic of fire ecology—I emailed my friend Gale, a Cleveland National Forest biologist living in Julian at the time. She told me that her house had escaped the rush of wind and flame by a mere two miles, but the town was reduced to a pre-modern state: no electricity in most of the region meant no well pumps working, no gas stations operating, and only candlelight at night for days. Another friend who had collected some of my paintings lost them as his house, built deep in the chaparral east of San Diego, burned down. More than three quarters of the 2003 wildfires burned in chaparral. A few months before the 2003 firestorms, over half the scrubland in San Diego County was estimated to be over fifty years old—a ticking bomb.[88]

This devastating fire season in southern California illuminated the ongoing debate among fire ecologists about how to protect life and property along the wildland interface, which in turn has led to intense study of the past. That the chaparral evolved with fire is agreed, but how the fire regime operated, how it structured the landscape, and what human influences fed it are still open questions.

Heated by the 2003 disasters, many fire ecologists aligned themselves with one or the other of two differing views of the historic fire regimes of California chaparral, and of how to manage fire country based on those regimes. In the model formulated by Richard Minnich of the University of California at Riverside, the fire regime under current management is different than that in precontact times, and wildfires are basically fuel-driven. On the other hand, Jon Keeley of the United States Geological Survey has developed a model in which today's wildfire patterns are similar to those of the past, and wildfires are dominantly wind-driven. Each model has thorough scientific evidence to support it, contained in piles of research papers full of charts, maps, and eloquent discussions, but the evidence used is sometimes completely contradictory.

"Who is right?" I thought to myself as I read the papers, trying to decide how to paint a landscape of the past. "Which model is closer to the truth?" The debate illuminates the problems associated with the study of historical ecology and the difficulties of reconstructing the past, even with mountains of evidence.

Minnich found, when looking at vegetation maps and aerial photographs of the U.S.-Mexican borderlands, that Baja California had numerous small fires, while San Diego County had huge wildfires.[89] Most contemporary fires in Baja were under five thousand acres, and few were over ten thousand; compare that with the two hundred and eighty thousand acres of the Cedar Fire in San Diego County. Under the Minnich model, "protectionist management" has led to the unusually

ALSO MAINTAINS A CERTAIN BALANCE BETWEEN OLD AND YOUNG TREES.

PATTERN OF
BURNS IN CHAPARRAL
LANDS OVER TIME

(REDRAWN FROM
SAN DIEGO COUNTY
WILDLAND FIRE TASK
FORCE 2003 MAP)

U.S.
SAN
DIEGO
COUNTY

MEXICO
NORTHERN
BAJA

PACIFIC
OCEAN

large, intense fires southern California has experienced in recent years. Key to Minnich's argument is what he observed to be the behavior of fires when they meet previous burns—they "lay down" at the borders, especially if these previous burns are less than twenty years old. W. V. Mendenhall, the first supervisor of the Angeles National Forest, said many settlers found that "fires were not extensive due to the fact they ran into older burns and checked themselves."[90] In the 1890s watchers on Mt. Wilson noted fires slowly burning for two to three months. During the same time fires in the San Jacinto Mountains were described as "scattered throughout the reserve in small tracts."[91] Before fire suppression became prevalent north of the border in the twentieth century, Minnich believes, there was an ever changing mosaic of burns, age-classes, and stand structures.

This is the pattern found in northern Baja today, as if the Mexican state were a mirror of California's past. The Mexican government does not attempt quick suppression of wildfires, as they believe that having several medium-sized fires in one season will burn the fuel and prevent one great fire. The fires burn for months in remote areas and eventually burn themselves out. José Luis Rosas, executive coordinator for the Baja California Civil Protection Agency, told reporters, "Well, let it burn. What's the problem?"[92] (Because there is less development in these rural areas, there is less property loss than north of the border: in October 2003, medium-sized wildfires destroyed only ten houses in Baja, compared to nearly three thousand in southern California.) A great patchwork of recent burns prevents the buildup of tall, solid brush that can carry blazes the size of the Cedar Fire.

Minnich notes that recently burned chaparral will not carry fire for about five years; from six to twenty years it may burn during extreme fire weather. After that until fifty years without a fire, it will burn well under normal conditions. After fifty years, dead branches accumulate and can burn very hot, creating intense fires that can easily get out of control.[93] As stands age, their flammability increases due to accumulating biomass and dead plant matter; numerous small burns preclude larger conflagrations, owing to the fragmentation of fuels. Thus fires under this regime, Minnich says, are self-limiting and self-organizing.

In Minnich's view, weather compounds today's fuel-driven catastrophic fires. In Baja California most fires occur in summer, with weak winds around ten miles per hour and 20 to 40 percent humidity. But fire-quenching in San Diego County results in a dangerous buildup of fuels that, given the chance, will burst into flame, no longer quenchable, when the Santa Ana wind season starts in the fall. Humidity then can be as low as 4 percent and winds over thirty miles per hour—wildfires get out of control and spread over huge areas. Most Los Angeles news reports of fires in the late nineteenth century were in July and August, not during severe fall weather.[94]

Not all chaparral researchers agree with the Minnich model. Jon Keeley and C. J. Fotheringham question whether fuel accumulation is important at all with respect to wildfire, and in particular whether Santa Ana-driven fires will lie down at young fuel patches.[95] Noting that many fires will, when driven by strong enough winds, readily burn through young stands and not stop at their boundaries for lack of fuel, they believe fire to be weather-driven. Whereas Minnich argues that huge firefighting efforts have shifted larger fires to fall, when Santa Ana winds whip up unstoppable firestorms, Keeley counters that Santa Ana-driven fires have always taken place in southern California, and the destruction they cause is not an artifact of firefighting.

Reading Fire History in Charcoal and Pollen

We can only speculate about brush fire intervals before fire suppression became the policy in California. Based on stand age structure, they ranged from every 40 to 100 years.[96] In Baja they occur about every 70 years, longer toward the arid interior.[97] As to particular type of chaparral, Minnich and Hong Chou further estimate the fire return interval for chamise chaparral to be every 72 to 77 years, and for mixed chaparral of ceanothus, scrub oak, and chamise to be every 58 years.[98] In the dry interior desert-edge chaparral and pinyon associations, fires may have been rarer—every 291 years.

Some of the little information we have about fire frequency in precontact California comes from charcoal deposited in the Santa Barbara Channel. Cores from these ocean deposits contain charcoal in layers of sediment that reflect yearly winter influx. The charcoal appears at a continuous "background" level, punctuated by small increases and occasional large peaks, some of which correlate with large fires in the Los Padres ranges just east of Santa Barbara. Large peaks dating back to the sixteenth century have been interpreted as evidence of huge smoke plumes being driven offshore by autumn fire-winds from conflagrations in the mountains. I do not see how these cores can give such well-defined results. Could numerous small fires produce the same peaks? How can wind-deposited and flood-deposited charcoal be distinguished from each other?

Pollen researcher Roger Byrne and his colleagues, analyzing the same cores, have said this distinction cannot yet be made, and the distance that charcoal can be moved by ocean currents is poorly understood. The area that could collect charcoal is huge and includes locations other than the Los Padres ranges—the Channel Islands, for instance.

Byrne pointed out that the peaks of charcoal recorded in precontact time were in gray layers of the core, indicating what he called "major fire-flood events," apparently caused by high winter flood deposits and turbidity current deposits. I believe this could represent El Niño rain events during Little Ice Age extremes sweeping large amounts of terrestrial charcoal from numerous small summer fires into the ocean.

Left: Chamise regrowing after a few years.
Right: Lush foothill needlegrasses and twining morning glories amid chamise regrowth after a burn.
OIL ON COTTON RAG PAPER, 5 ½ X 4 INCHES EACH, 2004

Interestingly, the Byrne study reports, "Apart from the gray layers, the average influx value for the prehistoric period is somewhat lower than for the modern period....The implication is that total burning was greater during the period 1931–1970 than in the prehistoric period sampled."[99] In other words, there may have been more fuel in the scrublands during the twentieth-century fire-suppression era, causing larger fires.

Evidence like these charcoal deposits can open up some intriguing clues to the past, but overinterpretation is a danger. I would like to see similar cores from the sea bottom off northern Baja California analyzed before more conclusions are drawn from the Santa Barbara Channel studies.

Lightning and Chaparral Fires

In San Diego County, lightning strikes more often inland, along the mountain crests, than on the coast, and summer thunderstorms surging up from the tropical Gulf of California account for five to thirty lightning fires per year. Lightning fires occur with some regularity in parts of California not subject to a summer monsoon: Santa Cruz County had thirty-four lightning fires from 1893 to 1979.[100] Fire scars on trees in chaparral indicate a fire every fifty years or less in Pinnacles National

LIGHTNING IGNITIONS COMMON ON MOUNTAINS IN CHAPARRAL AND CONIFEROUS FOREST.

SPOT-BURNING BY PEOPLE IN MOUNTAINS.

TRIBAL FIRE MANAGEMENT COMMON ON LOWLANDS IN GRASS-OAK HABITATS.

BIG GAME HERDS ALSO SIGNIFICANT IN LOWLANDS, OPENING UP BRUSH AND BROWSING TREES.

MODEL OF FIRE ECOLOGY IN DIFFERING TOPOGRAPHY OF THE COAST RANGES.

Monument, and on Junipero Serra Peak, in Monterey County.[101] Interior northern California national forests, which have extensive chaparral, have some of the highest lightning fire numbers in the state.[102]

Keeley argues that before Indian burning, California scrublands must have had a fire regime similar to today's—fires were few and large.[103] Minnich holds to the opposite claim, that even infrequent lightning-ignited fires could be significant in chaparral ecology.[104] As Minnich has pointed out, lone oaks sticking up amidst chaparral can act as lightning rods. Most lightning fires occur in humid weather in summer storm and fog periods, but they can "store" for weeks in logs and snags, waiting for dry weather to kick them up. Old oaks can be found in southern California with broken branches, basal fire wounds, and heart rot from lightning strikes.[105] Even in a drenching thunderstorm, a lightning strike could cause a fire inside a rotten oak trunk that within hours or days could ignite surrounding grass and chaparral.

Minnich reconstructed fires that occurred on Mt. Wilson in the San Gabriel Mountains in the late 1800s, before suppression: one fire persisted for months through the long dry season of summer, erratically smoldering and storing for long periods in logs and snags in woodland edges, then "running" through dry shrublands. Embers flew long distances to start secondary blazes—"spotting." The fires often spread in a web of meandering strips, leaving numerous islands. None was apparently larger than about seventeen thousand acres.[106] This is the same behavior that he found in Baja today, where fires have been known to last two months.

In Mediterranean Europe, lightning accounts for 2 to 10 percent of fires in oak and scrubland.[107] Until recently, shepherds burned scrub, grass, and savanna areas every three to five years to clear underbrush and increase pasturage for their herds. Aerial photographs of Crete from World War II suggest big fires were less common when this "occupational burning" was more common than it is today.

The point may be made that although lightning fires are rare in much of lowland California, they may have occurred just enough to promote a regular fire rotation in remote, rugged mountain ranges. Indian burning would have accelerated this cycle in many areas.

Fires Set by People

Indian burning may have been crucial in decreasing shrublands and woodlands, and in keeping valleys and lower slopes open and grassy, interacting in complex ways with elk herds that grazed there. In the mountains, Native people burned selected plant patches and set fires during game drives. Occasionally these mountain spot-burns got away and may have flamed over large areas. For example, Maria Solares, a Yokuts-Chumash woman, told ethnologist John P. Harrington that "some of the Indians were burning chamiso one day near Mt. Pinos to hunt cottontails and jackrabbits, and the fire got beyond their control."[108]

On the question of the influence of this practice, Keeley and Minnich are somewhat in agreement, but not all fire ecologists agree. Keeley summarizes the two camps.[109] One group believes Indians had only a minor effect on pristine vegetation, perhaps altering the landscape only in the vicinity of villages. The other group hypothesizes that Indian burning was pervasive and widespread, enough to significantly change grassland and scrubland patterns from their pre-human condition. Of course this picture is further complicated by trying to determine what a pre-human condition was for North America, as before and during the arrival of people, large herds of Pleistocene bison, horses, mammoths, camels, and other big game were having their own impacts on the vegetation, perhaps similar to the heavy grazing-browsing-trampling pressures seen in Africa. I wonder if these herds had the same effect on shrublands as did frequent fire: keeping them open and structured in a mosaic pattern. Even hungry, trampling elk herds during Holocene times may have opened up the landscape.

Keeley believes that Indian burning thinned out chaparral and coastal scrub over sizable portions of the landscape. The rugged interior ranges may have seen much less anthropogenic fire.[110] But on most areas, Keeley says that fires occurring more than one each decade would eliminate chaparral shrubs that reproduce by seed and thin the resprouters out into islands amid a matrix of grassland.

Minnich believes Indian burning had more effect on grasslands and coastal sage scrub and was less important in chaparral.[111] Increased burning by Native people may have led to "type conversion" of some shrublands: on the lower edges of chaparral slopes, frequent fires may have converted chaparral into coastal sage scrub or native bunchgrassland. I have often seen small-flowered melic grass as a chaparral edge species, its bunches filling in burned scrub temporarily if fires occur more than ten years apart; it might grow into a more permanent grassland if fires occurred more frequently.

Keeley and Minnich agree that weedy introduced annual grasses and mustards have added to massive fires and type conversion today in southern California. Weedy, fast-growing and fast-withering brome grasses, wild oats, and mustards may take over after a burn, aided by breaks in the chaparral created by roads and firefighters, and carpet the newly opened ground. This type of "flush and fade" fuel promotes more frequent fire, hinders the regrowth and recolonization of native grasses, shrubs, and wildflowers, and may negate the ability of young burn patches to stop wildfires from spreading over large areas. The situation is not helped when land managers reseed burns with such exotics as Italian ryegrass in an effort to stop erosion.

Adherents to the Keeley and Minnich fire regime models have almost opposite recommendations for ending today's massive firestorms. Under the Keeley model, where large fires driven by extreme fire weather are normal and happened regularly in the last several hundred years, fire suppression should be continued, with every effort made to save property. He advocates the building of buffer zones around urban areas where they meet fire-prone habitats, and he has recommended placing a greenbelt of golf courses and lawn parks on the edges of new developments to protect them from wildfires and ease access for firefighters.

According to the Minnich model, we are living in an unnatural fire regime caused by fire suppression, and we should try to reverse this trend and restore the landscape to a precontact condition through controlled burns throughout the state's chaparral, in order to create a patchwork of fuel ages that contain natural fuel breaks and thereby limit the spread of massive fires ignited during extreme fire weather. Northern Baja California makes a very good reference site, he says, because of the similarities—the chaparral does not stop at the border.

The Remembered Forest

Instead of locking forests into giant log-preserves or static wilderness areas, many Native Americans have a different way of being upon the land, a way that has helped shaped California for thousands of years. As we have seen, one part of this philosophy was to start fires in various plant communities, creating openings in the forest and brush and patches of early successional states.

Traditional ecological knowledge is being put into action in Plumas National Forest, as the United Maidu Nation makes agreements with the Forest Service to manage twenty-one hundred acres of their homeland. Their goal is not lumber, but the ground cover: basketry plants such as willows, medicinal plants, plants used for ceremonial purposes, and oaks used for food. The Maidu Stewardship Project area is in the Wolf Creek drainage, between the town of Quincy and the Lake Almanor reservoir in the Feather River watershed. I searched for mountain yellow-legged frogs along this creek in the 1990s and found nothing but overgrazed and highly eroded floodplains with helicopters carrying out pine logs overhead.

"We want to show we can bring the land back just by taking care of it," says Lorena Gorbet, a Maidu spokeswoman.[112] They have pruned willow and maple twigs for weaving materials, selectively tilled camas lily beds by digging in certain areas for the bulbs, and cultivated the oaks by encouraging large, low branches that would produce big acorn crops. Fire can be one of their most important tools. In the past they set annual low-intensity ground fires to encourage such basketry plants as beargrass. One of Gorbet's cousins remembered his grandfather using a forked stick to pull the slow-burning flames away from plants he wanted to keep unburnt. As recently as the 1970s Maidu people were given citations by the Forest Service for "illegal" burning. The Maidu plan on using ground fires again, as well as removing introduced weeds, replanting native grasses, willows, and aspens, and halting erosion on the floodplain. Students work to monitor these projects.

"The Remembered Forest" is a phrase the Klamath, Modoc, and Yahooskin tribes use today as a goal for the restoration of the forests on their Klamath Reservation in southern Oregon—forests continuous with ponderosa, lodgepole, and mixed conifer groves. The people here remember when they set fire to the old pine forests to renew berry crops and make flourishing wildlife habitat. They remember how fire sculpted the forest, lightly, clearing the ground of excess brush, forming over time patches of old, large ponderosas and small clusters of new trees in an irregular mosaic. The Klamath tribes are now restoring this complexity, reducing densities built up from fire suppression by removing some white fir stands (and leaving others), clearing saplings from around the huge old pines to protect them from fire, carrying out prescribed fires, and in turn renewing their own identity and continuity with the past. "As the true stewards of this land, the Klamath Tribes seek to reclaim our stewardship and, to the extent possible, return the forests and waters to their original splendor," says Klamath Tribes chairman Allen Foreman. "For we share a vision: 'When we heal the land, we also heal people.'"[113]

Living with Fire

Contrast this with the view of fire that is still dominant: as more conflagrations erupted with terrible predictability in southern California on October 25, 2007, I watched Katie Couric on the CBS *Evening News* talk of "war." The latest California wildfires were "man versus nature," nine thousand firefighters "battling the beast" and "launching a counterattack" with an "air war" of planes dropping water to save houses. "Evil devil winds" at 60 to 100 miles per hour (the Santa Anas) spread the numerous fires over seven hundred square miles, causing the largest evacuation in state history—"another brutal day on the front."

And with terrible predictability, megafires irrupted out of control in 2008 and 2009, causing both the largest single fire in state history—190 square miles burned in the Big Sur region—and the most fires to burn at one time in California, eight hundred. No amount of money, manpower, or technology thrown at the wildlands seems to be able to stop this new phenomenon.

The great wildfire debate will undoubtedly go on among ecologists, but both sides agree that rural migration out into the once remote firebelt has cost us dearly. Some cities will decide on whether to adopt a Rural Lands Initiative that limits the spread of houses into the remote indefensible backcountry where "intermix" wildfires around scattered houses are very difficult to fight. Buffer lands may be bought and developers offered incentives not to build in highly fire-prone areas. Fire-resistant house construction materials could also be used. Following the 2003 disaster, county supervisors in San Diego discussed adopting the Minnich model, proposing to control-burn twenty-seven thousand acres a year in a large rotation during cooler, safer weather periods.[114] Others in the West are even toying with ideas like "Wildland Fire Use," a carefully monitored let-it-burn policy in uninhabited lands, to reduce vegetative fuel.

California grasslands and scrublands, oak woodlands, and forests are complex and dynamic ecosystems, so we should remain open to as much evidence and as many points of view as possible in order to try to understand them. Fire is not "evil," but a process of cyclic renewal. Wildfire has scorched the landscape for thousands of years, and certain cultures have learned to live with it and use it—when will we?

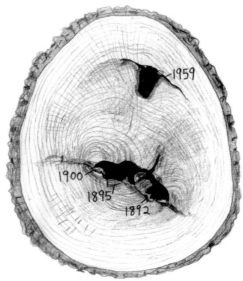

CUT SECTION OF OREGON OAK SHOWING 4 FIRE SCARS, HEALED OVER.
1878 - CENTER.
1985 - CUT.

1959
1900
1895
1892

Drawn from photo in T. R. Plumb and N. H. Pillsbury, eds., USDA Forest Service Symposium on Multiple-use Management of California's Hardwood Resources, 1987

NINE

WHERE DEER
AND ANTELOPE PLAYED
Cycles You Can See

"I have nowhere seen game as plentifully as in this valley. We killed an antelope in the morning. We could frequently see herds of deer and elk in different directions around us, as well as wild horses."

—*A. B. Clarke, on visiting the Central Valley in 1852*[1]

W e have seen how plants responded to fire and other forms of cyclic disturbance in the past and into the present. How did the native herds interact with these processes? Pronghorn antelope and mule deer introduce us to a past world where great herds roamed unfenced grasslands and oak-filled hills, dining on the juiciest forage, escaping mountains lions and coyotes, following disturbance patterns created on the landscape. Their behaviors, their daily life cycles, their ups and downs and historical patterns of change are much more easily observed than those of the oaks: their lifespan is much closer to our own. It is easy to grab binoculars and a sketchpad and observe a bit of normal mule deer, or even pronghorn activity, and in doing so we can catch a glimpse of the cycles that played through thousands of years, shifting with climate and geologic processes. We can imagine the daily events of Old California.

Pronghorn antelope in precontact Mojave Desert of San Bernardino County at sunset: a sandy flat with big galleta grass and creosote. OIL ON COTTON RAG PAPER, 6 X 15 INCHES, 1997

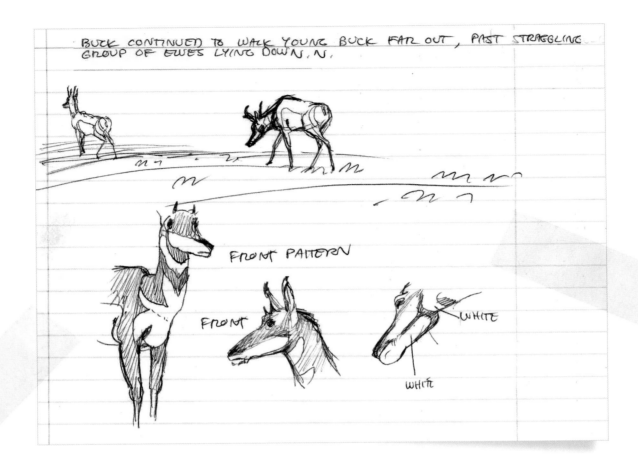

A Day among the Pronghorns

The policeman pulled his car up to mine and got out to walk towards me. I could now see he was actually a game warden, and he must have grown suspicious of me, spending so much time watching the herd of feeding antelope across the road.

"Hello, what are you up to?" he asked.

"Just sketching," I said.

"Ah, you've been here all day, so I was wondering."

That day I had decided to get up with the dawn and spend the entire day until dark watching and sketching a herd of antelope that had found a lush green alfalfa field within the Ash Creek National Wildlife Refuge area in Modoc County. It was human behavior the game warden was undoubtedly not used to seeing, but after peering into the back window of my car and seeing binoculars and a lunch, he bade me a good afternoon and drove off. I was happy that the California Department of Fish and Game was out watching for poachers, as this part of California is one of the last strongholds for antelope. That was the reason I was here: to get a feel for the small cycles of behavior, daily activity, and observable changes of a once widespread Old California animal.

The October rut was on and dominant males had established territories where bands of ten to fifteen does, yearlings, and kids fed. On the outskirts wandered single bucks and "bachelor bands." A territorial buck marked his ground with glands below the ear (under a black fur patch), urine, and large feces piles. He spent the entire day in a cycle of feeding—taking brief gulps of green alfalfa—bedding down with the females, and getting up to chase intruding males off. In this herd there were two lone young bucks who tried all day to approach the female band. If they grazed too close, the big buck loped towards them and then lowered his head in a walking threat, forcing the young bucks to move off to a respectful distance.

By the hot part of midday I thought the territorial buck had given up chasing the young males; he chewed his cud tolerantly as they walked by. But suddenly he up and strode steadily after a small-horned youngster, herding him off yet again. This continued into dusk as the herd gradually moved over the food patch, and then they walked over a rise and out of view. I packed up my spotting scope and sketchbooks and left for camp, happy knowing I had learned a little more about the daily life of these strange relics of a once diverse North American family of native antelopes, the Antilocapridae. Incidentally, although we call the pronghorns "antelopes" they are not true antelopes and are totally unrelated to the Old World antelopes, who fill a similar ecological niche but are in the family Bovidae.

A local fellow told me that a few weeks after the rut ended, two hundred to four hundred antelope would arrive here and aggregate on their winter range. Each buck would shed his black horn sheath,

BUCK

DOE

AREA BETWEEN
HORNS SOMETIMES
LIGHT BURNT OCHRE
ALSO.

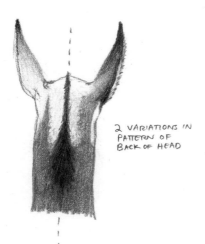

PATTERN
ON
UNDERSIDE
OF HEAD
AND NECK

ENDLESS
VARIATION
OF
NECK PATTERN

2 VARIATIONS IN
PATTERN OF
BACK OF HEAD

revealing a bony horn core that would then start regrowing a forked horn. By July the bucks' horns would be completely grown. Females often have small, unforked horns, as I saw while examining the band with the scope.

When I talked to a friend later about my day watching antelope, he exclaimed about how boring that sounded. But I discovered that even a seemingly quiet herd can reveal drama and interest when we put aside our busy schedules and activate our powers of observation.

Pronghorn History and Distribution

In the Golden State's past these swift-running herbivores apparently lived over much of the Central Valley, in grassy parts of the Sierran and Cascadean foothills up into the open ponderosa pine belt, on open lands in the Coast Ranges, and in southern California from the coast throughout the desert lowlands; they were premier grassland animals that preferred wide-open country. Driving throughout the West sketching wildlife, I often found pronghorn on the lonely grasslands of eastern New Mexico, all over Yellowstone National Park, and in the sagebrushy parts of Idaho, eastern Oregon, and Nevada. But they have largely disappeared in California west of the Sierra. In most places, only scraps of written descriptions and bits of archaeological evidence remain to tell us about these tan-and-white, long-legged, sheep-sized creatures that once moved abundantly through the state's bunchgrasslands and wildflower fields.

The bones of pronghorn have been recovered from shellmounds at west Berkeley and at Coyote Hills, on the eastern edge of San Francisco Bay, which shows that their range extended to the coast.[2] Father Crespí, in the late 1700s, saw antelope running together on mesas near present San Diego and found them numerous in the South Coast Ranges and Salinas Valley. Antelope were also sighted in 1846 near Olema, near the sea in Marin County.[3]

John Frémont, in his travels, noted that the Indians of the San Joaquin Valley would carry out hunting "drives" of antelope and jackrabbits.[4] This must have been very good habitat for the pronghorn—open and grown with tasty annual wildflowers in season—perhaps some of the densest populations of antelope in North America existed in this arid place. There were reports of herds of three thousand.[5]

Pronghorn Ecology

Precontact ecology of pronghorn in California must be deduced from studies of other regions where antelope are still plentiful. Judging from antelope behavior in other parts of the world, the herds followed the moisture content of green plants, dining on shrubs, forbs, and new green grass as it sprouted. In central California antelope may have eaten shrubs such as coyote brush, California sagebrush, and sages. When the wildflowers bloomed the antelope would have relied heavily on them for forage. Buckwheats, lupines, buttercups, clovers, California poppy, clarkia, milkvetches, and tarweeds were perhaps some of the most sought-after forbs. When their fine leaves were green, one-sided bluegrass and Idaho fescue were probably highly preferred grasses. In southern California prickly pear cacti were undoubtedly nibbled.

How pronghorn interacted with tule elk on the old rangelands can only be guessed at, but in Yellowstone National Park, where pronghorn still roam, the elk, which are generalist feeders, apparently leave enough "crumbs" for the small-bodied, more selective antelope to live on.[6] I wonder if grazing elk stimulated new green grass growth that benefited the pronghorn on California grasslands?

The rut took place in late August, September, and October, depending on location, and does gathered at kidding grounds in May or June. These were often hilly or shrubby areas, or places with tall grass or sedge clumps. The kids were too wobbly in their first few days to run, so they hid from predators by hugging the ground amid the tall vegetation while the mothers fed and watched at some distance, returning regularly to nurse them. Ninety percent of the kids may have been dropped in a ten-day period, apparently a strategy to swamp predators with so much prey that some kids were bound to survive.[7]

This was a dangerous time for the juveniles, as coyotes patrolled the areas, searching out the kids. While visiting Hart Mountain National Antelope Refuge, land in eastern Oregon specifically managed for the pronghorn, I learned that coyotes were a big problem here, taking so many kids that the antelope recruitment into adulthood was lowering. Coyotes specialized in searching out hidden kids, sometimes working in groups.[8]

I have talked with some biologists who dislike using the term "balance" in regard to nature, saying that this is an outdated concept of the guiding principle in ecosystems and has been superseded by random complexity. But I cannot help thinking of the wolf reintroduction program in

RUMP TAN ON
YOUNG – NOT HIGH
CONTRAST

Yellowstone National Park: biologists there noticed that after a few years the wolves had challenged and killed many of the local coyotes, and perhaps a rebalancing of predators was evident. With the reduction of the coyote population—small-prey specialists—by their larger cousins, antelope and other prey regained some strength in numbers. Wolves themselves had very rarely been observed to prey on adult antelope. This is just another question that remains to be investigated concerning the intricate relationships in a more "complete" ecosystem, where more niches are filled—a situation to which my mind often turns when thinking about Old California.

Other biologists have noticed that when rabbit populations cycle to abundant levels, this buffers the antelope kid population, as coyotes and bobcats take more rabbits and expend less time searching out kids. Coyotes will also kill adult antelope on occasion. And not to be forgotten, an even more complex ecosystem existed in California during the Pleistocene epoch, when mammoths and other megafauna roamed. Our small pronghorn antelope and perhaps two other related species lived throughout these millennia, filling the niches that various gazelles and antelopes of African savannas do today.

At day four after birth, pronghorn kids can outrun humans. Adult pronghorn can run at top speeds of sixty miles per hour and maintain a thirty-five mph run for several miles. White rump patches are flashed, with the hair raised to alert other herd members of incoming predators as the pronghorn flee "ridiculously too fast for any modern predator," as John Byers said while studying them in Montana.[9] In contrast, the top speeds of tule elk do not exceed thirty mph.

Big predators such as sabertooth cats and American lions probably did not pose much of a threat to adult antelope, but another Ice Age predator may have. Byers contends that the four-million-year history of pronghorns may have been shaped by highly cursorial predators such as the American cheetah. This fast cat lived on the North American continent during the Pleistocene and went extinct about ten thousand years ago. North American cheetahs may have been the "chief selecting agents," pushing pronghorn antelope to evolve their high-speed antipredator adaptation.

Antelope Watching Today

Antelope meat became abundant and cheap in markets in the 1850s.[10] The pronghorn were driven into the forested mountains (today they have been noted as high as 11,000 feet). The last pronghorn in the Central Valley was killed in the 1920s.[11] Though they were hunted out of western California, pronghorn remained in the Mojave and Colorado Deserts until the last were shot by hunters, apparently at Chuckwalla Bench (Riverside County) in the 1940s.[12] Fortunately they are gradually being reintroduced to former ranges across the state and can be observed now in old habitats that have not seen them in decades.

The best place to find pronghorn in California is in the northeast, in Modoc County, where large numbers inhabit the sagebrush valleys and juniper-dotted hills into northwestern Nevada and eastern Oregon.

YOUNGER EWE
(SHORTER FACE)

ONE
R EYE

While on a bicycle tour with my sister through the back roads of San Benito and eastern Monterey Counties one spring, I almost went into the shrubs when I spotted an antelope in the distance, grazing in a cow pasture among yellow Mediterranean mustards. I was thrilled to see in my binoculars this single buck antelope, like a ghost from the past, back in its former haunts despite the introduced flora and fauna around him. Cattle ranches along Mines Road (eastern Alameda County) and Carrizo Plain (Kern County), now a National Monument managed by the Bureau of Land Management, are some of the other places where these little "berrendos" (pintos) from early California can be seen. In western California they have been reintroduced by the California Department of Fish and Game in small numbers.

Sketching Deer

Those other small, hoofed, selective feeders, the deer, are still common across California and can be easily observed. During my stay at San Antonio Reservoir campground in the Monterey County Coast Range, the deer chewed on fallen blue oak acorns all morning, and I did a lot of sketching. Some deer stood up on their hind legs to reach dangling bunches of valley oak leaves on drooping twigs. The bucks this October were in rutting condition, their necks thick and a yellowish stain visible on the fur of their hind legs, caused by the animals squatting and urinating on the tarsal glands at the "knee" and rubbing their legs together—they attract females with this scent.[13] Yellow-billed magpies jumped on the deer's backs to pick off ticks in their fur. In the midday heat the deer bedded down in the shade of blue oaks, chewing cuds. By five o'clock they were all up, feeding, moving in small groups, the tall bucks raking the ceanothus bushes with their antlers, the young bucks playing and sparring by pushing and shoving their heads together. A knob-headed juvenile buck frolicked, ran, and galloped about in bursts, bucking with his head lowered. Large bucks with chunky bodies approached females at sunset, walking after them with heads low and snouts stretched out, in courtship posture. Other deer fed on large acorns littering the campground. At darkness the activity increased, the deer seldom staying in one place for long, moving back and forth between the oak groves and open grassy slopes.

American cheetah

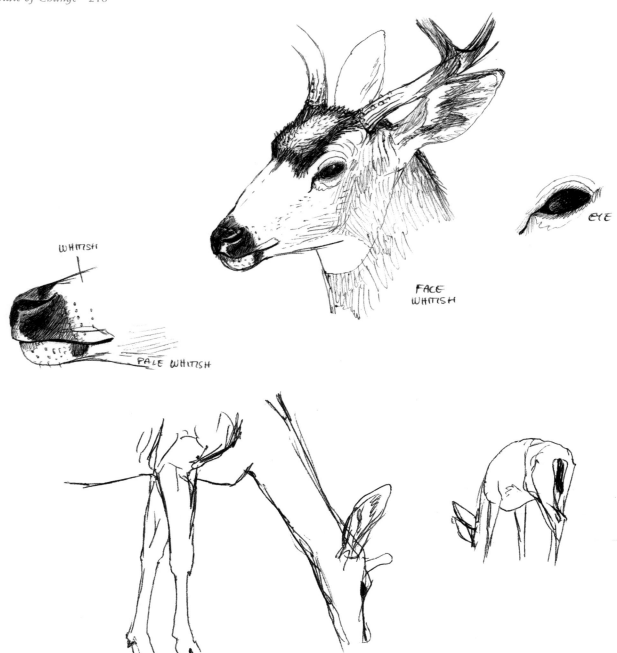

WHITISH

EYE

FACE
WHITISH

PALE WHITISH

JUV. ♀ WALKED FROM OPEN SLOPE INTO SHADY OAK-BAY WOODL. ON HILL.
ONLY ONE YOUNG ♂ SEEN NOW GRAZING. IN OPEN SUN,

I thought to myself as I drew with pencil on a pad of paper in the dusk light that if I were here a million years ago the same scenes would be playing themselves out, little daily feeding cycles within larger cycles of the annual rut.

Original Deer Numbers

Although no population estimates can be gleaned from historical accounts, there is much evidence that mule deer were numerous here before the arrival of Europeans, due largely to California's extraordinary plant and habitat diversity, and to Indian management of those varied habitats and plant resources. Unlike other parts of the country, where single mule deer subspecies are found, California also has an unusual diversity of deer types, adapted to the landscape in a cline of body sizes, color phases, and morphological characters to match the gradient of desert to scrub and oak to fir. Black-tailed deer, for example, a subspecies of mule deer, live in the moister northern California coastal region. Other races are adapted to the deserts and mountains.

Father Vicente Santa María, on the ship *San Carlos,* entered the San Francisco Bay in 1775 and noted the Indians wearing pelts of "otter and deer, which are plentiful in this region."[14] He found deer numerous on Angel Island. In his diary on December 4, 1774, Father Francisco Palóu noted that their party found "a dead deer partly eaten by a wolf" near Lake Merced. On the beaches of San Francisco they "did see many deer, encountering herds of 6 or 8 of them together." They found a tule raft and Indian trails as well. On December 11 near Aptos, in Santa Cruz County, they saw some Indians hunting deer in an arroyo. Smoke from a village came from the hills nearby.[15]

Russian explorer Otto von Kotzebue in November 1824 entered the Delta and later proclaimed:

> An abundance of deer, large and small [probably tule elk and mule deer], are to be
> met with all over the country, and geese, ducks, and cranes, on the banks of the rivers.
> There was such a superfluity of game, that even those among us who had never been
> sportsmen before, when once they took the gun in their hands, became as eager as the
> rest. The sailors chased the deer very successfully.[16]

Farther north, up the Sacramento River, he noted, "The steep banks sometimes opened to delightful plains, where the deer were grazing under the shade of luxuriant oaks."[17]

Deer Hunting the Old Way

Native people hunted deer with hidden snares along their trails, as well as with bows and arrows. Ishi, a Yahi man who survived colonialism late in his homeland of the Mount Lassen foothills, demonstrated hunting techniques to Saxton Pope, an interested medical doctor:

> Ishi was particularly careful in the observance of several essential precautions. He
> would eat no fish on the day prior to the hunt, because the odor would be detected by
> deer, he said; nor would he have the odor of tobacco smoke about him. The morning of
> the hunt Ishi bathed himself from head to foot, and washed his mouth. Eating no food,
> he dressed himself in a shirt, or breech clout...

> In hunting deer, Ishi used the method of ambush. It was customary in his tribe to
> station archers behind certain rocks or bushes near well-known deer trails. Then a
> band of Indians beat the brush at a mile or so distant, driving toward those in hiding.[18]

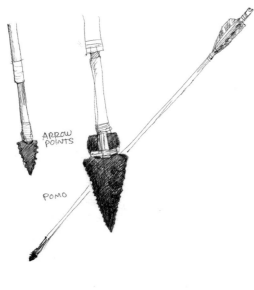

ARROW
POINTS

POMO

Ishi pointed out rock cairns in the bouldery canyons where he used to hunt, places where the archers hid in ambush. So as not to alert an animal to his presence, "In approaching game, Ishi would rather skirt an entire mountain than come up on the wind side," Pope said. Sometimes he waited at a deer lick for game to come. He could call in a doe by sucking air through a folded madrone leaf, imitating the bleat of a fawn. He also used a deer-head decoy, stuffed with leaves and twigs. Although he never used it, Ishi knew how to make an arrow poison out of rattlesnake venom and putrefying deer liver.

Pope thought Ishi's arrows would penetrate a deer at thirty yards with no problem, and if one struck the spine it could cause paralysis. The bow could also discharge farther than a hundred yards. Ishi said the best bow woods were juniper and incense cedar. He applied sinew from deer spines or legs to the bow's back with salmon-skin glue and used twined tendon strips to make the string. Arrow shafts were most often made of hazelnut, common reed, dogwood, mountain mahogany, or mock orange. He knapped arrowheads from bone, obsidian, or flint; obsidian was so valued that boulders of it were traded like money. The point was pressed with pine sap to the shaft and bound with sinew. When hunting, Ishi carried his bow and about a dozen arrows in a quiver made from a river otter skin over his left shoulder. He preferred to shoot while kneeling or squatting.

Archaeologists think the bow and arrow came into use in California perhaps one thousand to five hundred years ago.[19] Before that hunters used atlatls (spear-throwers) and four- to seven-foot-long darts with large points.

The Black-Tail Year

In Tilden Park I have been sketching deer since 1982. Watching the changing landscape through the seasons and how the deer responded became an interesting project on weekend hikes. Seeing little cycles helped me to picture the larger cycles of time that make up California's history.

Small, spotted fawns often appeared with their does in May. I surprised some hiding in willow copses at springs on the grassy slopes, and along well-used deer trails through the blackberry and oak groves. A doe in an oak woodland cautiously watched me, then lowered her head to nip the tip off a bracken fern. She raised her head, then took a bit of a poison oak shrub. A two-prong buck came up the trail and passed her, ignoring me. She then lowered her head and ate some low-growing blackberry and snowberry leaves. The flies bothered her and she often shook her ears, flopping them about, or

THE ANTLERS HAD BECOME POLISHED AND SHIN

reached back to nibble her flanks. I finally scared her accidentally with a quick movement, and she bounded off into the oaks and bays.

On May 11, 1985, I came upon a grass burn in Big Springs Canyon, full of newly emerging soap plants and annual lupines, most with their buds and new leaves chewed off by deer. On unburned grassy slopes I watched the deer closely crop the fine green bunches of foothill needlegrass.

The bucks had grown knobs in April; by June the large antlers were in velvet. In July of 1985 I made note of two large bucks in a grassy canyon, foraging together. Both had two prongs on each velvet antler. They had worked their way down from the ridgetop, eating green lupines and the leaves of mountain dandelion, California poppy leaves, and just a few tarweeds; occasionally they cropped blades of purple needlegrass on the lower slopes, where the bunches still had some green—they ignored it up on the ridge, where it was dry. They also grazed on some barely green mountain brome grass. They avoided the creeping wildrye on the canyon bottom though it was green—too coarse. I noticed how differently the deer and cattle foraged on adjacent pastures, the deer moving often, eating only some of each plant over a large area, leaving most of the plant untouched. The cattle took everything, not giving the plant much of a chance to regrow. Indeed, the impact of deer grazing was hardly noticeable at all. The bucks mostly shed the velvet off their antlers at the end of July.

By August, when the grasslands were hot and dry and green foods were scarcer, the deer had stripped the leaves off thimbleberry thickets under the oak canopy and nipped the flowers off bee plants and willow herbs. They took coffeeberry leaves, currants, and the leaves around the thorns on wild roses. Almost all the twig ends of the poison oak along the trails were chewed off now. The deer also gathered around the small arroyo willows along the creeks to browse on leaves up to four feet high. An old buckeye at the edge of the woodland was favored—it had a browseline—the deer stretched to get its leaves. They also strained to eat a green giant vetch vine hanging on an oak twig. The deer were quite selective, using their narrow muzzles to pick the best plant parts available.

By September the fawns had lost their spots. The rut was in progress now in this part of the state, and the bucks rubbed their antlers on willow limbs and trunks, making severe scrapes ten inches long that revealed the red-cream inner wood and left shreds of bark hanging. This did not kill the trees, however, and some sprouted leafy shoots next to the scrapes. The antlers had become polished and shiny since August, and the necks of the bucks swelled as a sign of breeding condition. At the woodland-grassland edges I also sometimes saw damaged coyote brush, the stems stripped of bark and the branches broken by bucks with their antlers as a means of advertising their presence.

Field notes: "Deer tracks common on grassy slopes."

During the day, young spike bucks dined on acorns under live oaks. At night the scene changed to one of high activity. Does fed in the inky blackness as I sat at a distance and attempted to watch the groups with binoculars. A magnificent older buck with thick antlers, long and spearlike, thrashed a hazelnut bush with quick jerky motions, grunting. He guarded the doe, who continued feeding on ground plants. A "teenager" spike buck approached cautiously and curiously. The big buck watched him and finally walked over, then trotted, causing the youngster to dash off in a rush of dry oak leaves. Ten minutes later he had to be chased off again. The old "master" buck never exerted himself much, and he always walked back to the vicinity of the doe to stand by her, or walk behind her with

NCE AUGUST, AND THE NECKS OF THE BUCKS SWELLED AS A SIGN OF BREEDING CONDITION.

HERDING

YOUNG BUCK

JUV. BLACKTAIL
AT SUGARLOAF
TROTTING AWAY
FAST LOOKING & ACTING
SOMEWHAT LIKE A
WHITETAIL

head low and neck stretched out, eliciting her urine so he could test her readiness for mating by its scent. When I returned at the height of the rut, I saw a frenzy of activity occurring under the stars as bucks chased does across fields and younger bucks hung out at the edges. I strained to make sketches on a pad of paper, fearing that using a flashlight to illuminate the page would scare the deer.

Biologist Valerius Geist learned by watching deer for long periods that these were not harems, but clans of related females that master bucks mingled with, tending as many does as possible in succession.

By November, when the first rains had caused the bunchgrasses to green up, the deer herds had become quiet again and were feeding on the new green needlegrass blades on the open hills. They would nip off the new leaves of soap plant all winter as well.

The park had hired a goatherd that fall so his herd could browse off the excess fire-fuel brush along the park border with Berkeley, and the goats did their job well, stripping the shrubs and weeds almost bare. After they left, plants started to resprout, as after a fire, and the deer came to take advantage of this new flush. I found them eating bracken ferns, which were among the first things to grow after the goats had passed through, and I wondered if long ago elk herds performed this heavy browsing-grazing sweep, followed by deer that took the daintier morsels.

In December, with the rains, the deer returned to the burn from the previous spring in Big Springs Canyon and ate the abundant resprouted green buckwheats, big squirreltail grass, and new growth of mountain brome, a soft-leaved grass they seemed to prefer over purple needlegrass. In other areas of the woodlands, I found deer "yards" created by heavy browsing: in their search for winter food the deer stripped the sword ferns and wood ferns of every pinnule, and the blackberries and poison oak of all leaves, but only in small spots under oaks and bays.

The wide green-up of January and February found the deer cropping down most of the soap plants out on the grassy hills, some green bunchgrass leaves (mountain brome and blue wildrye), and many growing rosettes of forbs, such as buttercups, wild pea, lupine, white yarrow, blue-eyed grass, and California poppy. Low live oaks were pruned into rounded shapes.

Two does in February came walking along a ridge of live oaks and grass. One touched the nose of the other, then jumped back and danced playfully. They continued walking along in single file.

By April, the deer were eating a large array of wildflowers, new shrub shoots, and tree browse. The cycle continued.

Deer, Fire, Oaks, and Chaparral

From my observations of local deer, I came to understand some of the broader patterns of animal interactions across the unique habitats of California. Today antelope thrive on rangelands that have been renewed by wildfire or grazing by larger ungulates, such as elk and bison; they fill the open-ground niche of selective feeders, while the deer fill a similar role in ecotones with woodland, forest, and scrubland. Chaparral fires and burned-over oak groves have benefited the "mulies" and "blacktails" enormously over the centuries.

Many deer populations seem to specialize in oak woodland and chaparral habitats, dining abundantly on oak leaves and various chaparral shrubs. Twenty to 80 percent of their diet is browse such as this.[20] Wildlife biologists in the North Coast Ranges have found that acorns are so important to the health of deer that more fawns are born in the spring after a good crop, and yearling bucks grow forked antlers instead of the usual spikes.[21] In much of California the health of the deer and the health of the oaks are interconnected—a bumper mast crop can extend the deer's food supply several months into the winter.

Deer have a relatively small digestive tract compared to sheep of similar size, so they must spend time selecting the greener and more nutritious parts of plants. Disturbances to the vegetation, such as elk grazing and Indian-set fires, probably increased regrowth and the growth of new successional plants and increased edges and ecotones between vegetation types, all of which provided deer with more high-quality feed.

Wildlife managers, trying to increase deer populations in California chaparral, have developed recommendations that include prescribed fires: scattered spot burns of five to one thousand acres each, leaving adequate heavier brush as cover for the deer. This was expected to quadruple the deer population as deer concentrated on the burn mosaic. Interestingly, this treatment is very similar to what Native Californians were doing for thousands of years—burning patches of landscape to increase the growth of tender new browse, forbs, and grass, increase ecotones, and keep the vegetation in a complex mosaic of successional states. No wonder early European and American travelers commented on the abundance of game animals throughout the state.

Not only does fire in chaparral affect deer populations and distribution, but the deer may influence the post-fire successional outcome of the plant community. Studies in Australian shrublands and woodlands indicate that if a burn patch is small, browsing by mammalian herbivores such as kangaroos and wallabies entering from nearby unburned areas has a profound effect on the size and species composition of plants; if the burn patch is somewhat larger, new growth satiates the herbivores, allowing many plants to escape browsing.[22] This may have happened often in California,

1535 — ONE WALKED INTO OAKS AGAIN, LEAVING 2 OUT IN GRASS NOW THEN 2 APPEARED ON HIGHER GRASSY HILL, GRAZING.

where after some fires the deer browse new shoots of chamise heavily enough to keep the bushes low and compact for many years.[23]

Ecologists have speculated on a possible "floral reticulum" of bare edges and unique herbaceous communities that might be created by the intense herbivory of rodents, rabbits, and jackrabbits as they enter new burns from the cover of adjacent dense chaparral. These animals browse heavily on seeds and seedlings just inside the boundaries of burn patches during the first few years after a fire, forming strips of distinctive regenerating floral communities. These narrow, selectively browsed areas disappear as the shrub community matures. The combination of fire with browsing by deer and small mammals may have created diverse floral "gardens" in early California shrub and oak habitats.[24]

Deer Numbers Today

Like the antelope, deer felt the impact of the gold rush as hunters, in response to heavy demand for meat to supply hungry immigrants, burst out into the woodlands and brushlands. A slew of men went to work commercially to procure game—deer, elk, grizzly bears, waterfowl—and they were wildly successful at what they did. In Colusa County, two hunters in the winter of 1856-57 took six hundred black-tailed deer skins.[25] In 1873 hunters at a six-day camp at Scott Mountain, in Siskiyou County, killed twenty to sixty deer daily. In 1878, 158 deer were taken in one day at Coffee Creek, in Trinity County. "Deer paths to the numerous licks below, near the stream, were cut by the deer from one to three feet deep along the hillsides," hunters said. The deer were apparently easy targets, and sometimes only the buckskins were taken. In 1880 an incredible

LIVE OAK SHAPED INTO HOUR-GLASS

2 EATING DOWN YOUNG OAK, 'PRUNING' BROWSE LINE.

SEVERAL YOUNG OAKS ON EDGE OF WOODLAND SHAPED INTO HOURGLASS FIGURES BY BROWSING. 3 DEER SURROUNDING BASAL BUSH AND REACHING IN TO EAT LEAVES

thirty-five thousand hides were hauled from Siskiyou, Trinity, and Shasta Counties and shipped to San Francisco. By 1881 no live deer were seen in the region, only carcasses stripped of their skins lying about on the ground.[26]

Bag limits were finally enacted in 1901.[27] But overhunting had reduced the deer herds to low numbers throughout the state in the last decades of the nineteenth century and first decades of the twentieth. Gradually deer increased, given this protection, and during the 1940s through 1960s their numbers peaked, perhaps beyond their original population size. In many areas they outgrew their supplies of high-quality foods, and disease and decline set in during the 1970s.[28]

Today numbers have recovered some, and deer have survived the population roller coaster of the last century. They are adaptable animals, among the few able to coexist easily with contemporary humans. Fortunately most types of mule deer and black-tailed deer are now abundant in California, and there are plenty of places to watch them and learn more about them—their behavior and interactions with the dynamic landscape can give the observer hours of entertainment and insight.

Natural History Observation

"Each species is a rare source of information, like a rare book. At present humanity has read, only partly, a few volumes and to a large extent human life has depended upon the knowledge so gained."

—*Robert C. Stebbins*

In the half-moonlight one night I lay in my sleeping bag, looking out over the blue oak savanna, barely able to make out the shapes of things, hearing the rustling of deer chasing deer, noting the subtle blue shades in the ochre grass and dark hues of the oak crowns. Starlight illuminated the timeless land of oaks and deer.

By the power of observation we can learn about the riches that remain in the Golden State, what our homeland was like centuries ago, and how we can restore species to their original ranges. Sometimes it is good to back away from the big picture—the vast stretches thousands of years back in time—as we look into early California. The plants and animals we watch in the natural world around us now, whether rare or common, often reveal hidden ecological gems. You may even begin to see the cycles of time on the landscape flow before your eyes.

Biology databases and surveys that reveal population trends, distribution shifts, and geological and climatic changes rely on observations of plants and animals, and for the historical ecologist, too, one of the first steps is information gathering. Anyone can do this—you do not need a degree, nor do you need to be a scientist, and your observations can be very important to future observers.

I met herpetologist Robert C. Stebbins at his home one day to share artwork, and we discussed the importance of getting young people outdoors to learn to look at things. Even a square foot of soil in a backyard can become fascinating if you take the time to observe it. He smiled broadly as he recalled taking groups of school kids to a meadow in Tilden Park to learn to map the webs of spiders that hung on tall grass stems and watch their locations change from week to week. The kids did not want to stop after their hour-long class—activating your powers of observation can be better than TV, they realized. We talked about how observing the natural world focuses the senses, develops patience, heightens environmental awareness, and increases a sense of place and belonging. He handed me a protocol he had developed with East Bay Municipal Utility District for training people about biological monitoring programs. In it, he said:

> Many of us as children start out with an interest in the wild creatures in our surroundings—from caterpillars to birds—but, all too often, the interest fades as prejudices or indifference of adults or peers and the insulation from nature that characterizes industrial society suppress such interest. However, fortunately, it can usually readily be revived with proper exposure and guidance.

Here I summarize my own interpretation of his curriculum. With simple tools, children and adults alike can record, for future observers, valuable information about the changing landscape.

Field Equipment

backpack or shoulder bag for carrying equipment

pencil, pen, eraser

clipboard with paper or blank notebook

maps

compass

binoculars

ruler

ELK COW AND FAWN

field guides—to birds, mammals, reptiles and amphibians, plants, stars, etc.

optional: camera

At the beginning stages you do not need to buy fancy equipment. GPS receivers and other such devices can always come later.

As you hike in a natural area or study an urbanized landscape and look for clues about the past, start by recording the date (day, month, and year) and time in your notebook or clipboard. Also look around at the weather—is it clear and sunny, overcast, or rainy? Is it cold or hot? In the future you can purchase a small thermometer to carry along with you to take more accurate measurements.

During some of my biological survey work for the United States Geological Service's Biological Research Division, I had a Kestrel handheld weather measuring device that recorded temperature, humidity, and wind speed; I held it in the shade of my body at three feet high to take readings, then used a mercury thermometer to take ground temperatures (ground temperature often differs from air temperature at head-level, and it can affect when lizards and snakes are active). I would also record cloud cover percentage. For now, you can estimate these measurements.

Next, record what landform you are standing on. Is the landscape flat or hilly? Are you within view of mountains, or are you in a river canyon? Even in a city you can see this information, and remnant topography can give clues about the old landscape later, when you investigate the history of an area. Use your compass to find north, then draw a simple map showing the hills, mountains, cliffs, rock outcrops, streams, or lakes within your view. If you have a map, you can locate yourself on it. Sometimes I use a clinometer, a device to measure the slope of a land surface or hillside that I am on, but this is not essential.

Is the soil fertile-black or alkaline-white, sandy or rocky or very fine, wet or dry? Without detailed knowledge of soil types, you can record some basic information. There are also small charts that tell you standardized size categories of different soil particles and rock fragments, such as silt, sand, gravel, pebbles, cobbles, and boulders.

You can begin to learn the different plant species present in your area. This takes time, as there are so many. A very good way to learn about a plant is to draw a simple diagram of its leaves and flowers. You can note flower color, plant height, and what growth stage it is in: is it lush and green, flowering, or dried out? If you have a plant guide with you, you can attempt to identify it and learn which plants have been in California for thousands of years and which have been introduced recently from other continents. You may even find a native relict plant growing in an empty lot in your city. You can record these locations on your map with a dot or number, with a key to these labels on the side of the map or on a separate sheet.

Your plant observations can be expanded to include information about plant communities. Record how abundant or rare the plant is, what other plants grow with it, what percentage of the ground is covered by grasses or herbs or shrubs, or what percentage of the sky is blocked out by the forest canopy. Record whether you are in a woodland or grassland, at a marsh or on a beach. If you are in an urban area, after a time the relict plants growing in yards or parks may begin to tell you more about past communities. Native oaks, for example, may suggest the area was a woodland years ago. If you have the time you can draw the extent of woodland or grassland on your map.

Use your binoculars to watch the animals you encounter: birds, squirrels, lizards, frogs in a pond. Using field guides you will gradually learn the species in your area, and you can record these in your notebook. You may also want to pinpoint the sightings on your map, especially if they seem to be uncommon species. Sketching the animals is a great way to learn more about them. You can also choose to sit and watch an animal and begin to learn its behavior: what it eats and how it interacts with its landscape, the weather, and other animals. I often do this, and learning how to hide myself so as not to disturb the animals has become a habit. If you do not see animals, you may see their sign, and this can tell equally interesting stories. Look for tracks, bits of fur or feathers, bones, scat (droppings), rubs or scratches on tree trunks, dust baths and mud wallows, nests, burrows, and browsed vegetation. Sketch them. Soon you may be able to tell the difference between human trails and animal trails. Field guides are available, such as *Mammal Tracks and Sign: A Guide to North American Species,* by Mark Elbroch (Stackpole Books, 2003).

If you encounter a waterway, there is a whole set of new observations you can make. Record what type of waterway it is: a pond, lake, creek, river, bog, wet meadow, spring, or ocean. In the city there are often remnant waterways, streams undergrounded in pipes, springs in boxes, or even telling soils or landforms, such as ravines now covered by houses, that may have once held springs and creeks. Many historic waterways have been drained, covered, or filled and built upon, so a lot of detective work may be needed to find their remnants.

As you will see in the chapter on salmon, you can get deeper into describing waterways, noting such details as substrate type (sandy, gravelly, full of cobbles), water velocity, temperature, channel width, and floodplain width.

Talk to local residents. Often you can get oral histories of what past landscapes looked like. I remember being on a plant walk in the East Bay on a trail beside a large reservoir. A man in our group recalled growing up near here and hiking in the original canyon before the dam went up, and he described to me the trees that used to grow along the stream, now flooded by a flat expanse of blue water.

You can collect stories of what happened in a place, the people and events, the ranches and buildings that came and went, for this is all part of our ecological history as well. If you are from a tribe native to the area, ask your elders the old names for places, where good plant gathering sites were, what stories occurred on the land.

This would also be a good place to mention any human impacts on the land. What are people using it for? Is it grazing land? A forest being logged? An empty lot with a "For Sale" sign? Is there a lot of garbage? Are there off-road vehicle tracks?

When your walk is finished, record the time and place, whether the walk was a loop or ended at a distance, and any other comments you might think of.

You have now begun to get closer to the landscape, and it has become less of an abstraction to you. After building up months and years and decades of such simple observations, you will begin to see the flow of time, the cycles of seasons, water table fluctuations, bird migrations, animals recolonizing old ranges, good wildflower years, droughts and El Niños, the effects of climate change, people's memories and stories, and more. Every place has a story, and you have begun to tap into it.

TEN

GREAT HERDS
Elk and Bison

On yet another sketching trip, at Hansen National Wildlife Refuge along the Columbia River in the Pacific Northwest, I observed Roosevelt elk in lush meadows and wet Douglas fir forests. The month was October and the rut was still on. I sat by my spotting scope along a dirt road and watched a giant seven-point bull elk walk by, his antlers so long they nearly touched his rump as he threw his head back to bugle. Elk cows grazed nearby. As night fell, an eerie mist rose from the river and the trees were silhouetted black against the pink clouds of sunset.

Incredible sounds came from the forest that night: against a background of hundreds of geese cackling in the distance, coyotes yelped, an owl hooted occasionally, and elk bugled—that indescribably wild whistle ending in a roar from the deep chest of an animal the size of a horse. And then came clashes of antlers, terrific cracking and echoing of two unseen opponents throwing their weight at each other in tests of strength.

This, I thought, must have been what primeval California was like, when elk filled the oak savannas, hills, and marshes. What if, in those days, I had been sitting on a hill overlooking a small cove in what would later become the city of San Francisco? I hoped to combine my field notes, sketches, photographs, and memories someday to paint a reconstruction of such a scene. So often, it takes diverse material from many geographical areas and many time periods to put a picture together and fill in the missing pieces. The story of big game herds in California, tule elk and bison, shows better than most the importance of knowing the history behind the ecology.

Elk Types

From Santa Barbara north, before 1850 elk roamed huge expanses along the California coast, over the Central Valley to the Sierra foothills, and on into northeastern California and Oregon. Although no records exist for the Sierra Nevada, we can speculate that elk wandered up the west slope in summer to forage on lush meadows, and herds certainly wintered in the foothills during times when flooding formed extensive lakes in the Central Valley. No sightings or bones from archaeological middens are recorded for the region south of the Tehachapi Range; the Los Angeles grasslands may have been too xeric to support elk.

Three subspecies of elk once inhabited California, and through successful conservation efforts they still do. The endemic tule elk, which inhabited the oak-grass valleys and hills, is lighter in color than other North American elk and has shorter antlers; old bulls sometimes develop palmate terminal points.

Antler growth and body size are sensitive indicators of nutrition, and tule elk thrive best when late summer forage is of high quality.[1] While volunteering for Fish and Game biologist Vern Bleich in Bishop one year, I used binoculars to count the number of tule elk with broken tines in a local herd. The elk were busy breaking into a lush alfalfa field, going after the choicest greens, away from the dry saltbush. "They have a nutritional deficiency here," commented Vern, explaining to me that they were probably not native to this desert region but were instead introduced into the Owens Valley in 1933 as part of an effort to restore their numbers throughout the state.

Thus descriptions of tule elk as "dwarf elk" compared to the large Rocky Mountain and Roosevelt forms are misleading. They may be based on observations of relict animals that survived the market hunting onslaught during and after the gold rush. Other observers found tule elk to be of substantial size. Market hunter H. C. Banta said that in the 1850s, "I found no difference in size between these elk and the Oregon, Washington, Wyoming, and Colorado elk, and felt sure that the bulls would weigh 700 to 800 pounds. They struck me as weighing about as much as an average steer and their horns were fully as big as any elk I have ever killed or seen in other states."[2]

Given access to prime range, tule elk can indeed grow huge. Wildlife biologist Dale McCullough told of a tule elk from Buttonwillow, in the San Joaquin Valley, that was transplanted to a Monterey golf course and "grew to very large size," looking more like a Rocky Mountain elk.[3] H. C. Bailey, living in the Colusa area, described elk there as having been "magnificent," sometimes having an antler spread of six feet across and a dressed weight of seven hundred pounds.[4] In recent times, California Department of Fish and Game records show tule elk bulls on Grizzly Island in Suisun Bay weighing up to 900 pounds. Cows weigh less, from 375 to 425 pounds.[5] I can only speculate that in the past, tule elk feeding all summer in the lush freshwater marsh edges of the Central Valley would have grown to truly impressive proportions.

Roosevelt elk are large, with darker pelage than the tule elk and heavy antlers that often have crowns of tines on their ends. They once ranged from Sonoma County north into Oregon, inhabiting meadows and forest openings in the North Coast Range to 7,000 feet elevation.[6] They can still be viewed at Prairie Creek Redwoods State Park, in Humboldt County.

The third subspecies of elk in California was the Rocky Mountain elk, the large-bodied type with long antlers that is famous today as the elk of Yellowstone National Park. It was noted in the Mount Shasta region, along the Pit River, and in Siskiyou County but was extirpated by 1873.[7] Since then, it has been reintroduced into northeastern California.

Highs and Lows: Elk Abundance

Tule elk were apparently common in Old California and may have been the dominant big game animal in original grasslands ecosystems. Trappers, hunters, explorers, and travelers frequently mentioned large herds: in 1845 "one herd of Elk had a grand appearance containing more than two thousand...head and covering the plain for more than a mile in length," according to James Clyman.[8] Market hunter Jonathan Watson said, of the San Joaquin Valley in the 1860s, "Elk were so plentiful there that we made corrals out of elk horns picked up on the plains."[9]

Not all researchers agree that precontact game numbers were high. In the view of geographer William Preston, big game numbers, including those for elk, were low due to overexploitation by Native people. He explains that the large herds seen by almost all first-contact travelers were "artificially high" because a "protohistoric plague" released in Latin America by the first explorers

HABITED CALIFORNIA, AND THROUGH SUCCESSFUL CONSERVATION EFFORTS THEY STILL DO.

A reconstruction of San Francisco around 1300 A.D. from Nob Hill, looking east across the bay toward Oakland, Berkeley, Emeryville, Albany, and Richmond. OIL ON PANEL, 11 x 21 INCHES, 2003

Antelope and tule elk herd on the plains of Sacramento in July. Great valley oaks tower over stands of creeping wildrye and, in the foreground, meadow barley bunches. OIL ON COTTON RAG PAPER, 6 X 12 INCHES, 2003

from Europe had swept through Native American populations even before Europeans came to California. As the "top predator," Native people, in the view of Preston and others, had overhunted big game animals before 1492 to the extent that they would have been marginal in early California, at least during the late Holocene.[10]

Much of the argument for this view comes from interpreting archaeological faunas in light of "optimal foraging" theory and "resource intensification" models. Anthropologist Jack Broughton, for example, examined numbers of food animal remains in the San Francisco Bay Area's Emeryville Shellmound, a midden long used by the local Ohlone people, with the assumption that the larger the prey, the higher the hunter's foraging efficiency. Bone counts for larger prey were said to decline over the period that the site was used, while those of smaller prey increased. This was interpreted to indicate that Native hunters had reduced the elk population so severely that they had to switch to smaller game.[11]

I would hesitate to make so many assumptions and interpretations about a death assemblage of animal bones where other factors may have been at work. Paleontological training leads me to consider the possibility that human behavioral and cultural traits would affect the choice of prey and the selection of parts of a kill; that new human cultures may have moved into the area; that other animals may have scavenged at the site; that the biology of prehistoric animals may have changed; and that the large-scale climatic fluctuations of the Holocene affected animal (and human) populations. In their work on environmental archaeology John Evans and Terry O'Connor said, "Human food debris...is never representative of the full biological community."[12] For those who are attempting to recreate past ecosystems, this is useful to keep in mind when tempted to depend heavily on quantitative studies of archaeofaunal remains.

The suggestion that epidemics reached California before European contact has also been disputed. Many of the early Spanish explorers depicted large native settlements with abundant game nearby. Crespí, for example, reported that soldiers told him of seeing smoke, presumably an indication of villages, all around the San Francisco Bay and that they often saw elk; Fages in 1770 described numerous villages in the Livermore Valley, a village of six hundred people at Santa Barbara—large by Native Californian standards—and "entire herds of elk" in the nearby Central Valley.[13]

Each species responds in unique ways to hunting pressures, and this further complicates the picture. Elk, unlike some Ice Age big game animals such as giant ground sloths, had a long association with hunting societies, having originated in Siberia-Beringia in the Pleistocene and then spread across Asia into Europe as well as to North America tens of thousands of years ago. North American elk are a fraction of the huge cline of ecotypes that have adapted to a variety of habitats in the New World and Old.[14] They may have coevolved with hunter-gatherers.

Data can yield surprisingly equivocal results. The debate about whether elk were rare or common prehistorically in the Yellowstone ecosystem still rages, with the same evidence yielding opposite interpretations: Charles Kay, using repeat photography, claimed that the lack of browselines in old pictures of conifers must indicate aboriginal overkill and rarity of elk;[15] Mary Meagher and Douglas Houston, however, showed old browselines in their repeat photography study and interpreted this to mean that elk were not rare.[16]

In developing models of historical ecology, each source of information reveals only a partial aspect of the past. As many other sources as possible should be integrated into the framework of data.

Following the Food

With so much evidence lost or open to wide interpretation, past ecosystems are very difficult to imagine. Even living ecosystems pose great challenges to decipher. Thirty years of intense research in East Africa, for example, have still not answered the many questions posed about the workings of the Serengeti Plain.[17] What causes the complex wanderings of grazing animals, zebras and wildebeests, across the grasslands and savannas? Herding may be an antipredator strategy, but food seems to be the single most powerful cause of local movements and long-distance migrations: grazers are constantly seeking the forage with the highest nutritional value, the most succulent greenery.

How did tule elk interact with the grasslands of early California? What were the seasonal movements of the herds like? How did the range ecology of those times differ from today? Reconstructing the food habits and movements of prehistoric elk is only guesswork, but clues can be found by studying elk today, as well as relict native plant communities.

Elk feed predominantly on grasses and sedges, but forbs are very important in the spring and summer, and they also favor the leaves of shrubs and trees throughout the year. In other words, elk are successful generalists, taking the best plant food available.

Although tule elk skulls are shorter than those of other elk, the tooth rows of grinding molars and premolars are longer, to accommodate chewing the fibrous plants of the semiarid California

Bull elk with antlers in velvet dines on new purple needlegrass blades in a burn.
OIL ON COTTON RAG PAPER, 4 X 6 INCHES, 2003

prairies.[18] A mosaic of patches of bunchgrasses, rhizomatous grass swards, and some annual grasses grew in Old California. Elk moved through this mosaic, choosing the most palatable species with the newest growth. Four days after the first rains in October, purple needlegrass began to green up, starting perhaps on ridgetops and warm south- and west-facing slopes. Elk may have concentrated in these spots to dine on green blades. During the winter rainy season, green bunchgrasses would be widespread, and elk could have dispersed over hills and plains. They may have selected particularly tender species ahead of coarse grasses: the small tufts of one-sided bluegrass that once were abundant on the slopes and flats of the California prairie; the soft, fine blades of junegrass, and the moist bunches of mountain bromegrass. This last grass, when grazed down early, will produce a luxuriant aftermath of foliage that is relished by grazing animals even in the dry season.

During the spring, elk probably turned to feeding on the abundant forbs whose flowers cloaked the prairies. In elk forage studies, I found long lists of California native annual and perennial forbs eaten by elk: buttercups, California poppies, owl's clover, soap plant, lupines, brodiaea, and many others. A feast of high-protein, nutrient-laden forbs allowed elk to put on weight before the summer dry season and shifted the grazing pressure away from the bunchgrasses as they put out seed stalks.

When the grassy hills dried out and spring wildflowers turned to dust, elk shifted again, to feed on green willow leaves in valleys. They also ate oak leaves and the leaves of small trees and shrubs such as ceanothus, currant and gooseberry, wild rose, and elderberry. Summer-green forbs may also

Tule elk herd on a summer slope of blue oak savanna in the South Coast Range.
OIL ON PANEL, 11 ½ X 17 ½ INCHES, 1997

have been important, such as buckwheats, the purple-flowered *Aster chilensis* and other asters, and the multitudes of aromatic tarweeds that grew among drying bunchgrasses. Dry purple needlegrass cured well in the summer and elk may have grazed it as a source of carbohydrate energy—good-quality hay. In some locations elk would have moved down to valley bottoms in the dry season as extensive patches of creeping wildrye provided much green forage. Marsh edges around the San Francisco Bay, and especially in the Central Valley, would have provided an abundance of luxuriant vegetation, green water-edge grasses such as bentgrass, sloughgrass, witchgrasses, knotgrass, and reedgrass, as well as sedges, rushes, green forbs, and willows.

In the fall, elk could gorge on acorns back in the uplands and travel to early green-up areas as the rains began to start the cycle again. Native Americans would have added a crucial food resource: burned fields. Fire removed old, dead leaves on perennial bunchgrasses and stimulated new growth of green leaves, even in an otherwise dry summer landscape. These green patches would have been highly attractive to elk, deer, and antelope, producing high-quality forage when nutritional resources were limited. A mosaic of burned and unburned grassland would keep elk moving.

Even so, the huge elk herds that were reported, sometimes numbering in the thousands, must have left some imprint on the land. If I could take a walk over the hills in Old California, I would see conspicuous trails leading to watering areas, some trampling and heavy grazing in favored spots, browselines in some places in the willow thickets, and large wallows where bull elk, during the rut, would roll and paw the mud. Purple needlegrass on heavily used areas like ridgetops might have formed a zootic climax, responding to elk grazing by reducing the diameter of individual bunches.

Many native plants have adaptations that allow them to disperse their seeds by hitching rides on the fur of passing elk or deer. Most tarweeds have achenes with gland-tipped hairs to stick to fur (and clothes). Cocklebur has hooked spines on its seeds and may have caught on elk fur around waterholes. Rancheria clover has numerous hairs on its seeds to catch on fur. The long, bristly awns of many native grasses also are easily caught in fur: needlegrasses, blue wildrye, and meadow barley often hitch rides on my socks.

In my wanderings through the oak and grass canyons of Tilden Regional Park, near Berkeley, I found an odd land feature. It was a depression about thirty or forty feet long, as if scooped out by a bulldozer. But it was old, with mature creeping wildrye growing over its banks, and small springs seeping water nearby. A creek ran next to it, but erosion did not cause this depression. After looking at it for long periods and noticing whitish soil in it, and even a strange species of tarweed that I had seen growing nowhere else, I decided that this could be an old mineral lick. Perhaps deer and elk over the centuries pawed it apart to supplement their diet with calcium, magnesium, or sodium, minerals rising out of the ground in solution from a fault.

In regard to the search for feeding grounds, the question of long-distance migration comes up. Many populations of Rocky Mountain elk migrate between high mountain ranges in summer and lower valleys in winter, when snow accumulates. Eastern elk apparently did not migrate.[19] Roosevelt elk in the Siskiyou Mountains, according to settlers, migrated to winter ranges at lower elevations.[20] A tally of dates and locations of tule elk sightings by early travelers shows no pattern of migration, however. Elk were seen on coastal hills in July as well as in December. They were found in abundance in the freshwater marshes of the Central Valley in April, June, and October. Similarly, in the Coast Ranges they seemed to occur at all seasons. Thus elk in much of California probably moved about locally in response to rains, burning, wildflower blooms, and wetland green-up, instead of making long migrations like the Serengeti wildebeest.

Daily and Yearly Cycles

And so life went on for the elk herds in Old California. They fed before first light and then each individual lay down to ruminate—chew its cud—for two hours or so. Then more feeding. At midday they idled about their bedding area, and in the afternoon feeding resumed, continuing intermittently through the night. Feeding and resting occupied 90 percent of the elk's day.

HERDING A COW   FACE OFF

SPIKE BUCK

BULLS STILL IN LONG WINTER WHITE COAT MOSTLY, SHEDDING OFF ON SIDES & FLANK, REMAINING ON BACK.

YOUNG BULL
HORNING COYOTE BR.

Bugling

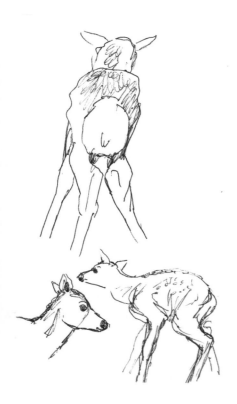

Newborn can barely stand

The rut began in July. Big bulls developed long, black neck hair that contrasted with their light body fur. They sought out herds of cows to join, chasing away lesser males. Their organlike bugles echoed through the oaks, ending in long squeals that carried far over the grasslands.

In August and September the rut peaked, and with necks extended and heads tilted up, showing off mighty racks of antlers, master bulls charged their challengers. If an intruder did not run off, the two might walk parallel to each other in display until one suddenly wheeled to face his opponent and, with terrific force, smashed his antlers into the other's.

By October the rut wound down. Bulls were exhausted from battling rivals. Cows now began to gather into larger winter herds. Bulls grouped into bachelor herds again.

When I was watching big game one May in Yellowstone National Park, a lone elk cow passed below the hill I was sitting on. With binoculars up, I sketched her. Her mouth was open, as if she were nervous. She looked about constantly until she entered a ravine full of Douglas fir and brush—she appeared to be seeking a hidden spot in order to drop her calf. I wondered at how difficult this must be, with grizzlies and a wolf pack in the vicinity, both sniffing the ground for every sign of calving. Such scenes must have been common in Old California.

The elk mother stayed alone with her new spotted calf, away from the herd, for two to three weeks. She fed as it lay hidden in brush or tall grass. When all was safe, the cow gave a special call and the calf jumped up and ran over to nurse. Then it sought cover again.

By the calf's second week it started to feed on green grass, and soon it was strong enough to run. The mother and young then joined the herd. The calf lost its spotted coat by July or August and was weaned by September or October.

The Survival of a Species

These daily and yearly cycles went on in California for tens of thousands of years and then were disrupted as, in the late 1700s and into the 1800s, Spanish rancheros hunted elk on horseback, lassoing them like cattle, taking their hides, and rendering their fat. Elk may have been able to hold their own in this period, coexisting with cattle and horse herds on open ranges.

Fur trappers took elk also, from the 1820s to 1840s, apparently decreasing their numbers in parts of the Sacramento Valley.[21] But it was not until the market hunting period during and after the gold rush that the elk population crashed. "In 1854," wrote market hunter H. C. Banta, "I found elk plentiful in the foothills west of the San Joaquin Valley, as well as in the tule swamp. Bob Dikemen and Lee Phillips were my hunting companions, and we practically finished up all the tule elk in that section between Martinez and San Joaquin City."[22] Elk disappeared from the San Francisco Bay Area by the 1860s. Roosevelt elk were driven from Sonoma County by about 1870.[23]

The tule elk's last stronghold was in the vast marshes of Tulare and Buena Vista Lakes, in the San Joaquin Valley, and they probably would have gone extinct there were it not for cattle baron Henry Miller, who in about 1874 found a few remaining elk while draining a marsh on his ranch—the last tule elk in the state. His decision to protect them led to a fifty-year effort, and the California Department of Fish and Game soon became involved.[24]

Elk were transplanted gradually to preserves, parks, and ranches across the state, and their numbers grew so that today there are now around three thousand—a far cry from Dale McCullough's estimated half-million before 1800.[25] Tule elk still carry the legacy of this population "bottleneck"—the term used when a significant percentage of a species is killed or otherwise prevented from reproducing—in their genes. The diversity of genetic types has been lost, and all tule elk today are directly related to the individuals from Henry Miller's ranch.[26] I can only speculate how elk herds across California may have differed slightly from one another. Subfossil bones from Pacifica, on the coast, show one skull character that approaches Roosevelt elk, yet other characters are like tule elk from the San Joaquin Valley.[27]

But overall the elk story in California is a very successful one. Biologists, hunters supportive of conservation measures, parks, groups such as the Rocky Mountain Elk Foundation, and private ranchers and landowners who do not mind elk herds wandering on their land have all contributed enormously to the growth of elk numbers. Elk are so successful that sometimes efforts to control their population growth must be put in effect—if only some of our other species that have been threatened or endangered had this problem!

Today elk can be easily seen at Point Reyes National Seashore (Marin County), Grizzly Island National Wildlife Refuge (Solano County), San Luis National Wildlife Refuge (Merced County), the Bureau of Land Management's Cache Creek Natural Area (Lake and Colusa Counties), and Prairie Creek Redwoods State Park (Humboldt County), among other places. One can follow the tracks of a herd of elk through the mud of a winter valley, feel the heat waves bounce off their backs in summer and watch kingbirds catch flies among their hooves, and in autumn hear the bugle of an unseen bull echo through the forests at dawn.

Where the Buffalo Roamed

California had other big "hoofstock" besides elk: the bison of the Modoc County region. It was on the northeastern sagebrush-grass plains and juniper hills that the only certain population of buffalo in California once roamed. Herds probably mixed with Rocky Mountain elk, pronghorn antelope, and Rocky Mountain mule deer.

An important question has often dogged me while walking around California grasslands: why were bison found only in this corner of the state during the last several thousand years, and not all over our grasslands? As it turns out, this is a good example of why the "history" is in "historical ecology."

I have spent a lot of time camping and hiking northeastern California's Modoc Plateau because of its remnant antelope herds and vast marshes filled with waterfowl, and I have come to know the peculiar type of cold-arid grassland that exists here. Mixed with pungent big sagebrush and scattered, dark green juniper, there is a grassland of bluebunch wheatgrass, one-sided bluegrass, Idaho fescue, prairie junegrass, and Thurber needlegrass, among others. This Great Basin community actually stretched, in varying form, in a broad arc across the interior West to the Rocky Mountain region, where it can still be found in places like Yellowstone National Park. A good place to see this habitat in fair condition is at Lava Beds National Monument in Modoc County.

Bison are grazers and would have selected for these grasses over shrub and tree browse. Bison herds were small and apparently transitory here, as they were in much of the West outside of their Great Plains core range. What kind of bison these were is a matter of debate. Although little evidence is left after colonial expansion and overhunting, some researchers speculate that the bison of the far West may have been a different subspecies than the Plains bison. Called the mountain bison or wood bison, this subspecies ranged in Oregon, Washington, Idaho, northern Nevada, Utah, and up into Canada. Early Euro-American travelers noted that it was darker in color and somewhat larger in size than the Plains bison, living in small bands of five to thirty animals in mountainous areas, timbered lands, meadows, and valley prairies.[28] Today this bison can only be seen at Wood Buffalo National Park, in Alberta.

Paleontologist Jerry MacDonald, however, after studying large series of bison skulls across the continent, concluded that skull measurements of bison from Malheur Lake, in southeastern Oregon, were closer to those of the Plains bison than the wood bison.[29] The presence in southeastern Oregon of the Plains bison would make sense, looking at the bluebunch wheatgrass steppe reaching from Wyoming and Colorado across to northeastern California.

What we do know for certain is that bison, of some kind, were present in Old California. The Northern Paiute and the Pit River tribes of northeastern California knew the bison well and told interviewers in the mid-twentieth century of how they used to hunt them with bows and arrows, although they said it was a difficult feat.[30] Bison once lived in Alturas Valley, Surprise Valley, the Madeline Plains, Hot Springs, Horse Lake Valley, Eagle Lake, Honey Lake, and a small permanent herd at Pine Creek Valley.[31] In the Smoke Creek Desert, in adjacent northwestern Nevada, many places—Buffalo Meadows and Buffalo Spring, for example—include "buffalo" in their names.

A hunter in 1871 told of finding weathered buffalo skulls as far west as the Sierra Nevada.[32] A buffalo wallow was described on the west shore of Honey Lake, with a trail leading southwest towards Plumas County over a low pass in the Sierra (about 5,000 feet in elevation). Bison were said to have taken the trail, but no one knew where it led.

Did bison cross over this low pass into the purple needlegrass habitats of western California? Most biologists writing of large mammal distribution in California deny that bison were found west of the Cascade-Sierra divide during the Holocene. But I have kept an open mind. Hiking the gentle Plumas County Sierra, where the transition begins to the Cascade volcanoes in the north, I found open ponderosa pine forest with a good grassy understory. This forest would not have been a big barrier to bison, considering that in other parts of the continent, such as Yellowstone National Park and in Canada, they regularly travel through conifer forest.

In the accounts of Spanish explorers there are some curious references to large animals that may not have been elk: Father Crespí, on October 11, 1769, traveling near the Pajaro River (Santa Cruz and

Monterey Counties) reported that soldiers showed him "various tracks that looked like cattle, and we suppose they are buffalo. I did not see any of the beasts myself, but the scouts reported that along the shore hereabouts they saw as many as twenty-one beasts together, of all colors, with calves at their feet like cows; also, that they had seen deer or stags, very big-bodies and with very large spreading antlers."[33] Pedro Fages, too, traveling in the 1770s from the San Francisco Bay to the Central Valley, looked upon the Sierra and told of hearing of "numerous wild buffaloes living in the dense parts of the forest."[34]

What were these beasts? Apparently not elk, as the soldiers identified those separately. Were they wild cattle, already spread from colonies in the Southwest?

Perhaps western California grasslands were too arid for bison, which are found today mostly in areas with higher summer rainfall. But in late prehistoric times it seems that bison were pushing the edges of the driest desert belts. In southeastern Nevada, bison bones have been found in an Indian rock shelter.[35] One hundred and twenty-eight miles east of this, a bison skull was picked up in Iron County, in far southwestern Utah, and evidence of bison has been found around Great Salt Lake as well.

In near-recent times bison trickled into arid grasslands in the American Southwest. Historians have found scattered accounts of bison or bison parts, such as hides and horns, in northern Mexico before 1600.[36] An 1806 document by an official at Monclova, Coahuila, tried to ban settlers from their incessant hunting of bison, called "cibolo."[37] There were also bison reports from Chihuahua, in semidesert grassland with cabbage palm and mesquite. Bison skeletal remains have been found in various archaeological sites west of the Rio Grande from before 1200, evidence to me of a range contraction perhaps related to the climatic fluctuations of the Medieval Warm Period and Little Ice Age—during times of increased moisture, the bison bands moved beyond the fringes of their core range as grassy areas expanded, but during dryer phases they shrank back. A dramatic increase in the number of bison bones recovered from archaeological sites in the Great Basin sagebrush steppe corresponded with greater grass abundance during the cooler, moister period from fifteen hundred to twelve hundred years ago.[38]

California bison could have been irregular wanderers, as many game herds probably were before fences and park boundaries. Father Francisco Garcés, traveling up the Colorado River into Arizona during 1775 and 1776, reported that in Yavapai country by Cataract Creek and the Grand Canyon in Coconino County the Indians had killed a buffalo, as well as stray cattle and deer, and shared the meat with him.[39]

Another explanation for the presence of bison in unexpected locations is the long-term multimillennial expansion that they may have undergone, described by Jerry MacDonald. Bison originated in Eurasia and during the late Pleistocene traveled across Beringia to North America, where they flourished as several species of Ice Age types, including *Bison antiquus*, which was abundant in California. Bison did not all go extinct with the rest of the megafauna, but certain populations did show range shrinkage and skeletal abnormalities due to inbreeding in small, isolated populations during the period from 12,000 to 6,000 years ago—a bottleneck which they survived. During this time bison body size decreased and horn size became smaller. Careful dating of 12,000 years' worth of skeletal remains shows the range of bison shrinking

SIZE COMPARISON

from continental proportions to the northern Great Plains by 7,000 to 5,000 years ago. This was their core area of survival during the Xerothermic mid-Holocene climatic crisis. After 5,000 B.P. their range may have expanded slowly as the climate became generally moister and cooler, and this is when our modern *Bison bison* appeared. MacDonald notes that their southward expansion accelerated by 3,000 B.P., and by 2,500 years ago they had begun to colonize outlying areas in a great range enlargement, to habitats such as the Great Basin steppes. The ancient bison had successfully adapted and evolved to the radically changed post–Ice Age climates and plant communities.[40]

Bison populations over the last few thousand years apparently fluctuated with long-term droughts and cold storms, but they were filtering in small numbers into the eastern United States, Mexico, northern Arizona, the grassier parts of the Great Basin, and possibly even western California. They may not have grazed east of the Mississippi until A.D. 1000.[41] Bison in eastern North America were apparently in the process of range expansion when Europeans first encountered them; evidence indicates that this great expansion might have continued steadily were it not for the Euroamerican settlers and hunters who cut it short.

I believe that bison may have been irregularly wandering into northeastern California (and perhaps farther west) in small groups for millennia. But then American settlers and travelers killed millions of buffalo between the 1860s and 1880s in their core range. According to MacDonald, this created a second Holocene bottleneck, which probably resulted in the loss of certain phenotypes (physical types) and behaviors. Their range has been fragmented and artificially regulated ever since. But they survive.

I pondered this while watching bison in Yellowstone National Park. Small groups of young bulls scattered with herds of elk among the cottonwoods on the flat. A group of cow bison with many orange calves grazed nearby. Two young bison romped together in play, loping after the elk and scattering them. Then the two butted heads. I could translate this scene into Modoc County five hundred years ago, to Honey Lake, Alturas, Lava Beds, and other places where I had spent so many hours watching and sketching mule deer and antelope.

Knowing something of the history, natural and human, of a region will certainly allow a curious naturalist to reconstruct the elements of the past. But not all questions can be answered. Whether bison were still living wild on the Modoc plains and lava rimrock lands just before the age of the rifle is now an undecipherable puzzle. Were they expanding their range naturally into California? Would climate change have affected them? Would increasing drought have pushed them back out?

The history of one species will often reveal something of the other species with which it interrelates. The next chapter examines the way that events such as the hunting out of elk or bison from a region, a disease hitting a species, or a sudden climatic turn can ripple across a landscape and change the lives of several other species.

ELEVEN

TOP PREDATORS

Interactions

nimals—and that includes humans—and plants do not exist in a vacuum. They interact with other species in a dynamic environment in ways that may change or be lost over time. Elk and deer were main prey animals in early California, but a varied array of predators also once inhabited our state. The landscape of Old California was inhabited by an array of predators, including coyotes, wolves, mountain lions, and even jaguars.

Wolves and Coyotes

Coyotes were apparently fairly common: their bones were found in archaeological deposits, and numerous explorers mentioned them. Pedro Fages in July 1769, in what is now San Diego, described "deer, antelope, conies [possibly cottontail rabbits], hares without number, wildcats, wolves, some bears, coyotes, and squirrels of three kinds."[1]

Old Sierra white wolf in the Kerrick Meadow area of North Yosemite Wilderness long ago.
OIL ON PANEL, 29 X 40 INCHES, 1996

The history of wolves in California is not so obvious. Some contemporary wildlife biologists attempting to reconstruct California's early fauna say that we had no wolves, but many observers in the 1800s mentioned both coyotes and wolves. Gray wolves roamed most of the state when explorers first arrived, according to a literature survey by biologist Robert Schmidt.[2] Russian explorer Otto von Kotzebue found two species of "wolves" (probably gray wolves and coyotes) while traveling from the San Francisco Bay to the Central Valley.[3] Other sightings occurred in Humboldt County in the 1820s, near Monterey Bay, and by San Gabriel Mission, east of Los Angeles.[4] From 1850 to 1900 trappers and railway survey naturalists sighted wolves in Shasta County and in the central Sierra Nevada above 6,000 feet.

Though wolves were reportedly common in the West in 1800, the highly efficient guns, traps, and poison that settlers used against them to protect their stock quickly reduced or eliminated the wolf population, as they did the grizzlies. Beginning in 1915, wolves were subject to the first federal predator-control measures. In California wolves now could only be found in the remotest parts: among the last records are a sighting in Modoc County in 1922, and a lone wolf trapped, also in 1922, in the Providence Mountains in the eastern Mojave Desert, a wildland of Joshua trees and barrel cactus. It was an old male, one hundred pounds, that had accidentally stepped into a coyote trap while chasing bighorn sheep.[5] The last confirmed native wolf was trapped in 1924 from Lassen County, an emaciated three-legged survivor very similar to the Plains wolf type. Wolves were eliminated from the western U.S. by the 1930s. Although some trickled into Montana from Canada, their rarity prompted biologists to protect them in 1974 under the Federal Endangered Species Act of 1973.[6]

We will never know what unique wolf genetics were lost in California—perhaps special ecotypes adapted to hunt elk in a Mediterranean climate. In Alaska, conditions allowed a glimpse of what had been lost over time when in 2007 scientists unearthed twenty-one frozen carcasses of Ice Age wolves from permafrost, dated seventeen thousand to forty-seven thousand years old: flesh was still present, giving genetic samples. The mitochondrial DNA showed lineages of wolves that matched none living. Compared to living wolf ecomorphs, these extinct types had larger jaws. Their bone-crushing teeth were adapted to take advantage of abundant megafaunal carcasses.[7]

Wolf Packs

Wolf packs consist of a dominant breeding pair and offspring of the current and previous years, and occasionally unrelated wolves. Juveniles may disperse from their packs between the ages of one to three years, and some individuals have been found to travel five hundred miles in a matter of months into new territory.[8] Packs usually number two to seven animals, although a pack of thirty-six wolves was reported in Alaska;[9] they may subdivide when the packs get too large. At times, a wolf group may lack a breeding pair. Sometimes there are temporary associations and lone wolves may also travel within the population.

The breeding season is January and February in the northern Rockies. In New Mexico and Mexico it is earlier, in December.[10] The pregnant female digs one or more dens into sandy or gravelly slopes or ridges. Whelping occurs in spring. By fall four to six pups travel with the pack.[11] Early Euro-American visitors to the Southwest noted wolf "runways": trails through oak-grass habitats, mountain ranges, and canyons that a pack would use regularly as it made a circuit of its hunting range.[12]

Viewing Wolves in the Wild

As I thought about wolf packs hunting tule elk through blue oak savanna runways, I wanted to see wolves in the wild for myself. Poring over books, articles, and scientific papers about wolves is no substitute for being in wolf habitat, seeing the animals themselves interacting with other animals, influencing whole communities of plants—and feeding the imagination with sights, smells, and sounds.

Wolves from Canada were successfully reintroduced in 1995 into Yellowstone National Park and central Idaho, yielding a look at predator-prey relationships that had not been seen in the lower forty-eight states in decades. I headed out there in May 1998 for an extended camping and sketching trip to watch megafauna in a semipristine ecosystem, and I was not disappointed.

The Yellowstone packs had been preying mostly on elk, often taking calves and cows, but some packs took as many bull elk.[13] They killed bison and moose more in late winter. They also took mule deer, white-tailed deer, bighorn sheep, and rarely, pronghorn antelope.[14] Packs killed an ungulate every one to five days. Of every hundred elk they chased, wolves killed only two or three. Herbivores are not always easy to kill: elk and bison that stand their ground against wolves had a much better chance of surviving than those that ran.[15] When elk were migrating, the wolf packs turned to other prey rather than follow them.[16]

Wolves also preyed on voles, ground squirrels, marmots, beavers, coyotes, grizzly bear cubs, badgers, skunks, sandhill cranes, ptarmigans, ravens, and golden eagles, but from 60 to 96 percent of their food consisted of larger animals.[17]

On a very cold morning I scanned a grassy valley in Yellowstone, watching for any wildlife. I was traveling with a group of like-minded observers. We had come from all over the country—some from England—to sit with spotting scopes and binoculars. A gray wolf began trotting about, hunting voles and ground squirrels. Sometimes it lunged, forelegs into the grass, almost like a coyote but without the elegant full-body dive. After fifteen minutes it caught a vole. Apparently not hungry enough to eat it immediately, the wolf used the rodent as a toy, letting it go and catching it again. Finally it ate it. After moving across the meadow, the wolf suddenly broke into a gallop, as if on cue from some unseen pack mate, and ran fast up a terrace, disappearing into the distance.

Four days later our group gathered before dawn on the roadside in the valley where the wolf had been chasing rodents. We waited for more sightings. Grazing elk were scattered on the grassy terrace and lower slopes—cows, a bull group in velvet, and a young elk group. A mule deer doe grazed near them.

Then we hushed as we heard faint howls up on the slopes somewhere in the Douglas fir forests. Almost immediately a single wolf answered from across the valley. A few minutes later more howling came from both slopes, low, long, steady, and eerie, as clouds swirled around the peak, breaking up only a little to reveal light blue sky.

Field notes, May 30, 1997:
0600: Elk grazing in Swan Lake Meadows.
0630: A young bull with velvet knobs disturbed on hill, running then standing. Wolf trotted past, same collared individual as last night, almost in same spot. Walked along base of hill through grass/sagebrush toward several elk (cows and one calf). About 500 feet from elk, wolf began to trot, staring intently at elk. They trotted quickly uphill into burned forest. Wolf trotted and loped at times up after them—not a real chase, but testing elk, which continued to trot away, not at top speed.

LYING DOWN

HUNTING VOLES

YOUNG THIN
2-TONE GRAY
WOLF

TRAVELING DOWN MEADOW

"HALF JUMP" AFTER VOLE,
ONLY FOREPARTS LEAVING
GROUND.

PLAYING WITH VOLE

EATING VOLE

Young female greeting more dominant pack member

The elk have amazingly keen senses and seemed to sense the coming of the wolves even before we heard the howling. The cow group became alert, heads up. The mule deer, the first to prick up her ears, galloped at full speed out of the open and into the forest. The young bulls trotted out of the valley, some hesitantly, some taking the lead. The remaining elk loped or trotted to the forest edge, lingering and then walking into cover.

Someone spotted a black wolf already in the valley, lying in the grass. A second black wolf trotted up. A third wolf, this one gray, joined them. More howling echoed into the valley, and one of the black wolves, a fairly dominant (beta) female, struck a classic pose while howling in return: snout in air and hind parts slightly crouched. The gray went off, exploring the valley, and swam across the cold river.

By 6:30 the whole pack was gathering—eight wolves coming out of the hills. A big greeting ceremony took place: two subordinate wolves moved with ears flat, heads low, and tails wagging toward another wolf, and they licked its mouth. Soon the alpha male and female arrived—the top dogs and breeding pair of the pack. With tails up they spent a long time greeting each of three less dominant members. At one point a dominant wolf pounced on a younger one, who rolled on its back, and they muzzled each other. Each of the alphas and betas briefly urinated with a leg up onto the bushes. The whole ceremony was complex and fast, a chain of behaviors that biologists label with such terms as "chin placed on back," "pin," and "tail tuck."

Gradually the displays lessened and the pack began to walk off toward the mountain slopes. They trotted as a unified body now, purposefully, only briefly broken up by a young wolf turning to

Field notes: "Size comparison: elk still look huge even with wolf."

the others in a play-invitation bow. None of the others joined the play, so the young wolf jumped up and ran back into line. They moved into the forest of firs and aspens, causing another elk herd to stop its grazing and move away. Soon all animals disappeared into the vast tracts of ridges and deep green.

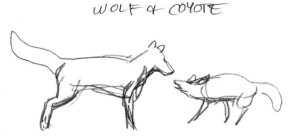

WOLF & COYOTE

Wolf Connections

In 2001, six years after wolves had been reintroduced to Yellowstone, elk numbers there had apparently changed little. Habitat use by elk, however, was another story and gives us a hint of the complex interrelations of predators, prey, and vegetation. With wolves hunting in the vicinity, hungry herds of elk moved off the aspen groves, which in turn allowed the heavily browsed aspen saplings to grow taller, replenishing the groves.[18] Aspen trees may be increasing in Yellowstone because of this interaction, although, as in the complex story of oaks in California, climate change and fire suppression may also play a part. One could guess that wolves (and indigenous bow hunters) played a similar role in precontact California, where large herds of elk might have heavily browsed riparian willow and cottonwood stands; wolves would scare elk out of watercourse forests, lessening their impact on the trees.

I am always delighted at the subtle ways in which everything in the natural world is connected, and often reminded that we too are wrapped in this web. When Euro-Americans killed off the wolf in California, a long-term ripple was started. In the absence of these predators to "herd" them, the elk moved around less and overbrowsed riparian resources, thus threatening their own range quality. As mentioned in chapter nine, the Yellowstone wolves may be helping the pronghorn antelope to

BLACK WOLF CHEWING BONE-

GRAY & WHITE CARRYING OFF BONE

BLACK WOLF CHEWING ON BONE.

Field sketches of wolves on their elk carcass

increase in numbers. Whether by "interference competition" with coyotes (wolves harass coyotes, compete with them for hunting areas, and cause the coyotes to shift their territories) or by direct predation, the wolves have reduced coyote numbers, which in turn may be allowing more newborn pronghorn to survive, as coyotes often kill large numbers of juveniles. This hypothesis has been called "mesopredator release," the coyote being a mid-level (meso) predator.

Other animals benefit too. As the wolf, the top predator, reduces coyote numbers (perhaps by as much as 50 percent in Yellowstone), small predators may be given the chance to increase: foxes, fishers, and wolverines, according to biologist Robert Crabtree of the Yellowstone Ecological Research Center.[19] In California, biologists have speculated that reduced numbers of San Joaquin kit foxes may be due to increased coyote predation on the little canids, again possibly because of the absence of wolves.[20]

Another avenue of research opened up by wolf reintroduction is the study of "trophic cascades." A trickle at the top of a series of trophic (food) relations can become a cascade as it affects other species; one keystone species, such as the wolf, can provide food for many lesser species in the ecological web. An example is the food that wolves supply to an array of scavengers, a supply that varies at different times of year. In winter wolves aggressively defend their kills, often chasing scavengers away; but in summer the pack often has pups to care for, and adults travel back and forth from a carcass with stomachs and mouths full of meat so that they can feed the pups by regurgitation. The carcass is thus sometimes left unattended and the scavengers have access.[21] Sometimes wolves cache parts of a carcass for later dining, especially if prey is not abundant. Scavengers often find these as well.

The Scavenger Guild

I sat on the roadside by my car, scanning the green ridges and flowing rivers by Slough Creek, in Yellowstone National Park. Coyotes howled in the hills and a sandhill crane landed in the grass of a flat. Then I spotted a fresh kill in the distance by a river bend. A wolf was feeding on a cow elk; the elk's hide had barely been torn yet.

The wolf-watching group gathered as word spread about the "action" at the carcass. A resident of Bozeman, Montana, told us she had seen the kill the day before while watching a grizzly. She said an elk herd came into view, running hard, a group of wolves chasing it. All the elk ran up a hill except for one cow, who ran downslope and away from the others. The wolves went after this one. One wolf grabbed the ham of the elk's hind leg with its jaws and held on, tucking its legs up as the elk kicked. She kicked the wolf off, but it ran up and bit again. She kicked it off three times—the wolf must have received a bruising! Finally the elk fell and the wolves made the kill.

CARCASS BY NOW MUCH EATEN: RIB CAGE EXPOSED, HIDE TORN OFF EXCEPT ON RUMP

2 BLACKS & A GRAY

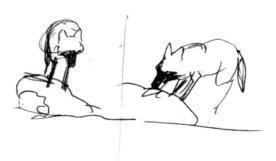

BLACK WOLF
RIPPING AT
CARCASS

Two black wolves now sat in the grass, waiting their turn, as a third, this one gray, fed on the carcass. It left and one black wolf went to feed. Dozens of ravens and two black-billed magpies also waited. The wolf would often chase the ravens, sending a cloud of black wings upward, but they landed persistently nearby. Each wolf soon tore off a bone to carry away, lying in the grass to gnaw on it. They returned and began tearing at the sides of the elk, and soon gaping red wounds were visible to us as we watched from a quarter-mile away. Nervous elk and antelope grazing on valley side slopes also watched the wolves for long periods.

As the wolves left to gnaw on a chunk, or nap, all the ravens leapt onto the carcass to feed, covering it. As the day grew hot the carcass bloated in the sun, but that did not stop a white wolf from yanking meat off of it. Later the wolf left and a coyote cautiously came by to feed, pulling at the carcass, looking around to check the surroundings after each bite. It then trotted off, stopping to mark a bone with urine. That afternoon I found a golden eagle sitting atop the elk body, pulling off strips of flesh. Twenty ravens waited around for their turn.

By five o'clock most of the carcass had been eaten; the rib cage was exposed and only the rump hide remained. A bald eagle was now on it, and the ravens loafed on the ground. A thundershower drenched the area and I left for camp.

The next morning a grizzly mother and cubs were eating at the carcass—they and the wolves must have been busy the night before, as the body was almost completely gone. The one small chunk that was left had been dragged two hundred feet, with room for two ravens to sit on it. The bears walked off and a lone black wolf came to take its turn. I was impressed at how quickly the elk was pulled apart, devoured, and scattered. It would be only dry bones and sinew in another day.

Back in the Golden State, I went to talk with Leslie Chow, a carnivore biologist with the U.S. Geological Survey at Yosemite National Park, about interactions in the past. "We just had a report of a wolverine up by Mule Pass!" he told me excitedly, savoring any possibility of seeing this highly secretive animal. Only two confirmed sightings exist for the whole park. Wolverines are carrion specialists, so they need large territories (several hundred square miles) in which to search out their food—they might walk fifty miles daily. Logging, ski resort development, other habitat fragmentation, and fur trapping (which was finally prohibited in 1970) have all hindered these solitary brown beasts, which are now rare. Leslie Chow speculates that in the past, the mountain-dwelling wolverines might have been attracted out onto the open Central Valley plains to scavenge on wolf- and grizzly-killed elk, deer, and antelope carcasses.

Order or Chaos at Isle Royale?

The pervasive influence of wolves in their ecosystems is becoming more apparent, although, as wolf researcher Rolf Peterson says, the paradoxical nature of ecological interrelationships is also more evident: "The longer one studies a particular living system, the less one can say with certainty about its behavior."[22] Ecologists have tried to fit nature into neat classification schemes and clean operating theories, but those studying wolves have sometimes been faced with "chaos."

On Isle Royale, in Lake Superior between Michigan and Ontario, Canada, a moose population free of predation was flourishing on the lush food supply provided by newly burned forests. In 1949 Canadian wolves colonized the island by crossing the ice of the frozen lake, giving scientists the opportunity to study predator-prey relations. The wolf and moose populations cycled through ups and downs into the 1960s and 1970s: when wildfires or intense windstorms opened up the forest and provided new food sources, the moose population increased, despite all "predatory obstacles."[23] But after three or four successive severe winters with deep snow, the wolves were able to "mow down" the moose; the packs killed one-fifth of them. Because fewer moose calves grew to adulthood and old age, wolves had less of their favorite and easiest prey—old moose. So wolf population peaks lagged behind moose peaks by about ten years in the cycle.

But wolves were found to be helping the forest recover from high moose numbers: tree ring studies showed that moose herbivory suppressed woody vegetation, but with increased wolf predation, the moose's favorite tree, balsam fir, was able to grow tall, beyond browse-height; the trees' growth rate cycled synchronously with the wolf population. With more trees available, the moose calves that did survive predation grew large and healthy. The wolf, in essence, had rejuvenated the moose population in a complex trophic cascade.

In the 1960s researchers had thought the wolf-moose system was in equilibrium, a natural balance. But all that changed when more years and decades of observation had piled up. In the 1980s canine parvovirus hit the wolves and their population crashed (the virus was carried by dogs and people). The great decades-long cycle then began all over again. Then in 1989, apparently due to unpredictable

Ravens

spring weather, tiny winter ticks infested the moose population so heavily that they killed more moose than the megafaunal wolf predators.

Rolf Peterson, noting "shock after shock" to this ecosystem as the years went by, began to question the entire notion of an "equilibrium system" in nature. Even the notion of a "dynamic equilibrium" might be false, he thought, as so many different influences knocked the animals and vegetation back and forth. "Disequilibrium system" or "discordant harmony" were more apt descriptions: "The longer we observe a system like Isle Royale, the more shocks we see; as variability increases, our interpretations become more circumspect, more cautious, more tentative."[24] Such unpredictability challenges conventional thinking, and language fails us when we try to describe the secrets of nature. We cannot know how the wolf-elk cycles impacted the grasslands and riparian thickets of California. The wolf is gone and native herbivores are reduced to tiny remnants, and we can only speculate. Because the area was so large, the cycles and disturbances may have been less severe. Drought, rather than snowfall, would have been a limiting factor on the lowland herds. But surely a "disquilibrium system" existed, a complex pattern of interactions and balances, and this included the human hunters, seed collectors, and vegetation burners.

Thankfully, we *can* look at the Northern Rocky Mountain Wolf Recovery success story: these furred shadows of the wild continue to run through parts of our country, and glimpses can still be caught of them. The wolf population in just one state, Montana, within the recovery program's region hovered around fifty in the 1990s but jumped to over two hundred and fifty in 2005.[25] I have heard talk of reintroducing wolves into the Sierra Nevada of California or even Tejon Ranch, in the Tehachapis, but I doubt this will happen anytime soon—wolves and humans still have a lot of "territoriality" issues to work out. One of my mentors, Dr. Dick Richardson of the University of Texas at Austin, said to me once, "Natural resource management is 98 percent human management and 2 percent trial and error."

Big Cats

Mountain lions, too, offer an example of trophic cascade interactions. Colleagues William Ripple and Robert Beschta theorize that black oaks in Yosemite Valley stopped recruiting when the government's predator-control measures led mule deer populations to irrupt in the early 1900s. The mouths of gluttonous deer kept the young oaks down. Deer-eating mountain lions stayed away from the areas around the Yosemite visitor centers, and the large deer herds devoured much of the acorn and sapling crop over the years. Researchers found that oaks were regenerating, however, in areas with cougar sign and lesser numbers of deer, and on areas that deer did not access, such as steep riverbanks cut off by highways.[26]

An ecosystem may be degraded when large carnivores are removed and the resultant lack of a "landscape of fear" leads to changes in ungulate behavior: deer begin to feed in one place instead of moving about and hiding for security. But as we have seen, this may be only one of many processes affecting oaks and deer in California, and trophic cascades may couple with fire, climate, and human development in ways that are tricky to untangle.

The processes of the world are like the strips of willow and rush, all tightly intertwined, that make up the weave of a basket: unravel it and you no longer have a basket; isolate one process in nature and your chances of understanding the way things work are slim.

More exotic felines roamed California in the early years of colonial expansion, apparently

In the past, a jaguar stalks through a coast live oak woodland in central California among sword ferns, poison oak, and hazelnut. OIL ON PAPER, 8 X 6 INCHES, 2005

disappearing with barely a whisper as Euro-American settlers began developing their habitats.

The jaguar, up from Mexico, inhabited parts of California. These big cats were found in the Colorado Desert—around Palm Springs, for example—and were last seen about 1860.[27] Hunters along the Colorado River in the 1830s reported seeing jaguars on islands in the delta area. Biologist C. Hart Merriam interviewed "Kammei" Indians (possibly Kamia or Kumeyaay) who knew of jaguars in the Cuyamaca Mountains of San Diego County.[28]

James Capen Adams, hunting grizzly bears with his dogs out of Fort Tejon in the Tehachapi Mountains, was camped in a gorge in rough country when a jaguar disturbed his horses—the next day he tracked it to a den in a cliff, where the cat had been eating bighorn sheep. A few nights later Adams was awakened by a roar, then saw the beast: "a spotted animal, resembling a tiger in size and form, with two young ones."[29] He found a male jaguar on another night. He could never manage to trap or shoot them.

More surprisingly, jaguars (often called tigers by English-speaking travelers) were reported as far north as Monterey and San Francisco in the 1820s.

Images come to my mind of solitary spotted cats wandering in dense oak woodlands and savannas and over the chaparral of rocky Coast Range hills, ambushing deer from thickets.

Those who are curious about the subtle interactions that occurred between jaguars and the native fauna of Old California will have to wait for further observations and speculations by those studying these great cats. I do not know if jaguars could ever return to California, but they are stalking up from Mexico into the timbered mountains of southern Arizona and New Mexico—there had been almost sixty sightings in the twentieth century as of 1997.[30]

TWELVE

GIANTS
IN THE SKY
Condors

Big Birdwatching

With binoculars and spotting scopes ready, we stood on a brushy mountain slope, gazing out into the deep vista, over hundreds of golden grassy hills rolling outward toward the vast San Joaquin Valley. The man with the New York accent teased Stephanie and me about our hair after two weeks of camping. We laughed. The woman who lived in nearby Frazier Park kindly invited us to stay with her when we came down next. We thanked her. The conversation lingered on as the heat waves began to pile up, obscuring the horizon, and the junipered mountain behind us became pungent with the aroma of sagebrush.

"There!" called someone from the group, pointing and raising his binoculars. We all jumped to attention and focused our optics on a black speck circling out over the grassy slopes.

"No, it's a TV."

That, I learned, is lingo for turkey vulture. The bird's V-shaped wing profile and tippy flight quickly identified it to the experts of the group.

Condors soaring. OIL ON PANEL, 8 ½ x 18 INCHES, 1999

We relaxed, chatted, watched scrub jays in a pinyon pine, reached into ice chests for sodas, waited.

"I have one," said the Frazier Park woman. From far off on the edge of the sky came a great black bird, soaring steadily and calmly with wings horizontal, still a mere speck.

"It's an adult, and it has a wing tag," said someone who was looking through a long scope.

The dark dot came closer, revealing slightly more detail. It bowed its wings downward briefly. This morning we were to finally see what had taken days of patience to find. The bird glided closer and closer, and then it was nearly overhead. White wing patches gleamed against huge black wings. Its flight was strong, easy, effortless, with no detectable movement except for the fluttering of huge, fingerlike primary feathers and a slight nod of the red head as the bird glanced down at us in passing.

The group was silent in awe, and after the black, gliding giant left for the southern horizon, we talked excitedly for hours, hoping for another view. The wing tag had identified the condor as AC-9, a male bird we were to see many times in the coming weeks.

The year was 1986, and I had come to watch the last wild lineage of condors in their holdout refuge around the borders of Los Padres National Forest in Kern County. This bird was a part of Old California, as symbolic as the grizzly but still extant, though on the verge of extinction.

My timing was fortunate, I later learned: the next year the wild condors were gone, the last birds of the population livetrapped in nets hidden on the grassy slopes we had watched, for a massive captive breeding program organized by biologists of the U.S. Fish and Wildlife Service. It was a last-ditch effort to save the species, as the wild population had been crashing to desperately low numbers: in 1985 only nine condors soared around Los Padres; in 1986, only six remained. Something was killing them off, and placing them safely into various special zoo havens seemed the best, although at the time very controversial, option. When we first saw AC-9, only three condors were left in the area, all adult males with small radio signal units attached to their upper wings so biologists could track their movements. Each would be captured as soon as possible.

Happily, two decades later the efforts of the condor recovery team seem to be on the road to success. The condors bred well in captivity and are now being released back into the wild in parts of their historic range—at Pinnacles National Monument in the South Coast Ranges, on the Big Sur coast, in Grand Canyon National Park and Baja California, and back to the Los Padres area. Once again condor watchers can see giant wings freely roaming expanses of blue sky.

These conservation efforts have been well summarized elsewhere (in the excellent *The California Condor: A Saga of Natural History and Conservation*, by Noel Snyder and Helen Snyder, for example), and in this chapter I wish to concentrate more on the hypothetical precontact world of the condor, based on hints in the literature, analogies with the still common Andean condor of South America, and hours of discussion that took place with experts and fellow watchers in the mid-eighties by the signpost at the entrance to the Los Padres National Forest, overlooking the vast feeding grounds of the wild condors.

The California condor survived the Pleistocene megafaunal extinctions that occurred about ten thousand years ago. It is not a relict, I believe, but a remnant of an adaptable raptor, one that shifted from competing with an array of other vultures for the carcasses of mammoths, giant bison, camels, and horses to a niche as top scavenger, dominating the common Holocene carrion of elk, deer, antelope, rodents, whales, and salmon.

RT FOOT

HOOD UP

YOU CAN SEE THROUGH THE NOSTRILS

DORSAL VIEW, HOOD UP.

Range and Habitat

Explorers, settlers, and early ornithologists found the California condor widely distributed in the western United States. Historic sight records ranged as far as Idaho and the Grand Canyon. Condor remains have been found in cave deposits and archaeological sites in New Mexico and western Texas.[1] Blackfoot Indians told of seeing the birds along the Rocky Mountains in Montana and Alberta. Lewis and Clark in 1805 and 1806 noted them several times along the lower Columbia River and along the seacoast at the river's mouth, feeding on fish. Other observers saw them attracted in great numbers to dead salmon strewn along streams.[2]

Condors undoubtedly fed on salmon runs along northern California rivers as well. Several sightings occurred in the redwood region, near Eureka, in the 1890s. Their core area was apparently always in California, with nesting from Santa Cruz south into the San Pedro Martir mountains of northern Baja California, and around the southern Sierra Nevada foothills. During the summer more may have traveled into the Sierra and northward, although Lewis and Clark saw them at Ft. Clatsop, in Oregon, earlier in the year, in January, February, and March.

Two or three hundred years ago, condors were a common sight soaring over the valley oaks and grasslands of the Sacramento Valley. They could be seen in the Coast Ranges over live oaks and bayshores. In the Napa Valley observers in 1845 said the "royal vulture" was "in great abundance" and in 1861 condors were called "one of the most characteristic land birds" at Monterey.[3] Pairs were seen along the Tuolumne River, groups in the foothills, and many around the giant sequoia forests and wet meadows of the Sequoia National Park region. In the 1860s they were described as "moderately abundant" in the San Joaquin Valley. A few wandered out into the Great Basin, the Owens Valley, and along the Colorado River.[4] Although they avoided the deserts for the most part, John van Dyke, exploring the Colorado Desert in the late 1800s, occasionally saw them wheeling high overhead, foraging away from their mountain roosts.[5]

From roosts and nesting cliffs in the rugged canyons and foothills of the San Gabriel Mountains, they foraged over the brushlands and grassland of the Los Angeles and San Bernardino plains. They visited the pine forests and meadows around Bear Valley, in the San Bernardino Mountains, and in 1893 one was seen in a cottonwood forest along the San Jacinto River in Riverside County. The chaparral slopes and canyons, the bouldery ridges and peaks, the grassy valleys and open potrero meadows, the mountainous groves of oak and spruce and pine on the ranges of Ventura, Santa Barbara, and Kern Counties were long the habitat of the condors, the last stronghold during their twentieth-century decline.

Raptor Scenes from Old California

Our group at the "sign site" by Los Padres National Forest looked through a window on the past—a small one I thought—and witnessed events very similar to the daily occurrences of Old California. Plenty of condor behavior could be seen each day as biologists placed a stillborn calf carcass on the Hudson Ranch, chained to the ground below our viewpoint, to attract the birds and capture them for the captive breeding program. Except for the long-gone grizzlies and wolves, these foothills on the west side of the San Joaquin Valley had a full array of predators and other scavengers as well.

I imagined that the carcasses were elk calves as I sat in a folding chair looking through spotting scopes and binoculars for hours each day in August and September 1986. I am always amazed at the wildlife that can be seen with some patience, especially with the many eyes of an interested group. The vast foraging grounds of the condor here were golden grasslands at 2,000 feet elevation, still covered with many native bunchgrasses, such as nodding needlegrass, one-sided bluegrass, and California melic. Grasshoppers called all through the dry grass. Milkweed and buckwheat bloomed despite the heat, attracting tarantula hawk wasps and small blue lycaenid butterflies to feed. Western whiptail lizards, blue-tailed, scratched the ground for insects in grass leaf litter.

Meadowlarks, mourning doves, and California ground squirrels fed in the dense grass. We saw a red-tailed hawk soar over the grassy slopes to catch a ground squirrel in its talons—it landed with it in a scrub oak. Western bluebirds were common in the grasslands, picking off insects on the ground and sometimes feeding on blue elderberries in canyons. One bluebird harassed a red-tailed hawk in flight and then got ahead of it—and the red-tail caught it in midair with a grab of its talons. Our group yelled with amazement at the aerial stunt.

Unlike most other grasslands in California, this one supported more golden eagles than any other raptor but kestrels. I have never seen so many—mostly younger birds with white tail bands, too inexperienced to have established territories and therefore often congregating at the carcasses. Eagles have not fared well over the last century, suffering from poisoning and shooting over much of their range. But here they rule, perhaps in precontact density, and I could glimpse a world filled with great raptors.

One day, exploring a grassy hill, I sat down to rest and then heard what sounded like a sailboat flapping in the wind over my head—a very loud noise! I looked skyward and saw a large brown eagle

A scene from the past, based on my 1986 field observations: an elk calf attracts condors, golden eagles,
a red-tailed hawk (left), and ravens. A condor on the right lands by an eagle, flashing its great wings.
The hill is clothed in nodding needlegrass and little one-sided bluegrass tufts.
COLORED PENCIL ON PAPER, 8 ½ X 11 INCHES, 1986

swooping directly towards me with wings folded, its feathers rushing in the air. It then veered off in a graceful curve, apparently just curious about my presence in its domain.

Golden eagles would gather at a carcass in midmorning, after the air warmed enough to carry them on the winds, and they stayed late in the day. Some fought on the ground for possession of the carrion, flapping and biting. But they usually followed a dominance hierarchy, one eagle feeding while the others waited their turn. One gluttonous eagle fed for five hours, finally waddling off down the slope and taking off with some difficulty. We saw as many as seven eagles around a carcass at one time. And at any time of day a lone eagle could be seen sailing over the grasslands, hunting ground squirrels.

Add the even larger condors to the scene, and a truly prehistoric scavenging ecology could be envisioned.

Scavenging Etiquette

Our group watched a single calf carcass for ten days below the viewpoint. Without grizzlies and wolves to tear it apart and carry off chunks, it remained intact for a long period. Condors always arrived later than eagles at the carcass. We watched and saw that which bird dominated depended

on the individuals and how hungry they were. One condor circled for twenty minutes over an eagle at the meat, casting a huge shadow on the grassy slope, then landed nearby. It sat for a while and then walked over to the carcass, suddenly opening its wings at the eagle— nine feet of flashy white on black was a good enough display to shake the raptor off its meal. The eagle flew downslope and landed, but the condor was not satisfied and jumped up to fly after it, landing near it and walking sideways in a lateral display designed to show off its great size. The eagle flew off, intimidated. The condor then walked, surprisingly fast, back up the hill to claim the carcass. Another eagle made a run at the feeding condor, but it did not budge and the eagle flew off.

But at other times the eagles dominated. A condor waiting to feed on the carcass while an eagle was pulling carrion from it finally made a run at the eagle. But the eagle ignored it and continued to feed. Sometimes we saw an eagle chase a condor. A researcher told us he saw one condor chase off five eagles.

Rarely, we saw a condor share the carcass with an eagle. The other condors sat nearby, some raising the black ruffs of feathers up their necks, preening, or taking short naps with head under wing, and others walked about, sticking their long thin necks into the grass to pick up bits of hide or even catch a grasshopper. A group of ravens flew up one day, landed in the grass, and waited their turn. We saw a poor red-tailed hawk land near a group of eagles and condors at the carcass but it looked puny in comparison.

One of our group saw another red-tailed hawk swoop at a condor. Ravens and kestrels also may pester condors in the air. Ornithologist William Dawson described three condors taking to the air and diving after a golden eagle in succession like "black thunderbolts" after a tiff at a carcass.[6]

Field sketches, 1986

Unlike African vultures, which feed in mad frenzies, crowding around a dead animal, the condors waited in an orderly manner, using more subtle tactics to vie for the prize—lateral displays, and sometimes little chases. When we could hide out next to the group, we would hear them make grunts and sometimes hisses. We saw only one, sometimes two, eat at a time, although one observer told us that in the early 1980s, when more condors were present, he had witnessed thirteen condors around a carcass, taking turns feeding in twos. One pair shoved another pair off with their wings; the eagles were kept off by the sheer numbers of condors. There are records of even larger numbers gathering at a carcass. Perhaps if food is scarce the rules are broken: an exceptional 1930s film from the Cuyama Valley, just north of our view site, shows a tumultuous condor group forming a mad scramble pileup on a sheep carcass.[7]

Sometimes an all-out fight occurred between two condors: one male ate at the carcass for a while but then raced at another male with its wings open. They had a standoff. After a few more chases, the first male chased the second into the air. Both flapped hard and long. "Two months of flapping done there," joked one researcher at his scope—condors usually only soar. They gained height fast. The two flapped deeply and kept close to each other, disappearing as dots over the horizon.

Mammalian scavengers also visited the carcass during our watch. A bobcat came once to eat at the carrion when no birds were present, but when the golden eagles arrived it had to retreat. The bobcat tried to rush at a big eagle, but to no avail. Coyotes, on the other hand, could dominate a carcass, but they usually came to feed at night, attempting to drag the carcass off. During the day the coyotes were busy inspecting ground squirrel holes in the open grassland, or getting curious about our condor-watching group—one day a coyote walked up to the door of the Englishman's car and barked at his wife.

A mountain lion came to feed at the carcass at night. A report came to us of a bald eagle coming to dine. The carcass was the social scene and focal feast of the region.

One scavenger notably absent from the area was the common turkey vulture—we saw only a few. Turkey vultures were present more in the lower foothills and on the valley floor, and researchers we talked with had seen them feed on the same carcasses as condors down in those habitats below us. But condor researcher Carl Koford had often seen vultures feeding, flying, and roosting with condors in the late 1930s and early 1940s in the same area as our view site.[8] Alexander Taylor, an author, collector, historian, and honorary member of the California Academy of Sciences, wrote in 1859 that "The 'condors' and turkey-buzzards often feed together over the same carcass, and generally in such cases do some fighting and biting; they may sometimes be seen soaring and circling together in the air."[9] No one could figure out why turkey vultures were not present at our site today.

It is rare for birds to have a sense of smell, and the turkey vulture is the only scavenging bird to have one. Thus it can find carrion sooner than condors and eagles. In earlier times, condors may have watched vultures as they soared about over the ridgelines—when a turkey vulture descended, the condors and eagles would follow. Indeed, in recent times researchers have watched condors make a beeline toward a group of circling turkey vultures.[10] In Central and South America, black vultures fly high and soar at a level above the turkey vultures, which make low-level traverses over forests to

Turkey vultures flying

locate the smells of carrion. When the turkey vultures turn to investigate these olfactory cues, the black vultures swarm down with them.

The condor researchers we talked with speculated that before the population crash, condors might have flown in a sort of formation stretching for miles, say ten soaring in a row, keeping an eye on each other until one went down to a find of carrion.

Dismantling a Carcass

Before 1870 antelope and elk were abundant in parts of the condor's range, and dead animals from predation, drought, or accident would have supplied scavengers with plenty of meat. Condors prefer large mammal carcasses, although they have been seen to feed on dead ground squirrels, jackrabbits, kangaroo rats, coyotes, skunks, and the like.[11]

An early ornithological account is perhaps exaggerated, but it gives the flavor of what could be seen in the old days:

> In searching for prey they soar to a very great altitude, and when they discover a wounded deer or other animal they follow its track, and when it sinks, precipitately descend on their object. Although only one is seen at first occupying the carcass, few minutes elapse before the prey is surrounded by great numbers, and it is devoured to a skeleton within an hour, even though it be one of the larger animals, as the elk or horse."[12]

Turkey vultures and ravens are often the first to find a carcass, but as condors arrive they dominate it. If no predator has started the process, a large group of condors will rip open the hide of a freshly dead animal. They eat the eyes and tongue first. They usually stand next to a carcass, reaching out and into the body, favoring the gut cavity and organs. Their bills are razor-sharp and slice meat from bone quickly. They can swallow large chunks. Their tongues have powerful retractor muscles and the backward-projecting spines at the tip help dislodge meat.

Golden eagles prefer flesh, often standing on a carcass and pulling up with their bills. Condors will, however, eat any part of the animal, including bits of hide and bone at the last. Condors can drag around a carcass the size of a deer and turn its skin inside out as they pull on it. As the body cavity is cleaned out, they pick out the muscles between the ribs and turn the leg hide inside out to get at the flesh. The carcass does not last long, maybe one to three days; after condors clean the bones, coyotes, bears, mountain lions, and in the old days wolves carry off the remainders. Bits of hide, hooves, the skull, and bone fragments lie scattered about. Finally, the carcass may be gone in a few days, with feathers on the trampled ground and unpalatable balls of grass fiber from the guts the only signs left of it.

Condors usually eat every two to three days and stay at a roost all day after a good meal. If it has fed heavily for several days, a condor will go without food for as long as two weeks, or even a month.

The Food Supply

In earlier times it was not unusual to find the great sky-fliers feeding along seacoasts on beached whales, sea lion carcasses, and dead fish. Alexander Taylor wrote:

> A few days ago we got within about seventy yards of a number of the male and female vultures. They were feeding on the carcass of a whale on the seashore, and must have

CONDOR NUMBERS MAY HAVE BUILT UP IN GOOD SCAVENGING AREAS—IN

been gorged....These huge creatures may often be seen fighting each other over a carcass on the beach; generally striking with the their outstretched wings, and running along the ground like the common turkey-buzzard.[13]

Spawned-out salmon provided a major food supply. At an archaeological site dated at between 10,000 and 7500 B.C. at Five Mile Rapids, along the Columbia River in Oregon, there are bones of California condors, bald eagles, gulls, and cormorants, all apparently attracted by salmon scraps left by humans fishing.[14] An early observer noted of the condor that "It is also met with near Indian villages, being attracted by the offal of the fish thrown around their habitations."[15] During the nesting season, females sought out calcium in the form of small bones they could swallow, as well as shells along shorelines. Pismo clamshells have been found at inland condor nests.[16]

Centuries ago, grizzlies, wolves, jaguars, and mountain lions would have regularly brought down big game, supplying carcasses to the condors, although at times at some risk to the birds. Grizzlies will remain nearby to guard a carcass. Mountain lions may leave their kills, but not always. A biologist told us about a lion that wandered in the Los Padres area for days until it caught a deer. The lion stayed around to eat its kill, resting in the shade of a tree during the heat of the day. When two turkey vultures arrived, the lion chased them off the carcass—they flew, but the lion leapt up eight feet and slammed one vulture down with its forepaws.

Indian burning may have increased the food supply for condors when animals died from smoke and flame. The opened-up brush probably provided better visibility to the condors for foraging, and condors would have benefited when burning resulted in an increase in deer numbers.

The Pomo, Miwok, Patwin, Yokuts, Nisenan, and other tribes took occasional condors from nests or snared them to make ceremonial regalia from the skin or feathers. The Monache, Tubatulabal, Miwok, and Yokuts sometimes raised eagles and condors for their feathers, then released them.[17] At the West Berkeley shellmound, long used by the Native people on that portion of the San Francisco bayshore, a complete condor was found that had been buried in a shallow pit and covered up, perhaps in a ritual context.[18] Though some would argue that Indians had a negative effect on condor populations, others find no evidence that this was the case.[19]

During the Spanish-Mexican period in California, when cattle were slaughtered for their hides and the bodies left on the range, condors and other scavengers undoubtedly benefited. Even after the gold rush, condors remained common. Alexander Taylor wrote, "Dr. Canfield tells me that he has seen as many as one hundred and fifty at one time and place, in the vicinity of antelopes he has killed."[20] Condor numbers may have built up in good scavenging areas—in the mid-twentieth century biologist Carl Koford reported seeing forty-two in one flock. Fish and Game employee Donald McLean sighted eighty-five condors in 1942 in the Antelope Valley feeding on a large dead steer; twenty-five to thirty stood around the carcass, and the remainder sat on grassy slopes nearby.[21]

Condor Legacy

The amount of landscape that a condor can cover in a day is remarkable. During our stay in the Los Padres area, two condors flew to the Sierra Nevada, then returned two days later, according to the radio telemetry biologist on duty. Condor ranges, including nesting areas and foraging grounds, are estimated to be as large as twelve thousand square miles.[22] Nesting pairs in the 1980s often flew together and had core areas of about sixteen hundred square miles. Nonbreeding condors and immatures wandered more widely. A bird may commute 125 to 150 miles a day between a foraging area and a roost.

In the air condors are graceful for their size (one condor measured nine feet, seven inches across). They soar with stability, constantly changing position gracefully, flapping rarely and with fluidity. They can fly at sustained speeds of up to eighty miles per hour.[23] We watched two condors take off from a carcass and flap and maneuver for a while under the dome of the sky, one partly closing its wings and diving at the other, almost hitting it but veering off to the side. Then they soared together out over the foothills.

Condors may skim over the ground just ten feet above the grass, looking for ground squirrels, but they usually soar at around five hundred feet, scanning larger areas. For best soaring they need sun-heated, rising air, or winds coming off ridges and hills; calm days over the Central Valley are not favorable. Rain grounds them—a group may be seen on the dirt or in low trees waiting out a storm. But the strong winds before storms are particularly favorable; the birds "appear most numerous and soar the highest" then, recalled an observer.[24]

Although they range widely, condors tend to develop specific routes between their roosts and foraging areas. Immature birds apparently learn foraging tactics and locations by watching and associating with adults. This lineage of long experience from thousands of years was broken when the last condors were taken out of the wild, and that has been a problem at times for those that have been reintroduced recently. Young, inexperienced condors have landed on house porches in the Tehachapi Mountains, begging for food from the inhabitants. After reintroductions at Grand Canyon National Park, condors congregated at viewpoints like pigeons, taking hot dogs from tourists, and rangers had to try to train both condors and people against this habit. Biologists hope the new condor generations will gradually learn a more natural behavioral pattern. Today adult birds "mentor" captive-bred juveniles for six months before the juveniles are released into the wild.[25]

Field sketches, 1986

Roosts and Nests

Our condor-watching group observed that on some days the condors would leave a carcass early. On other days they stayed until late afternoon, finally flapping up to catch a thermal and ride it smoothly off to a roost. They spent a lot of time on roosts—sometimes all day—preening, sunning with wings drooped, sleeping, stretching. They often gathered at stream pools to bathe and drink.

Most roosts are in conifers, such as ponderosa pines, Jeffrey pines, gray pines, Coulter pines, and pinyon pines, and in southern California, bigcone spruces as well. Cliffs are also favored. Turkey vultures used to roost with them in the canyons of Ventura County.[26] In redwood country, at Big Sur for example, condors prefer to roost in the top one-third of the tallest coast redwoods.[27]

Condors usually lay only one egg. They have a long incubation period and chicks depend on adults for a long time as well, factors that work against them in times of change.

They nest in many locations, often lofty but not always. There are accounts of nests found in small caves, in potholes, and on ledges on steep cliffs or slopes. Nests have been found behind rock slabs in talus piles, in crevices in boulders, and in burned-out holes a hundred feet up in the trunks of giant sequoias.[28] Alexander Taylor related that a ranchero in 1858 brought back a chick from the "hollow of a tall old robles-oak [possible a valley oak] in a steep barranca, near the summit of one of the highest peaks" in the Santa Lucia Range.[29] William Dawson climbed up a sandstone cliff strutting out of a "sea of chaparral" in eastern San Luis Obispo County to examine a nest cavity. He noted that though "turkey vultures were abundant about these cliffs," the condors "paid no heed whatever to them."[30]

The Decline, Fall, and Rise of the Condor

As my friend and I prepared to take leave of our camp and the condor-watching group at Los Padres that fall, the condors were gradually moving off to search out the gut piles left by deer hunters in the brushy mountain slopes above us. Little did we know at the time that this habit might be contributing to their downfall.

Biologists believe that condor numbers were once high, but that a continuous decline started with European settlement due to such practices as target shooting, egg collecting by hobbyists, and in the forty-niner era, killing the birds and using the quills of their large feathers to carry gold dust. Later, collisions with electrical lines became a problem, but even in remote areas without power lines condors were being discovered dead on the ground. As late as 1980 biologists had not pinpointed the main cause for the population crash. Some argued that what the condors needed was more land away from human disturbance, more pristine wilderness.[31]

But a more insidious form of disturbance, invisible on the surface of the land, was finally deduced to be the cause of the population freefall: poisoning. Strychnine had been used commonly in the late nineteenth and early twentieth centuries around the West to eliminate grizzlies, wolves, mountain lions, and coyotes from livestock ranges. The condors that fed on their carcasses were also poisoned. Later, coyotes and ground squirrels were poisoned with thallium and compound 1080. More condors died.

In the 1980s the first documented case of lead poisoning in condors was announced. Biologists realized that the scavenging birds had been eating fragments of lead bullets from animal carcasses since settlers first hunted deer and other game with guns. The lead caused paralysis of the digestive system, starvation, and death. Turkey vultures and golden eagles were also found to have high levels of lead in their blood. The condors we watched moving up to feed on hunter-shot deer may have been in danger of being poisoned. Like frogs poisoned by agricultural pesticides blown eastward into the remote mountains of Yosemite National Park, the condors in our wilderness areas were not truly safe from civilized ills.

The lead problem continued into the 1990s. Released captives suffered lead poisoning and had to be recaptured and detoxified. Currently, clean carcasses are often provided to released condors. The switch to nontoxic tin-tungsten-bismuth ammunition by sportsmen could help the situation. Hunter education is a priority.

The grassy slopes from which we scanned for black soaring wings have been purchased to become part of the Hopper Mountain National Wildlife Refuge Complex, and there are many

Giant forest of sequoias and sugar pines in the southern Sierra Nevada. Condors roosted and nested here in the past.
OIL ON PANEL, 21 X 48 ½ INCHES, 1999

new public viewpoints (see www.fws.gov/hoppermountain/Visitors for locations). From a low of twenty California condors in the 1980s, the population has now reached hundreds. Releases into the wild continue, due to the tremendous efforts of people in the U.S. Fish and Wildlife Service, U.S. Forest Service, National Park Service, California Department of Fish and Game, San Diego Wild Animal Park, Los Angeles Zoo, and Ventana Wilderness Sanctuary—it has been an amazing cooperative push.

The California condor once looked over the cliff of extinction, but unlike so many other once-abundant animals, it has returned. For me the best part is knowing that the last wild California condor, AC-9, caught in 1987, bred in captivity for fifteen years and was released back into the Los Padres area in 2002 to fly free again. He found a mate in January 2004, and that April the pair hatched the first wild chick. A window on Old California has reopened.

THIRTEEN

FIRST FISH
Salmon

Big Red

While conservation efforts have helped elk, wolves, and condors to increase in number, the populations of other important species that thrived in Old California are still plummeting. The great wild fish that once clogged our rivers and filled our coastal seas are facing extinction as I write. When people learn about the history, changes, and natural interactions of their local landscapes, when they adopt these landscapes as their true homelands and care for them, then hope may appear for these scaled sentinels, the salmon and steelhead.

The big rivers have taught me a lot about how landscape changes over time, but so have the smallest creeks. I recall a long line of children grasping a metal pipe carefully as we walked down a steep trail under a dark oak canopy, teachers and parents guiding us until we reached the creek at the canyon bottom. We all stood on the small wooden footbridge and gazed with wide eyes and pointing fingers at the tiny fish moving slowly in the run of clear water, fish that could fit easily into a kid's hand, fish in their own world so amazingly close to our school. I experienced a kind of awakening at being in the habitat of wild fish—little sticklebacks that fed on midge larvae, earthworms, and minute crustaceans in their aquatic world among the cobbles, dappled by the shade of alder trees.

Years later, standing on the green, grassy hills over the Carquinez Strait, I could imagine flooding fall rainstorms caught by the Sierran crest and funneled down a great network of forested rivers, swelling the flow of the combined Sacramento and San Joaquin Rivers with cold freshwater and causing a gargantuan run of large-bodied Chinook salmon—a million fish waiting in the estuary and surging through the straits on their migration to spawning streams. There are still people in Crockett who recall hearing firsthand about salmon so numerous that some spilled out onto the shore, attracting grizzlies to catch them.

What are these mysterious fish that used to be so abundant but are now on the verge of collapse? What secrets have they seen during their travels across the vast Pacific Ocean, boldly revealing themselves to us land dwellers, giving us a taste of something primordial as they throw themselves back up their natal streams?

In my quest to learn more about the anadromous fish—those that migrate between the streams and seas, the salmon and steelhead trout—I now continued the "fish watching" forays that had so captured my imagination on that childhood field trip.

Carquinez Strait, Contra Costa County side, five hundred years ago. Green slopes clothed in late-winter purple needlegrass above the migration route of millions of salmon: two Ohlone men survey the scene.
OIL ON COTTON RAG PAPER, 6 X 6 ½ INCHES, 2005

Coho Salmon

Being a lousy fisherman, I took binoculars instead of fishing gear and headed off to Lagunitas Creek. Dense redwoods and Douglas fir forests clothed the canyon, where the sun was out but the air temperature near freezing: December in Marin County. Sword ferns and tanbark oaks, hazelnuts, huckleberry bushes, and a white-flowering trillium grew on the forest floor. A varied thrush called its strange, long buzz deep in the firs, but otherwise the only noise was that of stream water rolling over riffles. I was the only salmon watcher today in Samuel P. Taylor State Park, yet the viewing was superb.

After some searching I found a large pool shaded by redwoods and red alders with a decaying fish on its shore. Several coho salmon (also called silver salmon) hung in the pool water. The "bucks" were bright, deep red, the color of old blood and rose petals, and they escorted dark brown females. Some fish had patches of white fungus; they had begun to decay even before they finished spawning. One red male lunged to the surface, creating a splash, just its head glinting out of the water.

I walked upstream along a smooth stretch of water deep in the canyon and found the spawners: several cohos paired off, males beside females. Some males splashed through the riffle below while I watched a female, her dark back spotted with olive-brown, shudder on her side, wagging her tail over the gravel on the stream bottom. Her silvery belly flashed like moonlight. A small cloud of

Grizzly mother and cubs dining on coho salmon in the past on Lagunitas Creek.
OIL ON COTTON RAG PAPER, 10 X 8 INCHES, 1998

silt trailed behind. The females had been digging redds, nests in the gravel where the eggs would be deposited as an accompanying male fertilized them. The redds were visible in the clear cold water—oval, ten feet long by five feet wide.

Eggs and alevins (tiny juveniles still attached to the yolk sacs they fed from) need clear, well-oxygenated water to breathe. Too much silt coming down a stream can clog the gills of juveniles and fill in the small spaces in the gravel where they thrive.

After laying eggs in the redds she had dug, the female coho would cover them with a light swish. The eggs would incubate for about thirty-eight days and hatch within the gravel, and alevins would stay in this all-important substrate for four to ten weeks. If a storm scoured the stream, they might all die. But if they survived, they would emerge and form groups of fry just over an inch long, growing larger in the stream as they fed on invertebrates.

The female might stay to guard the redd for a few days or weeks; the male would seek another female. Then both would die, a gift of ocean nutrients back to the stream. I saw a few salmon skeletons lying in pools. Raccoons slept curled up in Douglas fir branches, but they would be out tonight for the feast. People who in the 1930s lived along Big Creek, which drains to the ocean north of Santa Cruz, told of the rich smell of dead salmon that filled the deep, quiet redwood canyons there.[1]

Juveniles survive the summer in cold pools and deep runs; the more pools there are, the more coho juveniles, waiting for drifting insects. Fallen logs and branches offer good places to hide from predators: river otters, raccoons, mergansers (formerly called "fish ducks"), great blue herons, belted kingfishers, garter snakes, and large rainbow trout and steelhead. The juveniles cannot tolerate water temperatures over 70 degrees Fahrenheit, so the shade of riparian trees is critical for good rearing habitat.

During large winter storms they seek refuge in small, spring-fed tributaries, in side-channel pools, and in deep cover or under rocks and logs. The next spring, when they are a year old, the juveniles on some unknown cue migrate downstream, having survived the predation gauntlet. They often move at night, holding and feeding during the day. They linger by the ocean in the mouths of streams and in estuaries, and a magical transformation takes place: smolting. The juvenile parr marks along the sides disappear and the small fish turn into silvery, flashing sea-goers, ready to travel for sixteen to eighteen months, wandering widely off California and Oregon and to Alaska.

In the ocean they chase small fish schools, squid, shrimp, and crabs. Packs of hungry coho will sometimes slash, in a feeding frenzy, at anything that moves on the sea surface. In their third summer they gain a pound a week.[2] The nutrient-rich upwelling zone is an important feeding ground, and when upwelling decreases during El Niño–Southern Oscillation events, many salmon die.

In late summer of their third year, eight- to twelve-pound cohos gather at the mouths of streams and rivers, waiting and feeding in the estuaries or behind the lagoon sandbars that block entrance to the rivers. When heavy rains increase the flows, lowering the water temperatures, the salmon move up. The run at Lagunitas Creek begins in October or November, after the first heavy rain knocks the sandbar out at the mouth. The peak migration seems to occur during rising or falling flows.[3]

The up-migrating cohos, "twenty pounds of solid muscle that can swim 30 miles per hour, turn on a dime, and twist like an Olympic gymnast," are incredibly strong, jumping waterfalls as high as six feet tall and running rapids.[4] And so the cycle continues as the spawners change from silver to dark brown-red and seek their gravels again.

TWENTY POUNDS OF SOLID MUSCLE THAT CAN SWIM 30 MILES PER HOUR, TURN ON A DIME...

1400h -
REDD CA. 10 FT. LONG, 5 FT.
WIDE - OVAL. ♀ PERIODICALLY
DUG MORE AS SLOWLY MOVED
IN CIRCLE AROUND IT. NOW
NO ♂'S PRESENT.

IN
RUN
ABOVE
RIFFLE

← RIFFLE

↑
Carex SEDGE

♀ SHUDDERING ON SIDE,
WAGGING TAIL OVER REDD.
FLASHES SILVER BELLY -
CONSPICUOUS.
SILT TRAIL CLOUD BELOW

BIG ♂ SPLASHES UP QUICKLY
THRU SHALLOW RIFFLE.

♀ DARK OLIVE - BROWN, ♀
SLIGHT TINGE OF RED.
SPOTTED HEAVILY ON BACK.

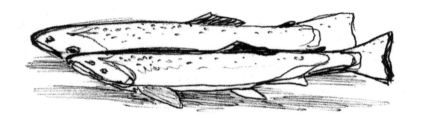

♂ FERTILIZING

♀ DIGGING
IN GRAVEL

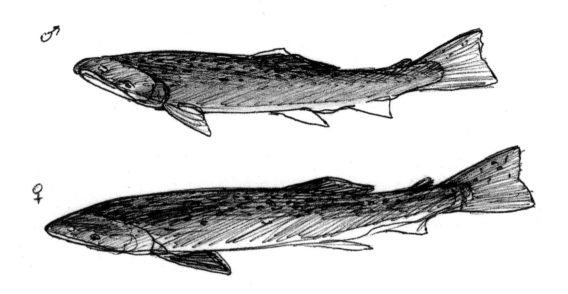

Laura Cunningham © 1998

Columbia River Coho Salmon ♀

Coho salmon male in spawning colors. OIL ON PAPER, 13 X 30 INCHES, 1998

Chinook Salmon

My next stop on the salmon-watching tour was to see the Chinook, or king, salmon, the largest salmon in the world and at one time California's most populous. Their runs filled every big river from San Francisco north to Alaska, and even south to the Ventura River in the 1800s.[5] They are today a rare sight, one that must be planned for, as a birdwatcher plans to find an unusual bird in its special location.

So I listened with interest when my friend Chandra described a September rafting trip on the Rogue River down a section in the Wild and Scenic Rivers System that no roads accessed. From their shore portage at Rainey Falls, sixty-five miles up the river, the group had watched as thirty-five-pound Chinook started to leap at dusk. Chandra exclaimed that in a stretch of rapids that river rafters would fear, salmon swam without effort. They would easily leap a dangerous obstacle impassable to boats.

ONE HUGE ♀ CHINOOK 3 TIMES LUNGED ON SURFACE HEAD & FOREPART OF BODY ONLY, APPEARING BLACKISH-BROWN. SPLASH

One jumped the entire eight feet of the falls, landing above on the rocks and powering through. The rafting group cheered. The fish were bright, silvery, still in ocean colors. One landed by Chandra's foot, beaching itself, then wriggled back into the water.

Chandra was awestruck. "Even running downriver, struggling with the rapids and not against them, I was terrified trying to keep the boat right." She was humbled by the power of the salmon to glide up the river and leap the falls.

My first day of Chinook viewing was not so romantic, although still exciting. I arrived in late December at the Nimbus Fish Hatchery along the American River east of Sacramento, below the towering Folsom Lake dam. The run had peaked in late November, and I found only a few leftover spawners along the riverbank, those that had not entered the artificial channel directing them up a watery cement ladder to the hatchery. But I got a flavor of what used to be a common scene on Central Valley rivers.

Huge fish a yard long swam about among the cobbles of the shallow blue riffle edge, their dorsal fins and tails shearing the water's surface. Most were dark brown, olive, or blackish with small spots, and I saw a few brighter, red-sided males. (Chinook have sometimes been called "black salmon" due to their dark color.) A large female lunged to the surface, showing her blackish brown head and foreparts and small silvery eye, looking like some strange water monster beyond my imagination. Males streaked through the shallows, splashing and biting each other. They were already in decay, showing white spots of worn flesh.

Three mossy dead salmon lay on the banks or in the shallows. A collection of gulls stood and fed on the small feast. Several double-crested cormorants fed in the river. Snowy egrets, great egrets, and bufflehead ducks also came to the site.

I walked into the hatchery viewing room as workers cut open a female Chinook to take out the thousands of neon red eggs tightly bundled within her belly. In her spawning colors, she was a beautiful, velvety chocolate brown with olive back and pink belly. A male lay on the metal table next to her—he was dark red and black, with fierce hooked jaw and sharp teeth. His gums were black, contrasting with the white gums of coho salmon—a good way to tell them apart. The hatchery would

Spawning Chinook, male above, female with eggs below. OIL ON PAPER, 8 x 9 ½ INCHES, 2005

raise the live eggs from the sacrificed female into juveniles and release them back into the river, an attempt at mitigating the damage caused by the dam that blocked their ancestral spawning grounds up in the Sierran canyons.

River Runs

The varied rivers and streams of California flow through pine-fir canyons and redwood forests, or through hills of oak and grass and chaparral. They may be spring-fed or from snowmelt, with headwaters in lava rock and black obsidian piles, in granitic crags and domes, or in soft, erodable sandstones. The Chinooks have adapted to these local differences by evolving many types of life histories. Stream-type Chinook adapted to run up rivers before full maturity. Juveniles of this type spend more than a year in freshwater, so they are already large when they move downriver. Ocean-type Chinooks spawn soon after running upstream, and juveniles spend only three to twelve months

Grizzlies gather to catch Chinooks moving over shallows on the Sacramento River.
OIL ON COTTON RAG PAPER, 7 ½ X 10 INCHES, 2005

in freshwater. They are smaller than the stream-type fish when they move down to the estuaries, taking advantage of the feeding grounds where the rivers mix with seawater.[6]

The Chinook population is further divided into separate runs—a river may have more than one, as the different strains take advantage of different water conditions in spring, summer, fall, or winter. Each is unique. Many river runs have been described as "evolutionarily significant units" (ESUs for short), important population segments with distinctive genetic legacies.

Fall-run fish are ocean types. Biologist Peter Moyle notes that more than other runs, the fall run strays to rivers other than those in which they are born, apparently an adaptation to colonize new areas after wet years increase flows or after a stream heals from a natural disaster, such as a great flood.[7] Historically, fall-run fish were the most abundant type in California. In the Sacramento Basin the fall run numbered a million spawners, an incredible surge of fish moving through the Carquinez Strait, spawning in lower main stem rivers and tributaries on the valley floor and lower foothills from 500 to 1,000 feet.[8]

There are late-fall and winter runs as well, each adapted to different parts of the river and different conditions, thus increasing the number of fish that can breed in the same inland waterways.

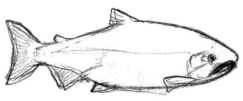

GIANT SALMON

Last, the calendar is rounded out by the spring run, stream-type fish that enter the rivers as immatures, migrating as far as they can go. Once numbering perhaps three to four hundred thousand in the Sacramento River drainage and over two hundred thousand up the San Joaquin branch, they began their upstream migration when the snowmelt waters rose and swelled the rivers in spring. They held through the summer in deep pools in foothill streams above 1,500 feet in the Sacramento Valley (probably higher in the San Joaquin Valley foothills) and traveled far up into the high-elevation streams to spawn.[9]

The young salmon that make it to the ocean morph into silvery bullets, and the various river runs meld and mix, chasing herring, anchovy, sardines, juvenile rockfish, sand lance, and other small fish as well as crustaceans in the productive upwelling belt off California. They form schools, plying the sea surface and swimming to three hundred feet deep.[10] At sea the salmon grow huge, 20 to 40 pounds (the world record was 126 pounds, caught in Alaska). El Niño events deal a hard blow to the salmon—in the past, commercial catches suddenly dropped as much as 70 percent, and the salmon hooked were as thin as snakes.[11]

STEELHEAD

Steelhead

More than a decade after the field trip that set me searching for anadromous fish, I descended the same trail through the live oaks, hiking along the metal pipe from some bygone day when a homestead in the Berkeley Hills relied on creek water for drinking. I had returned to Wildcat Creek, thankful that a regional park had spared this canyon the fate of the slope just to the west: row upon row of houses, line upon line of streets, and the creeks mostly buried in underground tunnels, lost to the kids who grow up there. And today I had just learned something equally wonderful from a local ranger-naturalist: a rare pure strain of steelhead had been found landlocked above the dam on San Leandro Reservoir and its creeks, several miles to the south. These native trout carried the genes of an ancient central California stock that was never mixed nor hybridized with the Canadian hatchery trout that were so often dumped in streams for sport fishing purposes in the past. In 1983 some of these fish had been transplanted into Wildcat Creek, brought back to a part of their home waters from which they had been extirpated by the forces of civilization—poaching, cattle grazing, pollution, dams, and where the creek enters San Pablo Bay, urbanization.

I reached the creek bottom, shaded by dense white and red alders, arroyo willows, stinging nettle, blackberry vines, and an occasional huge big-leaf maple. I found only goldfish in the water by the footbridge, exotics apparently washed down from above the Jewel Lake dam where they had been introduced. I explored the banks overgrown with thickets and fallen logs, looking for fish. I found raccoon and bobcat tracks in the mud. Then, in a large deep pool under leafy branches I saw them, none bigger than my hand, with spots on their sides—steelhead.

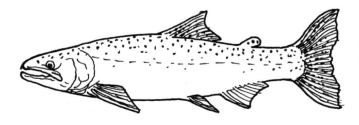

COASTAL RAINBOW
TROUT (STEELHEAD)
(*Oncorhynchus mykiss irideus*)

Writer Paul McHugh describes steelhead as "huge, sea-wandering rainbows," "silvery torpedoes" able to leap up the rapids far inland, farther than salmon.[12] They have evolved two ecotypes that can interbreed and even change into one another: anadromous forms (steelhead proper) and resident rainbow trout. Although they are very similar, sometimes you can tell a steelhead from a rainbow by the steelhead's smaller head, larger fins, thicker tail base, squarer tail, and generally larger body size (over sixteen inches).[13]

The "classic" rainbow trout can actually be resident (nonmigrating), anadromous (migrating between streams and the ocean), potamodromous (migrating within the river), estuarine, or coastal, and all forms may be present within a single stream. This plasticity gives the species the ability to live in many types of streams and rapidly recolonize areas after long droughts or when major floods or wildfires clog a stream with erosion sediments, causing local extinctions. Straying may be common. Subpopulations may exist in a given region. The native stocks have, over the centuries, become "fine-tuned" into numerous distinct runs spread out through the year so they do not compete for the same river resources.

Steelhead are still quite variable and complex in form and behavior, well adapted to the extremes of climate and hydrology in California. As with Chinook salmon, there are two behavioral types. The stream-maturing type (commonly called summer steelhead) enter freshwater when they are sexually immature, in the spring and early summer, and travel to the headwaters, where they hold in pools until mature and then spawn in fall and winter. This allows the adults to breed in tributaries that dry up in the summer. The ocean-maturing (winter steelhead) type, which migrates up in fall and winter, typically spawns quickly during January to March.[14]

In southern California, steelhead had to adapt to the climatic extremes of drought and wet years. The southern types have a shorter lifespan, yet they are productive. They can handle warmer waters with less shade; in Sespe Creek, off the Ventura River, they can tolerate temperatures as high as 80 degrees Fahrenheit.

In "staging areas" where sandbars block the rivers, the fish bunch up in the surf, waiting for the sandbar to breach with a winter storm. Big schools were documented waiting for the storm surge in such places as Morro Bay, off the Santa Ana River, and San Elijo beach, north of San Diego. Here they began to undergo the physiological changes necessary to osmoregulate in freshwater. Big shoals of steelhead gathered at river mouths, the fish so densely crowded that sunlight could not be seen between their bodies from beneath. They lined up into the current in shallow water, their silvery sides glinting in the sun.

The lagoons that form on the mouths of southern streams are key to the survival of these steelhead. Where sandbars partly or completely block the flow, the water is fairly warm, but not too warm for trout. Juveniles enter these highly productive lagoons and achieve extremely high growth rates, reaching sizes four to five times those of tributary-rearers before entering the ocean. (See chapter three for more on coastal lagoon habitats).

Southern streams often become intermittent in their lower reaches in the dry season, and juvenile steelhead sometimes must wait years for a big storm to breach the sandbar blocking access to the headwaters where they spawn.

In the past, the southern steelies then swam inland to places like the north fork of Matilija Creek, in Ventura County, where I spent weeks habitat-typing for the Department of Fish and Game in

1993. Clear water ran through cobbles and boulders shaded by live oak, maples, and sycamores, while the aromas of honeysuckle, sugarbush, toyon, and sage wafted through the canyons above. Surprises greeted me around every bend: a southern alligator lizard staring at me at eye level while hanging by its prehensile tail from a twig over the stream; a glade with a giant—man-sized—orange tiger lily; a goshawk diving through the riparian trees. This place looked to me like it might have a thousand years ago. But it is not—a small dam still cuts off most of this stream from the ocean-traveling steelhead.

Living River

> "The care of rivers is not a question of rivers, but of the human heart."
>
> —*Tanaka Shozo, nineteenth-century Japanese conservationist*

"Doesn't look too promising for the salmon in our area," a young man from Humboldt County in rubber waders and a baseball cap told me as we stood knee-deep in stream water.

"Why is that?" I asked. We had been climbing under fallen branches and over slippery waterfalls all day, measuring fish habitat.

"In the redwood forests some areas are clear-cut and eroded of any pools or hiding places for the salmon, but other streams have too much debris—they're clogged with logjams and the salmon can't pass." He took hold of the end of a tape measure and stretched it across the stream, as I recorded its width on a data sheet. I stuck a stadia rod down into a deep pool to measure the depth of the stream. He estimated the amount of tree cover shading the pool, and I wrote down the percentage of cobbles on the streambed. This particular stream was great salmonid habitat, we both agreed, and kept wading upstream in the icy clear water. The currents shaped channels, moved stones about, gouged out deep holes around bedrock and boulders—fish darted in front of us to hide under waterfalls.

Working as a fishery biology technician during the early 1990s, "habitat typing" various streams for the California Department of Fish and Game,[15] I was exploring the stream, quantifying the details of its condition so that restoration work could be planned.

Cover is crucial for the survival of both adult and juvenile salmon. Fish that migrate in summer need cold pools for holding, often with bedrock ledges or curtains of bubbles where water splashes from falls. Juveniles need slow-moving backwater and edgewater areas, often with branches or vegetation in the water for cover. An alder or Douglas fir falling into a stream causes the flow to scour a pool around it, creating good habitat. So important is this type of cover that fisheries biologists will carry out "Large Woody Debris" surveys in salmon streams. In restoration projects, elaborate

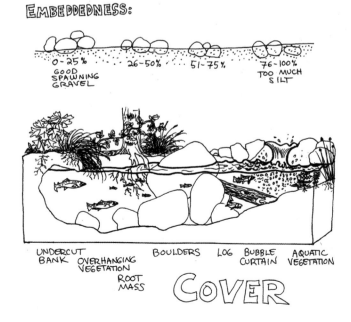

EMBEDDEDNESS:

0-25% GOOD SPAWNING GRAVEL   26-50%   51-75%   76-100% TOO MUCH SILT

UNDERCUT BANK   OVERHANGING VEGETATION   ROOT MASS   BOULDERS   LOG   BUBBLE CURTAIN   AQUATIC VEGETATION

COVER

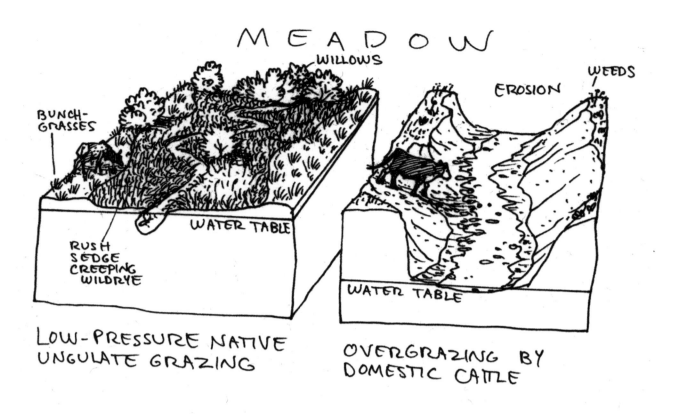

MEADOW

BUNCH-GRASSES

WILLOWS

RUSH SEDGE CREEPING WILDRYE

WATER TABLE

LOW-PRESSURE NATIVE UNGULATE GRAZING

EROSION

WEEDS

WATER TABLE

OVERGRAZING BY DOMESTIC CATTLE

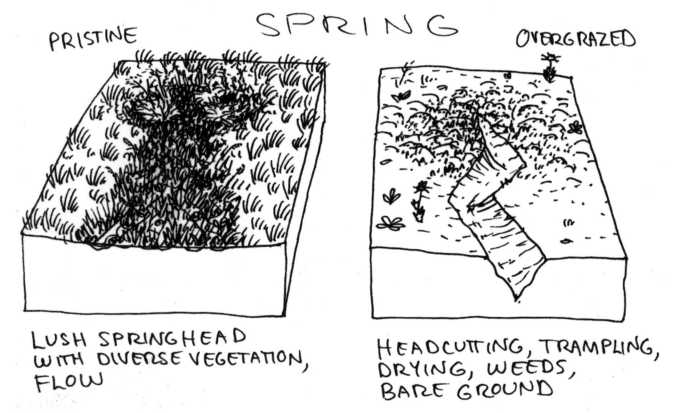

SPRING

PRISTINE

OVERGRAZED

LUSH SPRINGHEAD WITH DIVERSE VEGETATION, FLOW

HEADCUTTING, TRAMPLING, DRYING, WEEDS, BARE GROUND

How overgrazing erodes the landscape, dumping silt into salmon stream

methods have been developed to bolt and wire up logs and boulders to make "LWD" structures that will increase cover and pool habitat. Branches and twigs—"Small Woody Debris"—are also important, creating cover for small juveniles and the aquatic insects they feed on, and places to hide from the prowling, predatory Sacramento pikeminnow. Root wads and boulder clusters also provide good cover, the latter helping to stabilize gravel piles that the currents will slowly move downstream.

Riffles, where shallow water flows quickly over cobbles and boulders that break the surface, are factories of the aquatic invertebrate larvae that feed the growing salmon—caddisfly larvae, mayfly and stonefly nymphs, beetle larvae, and others.

Rivers are alive, constantly moving and shifting. Ideally, the lower flows in the heat of summer allow trees and shrubs to colonize and grow on banks and sandbars, shading the waters and stabilizing many banks. Currents gradually erode banks, contributing breeding gravels to the bed; storm surges scour the beds clean of fine sediment and distribute it down the channel.

But too much erosion, caused by logging, overgrazing, road building, excavation, grading, landslides on devegetated slopes, and bank destabilization due to tree removal, can dump unusually large amounts of silt and clay into streams. Too much silt in the current will settle into the gravel and "embed" the little stones, leaving no room nor oxygenated water flow for the salmon eggs and alevins—or worse, creating a cement. I picked up a little stone from the river to estimate the level of embeddedness marked on it while my coworker took the clipboard.

Dams, overfishing, urbanization, and hatchery fish competition have, in combination with erosion, conspired to eliminate and reduce salmon numbers throughout California. And the onslaught began early. By the 1890s, fishermen were stringing seines across the beaches where cohos lingered and sending their flesh to canneries.[16]

In the past, in years of good ocean productivity, California may have been home to a million coho spawners, but the numbers statewide have declined to less than five thousand.[17] They were found in coastal streams and rivers as far south as Scott Creek and Waddell Creek, in Santa Cruz County, with some spawning south to the Big Sur River, and as far north as Alaska and around the Pacific Rim to Japan. Lagunitas Creek now holds the largest single population of wild cohos in the state—about five hundred, 10 percent of the total California population.

The runs in streams that enter San Francisco Bay have dwindled to extinction: Alameda Creek had a run into the 1930s, Walnut Creek into the 1950s, and Corte Madera Creek into the 1960s.[18] Coho ascended the Eel and Klamath Rivers far into their headwaters. They were less common in the Sacramento River system, but they did spawn in the McCloud River and upper Sacramento before dams blocked access. Fisheries biologist Peter Moyle stated in 1991 that coho appear in only half of the 582 California coastal streams where their runs were documented in the past.[19]

No longer does the bay hold hundreds of thousands of big salmon bodies waiting for the Sacramento and San Joaquin Rivers to rise so they can pinch their way through the Carquinez Strait in runs so massive that they churn the water, spreading out and up into mountainous tributaries over three hundred miles away.

The Sacramento River Basin's fall Chinook run fell to an average of two hundred thousand fish in recent years, and in 2008 it crashed to a mere fifty-six thousand, forcing a ban on all commercial and sport fishing. The returns of the lower Yuba River (below the dam), a tributary of the Sacramento River, went into freefall: 3,842 Chinooks in 2003, 909 in 2006, and only 54 salmon in 2007.[20]

Resident rainbow trout forms once abounded "in every clear brook from the Mexican line northward to Mount Shasta" and further, but not east of the Cascades or the Sierra except as redband forms, which constituted distinct gene pools—the golden trout types in the Sierra Nevada, and redbands in Eagle Lake and Goose Lake, in northeastern California.[21]

No one knows how many unique stocks of rainbows have been lost—David Starr Jordan and Warren Barton Evermann describe a naturally landlocked form in Purisima Creek, San Mateo County, that was very small and especially brightly colored.[22] The McCloud River had large, unique redband trout weighing up to eight pounds with brick red bands along their sides; the Pit River may also have had a special redband population. The Sacramento system's coastal rainbow/steelhead trout naturally hybridized with them. Today, hatchery introductions threaten the McCloud River redband with genetic swamping.[23]

The Collapse of Commercial Catches

A sport-fishing neighbor once brought home a sea-caught Chinook, exhibiting it proudly, hanging it from a hook on the prow of his boat. These ocean fish are strong—"fighting a big Chinook is like hooking a train," one sportsman said.[24] My aunt and I walked over to study it, exclaiming at the fact that it reached three-quarters of her height. This enormous prize from the ocean was a thing of beauty in its sea colors, with flashing sides and glittering small scales. Every blue hue I could think of mingled on its head and back—cobalt, ultramarine, dark night blue, reflections of sky.

A whole industry once thrived on this ocean bounty. The first cannery opened in the Sacramento–San Joaquin Delta in 1864, followed by twenty more by 1881, packing nine million one-pound cans of salmon meat yearly, caught by gill nets in the river. By 1884 the commercial cannery catch had collapsed, however, as overharvesting and habitat degradation took their toll on the salmon. Small rebounds occurred on and off, but the decline set in for the long term—in 1918 only two hundred thousand pounds were canned, less in other years. The canneries had all closed by the 1930s[25] and all commercial salmon fishing was banned inside the Golden Gate by 1957.[26]

In 1919 a total of almost six million salmon were netted in the Sacramento, Eel, Klamath, and Smith Rivers; more than seven million were taken by trolling in the ocean, chiefly at Shelter Cove (off Humboldt County), in the vicinity of San Francisco, and in Monterey Bay.[27] Commercial salmon-trolling takes from the late 1950s to 1990 varied between 3.5 and 8 million pounds—that's pounds, not fish—annually.[28] The crash of 2008, however, brought a total ban on Chinook fishing off California—a first.

What caused this sad situation for the Chinook and the people who depend on them for a living, a population collapse like that of the passenger pigeon or Plains bison, a dire situation that has not yet been resolved? Will these runs go extinct in our lifetime? As a student of California's natural history, I've learned well that the factors are many and complex, and the solutions don't come easy.

Gold mining in the 1850s began the decline of these runs. Hydraulic miners spraying water at high pressure through giant nozzles to erode entire hillsides and extract gold from the gravel dumped literally tons of silt into the streams, embedding spawning gravel as well as diverting whole spawning streams for their water.

Agricultural water diversions then took their toll. Water ditches and irrigation canals, often with pumps, were built as early as the late 1800s, expanding into the 1920s.[29]

Then the massive Central Valley Project Act was passed by the state legislature in 1933, after the worst drought on record, setting off an unprecedented series of construction projects to build dams, diversions, pumps, and long canals to convert marshes and arid grasslands to orchards and giant farms. Thus began the "Dam Age." In fifty years the Central Valley Project became one of the largest artificial water storage and transport systems in the world. In 1951, the Feather River Project (later the State Water project) began delivering Shasta Dam water hundreds of miles to the south to irrigate the San Joaquin Valley desert areas. The California Aqueduct alone is 444 miles long.[30]

The McCloud, Pit, and Little Sacramento Rivers used to hold fifteen thousand spawning salmon—the huge Shasta Dam cut them off. The Feather River held eight to twenty thousand—Oroville Dam ended that run. The Yuba River had six to ten thousand—Englebright Dam stopped them. The American River had more than ten thousand—Folsom Dam blocked that run. The Sacramento Valley spring-run Chinooks now spawn only in a few minor streams: Deer Creek, Mill Creek, and Butte Creek. All in all, California claims more than fourteen hundred dams on its rivers and streams.

As late as 1945, more than fifty thousand spring-run salmon went up the San Joaquin River.[31] After 1920, canal diversions reduced the river flows, creating warm waters that are detrimental to salmon. Irrigation water put back into the river contained residues of selenium salts and agricultural chemicals. Then Friant Dam went up in 1942, completely cutting the salmon off. No fish ladder was built, and the stranded fish were finished off by herons, raccoons, and poachers. The run was gone forever.[32] By 1948 the Madera and Friant-Kern Canals were shipping the river south, completely drying up the channel for sixty miles below the dam. Later it became a channel for polluted agricultural runoff.

The spring-run Chinook were probably the most abundant run in the San Joaquin system, and perhaps in the entire Central Valley, taking advantage of vast reserves of snowmelt in the high mountains to keep their summering pools cold as they waited for fall, when they would access the nesting gravels.[33]

After spawning, the juveniles needed other kinds of habitat for feeding, growing, and hiding from predators. Peter Moyle speculates that large numbers of salmon juveniles once thrived in the pristine Valley and Delta, in the vast floodplains, overflow marshes, sloughs, and slow-moving river meanders that absorbed winter and spring freshets and meltwaters—a highly productive area of aquatic invertebrates and terrestrial insects.[34] The dense, shallow-water tulares and overhanging riparian jungles must have been a haven for growing fish. Before the agricultural projects, winter-run juveniles, for example, were seen to migrate into the Delta through Georgiana Slough, Sherman Lake, and Three Mile Slough with flood pulses.[35]

In the past, occasional salmon and other river fish, like sturgeon, would get landlocked in marshy overflow lakes left along the lower Sacramento River by receding winter floodwaters. Archaeological remains indicate that at Stone Lake, for example, two miles east of the river, the Cosumne Miwok fished for Sacramento perch, tule perch, hitch, hardhead, Sacramento sucker, and sometimes landlocked Chinook.[36]

But lately too much water has been pumped and diverted at the wrong times, and perhaps combined with a warming ocean temperature cycle, this has changed the conditions of the rich upwelling needed for fish growth.[37] The supply of freshwater in the West is like a precious mineral

Chinook salmon spawning on the San Joaquin River as it might have appeared before the Friant Dam.
OIL ON COTTON RAG PAPER, 8 X 20 INCHES, 2005

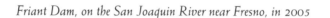

Friant Dam, on the San Joaquin River near Fresno, in 2005

that is fast dwindling, like gold or oil—the mines are playing out. Needless to say, the politics of irrigation has been a powerful force in the state's history, as I saw on the next river where I attempted to go salmon watching.

Klamath Riches

Driving beside the long, winding Klamath River in September, stopping overnight at a quiet campsite in a national forest, I would never have guessed that this river was one of the most controversial in the country and once was the third-largest producer of Pacific salmon. Now it is a microcosm for revealing the causes of salmon collapse.

On this trip my mother accompanied me, for she wanted to see the famous river too. She was always quite patient when I stopped to take some photos or pick a native grass stalk to examine. We drove from the coast through redwood canyons and over windy ridges with grassy balds and Oregon oak, reaching the Trinity River Fork and following it through Hoopa Valley to its confluence with the mighty Klamath.

Steelhead were reported to be running now, so there were many fly fishermen out on the river, which seemed low to me. The salmon would run later. Piles of berry-filled black bear scat lay on the cobble bars. The bears were said to come down at night from the forest, waiting for the coming feast.

From our camp along a small side creek to the Klamath, I walked along the river, watching a few spotted sandpipers on a bar, a dipper walking along the stony edge, and turkey vultures landing in black cottonwoods. I found more bear scat—in the past the grizzlies must have also been thick here when the salmon carcasses covered the banks. Patches of beautiful tall riparian forest lined the river on small flat areas—big-leaf maples turning yellow, tanbark oaks holding big acorns on their limbs. The poison oak leaves were red and the dogwood pink. A northern pygmy owl hooted that night.

The next day we drove east. The weather was sunny and bright now, and the vegetation drier— more sugar and ponderosa pines on the ridges, more patches of chaparral. We stopped at the Salmon River where it enters the Klamath. In California, this huge, cold, rocky river is second in size only to the Sacramento, and it is one of the few undammed large rivers in the state. Its waters were crystalline blue-green, clear down its depths to the underwater gravel floor. It still ran cold and deep from waters coming off the Salmon-Trinity Wilderness, so steelhead could run here even in July and August.

The spring run was apparently the main salmon run of the Klamath and Trinity in the past, more abundant than the fall run, possibly varying annually from one hundred thousand to a million.[38] The spring Chinook entered the river as immature fish in March, averaging eleven pounds, and held over the summer in large, deep pools filled with cold water from snowmelt. Today the spring run is on the verge of extinction, echoing the Sacramento situation. In August 2004 only 439 spring Chinook were counted coming back to the Salmon River.[39]

The Chinook were named "silvers" for their color. As they matured in the river they darkened; they were called "black salmon" by the Karuk people. Then they spawned in September and October in the upper reaches, the Scott and Shasta Rivers, and as far as the Williamson River in Oregon. Fry matured slowly in these cold headwater rivers and lakes. They averaged twenty pounds as adults.[40]

As the spring run trailed off, the fall run began moving. They appeared in July and peaked in August, and the run gradually ended in September and October.[41] The fall run was once incredibly abundant, with as many as a half-million Chinook. Salmon ascended the many large tributaries

of the Klamath, but most headed to the Klamath Lake area. As recently as 2001, a run of 200,000 fall Chinook was counted.[42] By fall 2006, the combined total count of Klamath River returning wild spawners was 30,400, triggering Governor Arnold Schwarzenegger's declaration of a "fishery resource disaster" for the Klamath salmon.[43]

Everglades of the West

In order to investigate the causes for this population crash, I had to go upriver. The upper Klamath is a whole different world. The river used to connect at its headwaters to a huge complex of shallow lakes, vast marshlands, and often flooded grasslands, all surrounded by an arid sea of sagebrush scrub, juniper woodland, and native dry grassland receiving only twelve inches of rain or so a year. The basin was filled by inflowing rivers and fault-fractured basalt lava beds that held and recharged groundwater. Oregon's Upper Klamath Lake, a large permanent lake, was about fifty-one thousand acres at its largest, fringed by eighty thousand acres of marshes and fed by long, cold, riparian-lined rivers. During peak flows of the Klamath River draining out of Upper Klamath Lake, winter and spring floodwaters used to overflow into Lower Klamath Lake. This shallow and cold body of water in California was ninety-four thousand acres in extent at its largest. In summer it shrank to as little as thirty thousand acres.

California condors, bad eagles, and gulls feast on spawned-out Chinook in a redwood-country stream of the past. OIL ON COTTON RAG PAPER, 10 X 4 INCHES, 2005

Next to it was Tule Lake, a similarly large and shallow lake that expanded and contracted greatly with flow variations in its water source, the Lost River. At times it spread over one hundred thousand acres, fluctuating down to fifty-five thousand. A natural slough connected the Lost River with the Klamath River during high water.[44]

The whole wetland system amounted to three hundred and fifty thousand acres; it was called the "Everglades of the West." Eighty percent of the waterfowl on the Pacific Flyway stopped here to feed and rest, in uncounted millions. Tule Lake once supported the largest nesting colony of ospreys in North America.[45]

Looking out on the lake as it reflected the blue sky of a clear October day, I marveled at thousands of white-fronted geese rising in wave after wave from a tule-lined slough, calling "kah-kah-kah" and settling out on the open water to join a group of pintails. Frost covered the wild barley tufts nearby. I had never seen so many red-tailed hawks—one on every telephone pole, as well as on irrigation pipes and lone junipers. A native muskrat poked its head out of the water by its burrow in a levee.

Before man-made water regulation, the lake and marsh complex regulated the Klamath River's annual flows, storing snowmelt and releasing it slowly during the dry summer. Unique among the rivers of north coastal California, the Klamath peaked in spring and stayed higher than other rivers in summer. Then the flows gradually diminished in September. This greatly benefited the anadromous fish populations traveling up from the ocean. During December to March, rainstorms dominated the river flow, mostly runoff from the lower basin rivers in their steep canyons, causing daily rises and short peaks in the main stem Klamath.[46] Human history has been closely tied to the Klamath River—from at least three thousand years ago onward, many permanent villages of plank houses occupied the river's edges, the largest next to rapids and confluences where the salmon were most easily fished.[47] Steelhead, lampreys, and sturgeon were also valued by the tribes there.

More than one hundred Karuk villages once lined the middle Klamath and lower Salmon Rivers, and many of their sites continue to hold importance for the tribe.[48] The Karuk held the spring Chinook in high esteem, and they addressed the first arrivals honorifically and allowed them to pass. Self-restraint was important and people did not even touch a salmon or steelhead until after the elaborate preparations and rituals of the First Salmon Ceremony. Then they were allowed to catch and eat them.[49] Lift-net or plunge-net scaffolds made of planks and poles tied with grapevines were set up along the river; the nets were woven of iris-leaf fibers.

Harpoons with detachable tips and toggle lines to hold the salmon were wielded along the creeks and river edges. Basketry traps six to seven feet long of split spruce poles were placed in the fish eddies. Downriver, the Yurok wove seines sixty feet long.[50]

The Karuk rebuilt a weir each year in late summer, when the flows were lower, moving between six different locations on a twenty-five-mile reach. Ceremony accompanied the construction, which took two weeks. The men fished salmon from the weir, which often had openings below platforms for spearing and netting, or had basketry traps built in. The weir was carefully monitored and opened after a set time to allow the bulk of the run to pass to upstream people and spawning grounds.

Fishing traditions stayed strong along the Klamath in the twentieth century and salmon, when available, are still an important food there. "In the old days I could dip out a hundred fish in two hours," recalled Earl Aubrey, a former Karuk tribal chairman.[51]

The Klamath River tribes roast fresh salmon on skewers placed alongside of coals and eat it fresh, but the fish can also serve as a crucial food store for the winter.[52] People use wooden-handled knives or bone awls to split both salmon and lampreys and smoke the strips over smoldering fires, often in smoke-huts, or hang them on scaffolds in the sun. After a few days they take the strips inside and hang them on drying racks to cure for eight to ten days.[53] In earlier times there might be as much as a ton of drying salmon hanging from the rafters of a successful family's house.[54] They layered the dried strips into large storage baskets. The Yurok and probably other tribes as well separated the layers with aromatic bay leaves.[55] To ensure that their supply of dried salmon would last long into the winter, they would place some in pits dug into the ground in the back of the house and lined with pine needles and maple leaves.[56] Sometimes they ground the dried fish into meal.[57] Other parts of the fish have uses too: salmon and sturgeon skins are made into glue.[58]

Soon after the gold rush erupted along the Klamath in 1850, raids began on the treasury of Klamath fish. From 1876 into the 1930s, several canneries processed tons of salmon netted out of the river. After the canneries closed, fishermen moved to offshore trolling. In 1933 the state made an attempt to ban Indian fishing, ignoring the onslaught of trollers out of Eureka.[59]

The "Age of Dams" struck the Klamath early. Copco Dam was built in 1917. Iron Gate Dam, built in 1962, blocked three hundred miles of the Klamath in what had been the main spring-run spawning region.[60] There are presently five dams on the Klamath main stem. The dams have halted the large spring freshets that swelled the river after rain events and allowed the salmon to move up. These floods once flushed silt out of the gravel and dug big pools out of the riverbed. But after the dams were built, river residents noticed the sandy banks growing over with vegetation. Willows grew taller than they had before, as flows became stabilized. The regulating effects of the headwater lakes were lost.[61] Below Iron Gate Dam a new pattern emerged: peak flows occurred in March, then quickly fell to persistent low summer levels as irrigation drew water out. After the Trinity Lake reservoir was filled in the 1960s, the Trinity River's snowmelt contribution to the Klamath main stem declined, further lowering spring flows.[62]

Much of the headwater river was diverted to farming in the Klamath Lakes Basin, starting as early as 1910.[63] The lakes became a soup of fertilizers, organochlorine pesticides, and sediments from agricultural runoff. The marshes had formerly filtered much of the extra silt: marsh peats absorbed large amounts of phosphorus and the tules, cattails, and bulrushes generally raised the water quality. With the destruction of the marshes, the great filters were lost, and massive blooms of blue-green algae in a monoculture spread in summer and fall, causing wide fluctuations in dissolved oxygen— the salmon could not breathe!

This runoff that collected in the remnant lakes and reservoirs all went down the Klamath main stem and affected the salmon migrating up to spawn, even in the undammed Salmon River: over half the spring Chinook found on 2004 carcass surveys were diseased with gill rot (*Columnaris*).[64]

Paul McHugh, searching for steelhead and salmon in the rugged watershed coming off the Trinity Alps and Yolla Bolly Wilderness, met an old-timer named Jim Smith who recalled the runs he witnessed just after World War II:

> From hundreds of yards away, you could hear a bedlam of splashing, like kids in a
> swimming pool. The river was a series of big deep pools and long stretches of gravel
> with just enormous redds of salmon. You could wade out into the middle and there

would be salmon spawning everywhere around you. If you stood still, you were like a tree or anything else: fish would drift into the eddy of your legs.

There'd be a pack of steelhead kind of idling downstream of a redd. One would reach in and lure the male off into an attack, and the rest of the steelhead would gobble up the salmon eggs. How could there be reproduction with that much predation? Well the reproduction was that much heavier. But personnel in the agencies don't believe me when I describe this because they have no experience or frame of reference for it; it just doesn't make sense to them.[65]

Smith went back to the stream one day in the sixties and found it dry. No salmon, no steelhead. In 1963 state water projects had reached the North Coast Range: the large Lewiston Dam had been completed, backing up the river into a large reservoir. A great tunnel was then dug to ship up to 90 percent of the Trinity River from here overland to Whiskeytown Reservoir, near Redding, and into the Sacramento River for increased agricultural use. Jim Smith rallied other local residents and fought to release more flows back into the Trinity channel. They succeeded—restoration groups and various agencies are now gradually working, besieged by droughts and political differences, to increase flows to the river.[66] (See the Friends of the Trinity River website, www.fotr.org, and for information on the Hoopa Tribe's efforts to increase flows in the Trinity, see their website at www.hoopa-nsn.gov.)

A river is a living, moving entity in a dynamic equilibrium: high floods cool the waters and low flows allow vegetation to grow. The dam and diversions on the Trinity almost killed it, lowering the flows so much that the gravel bars were left high and dry. Dense riparian thickets of willow and alder choked the small channel remaining—no scouring floods kept them in check. Gravel and cobble were prevented from entering the water. The Trinity needed increased flows and flushing pulses so that it could regulate itself again.[67]

In the Klamath River system, the combined effect of dams and huge water diversions was to cause water temperatures high enough to kill salmon eggs, even within the female's body. Gone were the thermal refugia—deep, cold pools, riparian-shaded waters, and areas of woody debris for cover—that were so important during drought years, when flows were naturally low.

Chronic poor land management has plagued the watershed—logging, overgrazing, and road construction have caused excessive siltation and landslides. Clear-cutting and road building on steep slopes have had especially severe impacts, causing some tributaries to go dry and filling up refugial pools with eroded silt.

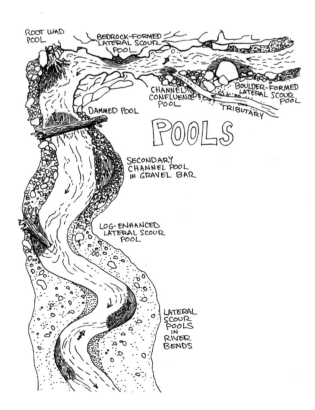

The Illusion of Abundance

Attempting to restore the fishery in the 1960s and 1970s, hatcheries released tens of thousands of artificially bred salmon. But the wild stocks continued to decline. Crashing low populations in the 1990s forced the local commercial fishery to close.[68] (Did anyone see the red flags and foretell that the entire state would be next?)

"They will be hatched by machinery and raised in ponds, and fattened on chopped liver, and grow flabby....Gross feeding and easy pond life enervate them and deprave him. The trout that the children will know only by legend is the gold-sprinkled living arrow of the white water; able to zigzag up the cataract; able to loiter in the rapids; whose dainty meat is the glancing butterfly." So wrote the Reverend Myron W. Reed in the late nineteenth century.[69] I have worked in hatcheries and I can't say I enjoyed the atmosphere: juvenile trout crowded into long concrete troughs devoid of any plant cover, nets overhead to keep the bird predators out, the stink of "fish chow" protein pellets spewed into the water by machine, the regular churning noise of pumps and filters.

Dumping hatchery fish in a stream or river to repopulate it is not the sustainable answer— only restoring ecosystem processes and linkages will give fish a chance to recover. To survive in continually shifting habitats, genetic variety is needed.

Only a small slice of genetic material is preserved by taking a few fish and artificially spawning them, ignoring the diversity present in a single river. Crowded together and fed, the hatchery fish lose adaptive robustness for surviving in the wild, but they will compete with wild fish by virtue of the sheer numbers of them dumped into the system. "Inbreeding depression," where genetic diversity is lost and vigor declines, is a problem. The hatcheries cannot imitate the kind of adaptive pressure forced by such habitats as heavy rapids or drying creeks. The hatchery fish may also introduce diseases to the streams.[70]

Wild fish advocate Freeman House has pointed out that hatchery releases give the illusion of abundance[71]—in 1978 more than three million hatchery salmon and trout were released into California waters, despite the fact that 95 percent of salmonid spawning habitat has been destroyed. Hatcheries can serve a purpose in restoration at times, but they are no substitute for habitat protection and restoration.

The Water Wars

In what seemed a final blow to the Klamath River fish populations, drought led the Bureau of Reclamation to cut flow from Iron Gate Dam from 1,000 cubic feet per second to 650 during the summer of 2002. More water was shunted into the main diversion canal to irrigate upper-basin agriculture than actually flowed in the riverbed. The impact on the salmon holding downriver and migrating up was devastating. In September the low, warm, deoxygenated water killed thirty-three thousand Chinooks and hundreds of coho and steelhead as they crowded together in the lower thirty miles of the river.[72] Conservationists' outcry led to lawsuits and court orders. Besides the salmon and steelhead, the sucker populations of the upper lakes and streams, already federally protected, had been further endangered by the draining of their spawning grounds.

Water wars erupted: river residents, the tribes, commercial fishing fleets, sportsmen and anglers, and environmental groups against upper-basin irrigation and agricultural groups. The situation devolved into angry demonstrations by, on one hand, groups supporting the Endangered Species Act, and on the other, farmers who believed that what was at stake was the most basic property rights of farm families. "People come first," one man scolded me.

What if the river could come first? Would benefits to people flow from it? Could we "modern" people learn to live with healthy landscapes like those that yielded such natural riches of fish in Old California?

The U.S. government appropriated $20 million to aid drought-stricken Klamath Basin farmers in 2001. Lowered crop prices and global competition have made it still more difficult for them to earn a living. This is presently not a very sustainable economy.[73] The Department of Interior was considering a program to buy the farms of willing sellers when their leases on National Wildlife Refuge lands expired, thereby making more water available for marsh restoration and Klamath River flows, but this program has been abandoned. Recommendations have been made to improve the efficiency of the irrigation process itself, and the use of water meters to keep track of the precious liquid has been suggested. Planning is currently distributed among numerous agencies and institutions across artificial bureaucratic boundaries; this could be improved.[74] In 2004 the Committee on Endangered and Threatened Fishes in the Klamath River Basin recommended planning a "water market," with water banks to buy, sell, and trade water in the basin, helping to reduce farmers' losses during droughts and enabling resource managers to buy water for wildlife.[75]

A Klamath Riverscape with People

These measures were inadequate in the face of the seemingly insurmountable polarizing issues, I thought. And then, downriver, I met a group of locals, Indian and non-Indian, who were taking matters into their own hands. I talked with Jack Ellwanger, then of the newly formed Klamath Restoration Council, about their activities and philosophy.

"We want to reconstruct the forest," he said. In tapping into the tribal knowledge of the Yurok, Karuk, Hoopa, and Tolowa people, combined with local land-based experience, he added, "We have something more valuable than gold." Old ties with the surrounding landscape are being rediscovered as people try to find more water for the river and salmon, and with the aid of the best of modern Western science, bioregional economic independence plans are being discussed.

The Karuk Tribe has decommissioned old dirt roads on the slopes above the river, fixing many sedimentation problems. But they have also found themselves tapping into their spiritual roots, Jack explained, regaining knowledge of how to take care of the land and its natural resources. In the past twenty years a revitalized culture has blossomed.

The council is managing a tribal, community-based demonstration riverside forest at Ti Bar, gradually reconstructing an ancient California ecosystem that showcases the interconnectedness of its constituents and the vitality of its processes.

Fire will play a big role—salmon depend on fire to maintain water levels, the group told me. Some people have noticed increased flows after forest fires. Fire reduces the mat of accumulated debris, so that more water filters into the ground, and fire thins the overcrowded trees, reducing transpiration of water into the atmosphere.[76] Forests and fish are interconnected.

Tribal knowledge of fire is far more intricate than once thought by outsiders, and the group will try to recreate the burning regime that once kept the forests healthy. "The tribes had five kinds of fire to manage with," Jack said: in understories, in the canopy, and at different times of the year.

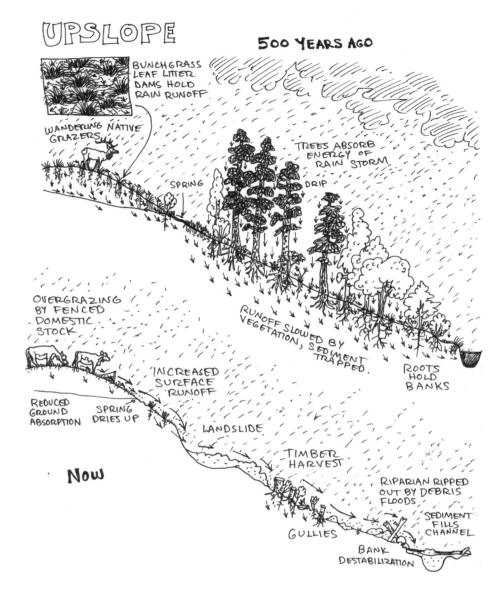

UPSLOPE

500 YEARS AGO

BUNCHGRASS LEAF LITTER DAMS HOLD RAIN RUNOFF

WANDERING NATIVE GRAZERS

TREES ABSORB ENERGY OF RAIN STORM

SPRING

DRIP

RUNOFF SLOWED BY VEGETATION, SEDIMENT TRAPPED.

ROOTS HOLD BANKS

OVERGRAZING BY FENCED DOMESTIC STOCK

INCREASED SURFACE RUNOFF

REDUCED GROUND ABSORPTION

SPRING DRIES UP

LANDSLIDE

TIMBER HARVEST

RIPARIAN RIPPED OUT BY DEBRIS FLOODS

SEDIMENT FILLS CHANNEL

Now

GULLIES

BANK DESTABILIZATION

Low-intensity fires were encouraged. One ceremony even included rolling a burning log downhill from a ridge. "What would the Forest Service think of that?" Jack laughed.

In the uplands of this demonstration forest, the group plans to recreate meadows, slope wetlands, and springs. These habitats once added much water to the main river and contributed to runoff floods that flushed the main channel, which today is laden with silt and algal blooms. These floods used to scour the riparian willows, keeping them small and encouraging many new shoots, which were valued as basketry material. Now they are old, tall, and "buggy," according to Karuk basket maker Laverne Glaze.[77] Native grasses will be replanted in the forest floor and river edges, acting as sponges to slow the runoff.

Beavers will be reintroduced to the river—the log-dammed ponds they create are extremely important as salmon rearing habitats; the endangered coho juveniles especially use them, and the dams are usually not a barrier to fish.[78] The logjams can store water to help stabilize stream flow, and they can help reduce peak flows during freshets. As early as 1828, fur trappers of the Hudson's Bay Company had nearly exterminated these soft-furred rodents in the Klamath region. Where beavers were trapped out, their dams fell apart and the small wetlands that had been created behind them dried out, allowing ranchers to move in to begin grazing the dry meadows that formed.[79]

Porcupines, too, will be brought back to the watershed—they help keep the forest clean, climbing the trees and eating excess twigs and branches. Roosevelt elk have been reintroduced successfully to the Ti Bar. Tribal knowledge says they are valuable in cleaning the forest of excess debris and keep some trees in check.

The group is seeking to recreate old cultural ties with this natural landscape as well: a Sacred Salmon Trail through the tribal lands, towns, and river landscapes will show people how everything is connected, and how we can live with the river, take care of it. They envision a biological-cultural corridor from the coast to the Marble Mountains where tourists could visit and learn, locals could manage the land, and salmon could thrive. A major goal of the council is to return indigenous land management practices to the region in areas now under the control of government agencies such as the Forest Service.

"Indians understand how to not overexploit the forest—to enhance it, not just have a monoculture," Jack Ellwanger said. "Conservationists have not been kind to the Indians either," he added, as we discussed the expense and misunderstandings created by the Western concept of wilderness. I admitted to him that I had been angry that although wilderness areas have been created to protect rocky peaks, environmental groups gave up the biologically rich valley floors to development. Designating an area as a wilderness can keep new roads and timber operations out of uplands such as the Salmon River watershed, but the "draw a line around it and protect it" method is not what the Klamath Restoration Council seeks. Theirs is a hands-on approach—the landscape is a home, not a distant "wild" park never to be touched by the hand of man. Active participation is needed in ecological processes, especially when for so many decades they have been knocked out of equilibrium.

Differences notwithstanding, the group seeks a consensus of all people involved, including the conservationists, the "back-to-the-land" folks from the city, the tribes, and others. The great thing is that anyone can get involved in restoring and living with Old California.

I think attitudes toward nature could be key to providing sustainable economies for our future. The tribal notion of personal and community responsibility for the entire natural system will serve us better than targeted management of a single species such as the spotted owl. Worse is the usual and continuing nineteenth-century style of maximum natural resource extraction and to-hell-with-the-future. Connectedness—seeing timber harvests as rearrangements of fish habitat, seeing fish as sustaining whole human economies far into the future—this is at the heart of the matter.[80]

What has been labeled an "ethnographic riverscape" emerges. Rain, trees, grasses, elk, beaver, marshes, fire, salmon, people—the landscape shows us its life-giving interconnections if we are open to observing them.

The Urban Creeks

Over the years I have crossed Wildcat Creek perhaps hundreds of times on my way to the grassy slopes on the other side of the canyon, and I always pause to appreciate its cycles. In July the water is low, and fish gather in pools; by September the reach by the footbridge is completely dry and I

Clean and cold, the way Chinook like it: a tributary of the Smith River in December with spawners.
OIL ON COTTON RAG PAPER, 6 ½ X 13 ½ INCHES, 2004

walk over the leaf-covered cobbles of the channel. Even the smaller pools dry up. I used to wonder where the fish went, and wondered still more when they returned after a few October rains started the flow back up. They must have come from some deep, out-of-the-way fish refuge pool somewhere, I thought. More storms in November fill the creek with rushing brown water. One December a fierce windstorm blew down several oaks and tree ceanothus into the creek, and I climbed through the branches to reach the other side of the trail. By February the alders had sprouted long, hanging aments full of pollen. In March the alders flushed light green with new leaves and the water ran cold and clear.

Some years are dry, some wet. Some years bring stunning events. A huge deluge came in February 1986, a powerful rainstorm that pummeled the hills and canyons for days. I pulled on a raincoat and hiked down to Wildcat Creek, slipping in the mud down the slope, grabbing branches dripping with rainwater, hoping I could make the hike. The creek was a monster. A swirl of brown floodwater roared down the channel, six feet higher than I had ever seen it, scraping the high banks and sweeping tree canopy branches. The footbridge was underwater. In the wider parts of the valley, where steep banks did not confine the flow, the floodwaters spread out over roads and the parking lots of the park headquarters. Afterward, when the flood had receded, I found the footbridge broken up and swept away, slammed into hardy alder tree trunks downstream with jams of other woody debris. The bank sides were scoured of vegetation, and the channel itself had dropped nearly a foot lower, dug out by rocks that had rolled down under the surge. New cobbles and gravel were deposited in the channel, and mounds of fresh silt piled up at the bases of the dense willows that clustered on the wider floodplains. That year the flow continued into September and did not dry up. What happened to the fish? Perhaps they sought refuge in small tributaries, perhaps some died. A few years later fish swam the pools again.

San Pablo Creek, just back of the Berkeley-Richmond hills, is larger than little Wildcat Creek, the next drainage to the west, and it flows perennially. On the floodplain a dense woodland of giant, white-trunked sycamores and Oregon ash trees grows, with huge valley oaks, tall willows, and buckeyes as well. White alders shade the stream. Hiking this urban creek one day, I glanced into a four-foot-deep lateral scour pool of swirling water and saw them: seven large trout side by side, all still except for the waving of their tails to hold position in the current. I made a sudden move and they scattered like darts. I moved closer, hiding on the bank, and they gradually returned to position—I could make out their gray spotted backs and gleaming pink-red sides.

This was not the first time I had seen these mysterious, quiet river creatures. They could be hatchery plants, eluding the hooks of sportsmen out in boats on the reservoir downstream, but I wondered if perhaps they were native steelhead from a stock landlocked by the building of San Pablo Dam in 1918.

Having recently returned from my trip to the Klamath region, I was thrilled more than ever by the possibility that a wild species straight from the depths of Old California had survived so close to my childhood home. I thought perhaps the lessons I had learned on the Klamath could come home: community responsibility for our own creeks and their connected watersheds.

And in fact people are actively working to restore the streams that flow into the San Francisco Bay. Community-based groups, such as the Urban Creeks Council, are rediscovering the value of open space in their neighborhoods and the beauty of restored creeks in downtown areas, and recognizing that steelhead are good indicators of healthy clean streams.

Those landlocked San Pablo Creek rainbow trout might be a unique native stock that could turn back into steelhead if the dam were removed. But dams are not the only problem. Overgrazing and, especially during the 1950s and 1960s, rapid urbanization have caused erosion and siltation on many Bay Area streams that once supported runs of steelhead and even coho salmon, such as Walnut Creek and San Pablo Creek. Complex flood control projects further hindered upstream movement of the fish. Alameda Creek once supported a run of two thousand steelhead, but warm waters and dams have reduced this to a mere remnant.[81]

Conventional Bureau of Reclamation flood control measures, however, missed Wildcat Creek. The stream still has a continuous riparian corridor down to the bay and can support native trout; locals rejoiced when landlocked rainbows in tributaries above San Leandro Reservoir were found by allozyme studies to be native, unmixed with hatchery plants, and thus fit to be reintroduced to the neighboring waters of the Wildcat Canyon and Tilden Regional Parks. The East Bay Regional Parks District developed a grazing management plan to benefit the creek and its new steelhead population. They fenced off the riparian zone, finally stopping the big cows from trampling the erodible creek banks. An upland rotation grazing plan was developed, the Wildcat Creek Grazing Management Demonstration Project, that aimed at increasing native perennial grasses on the slopes to reduce erosion and retain more groundwater.

Restoration groups on other creeks have used bioengineering to help stabilize banks and stop catastrophic flooding of their towns: instead of concrete, they use "cribbing," placing logs or live willow cuttings and blackberry patches on banks to form a wall. Structures made of native materials are fixed to banks—boulders, root wads, and logs. Mulching discourages heavy sheet erosion during rains. "Siltation baffles" of live willows have been planted within streams to trap the bedload of fine sediments that rains deliver and dissipate high-energy flows. Faulty culverts have been replaced or removed. The goal is to restore a state of dynamic equilibrium to the creek system, where excessive erosion or deposition does not happen.

Each urban creek has a community group forming around it. Schoolchildren have become stewards of their local creeks, with field trips to learn stream ecology. High school students have helped to clean garbage out of San Pablo Creek through its urban corridor, picking up shopping carts, fast food containers, and hypodermic needles. The stream has been adopted by the group San Pablo Watershed Neighbors Education and Restoration.

The Aquatic Outreach Institute in Richmond gives workshops on learning to identify animal tracks in riparian areas, map watersheds, identify plants, sample water quality, and more, including how schools can grow gardens without using pesticides that enter local creeks.

Ten years after my solo salmon-watching trip on Lagunitas Creek, a host of volunteer naturalists are leading "creek walks" to view spawning fish. The Lagunitas Creek watershed has great potential to aid the recovery of coho in California. It once supported a run estimated at five thousand, and in 1959 the largest coho caught in the state was retrieved from Lagunitas Creek: a fish thirty-six inches long, weighing twenty-two pounds.[82]

Habitat degradation has worsened since the 1960s, and the people living around Lagunitas Creek have decided to do something about it. The Salmon Protection and Watershed Network (SPAWN) formed to protect the Lagunitas watershed and its salmon and steelhead. The Lagunitas Creek system already has two large dams to make drinking water reservoirs, cutting off an estimated 50 percent of spawning habitat for cohos. So the SPAWN group works to increase the quality of the remaining habitat. During 1999 the group completed modification of a small but impassable concrete dam along the creek, building a fish ladder and jump pool and then planting native trees, shrubs, and grasses to stabilize the banks and provide shade to the creek. The network monitors numbers of salmon and counts their redds, checks water quality, and restores spawning and rearing habitat.

The Klamath River tribes are restrengthening their reciprocal connections with the land, and urban Californians are finding they too can place themselves in context with time and geography. They find that for sustainable survival, our sense of community must include the natural world. Urban planner Lev Kushner explains:

> By learning the shared history of the site, we come to understand it better and by doing so we claim part of it. While learning the history, we associate different pieces of the place's life and form links between the two. And so by teaching the history of a neighborhood to its residents, we come to feel a stronger bond with the place, that it is more than just a temporary residence in a constantly shifting world, but also a home for us. Understanding the past of the place fosters ownership and...all the positive spillover effects that come with it.[83]

What has most impressed me, on the Ti Bar demonstration forest, the Bay Area's urban creeks projects, and restoration projects underway throughout the rest of California, is the growing recognition of the multifaceted interconnections along the creeks and rivers—people are concerned not only with fish, but with slopes, estuaries, grass, trees, water—all are crucial. Working with them and caring for them can give a sense of place, an experience of local history unlike any other.

For more information, see:

Urban Creeks Council, www.urbancreeks.org

Creek maps for the San Francisco Bay Area
published by the Oakland Museum of California,
www.museumcastore.org/creekmaps.html

East Bay Municipal Utility District Education and Outreach,
www.ebmud.com

Friends of San Leandro Creek,
www.fslc.org

The Watershed Project
(www.thewatershedproject.org)

Friends of Strawberry Creek,
www.strawberrycreek.org

Friends of Five Creeks (Codornices, Village, Marin, Middle
(Blackberry), and Cerrito Creeks and their tributaries),
www.fivecreeks.org

Steelhead and Stream Recovery Coalition,
www.steelheadrecovery.org

California Trout, www.caltrout.org

RAINBOW TROUT FRY

Conclusion
RELOCALIZATION

"A science of land health needs, first of all, a base datum of normality,
a picture of how healthy land maintains itself as an organism."

—*Aldo Leopold, 1941*

But what is normality? What is natural? Can we hope to describe early conditions with reasonable confidence? As we have seen, California's landscape has changed constantly. But as we also know, a threshold was passed in the last few centuries when people began to alter the land in completely novel ways, adding new factors such as intensive hunting and fishing technologies, industrial toxins, huge population growth, water redistribution on the scale of agribusiness, clear-cutting, fencing, and mass carbon release. Is it still reasonable for us to try to attain a level of habitat health comparable to that of California's past landscapes? Is there a way we can learn to live with change? A recently developed strategy, "relocalization," emphasizes local economic communities over the trend to vast, abstract globalization. It could also work as a strategy to relate people to their local natural communities.

Relocalization seeks to increase local renewable energy sources (such as roof-top solar arrays), farmers' markets, and small local businesses, and reduce the need for long-distance transportation—in other words, sustainable self-sufficient local economies.[1] Planning for a healthy local native ecosystem as well can only benefit the community that lives in it. The challenge will be to define what a healthy natural community is, and our relation to it.

Studying the past in all its diversity, we have certainly not revealed all the secrets of Old California, but we have found patterns of natural variability in the landscape, a range of historic variation within which we can work towards restoring the land. Habitat restoration can be difficult, however—it took five thousand years or more to create many habitats, and there are no blueprints for us to follow.[2] We often do not take into account the rare and extreme events that influenced the species now present or absent. Restoring the processes that shape the land, such as fire or flood, may be more fruitful than trying to bring back a single fixed habitat.

The National Park Service, in trying to restore such places as the giant sequoia groves of Sequoia–Kings Canyon and Yosemite National Parks, has defined "natural" as "the dynamic conditions that would exist if the dominant Euro-American culture had never arrived, but Native Americans had continued to use the landscape."[3] But if we wish to treat ecosystems as museumlike settings, we will not be able to live *on* and *with* the land. Ecologic health makes no sense when we leave ourselves out of the picture.

One problem I see is forgetfulness of the past, a creeping skepticism—many could not guess or do not believe that California ever had the wealth of wildlife and plant resources it did. An almost nihilistic worldview can develop that denies such vast biodiversity and great abundance: "I don't see it now, so it must never have existed." But this dangerous attitude sets very low goals for our future.

Discussing the need for a long-term approach to working with fire in forests, ecologist Scott Stephens says, "Once you've got a system away from the high-severity fires, you have to have a long-term philosophy of putting fire back into that system every ten or twelve years. Because if you don't do that, we're going to be back in the same place in a hurry. I'm afraid that there's this notion that after twenty years of work, we'll have the problem licked. That's absurd. You can do some good work in twenty years, but this problem is never going away."[4]

Looking at the situation not as a problem but as a lifestyle might be part of the answer. Habitat restoration can be about restoring our own ways of living in nature, in balance. Many indigenous people see the concept of balance as an awareness of relationship and interdependence; too much of one thing can lead to imbalance and ill health.

That is what I have found, living next to a wetland that needs long-term, regular work to keep it healthy for the native fish and amphibians that inhabit it. One-time fixes won't do here. Living with the wetland day to day, not in a frantic way but in a relaxed manner with no deadlines, has worked well for me *and* the wetland. Changing landscape processes, such as fire, are a natural part of living; we can work with them as partners, not enemies.

One aspect of traditional Native life that everyone can learn from now is about our sense of time. And patience. In trying to work with Plumas National Forest, the Maidu tried to explain to federal employees that they foresaw a plan for regenerating the forest understory taking ninety-nine years to implement. At first that did not fit in with the mindset of annual budgets, intricate administrative regulations, and short-term, economically driven management policies. But to their credit, the Forest Service worked that long schedule into the plan.[5]

Long-term management should be the goal for all of us. All too often, however, we move about the country and never stay in one landscape long enough to connect deeply with it. I recall a discussion between my husband and me and an agency biologist about whether least Bell's vireos might be able to re-colonize the riparian land on our ranch. We explained our concerns about water development and urban growth that might take place around us in the future, and she seemed to empathize. But then she turned and laughed. "Well, by the time all that development happens it'll be time to move on anyway, right?"

Moving away from the problem was not the option we wanted to hear about. I have done enough moving across states, following jobs, to realize that asking people to stay put is not always the answer. But I also understand that wherever you live, you can gain an understanding of the local land quickly, within weeks. You can help out on restoration projects, get involved in conservation efforts, learn some history of the place, take some walks. Restoration can be reconnection, rebalancing.

In parts of Great Britain "heritage groups" have formed, in which "enthusiastic amateurs" and local residents get together to uncover, record, and celebrate the history, landscape, architecture, and wildlife of their community—in the process they discover more about their home and themselves.[6]

Most towns have parks or public lands where similar groups could be organized. And you can always get to know your backyard better—what did it look like a thousand years ago? How can you live in balance with it? We can all hone our powers of observation and begin to see the changes that gradually (or sometimes quickly) change our home ground and climate—kids can do this, nonscientists, anyone who is curious about the past and might want to know what the future will be like.

Some new (actually very old) philosophical ways that communities can relate to their landscape might also aid in relocalizing. The guiding principles of the Klamath Tribes could do us all well:[7]

PERMANENCE—Remembering our history and ancestors, thinking and planning for many future generations.

COLLABORATION—Working with our neighbors and community to bring back California landscapes to their fullest potential.

SENSE OF PLACE—Getting to know our land better, allowing it to inform our identity.

ECOLOGICAL HEALTH—The land can again be a living mosaic of healthy and abundant plant and animal communities.

BALANCE—Protecting these natural communities while generating a sound economy. "We will not take more than the land can endure."

HEALING—"When we heal the land, we also heal people."

I began my exploration of Old California by trying to imagine grizzly bears munching fallen acorns, digging brodiaea bulbs among the bunchgrasses, and taking siestas in the willow copses of the oak-dotted East Bay flat that is now car-filled El Cerrito Plaza. What I found as I dug deeper were many stories that people could tell me about the area—indeed, stories that the land itself revealed to me in relict plants, ancient shellmounds, fire scars on old tree trunks, hidden creeks and floodplains, and silvery trout nosing their way up next to city streets to find ancestral pools. The land has a memory.

Looking at such quiet landscapes as El Cerrito Plaza, the only visible movement today being bustling shoppers and car traffic, it is easy to underestimate natural processes of change on the land. After I moved to the Death Valley region, seemingly the ultimate in stable landscapes, stories of violent flux quickly revealed themselves to me.

August 15, 2004: the summer monsoon actively broiled up this year, building every day, exploding from a hurricane in the Caribbean—it traveled up Central America, along the spine of the Sierra Madre in Mexico, and into the Southwest in a giant swirl reaching over to Ohio. The day was dark and rainy at our ranch near Death Valley.

That evening, warm and humid air foretold interesting weather, the cloud cover thick. A terrific lightning show irrupted in the inky darkness. A shower dropped water on a nearby playa, bolts of lightning hitting close by. The pale flat flooded, becoming a lake. Then lightning hit everywhere: in the valley, in the clouds, and in the distance in every direction. We retreated inside.

Late that night a big flood pulse went down the Amargosa River by our place, the torrent widening out over its usual banks, moving cobbles and big branches, dropping silt piles. Extremely heavy rainfall hit Death Valley National Park, a year's worth of precipitation in an hour. Sheets of water from the storm poured onto the Funeral Mountains and soon intense flooding broke out of the normally arid hills.

A huge flash flood rolled angular rocks and mud down mountain canyons into Furnace Creek Wash. The surge dug out a new channel, broke up the highway, took buildings off their foundations, and turned over the car of some tourists attempting to drive through it. The floodwaters spread out over the fan in a wide, gray, wet debris wash. Rangers ran up but could only watch. My husband, Kevin, and I later hiked up the devastated ravine where a highway had once been, surveying the damage. As we walked I noticed large boulders embedded deep in the arroyo banks, rolled down by ancient floods and long buried, but now exposed by the flood.

The desert had seemed so stable and unchanging, but that was an illusion, the product of my short-sighted observation. Recent paleoclimatological studies measuring high stands of lakes in desert playas and flows in desert rivers, such as the Verde in Arizona, have shown that the "statistics of extreme flows derived from twentieth century records are not representative of all hundred-year episodes of the past 1,400 years...information of value for engineering applications as well as ecological understanding."[8] In our lifetimes we may not have even seen the largest flood events that could occur—and have occurred—in the desert. The past has witnessed natural events that would amaze us. These storms and floods may not have been out of the ordinary during the last thousand years, just during our brief human life spans.

In a philosophical moment on our walk through the changed landscape, Kevin mused, "We are born into a moving system, but we get fixated on abstractions of reality as a snapshot in time." I see it as cyclic: the future is not necessarily going to be worse, climate-wise, but events may recur that happened in the past, such as epic droughts or the mammoth floods that we see recorded in geologic sediments and biologic remains.

As the clouds parted and the sun came back out, I noticed snowy egret footprints running all over the muddy outflow channels and leftover pools by our stretch of the river. These floods have always happened and always will, and some animals have found new opportunities in them. We can too.

APPENDIX

Scientific Names of Species in This Book

abalone, black: *Haliotis cracherodii*

abalone, red: *Haliotis rufescens*

albacore: *Thunnus alalunga*

albatross, short-tailed: *Phoebastria albatrus*

alder, white: *Alnus rhombifolia*

alfileria (filaree): *Erodium cicutarium*

amaranth: *Amaranthus* spp.

anchovy, Japanese: *Engraulis japonicus*

anchovy, northern: *Engraulis mordax*

ant, harvester: *Messor* spp., *Pogonomyrmex* spp.

antelope (Ice Age): *Capromeryx minor*

antelope, pronghorn: *Antilocapra americana*

arrowgrass: *Triglochin maritima*

ash, Oregon: *Fraxinus oregona*

aster, Chilean: *Aster chilensis*

auklet, Cassin's: *Ptychoramphus aleuticus*

avocet, American: *Recurvirostra americana*

baby blue-eyes: *Nemophila* spp.

barley (annual): *Hordeum murinum, H. pusillum* (hare barley: *Hordeum murinum* ssp. *leporinum*)

barley, meadow: *Hordeum brachyantherum*

barley, Mediterranean: *Hordeum marinum* ssp. *gussonianum*

barracuda, California : *Sphyraena argentea*

bass, striped: *Morone saxatilis*

bass, white sea: *Atractoscion nobilis*

basswood: *Tilia*

bay-laurel, California: *Umbellularia californica*

bear, black: *Ursus americanus*

bear, grizzly: *Ursus arctos*

beargrass: *Xerophyllum tenax*

beaver: *Castor canadensis* (golden beaver: *Castor canadensis subauratus*)

bee plant: *Scrophularia californica*

bentgrass: *Agrostis exarata* (Diego bentgrass (thingrass): *Agrostis diegoensis* or *A. pallens*)

berry, bear (oso berry): *Oemleria cerasiformis*

berry, service-: *Amelanchier* spp.

bird's beak, salt marsh: *Cordylanthus maritimus* ssp. *palustris*

bison, ancient: *Bison alaskensis; B. antiquus; B. latifrons; B. priscus*

bitterbrush: *Purshia tridentata*

bitter-cress: *Cardamine oligosperma*

blackberry: *Rubus ursinus*

blackberry, Himalayan: *Rubus discolor*

blackbird, tricolored: *Agelaius tricolor*

blow wives: *Achyrachaena mollis*

blue dicks: *Dichelostemma pulchellum*

bluebird, western: *Sialia mexicana*

Alfileria

blueblossom: *Ceanothus* spp.

bluecurls, San Joaquin: *Trichostema ovatum*

blue-eyed grass: *Sisyrinchium bellum*

bluefin: *Thunnus thynnus*

bluegrass, one-sided (or malpais, steppe, or pine): *Poa secunda*

bonito, Pacific: *Sarda chiliensis*

boxelder: *Acer negundo* var. *californicum*

boxthorn: *Lycium californicum*

brittlebrush: *Encelia farinosa* and *E. californica*

brittlescale, Parish: *Atriplex parishii*

brodiaea: *Brodiaea* spp., *Dichelostemma* spp., *Triteleia* spp.

brome, Arizona: *Bromus arizonicus*

brome, Australian: *Bromus arenarius*

brome grass (or mountain brome or mountain bromegrass): *Bromus marginatus*

brome, red: *Bromus madritensis* ssp. *rubens*

brome, ripgut: *Bromus diandrus*

bromegrass, California: *Bromus carinatus*

buckeye: *Aesculus californica*

buckwheat: *Eriogonum* spp. (California buckwheat, bush buckwheat: *Eriogonum fasciculatum*)

bullfrog: *Rana catesbeiana*

bulrush (tule): *Schoenoplectus* spp. (alkali bulrush: *Schoenoplectus robustus*)

bur-reed: *Sparganium eurycarpum*

butter-and-eggs: *Linaria vulgaris*

buttercup, California: *Ranunculus californicus*

buttonbush: *Cephalanthus occidentalis*

cactus, beavertail: *Opuntia* spp.

calabazilla: *Cucurbita foetidissima*

camas: *Camassia* spp.

camel (Ice Age): *Camelops hesternus*

canegrass, bearded: *Bothriochloa barbinodis*

capybara: *Hydrochoerus hydrochaeris*

carp: *Cyprinus carpio*

caterpillar, tent: *Malacosoma* spp.

cattail: *Typha latifolia*

ceanothus, bigpod: *Ceanothus megacarpus*

ceanothus, greenbark: *Ceanothus spinosus*

ceanothus, wavyleaf: *Ceanothus foliosus*

cedar, incense: *Calocedrus decurrens*

chamise: *Adenostoma fasciculatum*

chat, yellow-breasted: *Icteria virens*

checker: *Sidalcea malviflora*

cheetah, American: *Acinonyx* or *Miracinonyx trumani*

chess, soft: *Bromus mollis*

chia: *Salvia columbariae*

chickaree squirrel: *Tamiasciurus douglasii*

chipmunk, alpine: *Tamias alpinus*

choke-cherry: *Prunus virginiana* var. *demissa*

cholla: *Opuntia prolifera*

cholla, cane: *Opuntia parryi*

chub, tui: *Gila bicolor*
clam, bent-nosed: *Macoma nasuta*
clam, gaper: *Schizothaerus nuttalli*
clam, Japanese littleneck: *Tapes semidecussata*
clam, Pismo: *Tivela stultorum*
clam, razor: *Siliqua patula*
clam, softshell: *Mya arenaria*
clam, Washington: *Saxidomus gigantea*
clapper rail, light-footed: *Rallus longirostris levipes*
clover: *Trifolium* spp.
clover, owl's: *Castilleja* spp., *Orthocarpus* spp. (purple owl's clover: *Castilleja exserta*; salt marsh owl's clover: *Castilleja ambigua*)
clover, rancheria: *Trifolium albopurpureum*
cocklebur: *Xanthium strumarium*
coffeeberry, California: *Rhamnus californica*
condor, California: *Gymnogyps californianus*
cordgrass: *Spartina foliosa* (Chilean cordgrass: *Spartina densiflora*)
cormorant, Brandt's: *Phalacrocorax penicillatus*
cormorant, double-crested: *Phalacrocorax auritus*
cormorant, pelagic: *Phalacrocorax pelagicus*
cottontail, Audubon: *Sylvilagus audubonii*
cottonthorn: *Tetradymia comosa*
cottonwood, Fremont: *Populus fremontii*
cow parsnip: *Heracleum lanatum*
cowbird, brown-headed: *Molothrus ater*
coyote: *Canis latrans*
coyote brush : *Baccharis pilularis*
coyote melon: *Cucurbita palmata*
crabgrass: *Cynodon dactylon*
crane, greater sandhill: *Grus canadensis tabida, G. c. rowani*
crane, lesser sandhill (little brown crane): *Grus canadensis canadensis*
crane, whooping: *Grus americana*
crayfish: *Procambarus clarkii*
cream cups: *Platystemon californicus*
croton: *Croton californicus*
cuckoo, yellow-billed: *Coccyzus americanus*
cucumber (wild): *Marah fabaceus*
curlew, long-billed: *Numenius americanus*
curly dock : *Rumex crispus*
currant: *Ribes* spp.
cypress, Sargent: *Cupressus sargentii*
dace, speckled: *Rhinichthys osculus*
dandelion, native: *Agoseris* spp., *Microseris* spp. ("mini-dandelion"); mountain dandelion: *Agoseris heterophylla*
deer, black-tailed: *Odocoileus hemionus columbianus*
deer, mule: *Odocoileus hemionus*
deerbrush: *Ceanothus integerrimus*
deerweed: *Lotus scoparius*
ditch-grass : *Ruppia maritima*
dock, curly: *Rumex crispus*

dogwood: *Cornus* spp.

dove weed: *Eremocarpus setigerus*

downingia: *Downingia bicornuta, D. pulchella*

dropseed: *Sporobolus* spp

duck, flightless diving: *Chendytes lawi*

duck, fulvous whistling: *Dendrocygna bicolor*

duck, wood: *Aix sponsa*

dunlin: *Calidris alpina*

eagle, golden: *Aquila chrysaetos*

eelgrass: *Zostera marina*

egret, cattle: *Bubulcus ibis*

egret, great: *Ardea alba*

egret, snowy: *Egretta thula*

elderberry: *Sambucus* spp. (blue elderbery: *Sambucus mexicana*)

elephant seal, northern: *Mirounga angustirostris*

elk: *Cervus elaphus*

elk, Rocky Mountain: *Cervus elaphus canadensis*

elk, Roosevelt: *Cervus elaphus roosevelti*

elk, tule: *Cervus elaphus nannodes*

evening primrose: *Oenothera* spp.

feathergrass: *Nassella cernua*

fern, bracken: *Pteridium aquilinum*

fescue, California: *Festuca californica*

fescue, Idaho: *Festuca idahoensis* (coastal California form: *Festuca idahoensis roemeri*)

fescue, meadow: *Festuca arundinacea*

fescue, red: *Festuca rubra*

fescue, six-weeks: *Vulpia octoflora*

fiddleneck: *Amsinckia* spp.

fig, Indian: *Opuntia ficus-indica*

filaree (alfileria): *Erodium cicutarium*

finch, house: *Carpodacus mexicanus*

fir, Douglas: *Pseudotsuga menziesii*

fir, red: *Abies magnifica*

fir, white: *Abies concolor*

fireweed: *Epilobium brachycarpum*

flycatcher, willow: *Empidonax traillii* (southwestern willow flycatcher: *Empidonax traillii extimus*)

flying fish, California: *Cypselurus californicus*

fox, kit (San Joaquin): *Vulpes macrotis mutica*

foxtail (introduced): *Vulpia myuros, V. bromoides*

foxtail grass (small foxtail): *Vulpia microstachys*

foxtail, annual (meadow foxtail): *Alopecurus saccatus*

foxtail, six-weeks: *Vulpia octoflora*

frankenia, Palmer's: *Frankenia palmeri*

frog, foothill yellow-legged: *Rana boylii*

fuchsia, California: *Epilobium canum*

fulmar: *Fulmarus glacialis*

galleta: *Hilaria* spp.

garibaldi: *Hypsypops rubicundus*

California Poppy CUNNINGHAM 98

garter snake, western terrestrial: *Thamnophis elegans*
gilia: *Gilia* spp.
goatgrass: *Aegilops* spp.
godwit, marbled: *Limosa fedoa*
goldenbush: *Isocoma menziesii; Ericameria* spp. (goldenbush endemic to Tulare Lake: *Isocoma bracteosa;*
    saw-toothed goldenbush: *Hazardia squarrosa*)
goldfields: *Lasthenia* spp. (goldfields, Fremont: *Lasthenia fremontii*)
gong (giant petrel): *Macronectes giganteus*
goose, Canada: *Branta canadensis* (Aleutian Canada goose: *Branta canadensis leucopareia;* cackling Canada goose:
    Branta canadensis minima)
goose, greater white-fronted: *Anser albifron*s (goose, tule: *Anser albifrons gambeli*)
goose, Ross's : *Chen rossii*
goose, snow: *Chen caerulescens*
gooseberry: *Ribes* spp.
goosefoot: *Chenopodium* spp.
gopher, pocket: *Thomomys bottae*
goshawk: *Accipiter gentilis*
grape, California wild: *Vitis californica*
grass, big squirreltail: *Elymus multisetus*
grass, brome: *Bromus marginatus*
grass, California Orcutt: *Orcuttia californica*
grass, grama : *Bouteloua* spp.
grass, hedgehog dogtail: *Cynosurus echinatus*
grass, pampas: *Cortaderia selloana*
grass, rabbitsfoot: *Polypogon* spp.
grass nut: *Triteleia laxa*
grasshopper, clear-winged: *Camnula pellucida*
grasshopper, desert: *Orphulella pelidna*
grasshopper, devastating: *Melanoplus devastator*
grasshopper, orange-winged: *Arphia conspersa ramona*
grasshopper, pallid-winged: *Trimerotropis pallidipennis*
grasshopper, rose-winged: *Dissosteira pictipennis*
grasshopper, short-horned: *Melanoplus aspasmus*
grasshopper, valley: *Oedaleonotus borckii*
grebe, eared: *Podiceps nigricollis*
grebe, western: *Aechmophorus occidentalis*
grizzly bear: *Ursus arctos*
grosbeak, blue: *Guiraca caerulea*
guillemot, pigeon: *Cepphus columba*
gull, California: *Larus californicus*
gull, western: *Larus occidentalis*
gumplant: *Grindelia* spp.
hairgrass, annual: *Deschampsia danthonioides*
hairgrass, European: *Aira caryophyllea*
hairgrass, slender: *Deschampsia elongata*
hairgrass, tufted: *Deschampsia caespitosa*
halibut, California: *Paralichthys californicus*
hardhead: *Mylopharodon conocephalus*
harrier, northern (marsh hawk): *Circus cyaneus*

hawk, Swainson's: *Buteo swainsoni*

hazelnut: *Corylus cornuta*

heath, alkali: *Frankenia grandifolia*

hemlock, mountain: *Tsuga mertensiana*

heron, black-crowned night-: *Nycticorax nycticorax*

heron, great blue: *Ardea herodias*

hitch: *Lavinia exilicauda*

horse (Ice Age): *Equus caballus, E. occidentalis*

huckleberry: *Vaccinium* spp.

hummingbird, Anna's: *Calypte anna*

ibis, white-faced: *Plegadis chihi*

Indian fig: *Opuntia ficus-indica*

Indian lettuce: *Claytonia* spp.

iodine bush: *Allenrolfea occidentalis*

jaguar: *Felis onca*

jaumea, fleshy: *Jaumea carnosa*

jay, magpie-: *Calocitta formosa*

jay, scrub: *Aphelocoma californica*

jimsonweed : *Datura wrightii*

jojoba: *Simmondsia chinensis*

junegrass, prairie: *Koeleria macrantha*

juniper: *Juniperus* spp. (juniper, California: *Juniperus californica*)

kangaroo rat: *Dipodomys* spp. (giant kangaroo rat: *Dipodomys ingens*; Heerman's kangaroo rat: *Dipodomys heermanni*)

kelp, giant: *Macrocystis* spp.

kestrel: *Falco sparverius*

killdeer: *Charadrius vociferus*

kite, white-tailed: *Elanus leucurus*

kit-kit-dizze: *Chamaebatia foliolosa*

knotgrass: *Paspalum distichum*

lagophylla: *Lagophylla dichotoma*

lamprey: *Lampetra similis*

lance, sand: *Ammodytes hexapterus*

lark sparrow: *Chondestes grammacus*

lemonadeberry: *Rhus integrifolia*

lettuce, Indian (miner's): *Claytonia* spp.

lily: *Lilium* spp.

lily, mariposa: *Calochortus* spp.

lion, mountain: *Felis concolor*

lizard, blunt-nosed leopard: *Gambelia silus*

lizard, coast horned: *Phrynosoma coronatum* (San Diego coast horned lizard: *Phrynosoma coronatum blainvillii*)

lizard, side-blotched: *Uta stansburiana*

lizard, western fence: *Sceloporus occidentalis*

lizard, western whiptail: *Cnemidophorus tigris*

llama (Ice Age): *Hemiauchenia macrocephala*

loon, red-throated: *Gavia stellata*

lotus (also see deerweed): *Lotus humistratus, L. strigosus, L. subpinnatus, L. wrangelianus*

lovegrass: *Eragrostis hypnoides*

lupine: *Lupinus* spp. (chick lupine: *Lupinus microcarpus*; dove lupine: *Lupinus bicolor*; silver lupine: *Lupinus albifrons*)

madrone: *Arbutus menziesii*
magpie-jay: *Calocitta formosa*
mahi mahi: *Coryphaena hippurus*
mahogany, mountain: *Cercocarpus* spp.
mallard: *Anas platyrhynchos*
mallow: *Sphaeralcea* spp.
mammoth, Columbian: *Mammuthus columbi*
mammoth, woolly: *Mammuthus primigenius*
mannagrass : *Glyceria occidentalis*
manzanita: *Arctostaphylos* spp.
maple, big-leaf: *Acer macrophyllum*
marlin, striped : *Tetrapturus audax*
matchweed: *Gutierrezia californica*
meadow foam: *Limnanthes* spp.
medusahead grass: *Taeniatherum caput-medusae*
melic, small-flowered: *Melica imperfecta*
melic, Torrey: *Melica torreyana*
mesquite, honey : *Prosopis glandulosa*
milkmaids: *Dentaria californica*
milkvetch: *Astragalus* spp.
milkweed: *Asclepias* spp. (woolly milkweed: *Asclepias vestita*)
miner's lettuce: *Claytonia* spp.
mink: *Mustela vison*
mock orange: *Philadelphus lewisii*
mockingbird: *Mimus polyglottos*
monkeyflower: *Mimulus guttatus*
moose: *Alces alces*
mosquitofish: *Gambusia affinis*
mountain lion: *Felis concolor*
mouse, pinyon: *Peromyscus truei*
mouse, salt marsh harvest: *Reithrodontomys megalotis limicola*
mule ears: *Wyethia angustifolia*
murre, common: *Uria aalge*
musk-ox, giant (Ice Age): *Symbos cavifrons*
muskrat: *Ondatra zibethicus*
mussel, bay: *Mytilus edulis*
mussel, California: *Mytilus californianus*
mustard, black: *Brassica nigra*
mustard, Mediterranean: *Hirschfeldia incana*
mustard, Saharan: *Brassica tournefortii*
needle-and-thread: *Hesperostipa comata*
needlegrass, foothill: *Nassella lepida*
needlegrass, giant (king): *Achnatherum coronatum*
needlegrass, nodding (feathergrass): *Nassella cernua*
needlegrass, purple : *Nassella pulchra*
needlegrass, western: *Achnatherum occidentale*
nettle, hedge: *Stachys* spp.
night-heron, black-crowned: *Nycticorax nycticorax*
nitgrass: *Gastridium ventricosum*

nutsedge: *Cyperus* spp.

oak, blue: *Quercus douglasii*

oak, California black: *Quercus kelloggii*

oak, coast live: *Quercus agrifolia*

oak, cork: *Quercus suber*

oak, Engelmann: *Quercus engelmannii*

oak, interior live: *Quercus wislizeni*

oak, live (Iberian): *Quercus rotundifolia* ·

oak, Oregon: *Quercus garryana*

oak, prickly: *Quercus coccifera*

oak, scrub: *Quercus berberidifolia*

oak, valley: *Quercus lobata*

oakworm, California: *Phryganidia californica*

oat, slender wild: *Avena barbata*

oat, wild: *Avena fatua*

oatgrass, California: *Danthonia californica*

onion (wild): *Allium* spp., *Muilla* spp.

oniongrass: *Melica californica*

ookow: *Dichelostemma congestum*

orca: *Orcinus orca*

orchardgrass: *Dactylis glomerata*

oso berry (bear berry): *Oemleria cerasiformis*

otter, river: *Lutra canadensis*

otter, sea: *Enhydra lutris*

owl, burrowing: *Speotyto cunicularia*

owl, California spotted: *Strix occidentalis occidentalis*

oyster, eastern (Virginia): *Crassostrea virginica*

oyster, European flat: *Ostrea edulis*

oyster, Japanese: *Crassostrea gigas*

oyster, Olympia: *Ostrea lurida*

pampas grass : *Cortaderia selloana*

parakeet, Carolina: *Conuropsis carolinensis*

parrot, thick-billed: *Rhynchopsitta pachyrhyncha*

pea, wild: *Lathyrus polyphyllus*

peccary : *Tayassu tajacu*

peccary, giant (Ice Age): *Platygonus compressus*

pelican, brown: *Pelecanus occidentalis*

pelican, white: *Pelecanus erythrorhynchos*

peppergrass: *Lepidium* spp.

perch, Sacramento: *Archoplites interruptus*

perch, tule: *Hysterocarpus traskii*

petrel, giant (gong): *Macronectes giganteus*

phacelia: *Phacelia californica, P. stellaris*

pickleweed: *Salicornia virginica* (annual pickleweed: *Salicornia bigelovii*)

pigweed : *Chenopodium* spp.

pika: *Ochotona princeps*

pikeminnow, Sacramento: *Ptychocheilus grandis*

pine, Coulter: *Pinus coulteri*

pine, gray: *Pinus sabiniana*

pine, Jeffrey: *Pinus jeffreyi*
pine, lodgepole : *Pinus contorta*
pine, ponderosa: *Pinus ponderosa*
pine, sugar: *Pinus lambertiana*
pintail, northern (sprig): *Anas acuta*
plantain, dwarf: *Plantago erecta*
plover, mountain: *Charadrius montanus*
plover, snowy: *Charadrius alexandrinus*
popcorn flower: *Plagiobothrys* spp.
poppy, bush: *Dendromecon rigida*
poppy, California: *Eschscholzia californica*
poppy, fire: *Papaver californicum*
porcupine: *Erethizon dorsatum*
prickly pear: *Opuntia* spp.
primrose, evening: *Oenothera* spp.
pronghorn antelope: *Antilocapra americana*
puffin, tufted: *Fratercula cirrhata*
pupfish: *Cyprinodon* spp. (Owens pupfish: *Cyprinodon radiosus*)
rabbitbrush: *Chrysothamnus nauseosus*
rat, giant kangaroo : *Dipodomys ingens*
rat, Heerman's kangaroo: *Dipodomys heermanni*
rattlesnake weed: *Chamaesyce albomarginata*
rattlesnake, western: *Crotalus viridis*
red maids: *Calandrinia* spp.
redwood, coast: *Sequoia sempervirens*
reed, common: *Phragmites australis*
reedgrass: *Phalaris arundinacea*
reindeer (Ice Age): *Rangifer tarandus*
rhino, woolly: *Coelodonta antiquitatis*
roach, California: *Lavinia symmetricus*
roadrunner: *Geococcyx californianus*
rose (wild): *Rosa* spp.
rush: *Juncus* spp. (Baltic rush: *Juncus balticus*)
rush-rose: *Helianthemum scoparium*
ryegrass, Italian: *Lolium perenne* ssp. *multiflorum*
sage, black: *Salvia mellifera*
sage, white: *Salvia apiana*
sagebrush, California: *Artemisia californica*
salamander, California tiger: *Ambystoma californiense*
salmon, Chinook (king): *Oncorhynchus tshawytscha*
salmon, coho (silver): *Oncorhynchus kisutch*
salmonberry: *Rubus spectabilis*
saltbush: *Atriplex* spp.
saltgrass: *Distichlis spicata*
saltwort: *Batis maritima*
sand lance: *Ammodytes hexapterus*
sandbass, spotted: *Paralabrax maculatofasciatus*
sandpiper, least: *Calidris minutilla*
sandpiper, western: *Calidris mauri*

sapsucker, red-breasted: *Sphyrapicus ruber*
sardine, California: *Sardinops sagax*
sardine, eastern: *Sardinops melanostictus*
scale broom: *Lepidospartum squamatum*
scoter, surf: *Melanitta perspicillata*
scoter, white-winged: *Melanitta fusca*
sea bass, white: *Atractoscion nobilis*
sea cow, Steller's: *Hydrodamalis gigas*
sea lavender: *Limonium*
sea lion, Steller's: *Eumetopias jubatus*
sea urchin, purple: *Strongylocentrotus purpuratus*
sea urchin, red: *Strongylocentrotus franciscanus*
sea-blite: *Suaeda* spp.
seal, Guadalupe fur: *Arctocephalus townsendi*
seal, northern elephant: *Mirounga angustirostris*
seal, northern fur: *Callorhinus ursinus*
sedge: *Carex* spp.
semaphoregrass, California: *Pleuropogon californicus*
sequoia, giant: *Sequoiadendron giganteum*
service-berry: *Amelanchier* spp.
shark, great white: *Carcharodon carcharias*
shark, leopard: *Triakis semifasciata*
shearwater, sooty: *Puffinus griseus*
sheephead: *Semicossyphus pulcher*
shoregrass: *Monanthochloe littoralis*
shrew, salt marsh wandering: *Sorex vagrans halicoetus*
shrimp, bay: *Crangon* spp.
shrimp, fairy: *Streptocephalus* spp., *Branchinecta* spp.
shrimp, ghost: *Callianassa*
shrub-ox (Ice Age): *Euceratherium collinum*
sloth, Harlan's ground : *Paramylodon harlani*
sloth, Shasta ground : *Nothrotheriops shastense*
sloughgrass: *Beckmannia syzigachne*
smoothhound, gray: *Mustelus californicus*
snake, western terrestrial garter: *Thamnophis elegans*
snipe, common: *Gallinago gallinago*
snowberry: *Symphoricarpos* spp.
snowbrush: *Ceanothus cordulatus*
soap plant: *Chlorogalum* spp.
sparrow, grasshopper: *Ammodramus savannarum*
sparrow, lark: *Chondestes grammacus*
sparrow, sage: *Amphispiza belli*
spearscale: *Atriplex triangularis*
spikerush: *Eleocharis palustris, E. macrostachya*
splitgrass: *Schismus barbatus*
sprangletop, bearded: *Leptochloa fascicularis*
sprig : *Anas acuta*
spruce, bigcone: *Pseudotsuga macrocarpa*
squirrel, Arctic ground: *Spermophilus parryii*

squirrel, California ground: *Spermophilus beecheyi*
squirrel, chickaree: *Tamiasciurus douglasii*
squirrel, San Joaquin antelope: *Ammospermophilus nelsoni*
squirreltail: *Elymus elymoides*
starling, European: *Sturnus vulgaris*
steelhead: *Oncorhyncus mykiss irideus*
stilt, black-necked: *Himantopus mexicanus*
strawberry (wild): *Fragaria* spp.
striped bass: *Morone saxatilis*
sturgeon, green: *Acipenser medirostris*
sturgeon, white: *Acipenser transmontanus*
sucker, Sacramento: *Catostomus occidentalis*
sugar bush: *Rhus ovata*
sumac, laurel: *Malosma laurina*
sun cup, California: *Camissonia bistorta*
sunflower: *Helianthus nuttallii*
swordfish : *Xiphias gladius*
sycamore, western: *Platanus racemosa*
tarweed: *Hemizonia* spp., *Holocarpha virgata*, *Madia* spp.teal, cinnamon: *Anas cyanoptera*
teal, green-winged: *Anas crecca*
tern, Forster's: *Sterna forsteri*
thimbleberry: *Rubus parviflorus*
thingrass (Diego bentgrass): *Agrostis diegoensis* or *A. pallens*
thistle: *Cirsium* spp.
thistle, prickly sow: *Sonchus asper*
thistle, tocalote: *Centaurea melitensis*
thrasher, LeConte's: *Toxostoma lecontei*
three-awn: *Aristida hamulosa*
three-awn, hook: *Aristida ternipes* var. *hamulosa*
threesquare, American: *Schoenoplectus pungens*
tidy-tips: *Layia platyglossa*
toad, Amargosa: *Bufo nelsoni*
toad, spadefoot: *Spea hammondii*
toad, western: *Bufo boreas*
tobacco: *Nicotiana attenuata*, *N. clevelandii*, *N. quadrivalvis*, and *N. obtusifolia*
tortoise, European land: *Emys orbicularis*
toyon: *Heteromeles arbutifolia*
treefrog, Pacific: *Hyla regilla*
trout, rainbow: *Oncorhynchus mykiss irideus*
trout, redband (McCloud River): *Oncorhynchus mykiss stonei*
tuctoria, Crampton's: *Tuctoria mucronata*
tule (bulrush): *Schoenoplectus acutus*, *S. californicus*
tule potato: *Sagittaria latifolia*
tumbleweed: *Salsola* spp.
tuna, skipjack: *Euthynnus pelamis*
tuna, yellowtail: *Thunnus albacares*
turbot, diamond: *Pleuronichthys guttulatus*
turtle, green sea: *Chelonia mydas*
velvetgrass: *Holcus lanatus*

verbena: *Verbena bracteata*

vetch, American: *Vicia americana*

vetch, giant: *Vicia gigantea*

vinegar weed: *Trichostema lanceolatum*

violet: *Viola pedunculata, V. douglasii*

vireo, least Bell's : *Vireo bellii pusillus*

vireo, warbling: *Vireo gilvus*

vole: *Microtus* spp. (California vole: *Microtus californicus*; spruce vole: *Phenacomys intermedius*)

vulture, black: *Coragyps atratus*

vulture, king: *Sarcorhamphus papa*

vulture, turkey: *Cathartes aura*

walnut, California black: *Juglans californica*

warbler, yellow: *Dendroica petechia*

wasp, tarantula hawk: *Pepsis* spp.

water cress : *Rorippa* spp.

weevil, California acorn: *Curculio uniformis*

whale, blue: *Balaenoptera musculus*

whale, gray: *Eschrichtius robustus*

whale, humpback: *Megaptera novaeangliae*

whale, right: *Balaena glacialis*

whispering bells: *Emmenanthe penduliflora*

whitethorn, chaparral: *Ceanothus leucodermis*

wildrye: *Leymus cinereus*

wildrye, blue: *Elymus glaucus*

wildrye, creeping: *Leymus triticoides*

wildrye, giant: *Leymus condensatus*

wildrye, Hansen's: *Elymus xhansenii*

willet: *Catoptrophorus semipalmatus*

willow: *Salix* spp. (arroyo willow: *Salix lasiolepis*)

willow herb: *Epilobium* spp.

winterfat: *Krascheninnikovia lanata*

wirerush: *Eleocharis* spp.

witchgrass: *Eragrostis* spp.

wolf, gray: *Canis lupus*

wolverine: *Gulo gulo*

woodpecker, acorn: *Melanerpes formicivorus*

woodpecker, black-backed: *Picoides arcticus*

woodpecker, Imperial: *Campephilus imperialis*

woodpecker, Nuttall's: *Picoides nuttallii*

yarrow, golden: *Eriophyllum confertiflorum*

yarrow, white: *Achillea millefolium*

yellowcarrot: *Lomatium* spp.

yerba santa: *Eriodictyon trichocalyx, E. crassifolium*

yucca, Whipple: *Yucca whipplei*

NOTES

Introduction

1. Valenciennes 1820
2. Conisbee 1996

One: Golden Bear

1. Bolton 1927
2. Sleeper 1976
3. Ibid.
4. Grinnell 1935
5. Ibid.
6. Ibid.
7. Ibid.
8. Sleeper 1976
9. Grinnell 1935, Storer and Tevis 1955
10. Sleeper 1976
11. Storer and Tevis 1955
12. Ibid.
13. Grinnell 1935
14. Sleeper 1976
15. Storer and Tevis 1955
16. Grinnell 1935
17. Storer and Tevis 1955
18. Sleeper 1976
19. Zwinger 1986
20. Grinnell 1935
21. Sleeper 1976
22. Storer and Tevis 1955
23. Murray 1995
24. Chapin 1971
25. Sleeper 1976
26. Storer and Tevis 1955
27. Semeniuk 2003, Gende and Quinn 2003
28. Kotzebue 1830
29. Grinnell 1935
30. Sleeper 1976
31. Grinnell 1935
32. Schoonmaker 1968
33. A. Murie 1981
34. Brewer 1949
35. Storer and Tevis 1955
36. Craighead, Sumner, and Mitchell 1995
37. Jepson 1901
38. Craighead, Sumner, and Mitchell 1995
39. Storer and Tevis 1955
40. Priestley 1937
41. Brewer 1949
42. Craighead, Sumner, and Mitchell 1995
43. Herrero 1985
44. Storer and Tevis 1955
45. Sleeper 1976
46. Storer and Tevis 1955
47. Ibid.
48. Ibid.
49. Halfpenny 1999
50. Craighead, Sumner, and Mitchell 1995
51. Grinnell 1935
52. Ibid.
53. Sleeper 1976
54. Storer and Tevis 1955
55. Gilbert 2002
56. Sleeper 1976
57. Chapin 1971
58. Sawyer 1922
59. Sleeper 1976
60. Chapin 1971
61. Sleeper 1976
62. Chapin 1971
63. Sleeper 1976

Two: Mysteries of Time and Climate

1. White, Mary 1998
2. deMenocal and Bloemendal 1991
3. Ibid.
4. Woolfenden 1996, Anderson, R.Y. 1990
5. Axelrod 1981
6. Broecker 2001
7. Axelrod 1981
8. Terasmae and Weeks 1979
9. Axelrod 1981
10. Emiliani 1972, Broecker 2001
11. Goudie 1977
12. Broecker 2001
13. Goudie 1977
14. Jones, Terry, et al. 2004
15. NOAA 2006
16. Goudie 1977
17. Stine 1996
18. Enzel et al. 1990
19. Zwinger 1986
20. Ibid.
21. Ibid.
22. Nelson 1989
23. Schoenman and Schoenman 1976
24. Short 1982
25. Audubon and MacGillivray 1839
26. Grinnell and Miller 1944, Small 1994
27. Kurten and Anderson 1980
28. Zwinger 1986
29. Millar and Woolfenden 1999
30. Ropelewski and Halpert 1990
31. Ware 1991
32. Wells 1990
33. Starr 1976
34. Farrior 2004
35. Minshall 1980
36. Ibid.
37. Martin 1997
38. Sund and Norton 1990
39. Skinner, John 1962
40. Ibid.
41. Ware 1991
42. Stowe 1979
43. Agostini 2005
44. Ibid.
45. Hollowed et al. 2001
46. Anderson, R. Y. et al. 1990
47. Sancetta et al. 1992
48. Sandweiss 2004
49. Takasuka et al. 2005
50. Stine 1996
51. NOAA 2006
52. Ibid.
53. Brower 2006
54. Dukes and Shaw 2007
55. Smith, Stanley, et al. 2009

Three: Shoreline Stories

1. Weber 1985
2. Fagan 2003
3. Goals Project 1999

4. Fagan 2003
5. Ibid.
6. Bolton 1930a
7. San Francisco Estuary Institute 1998
8. Skinner, John 1962
9. California Department Fish and Game Wildlife leaflet
10. Ibid.
11. Ibid.
12. Skinner, John 1962
13. Ibid.
14. Howell 1966
15. Goals Project 1999
16. Brewer 1949
17. McCawley 1996
18. Speth 1971
19. CNN, January 22, 2005
20. Goals Project 1999
21. Ibid.
22. Ibid.
23. Goals Project 2000
24. Ibid.
25. Zedler et al. 1992
26. Grossinger 2001
27. Holder 1906
28. Ibid.
29. Warme 1971
30. Cole and Wahl 1998
31. Skinner, John 1962
32. Ibid.
33. Power 1994, Fischer 2003
34. Evens 1988
35. Fischer 2003
36. Ainley et al. 1994
37. Gordon 1974
38. Grinnell and Miller 1944
39. Evens 1988, Kessel and Gibson 1994
40. Miller et al. 1961
41. Morejohn 1976
42. Ibid.
43. Guthrie 1980
44. Le Boeuf 1985, Grant and Cushing 1969
45. Ibid.
46. Lyman 1995
47. Ibid.
48. Kurten and Anderson 1980
49. Grant and Cushing 1969

50. Hubbs 1956
51. Ibid.
52. West and Simons 1979, Jones and Hildebrandt 1995
53. Le Boeuf and Bonnell 1980
54. Skinner, John 1962
55. Jones and Hildebrandt 1995, Le Boeuf and Bonnell 1980
56. Fischer 2003
57. Hildebrandt and Jones 1992
58. Le Boeuf 1985
59. Bleitz 1993
60. Fagan 2003
61. Stewart et al. 1993
62. Grant and Cushing 1969
63. Ibid.
64. Evens 1988
65. Grant and Cushing 1969
66. Evens 1988
67. Ibid.
68. Grant and Cushing 1969
69. Ibid.

Four: The Inland Marshes

1. Minnick and Bohn 1969
2. Bolton 1930a
3. Watson 1880
4. Katibah 1984
5. Kooser, Seabough and Sargent 1861
6. Leopold and Dasmann 1985
7. Dasmann 1981
8. Anderson, M. Kat, et al 1998
9. Woodward and Smith 1977
10. Preston 1981
11. Katibah 1984
12. Banks and Springer 1994
13. Preston 1981
14. Ibid.
15. Griggs 1983
16. Zwinger 1986
17. Grayson 1920
18. Ibid.
19. Fisher 1893
20. Banks and Springer 1994.
21. Remsen 1978
22. Grinnell 1944
23. Cassin 1865
24. Banks and Springer 1994
25. Small 1994

26. Cowan, John 1985
27. Welch 1927
28. Banks and Springer 1994
29. Ibid., Minshall 1980
30. Grinnell 1935
31. Skinner, John 1962
32. Dasmann 1981
33. Ibid.
34. Anderson, M. Kat 2005
35. Lawton et al. 1993
36. Anderson, M. Kat 2005

Five: River World

1. Mandel et al. 1989
2. Ibid.
3. Drost and Fellers 1996
4. Davidson, Carlos, et al. 2001
5. U.S. Geological Survey 2000
6. Thompson, Kenneth 1977
7. Ibid.
8. Barbour et al. 1993
9. McClurg 2000
10. Deane and Holing 1985
11. Meinecke 1936
12. McClurg 2000
13. Grossinger 1999
14. Woodward and Smith 1977
15. Dasmann 1965
16. Brewer 1949
17. Lummis 1902
18. Woodward and Smith 1977
19. Webb 1996, Webb et al. 2004
20. Barbour et al. 1993
21. Thompson, Kenneth 1977
22. Grossinger et al. 2006 and 2007
23. Deane and Holing 1985
24. Gaines 1977, Small 1994, Grinnell and Miller 1944
25. Garrett and Dunn 1981
26. Hanna in Gaines 1977
27. Deane and Holing 1985, Small 1994
28. Belding 1890
29. Harris, J. J. 1991
30. Laymon 1987, Small 1994, Grinnell and Miller 1944
31. Grinnell and Miller 1944
32. Small 1994
33. Franzreb 1987b, USFWS 2007
34. Franzreb 1987b

35. Gaines 1977

36. Grinnell and Miller 1944

37. Leahey 1982

38. Grinnell and Miller 1944

Six: California Grasslands

1. Anderson, Barbour, and Whitworth 1998

2. Mattoni and Longcore 1997

3. Grove and Racham 2001

4. Keeler-Wolf et al. 2007

5. translation in Johnson and Earle 1993

6. Galvin 1971

7. Thompson, R. A. 1902

8. Burcham 1957

9. Ibid.

10. Jackson, R. D. and Bartolome 2007

11. Bryant, E. 1849

12. Gordon 1974

13. Jackson, R. D. and Bartolome 2007

14. Burcham 1957

15. Dasmann 1965

16. Brewer 1949

17. D'Antonio et al. 2003

18. D'Antonio et al. 2007

19. Hendry 1931

20. Rice and Espeland 2007

21. Burcham 1957

22. Minnich and Dezanni 1998

23. Bartolome and Gemmill 1981

24. Sampson and McCarty 1930

25. Hull and Muller 1977

26. Bartolome and Gemmill 1981, D'Antonio et al. 2003

27. Holstein 2001

28. Clements 1934

29. Ibid.

30. Grove and Racham 2001

31. Bartolome, Klukkert and Barry 1986

32. Jackson, R. D. and Bartolome 2007

33. Watson 1880

34. Davidson and Moxley 1923

35. Abrams 1904

36. Hitchcock 1950, Crampton 1974, Munz and Keck 1963

37. Abrams 1904

38. Munz and Keck 1963

39. Ibid.

40. Davidson and Moxley 1923, Lathrop and Thorne 1968

41. Barry 1972

42. Watson 1880

43. Abrams 1904

44. Watson 1880

45. Twisselman 1967

46. Abrams 1904

47. Twisselman 1967

48. Munz and Keck 1963

49. Hickman 1993, Munz and Keck 1963

50. Ibid.

51. Crampton 1959

52. Sykes 2003

53. Jackson, R. D. and Bartolome 2007

54. Belk 1998, Simovich 1998

55. Preston 1981

56. Barbour and Witham 2004

57. Thorp and Leong 1998

58. Brewer 1949

59. Hoover 1935

60. Mayfield 1993

61. Hoover 1935

62. Ibid.

63. Twisselman 1967

64. Goodrich 1902

65. Saroyan 1937

66. Behr 1888

67. Bolton 1930a

68. Hamilton 1997, Schiffman 2000

69. Meinecke 1936

70. Storer 1965b

71. Schiffman 2007

72. Harrison, S. P. and Viers 2007, Schiffman 2007

73. Schiffman 2007

74. Fagan 2003

75. Anderson, M. Kat 1993

76. Ibid.

77. Lowry 1993

78. Schiffman 2007

79. Guthrie 1982

80. Thomasson 1978, Thomasson 1986

81. Barkworth and Everett 1986, Barkworth 1990

82. de Wet 1949, Dewey 1882, Doebley et al. 1992, Hartley 1961, Hartley 1973, Snyder, L. A. 1951, Stebbins 1972, Stebbins 1975, Stebbins and Tobgy 1944

83. Jepson 1901

84. Jefferson and Goldin 1989, and Jefferson personal communication 1989

85. Byrne personal communication 1989

86. Akersten, Foppe, and Jefferson 1989

87. Grove and Oliver Racham 2001

88. Grove and Racham 2001, Meagher and Houston 1998

89. Mol et al. 2003

90. Paddison 1999

91. van Staalduinen and Werger 2005

92. Huntsinger et al. 2007, Jackson, R. D. and Bartolome 2007

93. Edwards 1992

94. Fremontia vol. 20 No. 3, July 1992

95. Waller et al. 1985

96. Burcham 1957

97. White, K. L. 1967

98. D'Antonio et al. 2003

99. Dyer et al. 1996

100. Meagher and Houston 1998

101. Savory 1988

102. Kephart 2001

103. Reeves 2001

104. www.epa.gov/OWOW/NPS/Ecology/chap6wil

105. McClanahan 2000

106. Coughenour 1991

107. Winterhalder 1994

108. Morris 2001

109. Stromberg et al. 2007

110. www.cnga.org

111. Ibid.

Seven: The Oak

1. Basgall 2004

2. Gordon 1974

3. Kelly 2001, CalPIF 2002

4. Priestley 1937

5. Barker 1994

6. Pavlik et al. 1991

7. Gordon 1974

8. Brewer 1949

9. McArdle 1983

10. Timbrook et al. 1993

11. CalPIF 2002

12. Carmen 1988, McBride et al. 1990

13. Minnich and Vizcaino 1998

14. Brewer 1949

15. Bonnicksen 2000
16. Meyer 2001
17. Griffin 1988
18. Jepson 1923
19. Bonnicksen 2000, Sampson 1944
20. Jepson 1901
21. Preston 1981
22. Ibid.
23. Harris, W.N. 1902
24. Danielsen and Halvorson 1990
25. Nixon 2001
26. Griffin 1988, Lathrop and Arct 1987, Pavlik et al. 1991
27. Scott 1990, Oberbauer 1978
28. Griffin 1988
29. Mensing 1992
30. Bartolome et al. 1987, Matsuda and McBride 1986
31. Allen-Diaz and Bartolome 2001
32. Brown and Davis. 1990
33. Bartolome, et al. 2001, Mensing 1992
34. Griffin 1988, Davis et al. 1990
35. Grove and Racham 2001
36. Ibid.
37. Bartolome et al. 1987
38. Stine 1996
39. McPherson 1997
40. Grove and Racham 2001
41. Haggerty 1990
42. Bartolome et al. 2001
43. Gruell 2001, Anderson, Barbour, and Whitworth 1998
44. Bartolome et al. 1987
45. Pavlik et al. 1991

Eight: Fire

1. Wells 1962
2. Callaway and Davis 1993
3. Hutchings 1875
4. Anderson, M. Kat 1993, Lewis 1993, Bean and Lawton 1993
5. Young 1986
6. Gumprecht 2001
7. Davis n.d.
8. Guscio et al. 2007
9. Anderson 2005
10. Barry 2003
11. Anderson, Barbour, and Whitworth 1998; Reiner 2007
12. Johnson and Earle 1993
13. Johnson and Earle 1993
14. Ibid.
15. Bean and Lawton 1993
16. Lewis 1993
17. Ibid.
18. Anderson, M. Kat 2007
19. Benson 1969
20. Benson 1969, 1982
21. McBride and Heady 1968
22. McCawley 1996
23. Axelrod 1978
24. Mullally 1994
25. Minnich and Dezzani 1998, Keeley 2002
26. U.S. Forest Service 2000; Minnich and Dezzani 1998
27. Eliason and Allen 1997
28. Minnich and Dezzani 1998
29. Ibid.
30. McCarthy 1993
31. Show and Kotok 1924
32. Muir 1901
33. Muir 1894
34. Sudworth 1900
35. Bonnicksen 2000
36. Barbour et al. 1993
37. Bonnicksen 2000
38. Sudworth 1900
39. Gruell 2001
40. Baxley 1865
41. Lewis 1993
42. Anderson, M. Kat 2005
43. Brewer 1949
44. Ernst 1949
45. NPS 2004
46. San Francisco Chronicle, August 31, 1987
47. Minnich et al. 1995; Stephenson 1999; Skinner and Chang 1996; Barbour et al. 1993; Gruell 2001
48. Minnich et al. 1995; Garrison, Otahal, and Triggs 2001; Kauffman and Martin 1987; Skinner and Chang 1996
49. Skinner and Chang 1996
50. Bonnicksen 2000
51. Gruell 2001
52. Kinney 1996
53. Swetnam and Baisan 1989
54. Anderson, R. S. and Carpenter 1991; Woolfenden 1996
55. Gruell 2001
56. Vale and Vale 1994
57. Gruell 2001
58. Muir 1894
59. Swetnam 1993
60. Stephenson 1999
61. Priestley 1937
62. Biswell 1974
63. Sauer 1977
64. Biswell 1974; Sampson 1944
65. Sweeney 1985; Keeley and Keeley 1987
66. Keeley 2002; Keeley and Fotherigham 1998
67. Sampson 1944
68. Ibid.
69. U.S. Forest Service Cooperation 1920
70. U.S. Forest Service Cooperation 1920
71. Barbour et al. 1993
72. Minnich et al. 1995; Stephenson 1999
73. Beesley 1996
74. Gruell 2001
75. Ochert 2003
76. Stephenson 1999; Barbour et al. 1993; Bonnicksen 2000
77. Ochert 2003
78. Skinner and Chang 1996
79. Ochert 2003
80. Forecast Earth, The Weather Channel, July 28, 2007
81. Ochert 2003
82. NPS 2004
83. www.nps.gov/archive/yose/fire
84. Reiner 2007
85. Keeley 1990
86. Gruell 2001
87. Ochert 2003
88. Minnich 2003; San Diego County Wildland Fire Task Force 2003
89. Minnich 1989
90. Minnich 1983, 1989
91. Minnich 1983
92. Hernandez and Perry 2003
93. San Diego County Wildland Fire Task Force 2003
94. Minnich and Hong Chou 1997
95. Keeley and Fotheringham 2001b
96. Minnich 1989; Keeley et al. 1989
97. Minnich 1989

98. Minnich and Hong Chou 1997
99. Mensing et al. 1977
100. Greenlee and Langenheim 1990
101. Ibid.
102. Keeley 1977
103. Keeley 2002
104. Minnich 1989
105. Vogl 1977
106. Minnich 1983, 1989
107. Grove and Racham 2001
108. Timbrook et al. 1993
109. Keeley 2002
110. Ibid.
111. Minnich 1983
112. Little 2002
113. Wolf 2004
114. Downey 2003

Nine: Where Deer and Antelope Played

1. Dasmann 1965
2. Bickel 1976
3. Evens 1988
4. Lummis 1902b
5. Burcham 1957
6. Houston 1982
7. Einarsen 1948
8. Byers 1997
9. Ibid.
10. Meineke 1936
11. Dasmann 1965
12. Brown et al. 2006
13. Geist 1991
14. Paddison 1999
15. Palóu 1926
16. Bohn 1969
17. Ibid.
18. Heizer and Kroeber 1979
19. Frison 2004, Elsasser 1978, Fagan 2003
20. Urness 1981
21. Longhurst et al. 1979
22. Quinn 1986
23. Linsdale and Tomich 1953
24. Quinn 1986
25. California Fish and Game 1920b
26. Doney et al. 1916
27. Cornett et al. 1983
28. Leopold 1952

Ten: Great Herds

1. Geist 1991
2. Evermann 1915
3. McCullough 1969
4. California Fish and Game 1931
5. Suisun Ecological Workgroup 2003
6. Thomas and Toweill 1982
7. McCullough 1969
8. Ibid.
9. Sleeper 1976
10. Preston 1998, Geist 1996
11. Broughton 1999
12. Evans and O'Connor 1999
13. Priestley 1937
14. Geist 1991
15. Kay 1998
16. Meagher and Douglas Houston 1998
17. Sinclair and Arcese 1995
18. McCullough 1969
19. Geist, in Thomas and Toweill 1982
20. Adams, in Thomas and Toweill 1982
21. McCullough 1969
22. Evermann 1915
23. McCullough 1969, Skinner, John 1962
24. Evermann 1915, McCullough 1969
25. McCullough 1969
26. Matocq et al. 2002
27. McCullough 1965
28. Meagher 1978, Soper 1941
29. McDonald 1981
30. Riddell 1952
31. Merriam 1926
32. Ibid.
33. Paddison 1999
34. Priestley 1937
35. Bradley and Brechbill 1966
36. Reed 1952
37. Dobie 1953
38. Kinney 1996
39. Galvin 1967
40. McDonald 1981
41. Shay 1978

Eleven: Top Predators

1. Priestley 1937
2. Schmidt 1991
3. Kotzebue 1830
4. Schmidt 1991
5. Grinnell 1935
6. Sime et al. 2006
7. Van Valkenburgh et al. 2006
8. Sime et al. 2006
9. Mech 1970
10. Sime et al. 2006, Brown 1983
11. Mech 1970
12. Brown 1983
13. Meier 2003
14. U.S. Fish and Wildlife et al. 2000, Meier 2001, Boyd 2004
15. Robbins 1998
16. Smith, Douglas W. et al. 2000
17. Murie 1944, Mech 1970
18. Meier 2001, Ripple and Beschta 2007
19. Levy, Sharon 2004
20. Schmidt 1991
21. Boyd 2004
22. Peterson 1995
23. Ibid.
24. Ibid.
25. Sime et al. 2006
26. Ripple and Beschta 2008
27. Grinnell 1935
28. Merriam 1919
29. Hittel 1860
30. Stolzenburg 1997

Twelve: Giants in the Sky

1. Snyder and Snyder 2000
2. Koford 1950
3. Ibid.
4. Grinnell and Miller 1944
5. Van Dyke 1980
6. Dawson 1923
7. Snyder and Snyder 2000
8. Koford 1950
9. Whitney 1870
10. Kofford 1953
11. Snyder and Snyder 2000
12. Whitney 1870
13. Ibid.
14. Simons 1983
15. Whitney 1870
16. Koford 1950
17. Wilbur 1983, Simons 1983
18. Simons 1983
19. Wilbur 1983
20. Whitney 1870

21. Snyder and Snyder 2000
22. Ibid.
23. Ogden 1983
24. Whitney 1870
25. Rayl 2004
26. Koford 1950
27. www.ventanaws.org/fldnotes, accessed 2004
28. Snyder and Snyder 2000
29. Whitney 1870
30. Dawson 1923
31. Snyder and Snyder 2000

Thirteen: First Fish

1. Hoffman 1991
2. Waszozuk and Labignan 1996
3. SPAWN 2002
4. Waszczuk and Labignan 1996
5. Jordan 1892
6. Moyle 2002
7. Ibid.
8. Yoshiyama et al. 2001
9. Ibid.
10. Moyle 2002
11. Lufkin 1991
12. McHugh, Paul 1991
13. Steelquist 1992
14. Moyle 2002
15. See the California Salmonid Stream Habitat Restoration Manual, Flosi et al. 1997, for more information
16. Jordan 1892
17. Moyle 2002
18. Leidy 1984
19. Ibid.
20. Brown, Laura 2007
21. Jordan 1892; Moyle 2002
22. Jordan and Evermann 1904
23. Jordan and Evermann 1904; Moyle 2002
24. Waszczuk and Labignan 1996
25. Lufkin 1991; National Marine Fisheries Service 1996
26. National Marine Fisheries Service 1996
27. California Fish and Game 1920d
28. National Marine Fisheries Service 1996
29. Ibid.
30. McClurg 2000

31. Yoshiyama et al. 2001
32. Moyle 2002
33. Yoshiyama et el. 2001
34. Moyle 2002
35. National Marine Fisheries Service 1996
36. Schulz and Simons 1973
37. Fimrite 2008
38. Fall Newsletter of Salmon River Restoration Council, www.srrc.org, accessed 2004
39. Fall Newsletter SRRC; Moyle 2002
40. Fall Newsletter SRRC; Snyder, J. O. 1931
41. Snyder, J. O. 1931
42. Committee on Endangered and Threatened Fishes in the Klamath River Basin 2004
43. www.pcffa.org; ww.newportnewstimes.com/articles/2008/03/14/news/news03.txt, accessed June 2008
44. Stubbs and White 1993; Committee on Endangered and Threatened Fishes 2004
45. Committee on Endangered and Threatened Fishes 2004
46. Klamath Basin Coalition 2003; Williams, Ted 2003; Committee on Endangered and Threatened Fishes 2004
47. Fagan 2003
48. Salter 2003
49. Salter 2003; Kroeber 1925; Bell 1991
50. Kroeber 1925
51. Salter 2003
52. Kroeber 1925; Fagan 2003
53. Bell 1991
54. Heizer and Elsasser 1980
55. Heizer and Elsasser 1980; Kroeber 1925
56. Bell 1991
57. Kroeber 1925
58. Bell 1991
59. Pierce 1991
60. Pennington and Stercho 2004
61. Salter 2003
62. Committee on Endangered and Threatened 2004
63. Williams, Ted 2003
64. Pennington 2004; Stubbs and White 1993
65. McHugh, Paul 1991

66. McClurg 2000; McHugh, Paul 1991; www.klamathbasininfo.com, accessed 2004
67. McEwan and Jackson 1996
68. Moyle 2002.
69. Jordan 1892
70. Higgins 1991; Moyle 2002
71. House 1999
72. www.klamathbasin.info, accessed 2004; Committee on Endangered and Threatened Fishes in the Klamath River Basin 2004.
73. www.earthjustice.org, accessed 2004
74. See Klamath Basin Coalition, www.klamathbasin.info
75. Committee on Endangered and Threatened Fishes 2004
76. Villeponteaux 2004
77. Salter 2003
78. Flosi et al. 1997
79. Committee on Endangered and Threatened Fishes 2004
80. Hillman and Salter 1997
81. Hooper 1991
82. SPAWN 2002
83. Kushner 2002

Conclusion: Relocalization

1. For example, see relocalize.net and localharvest.org, and look into the Post Carbon Institute in Sebastopol, founded by Julian Darley, who coined the term "relocalization."
2. Zedler et al. 1992
3. Stephenson 1999
4. Ochert 2003
5. Little 2002
6. See for example www.leics.gov.uk/community_services/press_release/2002
7. Modified from Wolf 2004
8. Redmond 2009

BIBLIOGRAPHY

ABC News. 2004. KGO-TV Channel 7, Bay Area. July 25, 2004.

Abrams, L. 1904. *Flora of Los Angeles and vicinity.* Stanford, CA: Stanford University Press.

Adam, David P. 1975. A late Holocene pollen record from Pearson's Pond, Weeks Creek Landslide, San Francisco Peninsula, California. *United States Geological Survey Journal of Research* 3 (6): 721–731.

———. 1981. 130,000-year continuous pollen record from Clear Lake, Lake County, California. *Geology* 9 (8): 373–377.

———. 1985. Quaternary pollen records from California. Pollen records of late-Quaternary North American sediments. American Association of Spores and Pollen Foundation.

Agee, James K. 1993. *Fire ecology of Pacific Northwest forests.* Washington, D.C.: Island Press.

Agostini, Vera N. 2005. Climate, ecology, and productivity of Pacific sardine (*Sardinops sardax*) and hake (*Merluccius productus*). Ph.D. diss., University of Washington, Seattle.

Ainley, D. G., W. J. Sydeman, S. A. Hatch, U. W. Wilson. 1994. Seabird population trends along the West Coast of North America. In *A century of avifaunal change in western North America,* edited by Joseph R. Jehl and Ned K. Johnson. Proceedings of an International Symposium of the Cooper Ornithological Society at the Centennial Meeting, Sacramento, CA, April 17, 1993. Studies in Avian Biology No. 15. Lawrence, KS: Cooper Ornithological Society.

Ainley, D. G., W. J. Sydeman, and R. H. Parrish. 1991. Upwelling, offshore transport, and the availability of rockfish in central California. In *Proceedings of the seventh annual Pacific Climate (PACLIM) Workshop, Asilomar, California, April 1990,* edited by Julio L. Betancourt and Vera L. Tharp. Technical Report 26 of the Interagency Ecological Studies Program for the Sacramento-San Joaquin Estuary.

Akersten, W. A., T. M. Foppe, and G. T. Jefferson. 1989. New source of dietary data for extinct herbivores. *Quaternary Research* 30: 92–97.

Allen, Glover M. 1972. *Extinct and vanishing mammals of the western hemisphere, with the marine species of all the oceans.* New York: Cooper Square Publishers. Special Publication No. 11.

Allen, Helena G. 1974. San Bernardino County Museum commemorative edition. Redlands, CA: Allen-Greendale Publishers.

Allen-Diaz, B. H., and J. W. Bartolome. 1992. Survival of *Quercus douglasii* (Fagaceae) seedlings under the influence of fire and grazing. *Madrono* 39 (1): 47–53.

Alley, Donald W., D. H. Dettman, H. W. Li, and P. B. Moyle. 1977. Habitats of native fishes in the Sacramento River basin. In *Riparian forests in California: Their ecology and conservation,* edited by Anne Sands. Institute of Ecology Publication No. 15. Davis: Institute of Ecology, University of California, Davis.

Ambrose, R. F., J. M. Engle, J. A. Coyer, and B. V. Nelson. 1993. Changes in urchin and kelp densities at Anacapa Island, California. In *Third California Islands Symposium: Recent advances in research of the California islands,* edited by F. G. Hochberg. Santa Barbara: Santa Barbara Museum of Natural History.

Amme, David. 2003. Creating a native meadow. *Grasslands* 13 (summer): 1, 9–11. Newsletter of the California Native Grass Association.

Anderson, Bertin W., John Disano, Donald L. Brooks, and Robert D. Ohmart. 1984. Mortality and growth of Cottonwood on dredge-spoil. In *California riparian systems: Ecology, conservation, and productive management,* edited by Richard E. Warner and Kathleen M. Hendrix. Berkeley: University of California Press.

Anderson, M. Kat. 1993. Native Californians as ancient and contemporary cultivators. In *Before the wilderness: Environmental management by Native Californians,* edited by Thomas C. Blackburn and M. Kat Anderson. Ballena Press Anthropological Papers No. 40. Menlo Park, CA: Ballena Press.

———. 2005. *Tending the wild: Native American knowledge and the management of california's natural resources.* Berkeley: University of California Press.

———. 2007. Native American uses and management of California's grasslands. In *California grasslands ecology and management,* edited by M. R. Stromberg, J. D. Corbin, and C. M. D'Antonio. Berkeley: University of California Press.

Anderson, M. Kat, Michael G. Barbour, and Valerie Whitworth. 1998. A world of balance and plenty: Land, plants, animals, and humans in a pre-European California. In *Contested eden: California before the gold rush,* edited by Ramon A. Gutierrez and Richard J. Orsi. Berkeley: University of California Press.

Anderson, M. Kat, and Michael J. Moratto. 1996. Native American land-use practices and ecological impacts. In Sierra Nevada Ecosystem Project. Status of the Sierra Nevada, Vol. 2. Assessments and Scientific Basis for Management Options. Final Report to Congress. Wildlands Resources Center Report No. 37. Centers for Water and Wildland Resources, University of California, Davis.

Anderson, Nancy K. 1997. *Thomas Moran.* Washington, D.C.: National Gallery of Art, and New Haven: Yale University Press.

Anderson, Nancy K., and Linda S. Ferber. 1990. *Albert Bierstadt: Art and enterprise.* New York: Hudson Hills Press, in association with the Brooklyn Museum, Brooklyn, NY.

Anderson, R. S. 1990. Holocene forest development and paleoclimates within the central Sierra Nevada, California. *Journal of Ecology* 78: 470–489.

Anderson, R. S., and B. F. Byrd. 1998. Late-Holocene vegetation changes from the Las Flores Creek coastal lowlands, San Diego County, California. *Madrono* 45 (2): 171–182.

Anderson, R. S., and S. L. Carpenter. 1991. Vegetation change in Yosemite Valley, Yosemite National Park, California, during the Protohistoric period. *Madrono* 38 (1): 1–13.

Anderson, R. Y. 1990. Solar cycle modulations of ENSO: A possible source of climatic change. In *Proceedings of the sixth annual Pacific Climate (PACLIM) Workshop, March 5–8, 1989,* edited by J. L. Betancourt and A. M. Mackay. California Department of Water Resources, Interagency Ecological Studies Program Technical Report 23.

———. 1991. The role of direct observation in predicting climate change. In *Proceedings of the seventh annual Pacific Climate (PACLIM) Workshop, Asilomar, California, April 1990,* edited by Julio L. Betancourt and Vera L. Tharp. Technical Report 26 of the Interagency Ecological Studies Program for the Sacramento-San Joaquin Estuary.

Anderson, R. Y., B. K. Linsley, and J. V. Gardner. 1990. Expression of seasonal and ENSO forcing in climatic variability at lower than ENSO frequencies: Evidence from Pleistocene marine varves off California. *Palaeogeography, Palaeoclimatology, Palaeoecology* 78: 287–300.

Angel, M. 1882. *History of Placer County, California, with illustrations and biographical sketches of its prominent men and pioneers.* Oakland, CA: Thompson and West.

Applegate, R. D., L. L. Rogers, D. A. Casteel, and J. M. Novak. 1979. Germination of cow parsnip seeds from grizzly bear feces. *Journal of Mammalogy* 60 (3): 655.

Arnold, Caroline. 1993. *On the brink of extinction: The California condor.* A Gulliver Green Book. San Diego: Harcourt Brace.

Aschmann, H. H.. 1976. Man's impact on the southern California flora, p. 40—48. In *Symposium proceedings: Plant communities of southern California,* edited by J. Latting. Sacramento: California Native Plant Society. Special Publication No. 2.

———. 1977. Aboriginal fire use. In *Proceedings of the symposium on the environmental consequences of fire and fuel management in Mediterranean ecosystems,* edited by H. A. Mooney and C. E. Conrad. U.S. Forest Service General Technical Report WO-26.

Atsatt, S. R. 1913. The reptiles of the San Jacinto area of southern California. *University of California Publications in Zoology* 12 (3): 31–50.

Atwood, Todd C., Eric M. Gese, and Kyran Kunkel. 2004. Relative contributions of prey physical condition and habitat structure to predation by cougars and wolves in southwest Montana. In Rocky Mountain Wolf Recovery Team annual report 2004, by D. Boyd. A cooperative effort by the U.S. Fish and Wildlife Service, the Nez Perce Tribe, the National Park Service, and USDA Wildlife Services. www.westerngraywolf.fws.gov/. Accessed 2007.

Audubon, John James, and Alexander MacGillivray. 1839. *Ornithological biography.* New York: J. J. Audubon.

Audubon, John Woodhouse. 1906. *Audubon's western journal: 1849–1850. Being the MS record of a trip from New York to Texas, and an overland journey through Mexico and Arizona to the gold-fields of California.* Cleveland: Arthur H. Clark.

Auffenberg, Walter. 1994. *The Bengal monitor.* Gainesville: University Press of Florida.

Axelrod, Daniel I. 1975. Evolution and biogeography of Madrean-Tethyan sclerophyll vegetation. *Annals of the Missouri Botanic Garden* 62: 280–334.

———. 1978. The origin of coastal sage vegetation, Alta and Baja California. *American Journal of Botany* 65: 1117–1131.

———. 1981. Holocene climatic changes in relation to vegetation disjunction and speciation. *American Naturalist* 117 (6): 847–870.

Bagwell, Beth. 1982. *Oakland: The story of a city.* Novato, CA: Presidio Press.

Bahre, Conrad J. 1991. *A legacy of change: Historic human impact on vegetation of the Arizona borderlands.* Tucson: University of Arizona Press.

Banks, R. C., and P. F. Springer. 1994. A century of population trends of waterfowl in western North America. In *A century of avifaunal change in western North America,* edited by Joseph R. Jehl and Ned K. Johnson. Proceedings of an International Symposium of the Cooper Ornithological Society at the Centennial Meeting, Sacramento, CA, April 17, 1993. Studies in Avian Biology No. 15. Lawrence, KS: Cooper Ornithological Society.

Barbour, Michael G. 1996. California landscapes before the invaders. In Proceedings of the 1996 California Exotic Pest Plant Council Symposium, Vol. 2, edited by J. E. Lovich, J. Randall, and M. D. Kelly. http://ucce.ucdavis.edu/freeform/ceppc/documents/1996_Symposium_Proceedings1837.pdf or http://www.cal-ipc.org/symposia/archive/.

Barbour, Michael, and Jack Major, eds. 1988. *Terrestrial vegetation of California.* Sacramento: California Native Plant Society. Special Publication No. 9.

Barbour, Michael, Bruce Pavlik, Frank Drysdale, and Susan Lindstrom. 1993. *California's changing landscapes: Diversity and conservation of California vegetation.* Sacramento: California Native Plant Society. 2nd printing, 1996.

Barbour, Michael, and C. W. Witham. 2004. Islands within islands: Viewing vernal pools differently. *Fremontia* 32 (April).

Barker, Malcolm E. 1994. *San Francisco memoirs, 1835—1851: Eyewitness accounts of the birth of a city.* San Francisco: Londonborn Publications.

Barkworth, M. E. 1990. *Nassella* (Gramineae, Stipeae): Revised interpretation and nomenclatural changes. *Taxon* 39 (4): 597–614.

Barkworth, M. E., and J. Everett. 1986. Evolution in the Stipeae: Identification and relationships of its monophyletic taxa. In *Grass systematics and evolution,* edited by T. R. Soderstrom, K. W. Hilu, C. S. Campbell, and M. E. Barkworth. Washington, D.C.: Smithsonian Institution.

Barnhart, S. J., J. R. McBride, C. Cicero, P. Da Silva, and P. Warner. 1987. Vegetation dynamics of the northern oak woodlands. In USDA Forest Service Pacific Southwest Research Station, General Technical Report PSW-100.

Barnhart, S. J., J. R. McBride, and P. Warner. 1990. Oak seedling establishment in relation to environmental factors at Annadel State Park. In *Proceedings of the symposium on oak woodlands and hardwood rangeland management, October 31–November 2, 1990, Davis, California.* USDA Forest Service Pacific Southwest Research Station, General Technical Report PSW-126.

Barona Spirits Speak. 2004. Newsletter of the Barona Cultural Center and Museum. Reprinted in *News from Native California* 18 (1): 37–38.

Barry, W. J. 1972. *The Central Valley prairie.* Vol. 1 of *California Prairie Ecosystem.* Sacramento: State of California, Resources Agency, Department of Parks and Recreation.

———. 2003. California primeval grasslands and management in the State Parks system. *Grasslands* 13 (summer). Newsletter of the California Native Grass Association.

Bartlett, Richard A., and William H. Goetzmann. 1982. *Exploring the American West, 1803–1879.* Handbook 116, Washington, D.C.: Department of the Interior, National Park Service.

Bartolome, J. W. 1981. *Stipa pulchra,* survivor from the pristine prairie. *Fremontia* (April): 3–6.

———. 1987. California annual grassland and oak savanna. *Rangelands* 9 (3): 122–125.

Bartolome, J. W., and B. Gemmill. 1981. The ecological status of *Stipa pulchra* (Poaceae) in California. *Madrono* 28 (3): 172–184.

Bartolome, J. W., S. E. Klukkert, and W. J. Barry. 1986. Opal phytoliths as evidence for displacement of native Californian grassland. *Madrono* 33 (3): 217–222.

Bartolome, J. W., M. P. McClaran, B. H. Allen-Diaz, J. Dunne, L. D. Ford, R. B. Standiford, N. K. McDougald, and L. C. Forero. 2001. Effects of fire and browsing on regeneration of blue oak. In *Proceedings of the fifth symposium on oak woodlands: Oaks in California's changing landscape.* October 22–25, 2001, San Diego, California. USDA Forest Service Pacific Southwest Research Station, General Technical Report PSW-GTR-184.

Bartolome, J. W., P. C. Muick, and M. P. McClaran. 1987. Natural regeneration of California hardwoods. In USDA Forest Service Pacific Southwest Research Station, General Technical Report PSW-100.

Basgall, Mark E. 2004. Resource intensification among hunter-gatherers: Acorn economies from prehistoric California. In *Prehistoric California: Archaeology and the myth of paradise,* edited by L. Mark Raab and Terry L. Jones. Salt Lake City: University of Utah Press.

Bates, D. B. 1857. *Incidents on land and water, or four years on the Pacific Coast.* Boston: James French.

Baxley, H. W. 1865. *What I saw on the West Coast of South and North America and at the Hawaiian Islands.* New York: D. Appleton and Co.

Beals, R. L. 1933. Ethnology of the Nisenan. *University of California Publications in American Archaeology and Ethnology* 31 (6): 335–414.

Bean, L. J., and H. W. Lawton. 2003. Some explanations for the rise of cultural complexity in native California with comments of proto-agriculture and agriculture. In *Before the wilderness: Environmental management by Native Californians*, edited by Thomas C. Blackburn and M. Kat Anderson. Menlo Park, CA: Ballena Press.

Beard, Harry R. 1921. California sardine food products and their preparation. *California Fish and Game* 7 (4): 238–247.

Beesley, David. 1996. Reconstructing the landscape: An environmental history, 1820–1960. In Sierra Nevada Ecosystem Project. Status of the Sierra Nevada, Vol. 2. Assessments and Scientific Basis for Management Options. Final Report to Congress. Wildlands Resources Center Report No. 37. Centers for Water and Wildland Resources, University of California, Davis.

Beetle, A. A. 1947. Distribution of the native grasses of California. *Hilgardia* 17 (9): 309–358.

Behr, H. H. 1888. Changes in the fauna and flora of California. *Proceedings of the California Academy of Sciences*, 2nd ser. 1: 94–99.

———. 1891. Botanical reminiscences. *Zoe* 2: 2–6.

Belding, Lyman. 1890. *Land birds of the Pacific district*. San Francisco: California Academy of Sciences.

Belk, D. 1998. Global status and trends in ephemeral pool invertebrates conservation: Implications for Californian fairy shrimp. Pages 147–150 in *Ecology, conservation, and management of vernal pool ecosystems*, edited by C. W. Whitham, E. T. Bauder, D. Belk, W. R. Ferren, Jr., and R. Ornduff. Proceedings from a 1996 Conference, Sacramento, California. Sacramento: California Native Plant Society.

Bell, Maureen. 1991. *Karuk: The upriver people*. Happy Camp, CA: Naturegraph Publishers. Reprint, 2002.

Bellrose, Frank C. 1976. *Ducks, geese and swans of North America*. Washington, D.C.: Wildlife Management Institute and Harrisburg, PN: Stackpole Books. 3rd printing 1980.

Benedict, Nathan B. 1984. Classification and dynamics of subalpine meadow ecosystems in the southern Sierra Nevada. In *California riparian systems: Ecology, conservation, and productive management*, edited by Richard E. Warner and Kathleen M. Hendrix. Berkeley: University of California Press.

Bennett, Deb. 1998. *The conquerors: The roots of New World horsemanship*. Solvang, CA: Amigo Publications.

Benson, Lyman. 1969. *The native cacti of California*. Stanford, CA: Stanford University Press.

———. 1982. *The cacti of the United States and Canada*. Stanford, CA: Stanford University Press.

Bickel, Polly. 1976. Toward a prehistory of the San Francisco Bay Area: The archaeology of sites ALA-328, ALA-13, and ALA-12. Ph.D. diss., University of California, Berkeley.

Bicknell, S. H., A. T. Austin, D. J. Brigg, and R. P. Godar. 1992. Late prehistoric vegetation patterns at six sites in coastal California. Abstract in *Ecological Society of America 1992 Annual Meeting, Honolulu, Hawaii, August 9–13, 1992. Bulletin of the Ecological Society of America* 73 (2): 12.

Biswell, H. H. 1956. Ecology of California grasslands. *Journal of Range Management* 9: 19–24.

———. 1974. Effects of fire on chaparral. In *Fire and ecosystems*, edited by C. E. Athlgren. New York: Academic Press.

Blackburn, Thomas C., and M. Kat Anderson, eds. 1993. *Before the wilderness: Environmental management by Native Californians*. Menlo Park, CA: Ballena Press.

Blake, Emmet Ried. 1953. *Birds of Mexico: A guide for field identification*. Chicago: University of Chicago Press.

Blake, W. H. 1857. Geological report no. 1. Itinerary, or notes and general observations upon the geology of the route. Vol. 5, part 2 of *Explorations and surveys for a railroad route from the Mississippi River to the Pacific Ocean*. Washington, D.C.: U.S. War Department.

Blankinship, J. W., and Charles A. Keeler. 1892. On the natural history of the Farallon Islands. *Zoe* 3.

Bleitz, D. E. 1993. The prehistoric exploitation of marine mammals and birds at San Nicolas Island, California. In *Third California Islands Symposium: Recent advances in research of the California islands*, edited by F. G. Hochberg. Santa Barbara: Santa Barbara Museum of Natural History.

Bolander, H. N. 1870. *A catalogue of the plants growing in the vicinity of San Francisco*. San Francisco: A. Roman and Co.

Bolton, H. E. 1927. *Fray Juan Crespi*. Berkeley: University of California Press.

———. 1930a. *Anza's California expedition*. Volume III, *The San Francisco colony*. Diaries of Anza, Font, and Eixarch, and narratives by Palou and Moraga. Berkeley: University of California Press.

———. 1930b. *Anza's California expedition*. Volume IV, *Font's complete diary of the second Anza expedition*. Berkeley: University of California Press.

———. 1931. *Font's complete diary*. Berkeley: University of California Press.

Bond, W. J. 1980. Fire in senescent fynbos in the Swartberg. *South African Forestry Journal* 114: 68–71.

Bonnicksen, Thomas M. 2000. *America's ancient forests: From the Ice Age to the age of discovery*. New York: Wiley.

Borland, Hal. 1975. *The history of wildlife in America*. Washington, D.C.: National Wildlife Federation.

Bowermen, M. L. 1944. *The flowering plants and ferns of Mount Diablo, California: Their distribution and association into plant communities*. Berkeley: Gillick Press.

Boxt, Matthew A., L. Mark Raab, Owen K. Davis, and Kevin O. Pope. 1999. Extreme late Holocene climatic change in coastal southern California. *Pacific Coast Archaeological Society Quarterly* 35 (spring and summer).

Boyd, D., ed. 2004. Rocky Mountain wolf recovery team. Annual report. A cooperative effort by the U.S. Fish and Wildlife Service, the Nez Perce Tribe, the National Park Service, and USDA Wildlife Services. USFWS, Ecological Services, 100 N Park, Suite 320, Helena MT. 72 pp. www.westerngraywolf.fws.gov. Accessed 2007.

Bradley, W. G., and R. A. Brechbill. 1966. Evidence for modern bison in southern Nevada. *Journal of Mammalogy* 47 (2): 355.

Brandegee, T. S. 1891. The vegetation of "burns." *Zoe* 2: 118–122.

Brattstrom, B. H. 1988. Habitat destruction in California with special reference to *Clemmys marmorata*: A perpesctive [sic]. In *Proceedings of the conference on California herpetology*, edited by H. F. DeLisle, P. R. Brown, B. Kaufman, and B. M. McGurty. Southwestern Herpetologists Society Special Publication No. 4.

Brewer, William H. 1949. *Up and down California in 1860–1864: The journal of William H. Brewer, professor of agriculture in the Sheffield Scientific School from 1864 to 1903*. Edited by Francis P. Farquhar. Berkeley: University of California Press.

Brice, James. 1977. Lateral migration of the middle Sacramento River, California. US Geological Survey, Water Resources Investigations 77-43. Menlo Park, CA.

Brietler, Alex. 2004. Parasite with a purpose: Protection for lamprey considered. *Record Searchlight* (Redding, CA), December 12, 2004.

Brode, John M., and R. Bruce Bury. 1984. The importance of riparian systems to amphibians and reptiles. In *California riparian systems: Ecology, conservation, and productive management,* edited by Richard E. Warner and Kathleen M. Hendrix. Berkeley: University of California Press.

Brodhead, Michael J. 1973. *A soldier-scientist in the American Southwest: Being a narrative of the travels of Elliott Coues, assistant surgeon, USA, with his observations upon natural history.* Historical Monograph No. 1. Tucson: Arizona Historical Society.

Broecker, W. S. 2001. Glaciers that speak in tongues and other tales of global warming. *Natural History* (October 2001): 60–69.

Brothers, Timothy S. 1984. Historical vegetation change in the Owens River riparian woodland. In *California riparian systems: Ecology, conservation, and productive management,* edited by Richard E. Warner and Kathleen M. Hendrix. Berkeley: University of California Press

Broughton, Jack M. 1999. Resource depression and intensification during the late Holocene, San Francisco Bay. *University of California Anthropological Records* 32.

Brower, Kenneth. 2006. Disturbing Yosemite. *California* May–June 2006: 14–23, 41–44.

Brown, B. T. 1987. Breeding ecology of a willow flycatcher population in Grand Canyon, Arizona. *Western Birds* 18: 25–33.

Brown, Bruce. 1995. *Mountain in the clouds: A search for the wild salmon.* Seattle: University of Washington Press.

Brown, David E., ed. 1983. *The wolf in the Southwest.* Tucson: University of Arizona Press.

——. 1985. *The grizzly in the Southwest.* Norman: University of Oklahoma Press.

Brown, David E., Jorge Cancino, Kevin B. Clark, Myrna Smith, and Jim Yoakum. 2006. An annotated bibliography of references to historical distributions of pronghorn in southern and Baja California. *Bulletin* (Southern California Academy of Sciencs) 105 (1): 1–16.

Brown, Laura. 2007. Chinook salmon count way down: Scientists puzzled over slumping numbers on lower Yuba. *The Union* (Western Neavada County, CA), October 23, 2007. www.theunion.com/article/20071023/NEWS/110230159. Accessed June 2008.

Brown, R. W., and F. W. Davis. 1990. Historical mortality of valley oak (*Quercus lobata, Nee*) in the Santa Ynez Valley, Santa Barbara County, 1938–1989. In *Proceedings of the symposium on oak woodlands and hardwood rangeland management, October 31–November 2, 1990, Davis, California.* USDA Forest Service Pacific Southwest Research Station, General Technical Report PSW-126.

Browning, R. M. 1993. Comments on the taxonomy of *Empidonax traillii* (willow flycatcher). *Western Birds* 24: 241–257.

Bryant, E. 1849. *What I saw in California: Being the journal of a tour, in the years 1846, 1847.* New York: D. Appleton.

Bryant, H. C. 1921a. Klamath River salmon threatened with extermination. *California Fish and Game* 7 (1): 42.

——. 1921b. Salmon in the Eel River. *California Fish and Game* 7 (1): 52–53.

Bryant, Walter E. 1891. The "reed birds" of the San Francisco markets. *Zoe* 2: 142–145.

——. 1891. Notes on the land mammals of California. *Zoe* 2: 113.

Bunnell, Lafayette H. 1911. *Discovery of the Yosemite.* Los Angeles: G. W. Gerlicher. Reprint, Yosemite, CA: Yosemite Association, 1990.

Burcham, L. T. 1957. *California range land: An historico-ecological study of the range resources of California.* Sacramento: Department of Natural Resources, California Division of Forestry.

Burckle, L. H. 1993. Late Quaternary interglacial stages warmer than present. *Quaternary Science Reviews* 12: 825–831.

Bury, R. B. 1972. Habitats and home range of the Pacific pond turtle, *Clemmys marmorata,* in a stream community. Ph.D. diss., University of California, Berkeley.

Burtch, L. A. 1934. The Kern County elk refuge. *California Fish and Game* 20 (2): 140–147.

Butler, Michael J. A. 1982. Plight of the bluefin tuna. *National Geographic* (August 1982): 220–239.

Byers, John A. 1997. *American pronghorn: Social adaptations and the ghosts of predators past.* Chicago: University of Chicago Press.

Byrne, R., E. Edlund, and S. Mensing. 1990. Holocene changes in the distribution and abundance of oaks in California. In *Proceedings of the symposium on oak woodlands and hardwood rangeland management, October 31–November 2, 1990, Davis, California.* USDA Forest Service Pacific Southwest Research Station, General Technical Report PSW-126.

Byrne. R., J. Michaelsen, and A. Soular. 1977. Fossil charcoals as a measure of wildfire frequency in southern California. In *Proceedings of the Symposium on the Environmental Consequences of Fire and Fuel Management in Mediterranean Ecosystems,* ed. H. A. Mooney and C. E. Conrad, U.S.D.A. Forest Service, General Technical Report WO-3.

Calabi, Silvio. 1990. *Trout and salmon of the world.* Secaucus, NJ: Wellfleet Press.

California Fish and Game. 1916. *California Fish and Game* 2(3)

California Fish and Game. 1917. *California Fish and Game* 3 (4).

California Fish and Game. 1919. The Sacramento run of salmon. (No author). *California Fish and Game* 5 (4): 199.

California Fish and Game. 1920a. Forest fires destroy game. (No author). *California Fish and Game* 6 (1): 36–37.

California Fish and Game. 1920b. Mule deer on the Lassen forest. (No author). *California Fish and Game* 6 (3).

California Fish and Game. 1920c. Silver salmon at Monterey in 1920. (Author W.L.S.). *California Fish and Game* 6 (4).

California Fish and Game. 1920d. Ocean stream salmon catches. (Author W.L.S.). *California Fish and Game* 6 (4).

Callaway, R. M., and F. W. Davis. 1993. Vegetation dynamics, fire, and the physical environment in coastal central California. *Ecology* 74 (5): 1567–1578.

CalPIF (California Partners in Flight). 2002. Version 2.0. The oak woodland bird conservation plan: A strategy for managing and protecting oak woodland habitats and associated birds in California. S. Zack, lead author. Point Reyes Bird Observatory, Stinson Beach, CA.

Camp, C. L. 1915. *Batrachoseps major* and *Bufo cognatus californicus,* new amphibia from southern California. *University of California Publications in Zoology* 12 (12): 327–334.

Cane, Mark A. 1998. A role for the tropical Pacific. *Science* 282: 59–60.

Cardiff, S. W., and J. V. Rensen, Jr. 1981. Breeding avifaunas of the New York Mountains and Kingston Range: Islands of conifers in the Mojave Desert of California. *Western Birds* 12: 73–86.

Carmen, W. J. 1988. "Behavioral ecology of the California scrub jay (*Aphelocoma coerulescens Californica*): a non-cooperative breeder with close cooperative relatives." Ph.D. Dissertation. Berkeley: University of California Press.

Carey, Alan. 1986. *In the path of the grizzly*. Flagstaff, AZ: Northland Press.

Carothers, Steven W., and Bryan T. Brown. 1991. *The Colorado River through the Grand Canyon: Natural history and human change*. Tucson: University of Arizona Press.

Cassin, John. 1865. *Illustrations of birds of California, Texas, Oregon, British and Russian America*. Reprint, Austin: Texas State Historical Foundation, 1990.

Casteel, R. W. 1977. Late-Pleistocene and Holocene remains of *Hysterocarpus traski* (tule perch) from Clear Lake, California, and inferred Holocene temperature fluctuations. *Quaternary Research* 7: 133–143.

CFC (California State Board of Fish Commissioners). 1875. [3rd] Report of the Commissioners of Fish, State of California, for 1874 and 1875, Sacramento, California.

CFC (California State Board of Fish Commissioners). 1890. [11th] Biennial Report of the Commissioners of Fish, State of California, for 1888 and 1890, Sacramento, California.

Chamberlain, W. H., and H. L. Wells. 1879. *History of Sutter County, California*. Oakland, CA: Thompson and West. Reprint, Berkeley: Howell-North: Berkeley, 1974.

Chapin, Ray. 1971. *The grizzly bear in the land of the Ohlone Indians*. Cupertino: California History Center.

Cheatham, Wilma G. 1942. *The story of Contra Costa County for boys and girls*. San Francisco: Harr Wagner Publishing Co.

Clark, Frances N. 1926. The conservation of the grunion. *California Fish and Game* 12 (4): 162–166.

Cleland, Robert Glass. 1941. *The cattle on a thousand hills: Southern California 1850–80*. San Marino, CA: Huntington Library.

Clements, F. E. 1934. The relict method in dynamic ecology. *Journal of Ecology* 22 (1): 36–68.

Cole, K. L., and E. Wahl. 1998. A Holocene fossil pollen record from Los Penasquitos Lagoon, San Diego, California. www.palynology.org/content/abst/AASPabstr.98. Accessed 2003.

Committee on Endangered and Threatened Fishes in the Klamath River Basin. 2004. *Endangered and threatened fishes in the Klamath River Basin: Causes of decline and strategies for recovery*. Washington, D.C.: National Academies Press, and the National Research Council of the National Academies.

Conard, S. G. 1987. First year growth of canyon live oak sprouts following thinning and clearcutting. In USDA Forest Service Pacific Southwest Research Station, General Technical Report PSW-100.

Conard, S. G., Rod L. Macdonald, and Robert F. Holland. 1977. Riparian vegetation and flora of the Sacramento Valley. In *Riparian forests in California: Their ecology and conservation*, edited by Anne Sands. Institute of Ecology Publication No. 15. Davis: Institute of Ecology, University of California, Davis.

Conisbee, Philip. 1996. The early history of open-air painting. In *The light of Italy: Corot and early open-air painting*, edited by Philip Conisbee, Sarah Faunce, and Jeremy Stick. Washington D.C.: National Gallery of Art, and New Haven: Yale University Press.

Cook, Sherburne F. 1960. Colonial expeditions to the interior of California: Central Valley, 1800–1820. *University of California Anthropological Records* 16 (6): 239–292.

Cooper, William S. 1926. Vegetational development upon alluvial fans in the vicinity of Palo Alto, California. *Ecology* 7 (1): 1–30.

Cope, E. D. 1879. The fishes of Klamath Lake, Oregon. *American Naturalist* 13: 784–785.

———. 1884. Fishes of the recent and Pliocene lakes of the western part of the Great Basin, and of the Idaho Pliocene Lake. *Proceedings of the Academy of Natural Sciences of Philadelphia* 35 (1883): 134–167.

Corle. Edwin. 1949. *The Royal Highway*. Indianapolis: Bobbs-Merrill.

Cornett, D. C., W. M. Longhurst, R. E. Hafenfeld, T. P. Hemker, and W. A. Williams. 1983. The ecology and management of the Mineral King deer herd. Cooperative National Park Resources Studies Unit, University of California at Davis, Technical Report No. 14.

Cottam, G. 1987. Community dynamics on an artificial prairie. In *Restoration Ecology*, edited by W. R. Jordan, M. E. Gilpin, and J. D. Aber. Cambridge, UK: Cambridge University Press.

Coughenour, Michael B. 1991. Spatial components of plant-herbivore interactions in pastoral, ranching, and native ungulate systems. *Journal of Range Management* 44 (6): 530–542.

Courtois, Louis A. 1984. Temporal desert riparian systems: The Mojave River as an example. In *California riparian systems: Ecology, conservation, and productive management*, edited by Richard E. Warner and Kathleen M. Hendrix. Berkeley: University of California Press.

Cowan, I. M. 1936. Distribution and variation in deer (genus *Odocoileus*) of the Pacific Coast region of North America. *California Fish and Game* 22: 155–246.

———. 1940. Distribution and variation in the native sheep of North America. *American Midland Naturalist* 24 (3): 505–580.

Cowan, John B. 1985. Waterfowl history in the Sacramento Valley. *Outdoor California* (January–February 1985): 1–7.

Cox, George W. 1984. Mounds of mystery. *Natural History* (June 1984): 36–45.

———. 1986. Mima mounds as an indicator of the presettlement grassland-chaparral boundary in San Diego County, California. *American Midland Naturalist* 116 (1): 64–77.

Craighead, F. C., Jr. 1979. *Track of the grizzly*. San Francisco: Sierra Club Books.

Craighead, J. J., F. C. Craighead, Jr., R. L. Ruff, and B. W. O'Gara. 1973. Home ranges and activity patterns of non-migratory elk of the Madison drainage herd as determined by biotelemetry. Wildlife Monograph No. 33. Washington, D.C.: Wildlife Society.

Craighead, J. J., J. S. Sumner, and J. A. Mitchell. 1995. *The grizzly bears of Yellowstone: Their ecology in the Yellowstone ecosystem, 1959–1992*. Washington, D.C.: Island Press, with the Craighead Wildlife-Wildlands Institute.

Craighead, J. J., J. S. Sumner, and G. B. Scaggs. 1982. A definitive system for analysis of grizzly bear habitat and other wilderness resources. University of Montana Foundation, Wildlife-Wildlands Monographs No. 1: 1–251.

Crain, Jim. 1994. *California in depth: A stereoscopic history*. San Francisco: Chronicle Books.

Crampton, Beecher. 1959. The grass genera Orcuttia and Neostapfia: A study in habitat and morphological specialization. *Madrono* 15 (4): 97–128.

———. 1974. *Grasses in California*. Berkeley: University of California Press.

CSHA (California State Historical Association). 1929. Millerton: Landmark of a vanished frontier. *California History Nugget* 2: 114–117.

Curry, Robert. 2000. An expert speaks out against the Potter Valley Project. *Eel River Reporter,* Spring 2003. www.eelriver.org. Accessed 2004.

Curson, Jon, David Quinn, and David Beadle. 1994. *Warblers of the Americas: An identification guide.* Boston: Houghton Mifflin.

Cutright, Paul Russell. 1969. *Lewis and Clark: Pioneering naturalists.* Lincoln: University of Nebraska Press. Reprint, Lincoln: Bison Books in cooperation with University of Illinois, 1989.

D'Antonio, C. M., Susan Bainbridge, Coleman Kennedy, James Bartolome, and Sally Reynolds. 2003. *Ecology and restoration of California grasslands with special emphasis on the influence of fire and grazing on native grassland species.* Unpublished manuscript. University of California, Berkeley. www.elkhornsloughctp.org/uploads/1126128955CROWNGrassReview.pdf. Accessed 2007.

D'Antonio, C. M., S. F. Enloe, and M. J. Pitcairn. 2007. Exotic plant management in California annual grasslands. In *California grasslands ecology and management,* edited by M. R. Stromberg, J. D. Corbin, and C. M. D'Antonio. Berkeley: University of California Press.

D'Antonio, C. M., C. Malmstrom, S. A. Reynolds, and J. Gerlach. 2007. Ecology of non-native speices in California grassland. In *California grasslands ecology and management,* edited by M. R. Stromberg, J. D. Corbin, and C. M. D'Antonio. Berkeley: University of California Press.

Dana, R. H. 1840. *Two years before the mast.* New York: Harper and Brothers.

Danielsen, K. C., and W. L. Halvorson. 1990. Valley oak seedling growth associated with selected grass species. In *Proceedings of the symposium on oak woodlands and hardwood rangeland management, October 31–November 2, 1990, Davis, California.* USDA Forest Service Pacific Southwest Research Station, General Technical Report PSW-126.

Dary, David A. 1974. *The buffalo book.* New York: Avon Books.

Dasmann, Raymond F. 1965. *The destruction of California.* New York: MacMillan.

——. 1981. *California's changing environment.* Boston: Heinle and Heinle.

Davidson, A., and G. L. Moxley. 1923. *Flora of Southern California.* Los Angeles: Times-Mirror Press.

Davidson, Carlos, H. Bradley Shaffer, and Mark R. Jennings. 2001. Declines of the California red-legged frog: Climate, UV-B, habitat, and pesticides hypotheses. *Ecological Applications* 11 (2): 464–479.

Davis, O. K. n.d. History of borderland wetlands. Current Palynological Investigations at the University of Arizona. www.geo.arizona.edu/palynolog/restopcs. Accessed 2003.

——. 1987. Spores of the dung fungus *Sporormiella:* Increased abundance in historic sediments and before Pleistocene megafaunal extinction. *Quaternary Research* 28: 290–294.

——. 1992. Rapid climatic change in coastal southern California inferred from pollen analysis of San Joaquin Marsh. *Quaternary Research* 37 (1): 89–100.

Davis, O. K., and M. J. Moratto. 1988. Evidence for a warm dry early Holocene in the western Sierra Nevada of California: Pollen and plant macrofossil analysis of Dinkey and Exchequer Meadows. *Madrono* 35 (2): 132–149.

Dawson, W. L. 1923. *The birds of California.* San Diego: South Moulton.

de Wet, J. M. J. 1949. Cytogenetic and morphological evidence for generic and subgeneric relationships in the genus *Danthonia.* Ph.D. diss., University of California, Berkeley.

——. 1986. Hybridization and polyploidy in the *Poaceae.* In *Grass systematics and evolution,* edited by T. R. Soderstrom, K. W. Hilu, C. S. Campbell, and M. E. Barkworth. Washington, D.C.: Smithsonian Institution.

Deane, James G., and Dwight Holing. 1985. Ravage the rivers, banish the birds. *Defenders* (May/June 1985).

DeLong, Jay. 1999. Walking in 100-year-old footsteps in southern Oregon. North American Native Fish Association, www.nanfa.org/NANFAregions/or_wa/klamath/klamath.htm. Accessed 2005.

deMenocal, Peter, and Jan Bloemendal. 1991. High- and low-latitude climate interactions: Evidence for enhanced aridity of Asian monsoon dust source areas after 2.4 MYr from ODP Leg 117 magnetic-susceptibility data. In *Proceedings of the seventh annual Pacific Climate (PACLIM) Workshop, Asilomar, California, April 1990,* edited by Julio L. Betancourt and Vera L. Tharp. Technical Report 26 of the Interagency Ecological Studies Program for the Sacramento-San Joaquin Estuary.

Derby, George H. 1852. Report to the secretary of war, communications in compliance with a resolution of the Senate: A report on the Tulare Valley. Senate Executive Document no. 110, 32nd Congress, 1st session.

Desante, D. F., and T. L. George. 1994. Population trends in the landbirds of western North America. In *A century of avifaunal change in western North America,* edited by Joseph R. Jehl and Ned K. Johnson. Proceedings of an International Symposium of the Cooper Ornithological Society at the Centennial Meeting, Sacramento, CA, April 17, 1993. Studies in Avian Biology No. 15. Lawrence, KS: Cooper Ornithological Society.

Dewey, D. R. 1882. Genomic and phylogenetic relationships among North Amercian perennial Triticeae. In *Grasses and grasslands: Systematics and ecology,* edited by J. R. Estes, R. J. Tyrl, and J. N. Brunken. Norman: University of Oklahoma Press.

Diffendorfer, J. 2003. Mammals. In *A summary of affected flora and fauna in the San Diego County fires of 2003.* San Diego Biological Resources Researchers, November 14, 2003.

Digital Library Project. 2003. California Dams database. Digital Library Project, University of California, Berkeley. http://elib.cs.berkeley.edu/dams/. Accessed February 2003. Based on "Dams within the jurisdiction of the State of California," Bulletin 17, Department of Water Resources, 1993.

Dobie, J. F. 1953. Bison in Mexico. *Journal of Mammalogy* 34 (1): 150–151.

Dodge, J. M. 1975. Vegetational changes associated with land use and fire history in San Diego County. Ph.D. diss., University of California, Riverside.

Doebley, J., R. von Bothmer, S. Larson. 1992. Chloroplast DNA variation and the phylogeny of *Hordeum (Poaceae). American Journal of Botany* 79 (5): 576–584.

Domico, Terry. 1988. *Bears of the world.* New York: Facts on File.

Dorn, Ronald I., A. J. T. Jull, D. J. Donahue, T. W. Linick, and L. J. Toolin. 1990. Latest Pleistocene lake shorelines and glacial chronology in the Western Basin and Range Province, USA: Insights from AMS radiocarbon dating of rock varnish and paleoclimatic implications. *Palaeogeography, Palaeoclimatology, Palaeoecology* 78: 315–331.

Doughty, Robin W. 1989. *Return of the whooping crane.* Austin: University of Texas Press.

Douros, W. J. 1993. Prehistoric predation on black abalone by Chumash and sea otters. In *Third California Islands Symposium: Recent advances in research of the California islands,* edited by F. G. Hochberg. Santa Barbara: Santa Barbara Museum of Natural History.

Downey, Dave. 2003. Panel proposes burning 27,000 acres annually. *San Diego Union-Tribune*, November 22, 2003.

Downie, Scott. 1991. North coast salmon and steelhead and their habitat. In *California's salmon and steelhead: The struggle to restore an imperiled resource*, edited by Alan Lufkin. Berkeley: University of California Press.

Drost, Charles A., and Gary M. Fellers. 1996. Collapse of a regional frog fauna in the Yosemite area of the California Sierra Nevada, USA. *Conservation Biology* 10: 414–425.

Du Bois, C. 1935. Wintu ethnography. *University of California Publications in American Archaeology and Ethnology* 36: 1–148.

Dukes, J. S., and M. R. Shaw. 2007. Responses to changing atmosphere and climate. In *California grasslands ecology and management*, edited by M. R. Stromberg, J. D. Corbin, and C. M. D'Antonio. Berkeley: University of California Press.

Duncan, D. A., N. K. McDougald, and S. E. Westfall. 1987. Long-term changes from different uses of foothill hardwood rangelands. In USDA Forest Service Pacific Southwest Research Station, General Technical Report PSW-100.

Dwire, K. A. 1984. What happens to native grasses when grazing stops? *Fremontia* (July 1984): 23–25.

Dyer, A. R., H. C. Fossum, and J. W. Menke. 1996. Emergence and survival of *Nassella pulchra* in a California grassland. *Madrono* 43 (2): 316–333.

Eberts, Mike. 1996. *Griffith Park: A centennial history*. Los Angeles: Historical Society of Southern California, and Spokane, WA: Arthur H. Clark.

Edwards, Stephen W. 1988. Giant redwoods of the East Bay hills. *The Four Seasons* 8 (2): 5–19.

——. 1989. Ten splendid grasses. *The Four Seasons* 8 (3): 17–24.

——. 1992. Observations on the prehistory and ecology of grazing in California. *Fremontia* 20 (1): 3–11.

——. 1990. The East Bay's richest grassland: A Pleistocene relict? *The Four Seasons* 8 (4): 23–32.

Egenhoff, Elisabeth L. 1952. Fabricas: A collection of pictures and statements on the mineral materials used in building in California prior to 1850. Supplement to the *California Journal of Mines and Geology* (April 1952). San Francisco: Division of Mines.

Einarsen, Arthur. 1948. The pronghorn antelope and its management. Corvallis: Oregon Cooperative Fish and Wildlife Research Unit, Oregon State University.

Eliason, Scott A., and Edith B. Allen. 1997. Exotic grass competition in suppressing native shrubland re-establishment. *Restoration Ecology* 5 (3): 245–255.

Elliot, W. W. 1882. *History of Fresno County, California, with illustrations*. San Francisco: W. Elliot and Co. Reprint, Fresno, CA: Valley Publishing: Fresno, 1973.

Elliott, B. G. 1981. Defensive behavior of an immature California condor. *Western Birds* 12: 139–140.

Ellis, S. N. L. 1920. Salmon fishing at Mendota weir. *California Fish and Game* 6 (3): 120–121.

Elsasser, Albert B. 1978. Development of regional prehistoric cultures. In *Handbook of North American Indians*, Vol. 8, *California*, by Robert F. Heizer. Washington, D.C.: Smithsonian Institution.

Emiliani, C. 1972. Quaternary hypsithermals. *Quaternary Research* 2: 270–273.

Enzel, Y., R. Y. Anderson, W. J. Brown, D. R. Cayan, and S. G. Wells. 1990. Tropical and subtropical moisture and southerly displaced North Pacific storm track: Factors in the growth of late Quaternary lakes in the Mojave Desert. In *Proceedings of the sixth annual Pacific Climate (PACLIM) Workshop, March 5–8, 1989*, edited by J. L. Betancourt and A. M. Mackay. California Department of Water Resources, Interagency Ecological Studies Program Technical Report 23.

Ernst, E. F. 1949. Vanishing meadows in Yosemite Valley. *Yosemite Nature Notes* 28 (5): 34–41.

Evans, John, and Terry O'Connor. 1999. *Environmental archaeology: Principles and methods*. Thrupp, UK: Sutton Publishing Limited.

Evans, R. A., H. H. Biswell, and D. E. Palmquist. 1987. Seed dispersal in *Ceanothus cuneatus* and *C. leucodermis* in a Sierran oak-woodland savanna. *Madrono* 34 (4): 283–293.

Evans, Willis A., Orthello L. Wallis, and Glenn D. Gallison. 1961. Fishes of Yosemite National Park. *Yosemite* 23 (1): 1–30.

Evens, Jules. 1988. The *natural history of the Point Reyes peninsula*. Point Reyes Natural History Association.

Evermann, B. W. 1915. An attempt to save California elk. *California Fish and Game* 1 (3): 85–96.

Evermann, B. W., and S.E. Meek. 1897. A report upon salmon investigations in the Columbia River Basin and elsewhere on the Pacific Coast in 1896. *Bulletin of the United States Fish Commission* 17: 15–84.

Faber, Phyllis M. 1997. *California's wild gardens*. Sacramento: California Native Plant Society and California Department of Fish and Game.

Fagan, Brian. 2000. *The little ice age: How climate made history 1300–1850*. New York: Basic Books.

——. 2003. *Before California: An archaeologist looks at our earliest inhabitants*. Lanham, MD: Rowman and Littlefield, and Walnut Creek, CA: AltaMira Press.

Fairbridge, R. W. 1972. Climatology of a glacial cycle. *Quaternary Research* 2: 283–302.

Farrior, Michael L. 2004. *The history of the Tuna Club, 1898–1998*. Avalon, Santa Catalina Island, CA: Tuna Club Foundation.

Fellers, Gary M., and Kathleen L. Freel. 1995. A standardized protocol for surveying aquatic amphibians. Technical Report NPS/WRUC/NRTR-95-01. United States Department of the Interior, National Park Service and National Biological Service, and University of California, Davis.

Ferrier, Gary J., and Edwards C. Roberts, Jr. 1973. The Cache Creek tule elk range. *Cal-Neva Wildlife* 1973: 25–34.

Fimrite, Peter. 2008. All salmon fishing banned on West Coast. *S.F. Gate*, May 2, 2008. http://www.sfgate.com/cgibin/article.cgi?f=/c/a/2008/05/02/BABT10F7PE. DTL&tsp=1. Accessed June 2008.

Fink, Augusta. 1966. *Time and the terraced land: Palos Verdes peninsula*. Berkeley: Howell-North Books.

Fischer, Douglas. 2003. Mystic sentinels: Farallones ecology shrouded for eons. *Oakland Tribune*, August 18, 2003.

Fisher, A. K. 1893. Report on birds. In *The Death Valley expedition: A biological survey of parts of California, Nevada, Arizona, and Utah*, Part 2, North American Fauna 7. Washington, D.C.: U.S. Department of Agriculture.

Fleck, Richard F. 1980. *Mountaineering essays, by John Muir*. Salt Lake City: Peregrine Smith Books.

Fletcher, M. 1983. A Flora of Hollister Ranch, Santa Barbara County, California. The Herbarium, Department of Biological Sciences, University of California, Santa Barbara, Publication No. 2.

Flett, M. A., and S. S. Sanders. 1987. Ecology of a Sierra Nevada population of Willow flycatchers. *Western Birds* 18: 37–42.

Flosi, Gary, Scott Downie, James Hodelain, Michael Bird, Robert Coey, and Barry Collins. 1997. *California salmonid stream habitat restoration manual.* Third edition. State of California, The Resources Agency, California Department of Fish and Game, Inland Fisheries Division.

Franklin, Jerry F., and C. T. Dyrness. 1973. Natural vegetation of Oregon and Washington. USDA Forest Service General Technical Report PNW-8. Pacific Northwest Forest and Range Experiment Station, Forest Service, Portland, Oregon.

Franzreb, K. E. 1987a. Perspectives on managing riparian ecosystems for endangered bird species. *Western Birds* 18: 3–9.

——. 1987b. Endangered status and strategies for conservation of the Least Bell's vireo (*Vireo bellii pusillus*) in California. *Western Birds* 18: 43–49.

Franzreb, K. E., and S. A. Laymon. 1993. A reassessment of the taxonomic status of the Yellow-billed cuckoo. *Western Birds* 24: 17–28.

Freeman, Jim. 1971. *California steelhead fishing.* San Francisco: Chronicle Books.

Frison, George C. 2004. *Survival by hunting: Prehistoric human predators and animal prey.* Berkeley: University of California Press.

Fultz, Francis Marion. 1927. *The Elfin Forest of California.* Los Angeles: Times-Mirror Press.

Gaines, David. 1974. A new look at the nesting riparian avifauna of the Sacramento Valley, California. *Western Birds* 5: 61–80.

——. 1977. The valley riparian forests of California: Their importance to bird populations. In *Riparian forests in California: Their ecology and conservation,* edited by Anne Sands. Institute of Ecology Publication No. 15. Davis: Institute of Ecology, University of California, Davis.

——. 1984. Decline, status, and preservation of the Yellow-billed cuckoo in California. *Western Birds* 15: 49–80.

——. 1988. *Birds of Yosemite and the East Slope.* Lee Vining, CA: Artemisia Press. 2nd printing 1992.

Gales, Donald M. 1988. *Handbook of wildflowers, weeds, wildlife, and weather of the South Bay and Palos Verdes peninsula.* Palos Verdes Peninsula, CA: FoldaRoll Co.

Galvin, John, ed. 1967. *A record of travels in Arizona and California, 1775–1776, Fr. Francisco Garces.* San Francisco: John Howell.

——, ed. 1971. *The first Spanish entry into San Francisco Bay, 1775; the original narrative, hitherto unpublished, by Vicente Maria, and further details by participants in the first explorations of the bay's waters.* San Francisco: John Howell.

Garrett, Kimball, and Jon Dunn. 1981. *Birds of southern California.* Los Angeles: Los Angeles Audubon Society.

Garrison, B. A., and S. A. Laymon. 1987. Bank swallow distribution and nesting ecology on the Sacramento River, California. *Western Birds* 18: 71–76.

Garrison, B. A., C. D. Otahal, and M. L. Triggs. 2001. Age structure and growth of California black oak (*Quercus kelloggii*) in the central Sierra Nevada, California. In *Proceedings of the fifth symposium on oak woodlands: Oaks in California's changing landscape.* October 22–25, 2001, San Diego, California. USDA Forest Service Pacific Southwest Research Station, General Technical Report PSW-GTR-184.

Gayton, A. H. 1946. Culture-environment integration: External references in Yokuts life. *Southwestern Journal of Anthropology* 2 (3): 252–268.

——. 1948. Yokuts and Western Mono ethnography. *Anthropological Records* 10 (1, 2).

Gerdts, William H., and Will South. 1998. *California impressionism.* New York: Abbeville Press Publishers.

Geist, Valerius. 1991. *Elk country.* Minocqua, WI: North Word Press, Inc.

——. 1996. *Buffalo nation: History and legend of the North American bison.* Stillwater, MN: Voyageur Press.

Gende, Scott M., and Thomas P. Quinn. 2003. Fin tuning. *Natural History* (April 2003): 24.

Gilbar, Steven. 1998. *Natural state: A literary anthology of California nature writing.* Berkeley: University of California Press.

Gilbert, Barrie. 2002. Emerging from the dark side: A re-interpretation of grizzly-human relationships based on current and historic evidence. Abstract No. 60. 14th International Bear Association Conference, Steinkjer, Norway.

Gilliam, Harold. 1969. *Between the devil and the deep blue bay: The struggle to save San Francisco Bay.* San Francisco: Chronicle Books.

Glassow, M. A. 1980. Recent developments in the archaeology of the Channel Islands. In *The California islands: Proceedings of a Multidisciplinary Symposium,* edited by Dennis M. Power. Santa Barbara: Santa Barbara Museum of Natural History.

——. 1993. The occurrence of red abalone shells in northern Channel Island archaeological middens: Implications for climatic reconstruction. In *Third California Islands Symposium: Recent advances in research of the California islands,* edited by F. G. Hochberg. Santa Barbara: Santa Barbara Museum of Natural History.

Goals Project. 1999. Baylands Ecosystem Habitat Goals. A report of habitat recommendations prepared by the San Francisco Bay Area Wetlands Ecosystem Goals Project. San Francisco: United States Environmental Protection Agency, and Oakland: San Francisco Bay Regional Water Quality Control Board.

Goals Project. 2000. Baylands Ecosystem Species and Community Profiles: Life histories and environmental requirements of key plants, fish, and wildlife. Prepared by the San Francisco Bay Area Wetlands Ecosystem Goals Project. P. R. Olofson, editor. Oakland: San Francisco Bay Regional Water Quality Control Board.

Goldwasser, Sharon, David Gaines, and Sanford R. Wilbur. 1980. The Least Bell's vireo in California: A de facto endangered race. *American Birds* 34 (5): 742–745.

Goodrich, F. M. 1902. Kings County and Hanford. *Out West: A Magazine of the Old Pacific and the New,* edited by Charles F. Lummis. Vol. 17. Los Angeles: Out West Magazine Company.

Goodridge, J. D. 1991. One hundred years of rainfall trends in California. In *Proceedings of the seventh annual Pacific Climate (PACLIM) Workshop, Asilomar, California, April 1990,* edited by Julio L. Betancourt and Vera L. Tharp. Technical Report 26 of the Interagency Ecological Studies Program for the Sacramento-San Joaquin Estuary.

Gordon, Burton L. 1974. *Monterey Bay Area: Natural history and cultural imprints.* Pacific Grove, CA: Boxwood Press.

Goudie, Andrew S. 1977. Environmental change. Oxford, UK: Clarendon Press.

Gould, F. W., and R. Moran. 1981. The grasses of Baja California, Mexico. San Diego Society of Natural History, Memoir No. 12.

Graham, A. 1999. *Late Cretaceous and Cenozoic history of North American vegetation.* New York: Oxford University Press.

Grant, Campbell, and John E. Cushing, eds. 1969. *The marine mammals of the north-western coast of North America and the American whale fishery,* by Charles M. Scammon. San Francisco: John H. Carman and Co., 1874. Facsimile edition, Riverside, CA: Manessier Publishing Co.

Grave, Ken. 1997. Working together for fishery enhancement. *Fish Trails: A Newsletter from Rowdy Creek Fish Hatchery* 1 (4).

Gray, M. Violet, and James M. Greaves. 1984. Riparian forest as habitat for the Least Bell's vireo. In *California riparian systems: Ecology, conservation, and productive Management*, edited by Richard E. Warner and Kathleen M. Hendrix. Berkeley: University of California Press.

Grayson, A. J. 1920. Game in the San Joaquin Valley in 1853. *California Fish and Game* 6 (3): 104–107.

Grayson, Donald K. 1993. *The desert's past: A natural prehistory of the Great Basin*. Washington, D.C.: Smithsonian Institution.

Greaves, J. M. 1987. Nest-site tenacity of Least Bell's vireo. *Western Birds* 18: 50–54.

Green, L., and J. R. Bentley. 1957. Seeding and grazing trials of *Stipa* on foothill ranges. U.S. Forest Service Research Note 128.

Greenlee, J. M., and J. H. Langenheim. 1990. Historic fire regimes and their relation to vegetation patterns in the Monterey Bay Area of California. *American Midland Naturalist* 124 (2): 239–253.

Griffin, J. R. 1988. Oak woodlands. In *Terrestrial vegetation of California*, edited by M. G. Barbour and J. Major. Sacramento: California Native Plant Society. Special Publication No. 9.

Griggs, F. T. 1981. Life histories of vernal pool annual grasses. *Fremontia* 9 (1): 14–17.

———. 1983. Creighton Ranch Preserve: A relict of Tulare Lake. *Fremontia* 10 (4): 3–8.

Grime, J. P., and P. S. Lloyd. 1973. *An ecological atlas of grassland plants*. London: Edward Arnold Publishers Limited.

Grinnell, Joseph. 1914. An account of the mammals and birds of the lower Colorado Valley. *University of California Publications in Zoology* 12 (4): 51–294.

———. 1935. *Fur-bearing mammals of California*. Berkeley: University of California Press.

Grinnell, Joseph, and Charles L. Camp. 1917. A distributional list of the amphibians and reptiles of California. *University of California Publications in Zoology* 17 (10): 127–208.

Grinnell, Joseph, and A. H. Miller. 1944. The distribution of the birds of California. *Pacific Coast Avifauna* 27.

Grinnell, Joseph, and M. Wythe. 1927. Directory to the bird-life of the San Francisco Bay region. *Pacific Coast Avifauna* 18.

Grossinger, Robin. 1999. Seeing time: A historical approach to restoration. *Ecological Restoration* 17 (4): 251–252.

———. 2001. Documenting local landscape change: The San Francisco Bay Area Historical Ecology Project. In *The Historical Ecology Handbook*, edited by Dave Egan and Evelyn Howell. Washington, D.C.: Island Press.

Grossinger, R. M., R. A. Askevold, C. J. Striplen, E. Brewster, S. Pearce, K. N. Larned, L. J. McKee, and J. N. Collins. 2006. Coyote Creek watershed historical ecology study: Historical condition, landscape change, and restoration potential in the eastern Santa Clara Valley, California. Prepared for the Santa Clara Valley water district. A Report of SFEI's historical ecology, watersheds, and wetlands science programs. SFEI Publication No. 426. Oakland: San Francisco Estuary Institute.

Grossinger, Robin M., Charles J. Striplen, Ruth A. Askevold, Elise Brewster, and Erin E. Beller. 2007. Historical landscape ecology of an urbanized California valley: Wetlands and woodlands in the Santa Clara Valley. *Landscape Ecology* 22: 103–120.

Grove, A. T., and Oliver Racham. 2001. *The nature of Mediterranean Europe: An ecological history*. New Haven, CT: Yale University Press.

Gruell, George E. 2001. *Fire in Sierra Nevada forests: A photographic interpretation of ecological change since 1849*. Missoula, MT: Mountain Press Publishing Co.

Guerriero, Michael. 2003. The Van Duzen River hit hard by MAXXAM. *Eel River Reporter*, Spring 2003, Friends of the Eel River. www.eelriver.org. Accessed 2004.

———. 2004. The Eel River Estuary grows as old levees break down. *Eel River Reporter*, Winter 2004, Friends of the Eel River. www.eelriver.org. Accessed 2004.

Gumprecht, Blake. 2001 (1999). *The Los Angeles River: Its life, death, and possible rebirth*. Baltimore: John Hopkins University Press.

Guscio, C. Gregory, Blake R. Hossack, Lisa A. Eby, and Paul Stephen Corn. 2007. Post-breeding habitat use by adult Boreal toads (*Bufo boreas*) after wildfire in Glacier National Park, USA. *Herpetological Conservation and Biology* 3 (1): 55–62.

Guthrie, D. A. 1980. Analysis of avifaunal and bat remains from midden sites on San Miguel Island. In *The California islands: Proceedings of a Multidisciplinary Symposium*, edited by Dennis M. Power. Santa Barbara: Santa Barbara Museum of Natural History.

———. 1982. Mammals of the Mammoth Steppe as paleoenvironmental indicators. In *Paleoecology of Beringia*, edited by D. M. Hopkins, J. V. Matthews, Jr., C. E. Schweger, and S. B. Young. New York: Academic Press.

———. 1990. *Frozen fauna of the Mammoth Steppe: The story of Blue Babe*. Chicago: University of Chicago Press.

Gutierrez, Ramon A., and Richard J. Orsi, eds. 1998. *Contested eden: California before the gold rush*. Berkeley: University of California Press.

Haggerty, P. K. 1990. Fire effects in blue oak woodland. In *Proceedings of the symposium on oak woodlands and hardwood rangeland management, October 31–November 2, 1990, Davis, California*. USDA Forest Service Pacific Southwest Research Station, General Technical Report PSW-126.

Halfpenny, Jim. 1999. Bear art. *Bears and Other Top Predators* 1 (1).

Hall, E. R. 1927. The deer of California. *California Fish and Game* 13: 233–256.

Hall, Raymond. 1936. The grizzly bear of California. *California Fish and Game*.

———. 1946. *Mammals of Nevada*. Berkeley: University of California Press.

Hall, Raymond, and K. R. Kelson. 1959. *The Mammals of North America*. New York: Ronald Press Co.

Haller, Stephen A. 1997. *Post and park: A brief illustrated history of the Presidio of San Francisco*. San Francisco: Golden Gate National Parks Association.

Hallock, R. J. 1991. The Red Bluff Diversion Dam. In *California's salmon and steelhead: The struggle to restore an imperiled resource*, edited by Alan Lufkin. Berkeley: University of California Press.

Hallock, R. J., and D. H. Fry. 1967. Five species of salmon, *Oncorhynchus*, in the Sacramento River, California. *California Fish and Game* 53: 5–22.

Hamilton, J. G. 1997. Changing perceptions of pre-European grasslands in California. *Madrono* 44 (4): 311–333.

Hanes, T. L. 1977. California chaparral. In *Terrestrial Vegetation of California*, edited by M. G. Barbour and J. Major. Edition 1988, pp. 417–469.

———. 1984. Vegetation of the Santa Ana River and some flood control implications. In *California riparian systems: Ecology, conservation, and productive management*, edited by Richard E. Warner and Kathleen M. Hendrix. Berkeley: University of California Press.

———. 1988. Chaparral. In *Terrestrial Vegetation of California*, edited by M. G. Barbour and J. Major. Sacramento: California Native Plant Society. Special Publication No. 9.

Harrington, J. P. 1932. Tobacco among the Karok Indians of California. *Bureau of American Ethnology Bulletin* 94. Washington, D.C.: Smithsonian Institution.

Harris, David. 1993. *Eadweard Muybridge and the photographic panorama of San Francisco, 1850–1880*. Montreal: Centre Canadien d'Architecture and Cambridge, MA: MIT Press.

Harris, J. J. 1991. Effects of brood parasitism by Brown-headed cowbirds on Willow flycatcher nesting success along the Kern River, California. *Western Birds* 22: 13–26.

Harris, J. J., S. S. Sanders, and A. A. Flett. 1987. Willow flycatcher surveys in the Sierra Nevada. *Western Birds* 18: 27–36.

Harris, W. N. 1902. The Laguna de Tache Grant. In *Out West: A Magazine of the Old Pacific and the New*, edited by Charles F. Lummis. Vol. 17, No. 5, pp. 652–645. Los Angeles: Out West Magazine Company.

Harrison, Peter. 1987. *Seabirds of the world: A photographic guide*. Princeton, NJ: Princeton University Press. 3rd printing 1996.

Harrison, S. P., and J. H. Viers. 2007. Serpentine grasslands. In *California Grasslands Ecology and Management*, edited by M. R. Stromberg, J. D. Corbin, and C. M. D'Antonio. Berkeley: University of California Press.

Hartley, W. 1961. Studies on the origin, evolution, and distribution of the *Gramineae*. IV. The genus *Poa*. *Australian Journal of Botany* 9: 152–162.

———. 1973. Studies on the origin, evolution, and distribution of the *Gramineae*. V. The subfamily festucoideae. *Australian Journal of Botany* 21: 201–234.

Heady, H. F. 1977. Valley grassland. In *Terrestrial vegetation of California*, edited by M. G. Barbour and J. Major. New York: Wiley-Interscience: pp. 491–514.

Heizer, Robert F. 1978. *Handbook of North American Indians*. Vol. 8, *California*. Washington, D.C.: Smithsonian Institution.

Heizer, Robert F., and Albert B. Elsasser. 1980. *The natural world of the California Indians*. Berkeley: University of California Press.

Heizer, Robert F., and Theodora Kroeber. 1979. *Ishi the last Yahi: A documentary history*. Berkeley: University of California Press.

Henderson, Jim. 2004. Klamath River dams: Opposition to relicensing grows. *The River Voice* 1 (2). www.srrc.org (Salmon River Restoration Council). Accessed 2004.

Hendry, George W. 1931. The adobe brick as a historical source. *Agricultural History* 5: 110–127.

Hernandez, Daniel, and Tony Perry. 2003. "Natural burn" cited as deterring big fires. *Los Angeles Times* News Service, November 9, 2003.

Herrero, Stephen. 1985. *Bear attacks: Their causes and avoidance*. New York: Lyons and Burford, Publishers.

Herrington, William C. 1926. Depletion of Pismo clam in California. *California Fish and Game* 12 (3): 117–124.

Hershey, Marvin C. 1973. The silver salmon of Muir Woods. Muir Woods-Point Reyes Natural History Association.

Hesseldenz, Thomas F. 1984. Developing a long-term protection plan for the McCloud River, California. In *California riparian systems: Ecology, conservation, and productive management*, edited by Richard E. Warner and Kathleen M. Hendrix. Berkeley: University of California Press.

Hickman, James C. 1993. *The Jepson manual: Higher plants of California*. Berkeley: University of California Press.

Higgins, Patrick. 1991. Why all the fuss about preserving wild stocks of salmon and steelhead? In *California's salmon and steelhead: The struggle to restore an imperiled resource*, edited by Alan Lufkin. Berkeley: University of California Press.

Hildebrandt, W. R., and T. L. Jones. 1992. Evolution of marine mammal hunting: A view form the California and Oregon coasts. *Journal of Anthropological Archaeology* 11: 360–401.

———. 1995. Reasserting a prehistoric tragedy of the Commons: Reply to Lyman. *Journal of Anthropological Archaeology* 14: 78–98.

Hill, Mary. 1975. *Geology of the Sierra Nevada*. Berkeley: University of California Press.

Hillman, Leaf G. 2004[?]. Variations between Euro-American and Native American thought and perceptions: The cultural and spiritual in Karuk land management. Pelican Network, 2004.

Hillman, Leaf G., and John F. Salter. 1997. Karuk environmental stewardship: Steps toward tribal/agency co-management. A paper jointly written and presented at the International Conference on Creativity and Innovation at Grassroots for Sustainable Natural Resource management, Indian Institute of Management, Ahmedabad, India, January 11–14, 1997.

Hinds, Norman. 1952. Evolution of the California landscape. San Francisco: State of California, Division of Mines, Bulletin 158.

Hitchcock, A. S. 1950. Manual of the grasses of the United States. Washington, D.C.: U.S. Government Printing Office. U.S. Department of Agriculture Miscellaneous Publication No. 200. 2nd edition revised by Agnes Chase, New York: Dover Publications,1971.

Hittell, Theodore H. 1860. *Adventures of James Capen Adams, Mountaineer and Grizzly Bear Hunter of California*. San Francisco: Towne and Bacon.

Hittle, John S. 1966. *The resources of California: Comprising agriculture, mining, geography, climate, commerce, and the past agricultural development of the state*. San Francisco: A. Roman.

Hobbs, N. T., D. L. Baker, J. E. Ellis, and D. M. Swift. 1981. Composition and quality of elk winter diets in Colorado. *J. Wildlife Management* 45 (1): 156–171.

Hoffman, Eric. 1991. Saving the steelhead. In *California's salmon and steelhead: The struggle to restore an imperiled resource*, edited by Alan Lufkin. Berkeley: University of California Press.

Hoffmeister, Donald F. 1986. Mammals of Arizona. Tucson: University of Arizona Press and Arizona Game and Fish Department.

Holder, Frederick C. 1906. *Life in the open: Sport with rod, gun, horse and hound in southern California*. New York: G. P. Putnam's Sons, The Knickerbocker Press.

Holing, Dwight. 1988. *California wild lands: A guide to the Nature Conservancy preserves*. San Francisco: Chronicle Books.

Holland, Robert, and Subodh Jain. 1988. Vernal pools. In *Terrestrial vegetation of California*. Sacramento: California Native Plant Society. Special Publication No. 9.

Holland, V. L., and David J. Keil. 1995. *California vegetation*. Dubuque, IA: Kendall/Hunt Publishing Co.

Hollowed, A. B., S. R. Hare, and W. S. Wooster. 2001. Pacific basin climatic variability and patterns of northeast Pacific marine fish production. *Progress in Oceanography* 49: 257–282.

Holstein, Glen. 1984. California riparian forests: Deciduous sslands in an evergreen sea. In *California riparian systems: Ecology, conservation, and productive management*, edited by Richard E. Warner and Kathleen M. Hendrix. Berkeley: University of California Press.

———. 2001. Pre-agricultural grassland in central California. *Madrono* 48 (4): 253–264.

Hooper, William, Jr. 1991. Urban stream restoration. In *California's salmon and steelhead: The struggle to restore an imperiled resource*, edited by Alan Lufkin. Berkeley: University of California Press.

Hoover, Robert F. 1935. Character and distribution of the primitive vegetation of the San Joaquin Valley. Ph.D. diss., University of California, Berkeley.

———. 1970. The vascular plants of San Luis Obispo County, California. Berkeley: University of California Press.

House, Freeman. 1999. *Totem salmon: Life lessons from another species*. Boston: Beacon Press.

Houston, D. B. 1982. *The northern Yellowstone elk*. New York: Macmillan Publishing Co.

Howard, Hildegarde. 1937. A Pleistocene record of the passenger pigeon in California. *Condor* 30: 12–14.

———. 1955b. Fossil birds, with especial reference to the birds of Rancho La Brea. Science Series No. 17: 16-40. Los Angeles: Natural History Museum of Los Angeles County.

Howard, Walter E. 1953. Rodent control on California ranges. *Journal of Range Management* 6: 423-434.

Howell, John Thomas. 1970. *Marin flora*. Berkeley: University of California Press.

Hubbs, C. L. 1956. Back from oblivion: Guadalupe fur seal: Still a living species. *Pacific Discovery* (November–December 1956): 14–21.

Hubbs, C. L., and R. R. Miller. 1948. The Great Basin: With emphasis on glacial and postglacial times. II. The zoological evidence: Correlation between fish distribution and hydrographic history in the desert basins of the Western United States. *Bulletin of the University of Utah* 38 (20). Reprint.

Huffman, Margaret. 1998. *Wild heart of Los Angeles: The Santa Monica Mountains*. Niwot, CO: Roberts Rinehart Publishers.

Hull, J. C., and C. H. Muller. 1977. The potential for dominance by *Stipa pulchra* in a California grassland. *American Midland Naturalist* 97: 147-175.

Hunt, G. L., Jr., R. L. Pitman, and H. Lee Jones. 1980. Distribution and abundance of seabirds breeding on the Channel Islands. In *The California islands: Proceedings of a Multidisciplinary Symposium*, edited by Dennis M. Power. Santa Barbara: Santa Barbara Museum of Natural History

Hunter, W. C., R. D. Ohmart, and B. W. Anderson. 1987. Status of breeding riparian-obligate birds in Southwestern riverine systems. *Western Birds* 18: 10–18.

Huntsinger, L., J. W. Bartolome, C. M. D'Antonio. 2007. Grazing management on California's Mediterranean grasslands. In *California grasslands ecology and management*, edited by M. R. Stromberg, J. D. Corbin, and C. M. D'Antonio. Berkeley: University of California Press.

Huntsinger, L., M. P. McClaran, A. Dennis, and J. W. Bartolome. 1996. Defoliation response and growth of *Nassella pulchra* (A. Hithc.) Barkworth from serpentine and non-serpentine populations. *Madrono* 43 (1): 46–57.

Hutchings, J. M. 1875. *Scenes of Wonder and Curiosity in California*. New York and San Francisco: A. Roman and Co.

Ivey, G. 1984. Some recent nesting records for the Snowy plover in the San Joaquin Valley, California. *Western Birds* 15: 189.

Jackson, Donald, and Mary Lee Spence, eds. 1970. *The expeditions of John Charles Fremont*. Vol. 1, *Travels from 1838 to 1844*. Urbana: University of Illinois Press.

Jackson, Joseph H., ed. 1949. *Gold rush album*. New York: Bonanza Books.

Jackson, R. D., and J. W. Bartolome. 2007. Grazing ecology of California grasslands. In *California grasslands ecology and management*, edited by M. R. Stromberg, J. D. Corbin, and C. M. D'Antonio. Berkeley: University of California Press.

Jefferson, G. T., and J. L. Goldin. 1989. Seasonal migration of *Bison antiquus* from Rancho La Brea, California. *Quaternary Research* 31: 107–112.

Jehl, Joseph R., Jr., and Ned K. Johnson, eds. 1993. *A century of avifaunal change in western North America*. Proceedings of an International Symposium of the Cooper Ornithological Society at the Centennial Meeting, Sacramento, CA, April 17, 1993. Studies in Avian Biology No. 15. Lawrence, KS: Cooper Ornithological Society.

Jenkins, Ken L. 1995. *Black bear reflections*. Merrillville, IN: ICS Books, Inc.

Jennings, M. R. 1983. An annotated checklist of the amphibians and reptiles of California. *California Fish and Game* 69: 151–171.

———. 2003. Information of the native frogs of California. Identification and Ecology of Sensitive Amphibians and Reptiles of the Southern California Region, a conference workshop of the Wildlife Society, Western Section, May 8-10, 2003.

Jepson, Willis L. 1893. The riparian botany of the Lower Sacramento. *Erythea* 1: 242.

———. 1901. *A Flora of Western Middle California*. Berkeley: Encina Publishing Company.

———. 1923. *The Trees of California*. 2nd edition. Berkeley: Sather Gate Book Shop.

Jezek, George R., and Roger M. Showley. 2000. *San Diego: Then and now*. San Diego: George Ross Jezek Photography and Publishing.

Jimmerson, T. M., and S. K. Carothers. 2001. Northwest California oak woodlands: Environment, species composition, and ecological status. In *Proceedings of the fifth symposium on oak woodlands: Oaks in California's changing landscape*. October 22–25, 2001, San Diego, California. USDA Forest Service Pacific Southwest Research Station, General Technical Report PSW-GTR-184.

Johnson, B. L. 1972. Polyploidy as a factor in the evolution and distribution of grasses. In *The Biology and Utilization of Grasses*, edited by V. B. Youngner and C. M. McKell. New York: Academic Press.

Johnson, Drew Heath, and Marcia Eymann, eds. 1999. *Silver and gold: Cased images of the California gold rush*. Iowa City: University of Iowa Press and Oakland: Oakland Museum of California.

Johnson, J. R., and D. D. Earle. 1993. Vegetation burning by the Chumash. In *Before the wilderness: Environmental management by Native Californians*, edited by Thomas C. Blackburn and M. Kat Anderson. Menlo Park, CA: Ballena Press.

Johnson, N. K. 1994. Pioneering and natural expansions of breeding distributions in western North American birds. In *A century of avifaunal change in western North America*, edited by Joseph R. Jehl and Ned K. Johnson. Proceedings of an International Symposium of the Cooper Ornithological Society at the Centennial Meeting, Sacramento, CA, April 17, 1993. Studies in Avian Biology No. 15. Lawrence, KS: Cooper Ornithological Society.

Johnson, N. K., and K. L. Garrett. 1974. Interior bird species expand breeding ranges into southern California. *Western Birds* 5: 45–56.

Johnson, Paul C., ed. 1964. *The California missions: A pictorial history*. Menlo Park, CA: Lane Book Co.

———. 1970. *Pictorial history of California*. New York: Bonanza Books.

———. 1973. *The early Sunset magazine, 1898–1928*. San Francisco: California Historical Society.

Jones, Harvey L. 1995. *Twilight and reverie: California tonalist painting, 1890–1930. Oakland:* Oakland Museum of California.

———. 1998a. The Hessian party: Charles Christian Nahl, Arthur Nahl, and August Wenderoth. In *Art of the gold rush,* edited by Janice T. Druesbach, Harvey L. Jones, and Katherine Church Holland. Oakland: Oakland Museum of California; Sacramento: Crocker Art Museum; and Berkeley: University of California Press.

———. 1998b. Arthur Mathews. In *Plein air painters of California: The north,* edited by Ruth Lilly Westphal. Irvine, CA: Westphal Publishing.

Jones, T. L., and W. R. Hildebrandt. 1995. Reasserting a prehistoric tragedy of the Commons: Reply to Lyman. *Journal of Anthropological Archaeology* 14: 78–98.

Jones, Terry L., Janet L. McVickar, Andrew York, Gary M. Brown, W. Geoffrey Spaulding, Phillip L. Walker, L. Mark Raab, and Douglas J. Kennett. 2004. Environmental imperatives reconsidered: Demographic crises in western North America during the Medieval Climatic Anomaly. In *Prehistoric California: Archaeology and the myth of paradise,* edited by L. Mark Raab and Terry L. Jones. Salt Lake City: University of Utah Press.

Jordan, David Starr. 1892. Salmon and trout of the Pacific Coast. Bulletin No. 4 of the Board of Fish Commissioners, State of California. Sacramento: State Office.

Jordan, David Starr, and Barton W. Evermann. 1904. *American food and game fishes: A popular account of all the species found in America north of the equator, with keys for ready identification, life histories, and methods of capture.* New York: Doubleday, Page and Co.

Juniper, Tony, and Mike Parr. 1998. *Parrots: A guide to parrots of the world.* New Haven, CT: Yale University Press.

Katibah, Edwin F. 1984. A brief history of riparian forests in the central valley of California. In *California riparian systems: Ecology, conservation, and productive management,* edited by Richard E. Warner and Kathleen M. Hendrix. Berkeley: University of California Press.

Kauffman, J. B., and R. E. Martin. 1987. Effects of fire and fire suppression on mortality and mode of reproduction of California black oak (*Quercus keloggii* Newb). In USDA Forest Service Pacific Southwest Research Station, General Technical Report PSW-100.

Kay, Charles E. 1998. Are ecosystems structured from the top-down or bottom-up: A new look at an old debate. *Wildlife Society Bulletin* 26 (3): 484–498.

Keator, G. 1989. The Brodiaeas. *Four Seasons* 8 (3): 4–11.

Keeler, Chas. A. 1891. The nesting time of birds about San Francisco Bay. *Zoe* 2: 167–172.

Keeler-Wolf, T., J. M. Evens, A. I. Solomeshch, V. L. Holland, and M. G. Barbour. 2007. Community classification and nomenclature. In *California grasslands ecology and management,* edited by M. R. Stromberg, J. D. Corbin, and C. M. D'Antonio. Berkeley: University of California Press.

Keeley, J. E. 1977. Fire-dependent reproductive strategies in *Arctostaphylos* and *Ceanothus.* In *Proceedings of the symposium on the environmental consequences of fire and fuel management in Mediterranean ecosystems,* edited by H. A. Mooney and C. E. Conrad. USDA Forest Service General Technical Report WO-26.

———. 1990. The California valley grassland. Reprinted from *Endangered plant communities of southern California,* edited by Allan S. Schoenherr. Southern California Botanists, Special Publication No. 3.

———. 2000. Chaparral. In *North American terrestrial vegetation,* 2nd edition, edited by M. G. Barbour and W. D. Billings. Cambridge, UK: Cambridge University Press.

———. 2002. Native American impacts on fire regimes of the California coastal ranges. *Journal of Biogeography* 29: 303–320.

Keeley, J. E., and S. C. Keeley. 1987. Role of fire in the germination of chaparral herbs and suffrutescents. *Madroño* 34 (3): 240–249.

Keeley, J. E., and C. J. Fotheringham. 1998. Smoke-induced seed germination in California chaparral. *Journal of Ecology* 79.

Keeley, J. E., and C. J. Fotheringham. 2001a. Historic fire regime in southern California shrublands. *Conservation Biology* 15 (6): 1536–1548.

Keeley, J. E., and C. J. Fotheringham. 2001b. History and management of crown-fire ecosystems: A summary and response. *Conservation Biology* 15 (6): 1561–1567.

Keeley, J. E., P. H. Zedler, C. A. Zammit, and T. H. Stohlgren. 1989. Fire and demography. In *The California chaparral: Paradigms reexamined,* edited by S. C. Keeley. Science Series No. 34. Los Angeles: Natural History Museum of Los Angeles County.

Keller, E. A. 1977. A fluvial system: Selected observations. In *Riparian forests in California: Their ecology and conservation,* edited by Anne Sands. Institute of Ecology Publication No. 15. Davis: Institute of Ecology, University of California, Davis.

Kelley, Donald G., Jack W. Edgemond, and W. Drew Chick. 1931. *Three scout naturalists in the National Parks.* New York: Brewer, Warren, and Putnam.

Kelly, N. M. 2001. Monitoring Sudden Oak Death in California using high resolution imagery. In *Proceedings of the fifth symposium on oak woodlands: Oaks in California's changing landscape.* October 22–25, 2001, San Diego, California. USDA Forest Service Pacific Southwest Research Station, General Technical Report PSW-GTR-184.

Kenney, J. P. 1980. Rising from the ashes: After the Santa Monicas blaze. *Sierra* March/April 1980: 24–28.

Kephart, Paul. 2001. Resource management demonstration at Russian Ridge Preserve. *Grasslands* 11 (1): 1, 8–11.

Kessel, Brina, and Danial D. Gibson. 1994. A century of avifaunal change in Alaska. In *A century of avifaunal change in western North America,* edited by Joseph R. Jehl and Ned K. Johnson. Proceedings of an International Symposium of the Cooper Ornithological Society at the Centennial Meeting, Sacramento, CA, April 17, 1993. Studies in Avian Biology No. 15. Lawrence, KS: Cooper Ornithological Society.

Kimball, Sandy. 1987. *Moraga's pride: Rancho Laguna de los Palos Colorados.* Moraga, CA: Moraga Historical Society.

King, Chester. 1978. Protohistoric and historic archaeology. In *Handbook of North American Indians,* Vol. 8, *California,* by Robert F. Heizer. Washington, D.C.: Smithsonian Institution.

———. 1993. Fuel use and resource management: Implications for the study of land management in prehistoric California and recommendations for a research program. In *Before the wilderness: Environmental management by Native Californians,* edited by Thomas C. Blackburn and M. Kat Anderson. Menlo Park, CA: Ballena Press.

King, Clarence. 1872. *Mountaineering in the Sierra Nevada.* Boston: James R. Osgood and Co. Reprint, New York: Penguin Books, 1989.

King, Judith E. 1983. *Seals of the world.* Comstock Book Series, Natural History Museum Publications. Ithaca, NY : Comstock Publishing Associates, a division of Cornell University Press.

Kinney, William C. 1996. Conditions of rangelands before 1905. In Sierra Nevada Ecosystem Project. Status of the Sierra Nevada, Vol. 2. Assessments and Scientific Basis for Management Options. Final Report to Congress. Wildlands Resources Center Report No. 37. Centers for Water and Wildland Resources, University of California, Davis.

Klamath Basin Coalition. 2003. Vision 2004. www.klamathbasin.info. Accessed 2004.

Klein, M., and K. Williams. 2003. Invertebrates. In *A summary of affected flora and fauna in the San Diego County fires of 2003.* San Diego Biological Resources Researchers, November 14, 2003.

Koehler, P. A., and R. S. Anderson. 1994. The paleoecology and stratigraphy of Nichols Meadow, Sierra National Forest, California, USA. *Palaeogeography, Palaeolimatology, Palaeoecology* 112: 1–17.

Koenig, W. D., W. J. Carmen, M. T. Stanback, and R. L. Mumme. 1990. Determinants of acorn productivity among five species of oaks in central coastal California. In *Proceedings of the symposium on oak woodlands and hardwood rangeland management, October 31–November 2, 1990, Davis, California.* USDA Forest Service Pacific Southwest Research Station, General Technical Report PSW-126.

Koford, Carl B. 1950. The natural history of the California condor (*Gymnogyps californianus*). Ph.D. diss., University of California, Berkeley.

———. 1953. The California condor. *National Audubon Society Research Report* 4: 1– 154.

Kondolf, G. Mathias, and Robert R. Curry. 1984. The role of riparian vegetation in channel bank stability: Carmel River, California. In *California riparian systems: Ecology, conservation, and productive management,* edited by Richard E. Warner and Kathleen M. Hendrix. Berkeley: University of California Press.

Kooser, B. J., S. Seabough, and F. L. Sargent. 1861. Notes on trips of the San Joaquin Valley Agricultural Society's Visiting Committee on Orchards and Vineyards. In *Transactions and second annual report of the San Joaquin Valley Agricultural Society,* edited by J. A. Anderson. Stockton, CA: Stockton Democrat Job Office Print.

Kotzebue, Otto von. 1821. *Voyage of discovery into the South Sea and Beering's Straits [sic], for the purpose of exploring a north-east passage, undertaken in the years 1815–1818, at the expense of His Higness the Chancellor of the Empire, Count Romanzoff, in the ship Rurick, under the command of the lieutenant in the Russian Imperial Navy, Otto von Kotzebue.* London: Printed for Longman, Hurst, Rees, Orme, and Brown.

———. 1830. *A new voyage round the world, in the years 1823, 24, 25, and 26.* Two volumes. London: Henry Colburn and R. Bentley.

Kroeber, A. L. 1925. *Handbook of the Indians of California.* Bureau of American Ethnology, Smithsonian Institution, Bulletin 78. Reprint, New York: Dover, 1976.

———. 1976. *Yurok myths.* Berkeley: University of California Press.

Kroeber, A. L., and E. W. Giffird. 1949. World renewal: A cult system of native northwest California. *Anthropological Records* 13: 1–154.

Kroeber, Theodora. 1961. *Ishi in two worlds: A biography of the last wild Indian in North America.* Berkeley: University of California Press.

Kurten, Bjorn, and Elaine Anderson. 1980. *Pleistocene mammals of North America.* New York: Columbia University Press.

Kurutz, K. D., and Gary Kurutz. 2000. *California calls you: The art of promoting the Golden State, 1870 to 1940.* Sausalito, California: Windgate Press.

Kushner, Lev. 2002. Marking time: Rethinking the presentation of history in urban places. M.S. thesis, University of California, Berkeley.

Lathrop, E. W., and M. J. Arct. 1987. Age structure of Engelmann oak populations on the Santa Rosa Plateau. In USDA Forest Service Pacific Southwest Research Station, General Technical Report PSW-100.

Lathrop, E. W., and C. D. Osborne. 1990. Influence of fire on oak seedlings and saplings in southern oak woodland on the Santa Rosa Plateau Preserve, Riverside County, California. In *Proceedings of the symposium on oak woodlands and hardwood rangeland management, October 31–November 2, 1990, Davis, California.* USDA Forest Service Pacific Southwest Research Station, General Technical Report PSW-126.

Lathrop, E. W., C. Osborne, A. Rochester, K. Yeung, S. Soret, and R. Hopper. 1990. Size class distribution of *Qurecus engelmannii* (Engelmann oak) on the Santa Rosa Preserve, Riverside County, California. In *Proceedings of the symposium on oak woodlands and hardwood rangeland management, October 31-November 2, 1990, Davis, California.* USDA Forest Service Pacific Southwest Research Station, General Technical Report PSW-126.

Lathrop, E. W., and R. F. Thorne. 1968. Flora of the Santa Rosa Plateau of the Santa Ana Mountains, California. *Aliso:* 17–40.

Latta, Frank F. 1977. *Handbook of the Yokuts Indians.* Sacramento: Bear State.

Lawton, H. W., P. J. Wilke, M. DeDecker, and W. M. Mason. 1993. Agriculture among the Paiute of Owens Valley. In *Before the wilderness: Environmental management by Native Californians,* edited by Thomas C. Blackburn and M. Kat Anderson. Menlo Park, CA: Ballena Press.

Lawton, Harry W., Philip J. Wilke, Mary DeDecker, and William M. Mason. 1993. Agriculture among the Paiute of Owens Valley. In *Before the wilderness: Environmental management by Native Californians,* edited by Thomas C. Blackburn and M. Kat Anderson. Menlo Park, CA: Ballena Press.

Laycock, George. 1986. *The wild bears.* New York: Outdoor Life Books.

Laymon, Steven A. 1984a. Photodocumentation of vegetation and landform change on a riparian site, 1880–1980: Dog Island, Red Bluff, California. In *California riparian systems: Ecology, conservation, and productive management,* edited by Richard E. Warner and Kathleen M. Hendrix. Berkeley: University of California Press.

———. 1984b. Riparian bird community structure and dynamics: Dog Island, Red Bluff, California. In *California riparian systems: Ecology, conservation, and productive management,* edited by Richard E. Warner and Kathleen M. Hendrix. Berkeley: University of California Press.

———. 1987. Brown-headed cowbirds in California: Historical perspectives and management opportunities in riparian habitats. *Western Birds* 18: 63–70.

Laymon, Steven A., and M. D. Halterman. 1987. Can the western subspecies of the Yellow-billed cuckoo be saved from extinction? *Western Birds* 18: 19–25.

Le Boeuf, Burney J. 1981. Mammals. In *The natural history of Año Nuevo,* edited by Burney J. Le Boeuf and Stephanie Kaza. Pacific Grove, CA: Boxwood Press. 2nd printing, 1985.

Le Boeuf, Burney J., and M. L. Bonnell. 1980. Pinnepeds of the California islands: Abundance and distribution. In *The California islands: Proceedings of a Multidisciplinary Symposium,* edited by Dennis M. Power. Santa Barbara: Santa Barbara Museum of Natural History

Le Boeuf, Burney J., and Stephanie Kaza, eds. 1985. *The Natural History of Año Nuevo.* Pacific Grove, CA: Boxwood Press. 2nd printing, 1985.

Leahy, Christopher. 1982. *The birdwatcher's companion: An encyclopedic handbook of North American birdlife.* New York: Hill and Wang.

LeFee, Scott. 2003. October's wildfires changed the face of Cuyamaca's conifer forests, maybe forever. *San Diego Union-Tribune,* December 31, 2003.

Leidy, R. A. 1984. Distribution and ecology of stream fishes in the San Francisco Bay drainage. *Hilgardia* 52 (8): 1–175.

Leidy, R. A., and E. G. White. 1998. Toward an ecosystem approach to vernal pool compensation and conservation. Pages 263–273 in *Ecology, conservation, and management of vernal pool ecosystems,* edited by C. W. Witham, E. T. Bauder, D. Belk, W. R. Ferren, Jr., and R. Ornduff. Proceedings from a 1996 Conference, Sacramento, California. Sacramento: California Native Plant Society.

Lentz, J. E. 1993. Breeding birds of four isolated mountains in southern California. *Western Birds* 24: 201–234.

Leopold, A. Starker. 1959. *Wildlife of Mexico.* Berkeley: University of California Press. 2nd printing, 1972.

Leopold, A. Starker, and Raymond Dasmann. 1985. *Wild California: Vanishing lands, vanishing wildlife.* Berkeley: University of California Press.

Leopold, A. Starker, W. M. Longhurst, and R. F. Dasmann. 1952. A survey of California deer herds, their ranges and management problems. Game Bulletin 6. Sacramento: California Department of Fish and Game.

Lesley, Cecil. No date. Project tour hosted by the Bureau of Reclamation for Humboldt University. www.klamathbasincrisis.org/tours/humboldtprojecttour. Accessed 2004.

Levy, R. 1978. Eastern Miwok. In *Handbook of North American Indians*, Vol. 8, *California*, by Robert F. Heizer. Washington, D.C.: Smithsonian Institution.

Levy, Sharon. 2004. A top dog takes over. *National Wildlife* (August/September 2004). www.nwf.org/nationalwildlife/article.cfm?articleId-69. Accessed 2007.

Lewis, Henry T. 1993. Patterns of Indian burning in California: Ecology and ethnohistory. In *Before the wilderness: Environmental management by Native Californians*, edited by Thomas C. Blackburn and M. Kat Anderson. Menlo Park, CA: Ballena Press.

Linley, B. K. 1991. The Younger Dryas and millenial-scale oceanographic variability in the Sulu Sea, tropical western Pacific. In *Proceedings of the seventh annual Pacific Climate (PACLIM) Workshop, Asilomar, California, April 1990*, edited by Julio L. Betancourt and Vera L. Tharp. Technical Report 26 of the Interagency Ecological Studies Program for the Sacramento-San Joaquin Estuary.

Linsdale, Jean M. 1937. Observations on waterfowl in California. *California Fish and Game* 12: 2–36.

———. 1946. *The California ground squirrel: A record of observations made on the Hastings Natural History Reservation*. Berkeley: University of California Press.

Linsdale, Jean M., and P. Q. Tomich. 1953. *A herd of mule deer*. Berkeley: University of California Press.

Little, Jane Braxton. 2002. Maidu Stewardship Project: Restoring the understory. *Forest Magazine* (summer 2002). Forest Service Employees for Environmental Ethics. www.fseee.org. Accessed 2007.

Lloret, F., and P. H. Zedler. 1991. Recruitment pattern of *Rhus integrifolia* populations in periods between fire in chaparral. *Journal of Vegetation Science* 2: 217–230.

Lo Piccollo, M. 1962. Some aspects of the range cattle industry of Harney County, Oregon, 1870–1900. M.S. thesis, University of Oregon, Eugene.

Logsdon, H. S. 1973. Movements of the Roosevelt elk. *Cal-Neva Wildlife* 1973: 44–52.

Longhurst, W. M., G. E. Connoly, B. M. Browning, and E. O. Garton. 1979. Food interrelationships of deer and sheep in parts of Mendocino and Lake Counties, California. *Hilgardia* 47 (6): 191–247.

Loomis, B. F. 1926. *Pictorial history of the Lassen volcano*. Anderson, CA: California History Books.

Loud, Llewellyn L. 1924. The Stege mounds at Richmond, California. *University of California Publications in American Archaeology and Ethnology* 17.

Lovich, Jeffrey. 1999. Functional ecology of the Desert tortoise and threats to their survival. Desert Tortoise Council, 8th Annual Desert Tortoise Surveying, Monitoring, and Handling Techniques Workshop, Ridgecrest, CA, October 23–24, 1999.

Lowry, Judith Larner. 1993. *Notes on native grasses*. Bolinas, CA: Larner Seeds.

Lufkin, Alan, ed. 1991. *California's salmon and steelhead: The struggle to restore an imperiled resource*. Berkeley: University of California Press.

Lummis, Charles F., ed. 1902a. *Out West: A Magazine of the Old Pacific and the New*, Vol. 17. Los Angeles: Out West Magazine Company.

———. 1902b. Bakersfield, Kern County. *Out West: A Magazine of the Old Pacific and the New*, edited by Charles F. Lummis. Vol. 17. Los Angeles: Out West Magazine Company.

Lyman, R. L. 1995. On the evolution of marine mammal hunting on the West Coast of North America. *Journal of Anthropological Archaeology* 14: 45–77.

MacPhail, Elizabeth C. 1979. *The story of New San Diego and its founder Alonzo E. Horton*. San Diego: San Diego Historical Society. 2nd printing, 1989.

Major, J., and W. T. Pyott. 1959. Buried, viable seeds in two California bunchgrass sites and their bearing on the definition of a flora. *Vegetatio* 13: 253–280.

Mandel, Stephanie, Otis Wollan, Terry Wright, Eric Peach, Jerry Meral, and others. 1989. *The American River: North, Middle and South Forks*. Auburn, CA: Wilderness Conservancy and Protect American River Canyons.

Manly, William Lewis. 2001 [1894]. *Death Valley in '49*. Edited by LeRoy and Jean Johnson. Berkeley: Heyday Books, and Santa Clara, CA: Santa Clara University.

Margolin, Malcolm. 1989. *Monterey in 1786: The journals of Jean Francois de La Perouse*. Berkeley: Heyday Books.

Martin, Glen. 1997. Exotic fish head north. *San Francisco Chronicle*, September 3, 1997.

———. 2001. Carrizo Plain now a national monument, but conflict over cattle grazing continues. *San Francisco Chronicle*, February 12, 2001.

Marzluff, J. M., R. B. Boone, and G. W. Cox. 1994. Historical changes in populations and perceptions of native pest bird species in the West. In *A century of avifaunal change in western North America*, edited by Joseph R. Jehl and Ned K. Johnson. Proceedings of an International Symposium of the Cooper Ornithological Society at the Centennial Meeting, Sacramento, CA, April 17, 1993. Studies in Avian Biology No. 15. Lawrence, KS: Cooper Ornithological Society.

Matocq, Marjorie, Dale McCullough, Jonathan Ballou, and Karen Jones. 2002. Founder events, bottlenecks, and genetic diversity in the Tule elk: Theoretical predictions meet reality. Abstract in Conservation Genetics, Society for Conservation Biology 16th Annual Meeting, July 14–July 19, 2002. http://www.ukc.ac.uk/anthropology/dice/scb2002/abstracys/Tuesday/cgtwo.html. Accessed February 2003.

Matsuda, K., and J. R. McBride. 1986. Difference in seedling growth morphology as a factor in the distribution of three oaks in central California. *Madrono* 33 (3): 207–216.

Mattoni, Rudi, and Travis R. Longcore. 1997. The Los Angeles coastal prairie, a vanished community. *Crossosoma* 23 (2): 71–102.

Mayfield, Thomas Jefferson. 1993. *Indian summer: Traditional life among the Choinumne Indians of California's San Joaquin Valley*. Recorded by Frank Latta in 1871. Berkeley: Heyday Books, and San Francisco: California Historical Society.

McAllister, M. H. 1919. Elk in Shasta County. *California Fish and Game* 5 (2): 98.

McArdle, Phil, ed. 1983. *Exactly opposite the Golden Gate: Essays on Berkeley's history, 1845–1945*. Berkeley: Berkeley Historical Society.

McBride, J. R. 1974. Plant succession in the Berkeley Hills, California. *Madrono* 22 (7): 317–380.

McBride, J. R., and H. F. Heady. 1968. Invasion of grassland by *Baccharis pilularis* DC. *Journal of Range Management* 21: 106–108.

McBride, J. R., E. Norberg, S. Cheng, and A. Mossadegh. 1990. Seedling establishment in Coast Live Oak in relation to seed caching by jays. In *Proceedings of the symposium on oak woodlands and hardwood rangeland management, October 31–November 2, 1990, Davis, California*. USDA Forest Service Pacific Southwest Research Station, General Technical Report PSW-126.

McCarthy, Helen. 1993. Managing oaks and the acorn crop. In *Before the wilderness: Environmental management by Native Californians*, edited by Thomas C. Blackburn and M. Kat Anderson. Menlo Park, CA: Ballena Press.

McCawley, William. 1996. *The first Angelinos: The Gabrielino Indians of Los Angeles*. Banning, CA (Morongo Indian Reservation): Malki Museum Press and Novato, CA: Ballena Press.

McClanahan, Mary. 2000. Holistic resource management unproven in California rangeland. *Grassland* 10 (3): 4–5.

McClane, A. J. 1974. *McClane's field guide to freshwater fishes of North America*. New York: Holt, Rinehart and Winston.

McClatchie, A. J. 1895. *Flora of Pasadena and vicinity*. Los Angeles: Barnes and Neuner Co.

McClung, Robert M. 1969. *Lost wild America: The story of our extinct and vanishing wildlife*. New York: William Morrow and Co.

McClurg, Sue. 2000. *Water and the shaping of California*. Berkeley: Heyday Books and Sacramento: Water Education Foundation.

McCullough, Dale R. 1965. Elk deposit on the San Francisco peninsula. *Journal of Mammalogy* 46 (2): 347–348.

———. 1969. *The Tule elk: Its history, behavior, and ecology*. Berkeley: University of California Press.

McDaniel, Bruce W. 1926. *Dune and desert folk*. Los Angeles: Swetland Publishing Co.

McDonald, Jerry N. 1981. *North American bison: Their classification and evolution*. Berkeley: University of California Press.

McEwan, Dennis, and Terry Jackson. 1996. *Steelhead restoration and management plan for California*. Sacramento: California Department of Fish and Game.

McGinnis, Samuel M. 1984. *Freshwater fishes of California*. Berkeley: University of California Press.

McHugh, Paul. 1991. Steelies. In *California's salmon and steelhead: The struggle to restore an imperiled resource*, edited by Alan Lufkin. Berkeley: University of California Press.

McHugh, Tom. 1972. *The time of the buffalo*. New York: Alfred A. Knopf.

McIntyre, Rick. 1990. *Grizzly cub: Five years in the life of a bear*. Portland, OR: Alaska Northwest Books.

McNaughton, S. J. 1968. Structure and function in California grasslands. *Ecology* 49 (5): 962–972.

———. 1983. Serengeti grassland ecology: The role of composite environmental factors and contingency in community organization. *Ecological Monographs* 53 (3): 291–320.

McPherson, Guy R. 1997. *Ecology and management of North American savannas*. Tucson: University of Arizona Press.

Meagher, M. M. 1978. Bison. In *Big game of North America: Ecology and management*, edited by J. L. Schmidt and D. L. Gilbert. Harrisburg, PA: Stackpole Books.

Meagher, M. M., and Douglas B. Houston. 1998. *Yellowstone and the biology of time: Photographs across a century*. Norman: University of Oklahoma Press.

Mech, L. David. 1970. *The wolf: The ecology and behavior of an endangered species*. Minneapolis: University of Minnesota Press.

Meents, Julie K., Bertin W. Anderson, and Robert D. Ohmart. 1984. Sensitivity of riparian birds to habitat loss. In *California riparian systems: Ecology, conservation, and productive management*, edited by Richard E. Warner and Kathleen M. Hendrix. Berkeley: University of California Press.

Meier, T., ed. 2001. Rocky Mountain Wolf Recovery Team annual report. A cooperative effort by the U.S. Fish and Wildlife Service, the Nez Perce Tribe, the National Park Service, and USDA Wildlife Services. www.westerngraywolf.fws.gov. Accessed 2007.

———. 2003. Rocky Mountain Wolf Recovery Team annual report. A cooperative effort by the U.S. Fish and Wildlife Service, the Nez Perce Tribe, the National Park Service, and USDA Wildlife Services. www.westerngraywolf.fws.gov. Accessed 2007.

Meinecke, E. P. 1936. Changes in California wild life since the white man. *Transactions of the Commonwealth Club of California* 30 (7).

Mensing, S. A. 1998. 560 years of vegetation change in the region of Santa Barbara, California. *Madrono* 45 (1): 1–11.

———. 1992. The impact of European settlement on blue oak (*Quercus douglasii*) regeneration and recruitment in the Tehachapi Mountains, California. *Madrono* 39 (1): 36–46.

Mensing, S. A., J. Michaelsen, and R. Byrne. 1999. A 560-year record of Santa Ana fires reconstructed from charcoal deposited in the Santa Barbara Basin, California. *Quaternary Research* 51: 295–305.

Merriam, C. H. 1899. Results of a biological survey of Mount Shasta, California. *North American Fauna* 16.

———. 1905. A new elk from California, *Cervus nannodes*. *Proceedings of the Biological Society of Washington* 18: 23–25.

———. 1914. Preliminary report on the discovery of human remains in an asphalt deposit at Rancho La Brea. *Science*, n.s., 15 (1023): 198–203.

———. 1918. Review of the grizzly and big brown bears of North America. *North American Fauna* 4: 1–136. Washington, D.C.: U.S. Government Printing Office.

———. 1919. "Is the Jaguar Entitled to a Place in the California Fauna?" *Journal of Mammalogy* 1 (1), Nov. 1919.

———. 1921. A California elk drive. *Scientific Monthly* 13 (5): 465–475.

———. 1926. The buffalo in northeastern California. *Journal of Mammalogy* 7: 211–214.

Meyer, V. C. 2001. Soil moisture availability as a factor affecting valley oak (*Quercus lobata* Nee) seedling establishment and survival in a riparian habitat, Cosumnes River Preserve, Sacramento County, California. Abstract in Oaks in California's Changing Landscape, 5th Symposium on Oak Woodlands, October 22–25, 2001, Bahia Resort Hotel, San Diego, California. University of California Integrated Harwood Range Management Program, University of California, Berkeley. http://danr.ucop.edu/ihrmp/proceed/symproc49.html. Accessed December 2003.

Millar, C. I., and W. B. Woolfenden. 1999. The role of climate change in interpreting historical variability. *Ecological Applications* 9 (4): 1207–1216.

Miller, Loye. 1925. Chendytes, a diving goose from the California Pleistocene. *Condor* 27: 145–147.

Miller, Loye, E. D. Mitchell, and Jere H. Lipps. 1961. New light on the flightless goose *Chendytes lawi*. Los Angeles County Museum Contributions in Science No. 43: 3–11.

Minnich, R. A. 1977. The geography of fire and Big-cone Douglas-fir, Coulter pine and western conifer forests in the east Transverse Ranges, southern California. In *Proceedings of the symposium on the environmental consequences of fire and fuel management in Mediterranean ecosystems*, August 1–5, 1977, Palo Alto, California, edited by H. A. Mooney and C. E. Conrad. USDA Forest Service General Technical Report WO-3.

——. 1983. Fire mosaics in southern California and northen Baja California. *Science* 219: 1287–1294.

——. 1989. Chaparral fire history in San Diego County and adjacent northern Baja California: An evaluation of natural fire regimes and the effects of suppression management. In *The California chaparral: Paradigms reexamined*, edited by S. C. Keeley. Science Series No. 34. Los Angeles: Natural History Museum of Los Angeles County.

——. 2003. Fire is inevitable but we can mitigate the damage. *San Diego Union-Tribune*, November 2, 2003.

Minnich, R. A., M. G. Barbour, J. H. Burk, and R. F. Fernau. 1995. Sixty years of change in Californian conifer forests of the San Bernardino Mountains. *Conservation Biology* 9 (4): 902–1914.

Minnich, R. A., and R. J. Dezzani. 1998. Historical decline of coastal sage scrub in the Riverside-Perris Plain, California. *Western Birds* 29: 366–391.

Minnich, R. A., and E. Franco-Vizcaino. 1998. *Land of chamise and pines: Historical descriptions of northern Baja California*. Berkeley: University of California Press.

Minnich, R. A., and Y. Hong Chou. 1997. Wildland fire patch dynamics in the chaparral of southern California and northern Baja California. *International Journal of Wildland Fire* 7 (3): 221–248.

Minnick, Roger, and Dave Bohn. 1969. *Delta west: The land and people of the Sacramento-San Joaquin Delta*. Berkeley: Scrimshaw Press.

Minshall, Herbert L. 1980. *Window on the sea: A nostalgic view of the changing coastal environment of the two Californias*. La Jolla, CA: Copley Books.

Moffitt, James. 1934. History of the Yosemite elk herd. *California Fish and Game* 20 (1): 37–51.

Mol, Dick, Alexei Tikhonov, Johannes Van Der Plicht, Ralf-Dietrich Kahlke, Regis Debruyne, Bas Van Geel, Jan Peter Pals, Christian De Marliave, and Jelle W. F. Reumer. 2003. Results of the CERPOLEX/Mammuthus expeditions on the Taimyr Peninsula, arctic Siberia, Russian Federation. Abstracts in the Third International Mammoth Conference, May 2003, Dawson City, Yukon Territory, Canada. www.yukonmuseums.ca/mammoth. Accessed 2005.

Monson, Gale, and Lowell Sumner, eds. 1985. *The desert bighorn: Its life history, ecology, and management*. Tucson: University of Arizona Press.

Morejohn, G. Victor. 1976. Evidence of the survival to recent times of the extinct flightless duck *Chendytes lawi* Miller. *Smithsonian Contributions to Paleobiology* 27: 207–211.

Moritz, M. A. 2003. Spatiotemporal analysis of controls on shrubland fire regimes: Age dependency and fire hazard. *Ecology* 84 (2): 351–361.

Morris, Joe. 2001. Holistic management response. *Grasslands* 11 (2): 11.

Morrison, Susan D. 1989. *The passenger pigeon*. New York: Crestwood House.

Moyle, Peter B. 1973. Recent changes in the fish fauna of the San Joaquin River system. *Cal-Neva Wildlife* 1973: 60–63.

——. 2002. Inland fishes of California. Berkeley: University of California Press.

Muir, John, ed. 1888. *Picturesque California and the region west of the Rocky Mountains, from Alaska to Mexico*. Reprinted as *West of the Rocky Mountains*, Philadelphia: Running Press, 1976.

——. 1894. *The mountains of California*. New York: Century Co. Reprint, New York: Penguin Books, 1985.

——. 1901. *Our national parks*. Boston: Houghton Mifflin.

Mullally, Don P. 1994. Some results and implications of the 1947–1951 drought near Los Angeles. *Crossosoma* 20 (1): 49–74.

Munz, P. A., and D. D. Keck. 1963. *A California flora*. Berkeley: University of California Press.

Murie, Adolph. 1944. *The wolves of Mount McKinley*. Seattle: University of Washington Press.

——. 1981. *The grizzlies of Mount McKinley*. Preface by J. O. Murie. USDI, National Park Service, Science Monographs Series 14: 1–251.

Murie, O. J. 1951. *The elk of North America*. Washington, D.C.: Wildlife Management Institute and Harrisburg, PN: Stackpole Books.

Murphy, Dennis. 1985. The biology and conservation of grasslands on serpentine soil in the San Francisco Bay Area. General Meeting of the California Native Plant Society, Berkeley, California, October 23, 1985.

Murray, John A. 1995. *Grizzly bears: An illustrated field guide*. Dublin, Ireland: Roberts Rinehart Publishers.

Myers, Kirk. 1994. *When Old Town was young: The early decades of Old Pasadena*. Pasadena: Kirk Myers.

Napa River Flood Protection Project. 2002. Progress and plan summary. Napa, CA: Napa County Flood Control and Water Conservation District. www.napaflooddistrict.org.

Nash, Steven A. 1995. *Facing eden: 100 years of landscape art in the Bay Area*. San Francisco: Fine Arts Museums of San Francisco and Berkeley: University of California Press.

National Marine Fisheries Service. 1996. NMFS proposed recovery plan for the Sacramento River winter-run Chinook salmon. NMFS Southwest Region, Long Beach, California. 250 pp.

NCHRSP [Northern California Historical Records Survey Project]. 1940. Inventory of the county archives of California. No. 10, Fresno County (Fresno). Division of Professional and Science Projects, Work Projects Administration, July 1940. San Francisco: Northern California Historical Records Survey Project.

Neasham, V. Aubrey. *Wild legacy: California hunting and fishing tales*. Berkeley: Howell-North Books.

Ne'em, G., J. Fotheringham, and J. E. Keeley. 1999. Patch to landscape patterns in post fire recruitment of a serotinous conifer. *Plant Ecology* 145: 235–242.

Nelson, A. R. 1992. Discordant 14C ages from buried tidal-marsh soils in the Cascadia subduction zone, southern Oregon coast. *Quaternary Research* 38: 74–90.

Nelson, E. W. 1925. Distribution of the Pronghorned antelope in California. *California Fish and Game* 11 (4): 154–157.

Nelson, E. W. 1989. The Imperial ivory-billed woodpecker, *Campephilus imperialis* (Gould). *The Auk* 15 (3): 217–223.

Nelson, L. L., and E. B. Allen. 1993. Restoration of *Stipa pulchra* grasslands: Effects of Mycorrhizae and competition from Avena barbata. *Restoration Ecology* (March 1993): 40–50.

Nelson, N. C. 1910. The Ellis Landing shellmound. *University of California Publications in American Archaeology and Ethnology* 7: 309–356.

Nevins, Allan. 1983. *Fremont: Pathmaker of the West*. Lincoln: University of Nebraska Press.

Newberry, J. S. 1857. Report upon the mammals. Vol. 6, part 4, no. 2, p. 35–72 of *Reports of explorations and surveys, to ascertain the most practicable and economical route for a railroad from the Mississippi River to the Pacific Ocean*. Washington, D.C.: U.S. War Department.

Newland, Joseph N. 1996. *Impressions of California: Early currents in art, 1850–1930*. Irvine, CA: Irvine Museum.

Nickel, Douglas R. 1999. *Carleton Watkins: The art of perception*. San Francisco: San Francisco Museum of Modern Art.

Nielson, J. A. 1981. *Flora of the Mayacmas Mountains*. Napa, CA: Ecoview Environmental Consultants.

Nilsen, E. T., P. W. Rundel, and M. R. Sharifi. 1984. Productivity in native stands of *Prosopis glandulosa* mesquite in the Sonoran Desert of southern California and some management implications. In *California riparian systems: Ecology, conservation, and productive management*, edited by Richard E. Warner and Kathleen M. Hendrix. Berkeley: University of California Press.

Nixon, K. C. 2001. The oak (*Quercus*) biodiversity of California and adjacent regions. In *Proceedings of the fifth symposium on oak woodlands: Oaks in California's changing landscape*. October 22–25, 2001, San Diego, California. USDA Forest Service Pacific Southwest Research Station, General Technical Report PSW-GTR-184.

Nixon, K. C., and K. P. Steele. 1981. A new species of *Quercus* (Fagaceae) from southern California. *Madrona* 28 (4): 210–219.

NOAA [National Oceanic and Atmospheric Administration]. 2004. www.beringclimate.noaa.gov/reports/np-04.htm. Accessed 2007.

———. 2006. Paleo perspectives. www.ncnd.noaa.gov/paleo/persectives. Accessed 2007.

Noon, Patrick. 2003. *Crossing the Channel: British and French painting in the age of romanticism*. London: Tate Publishing.

Norelli, Martina R. 1975. American wildlife painting. Watson-Guptill Publications.   Reprint, New York: Galahad Books, 1982.

NPS [National Park Service]. 2004. Final Yosemite fire management plan environmental impact statement. www.nps.gov/archives/yos/planning/fire. Accessed 2007.

OES. 1920. *California Fish and Game* 6 (4): 182.

Oberbauer, T. A. 1978. Distribution of dynamics of San Diego County grasslands. M.S. thesis, San Diego State University, San Diego, California. 120 pp.

———. 2003. Vegetation communities affected. In *A summary of affected flora and fauna in the San Diego County fires of 2003*. San Diego Biological Resources Researchers, November 14, 2003.

Oberholser, Harry C. 1900. Notes on some birds from Santa Barbara Islands, California. *Proceedings of the United States National Museum* 22: 229–234.

O'Brien, R. 1951. California called them: A saga of golden days and roaring camps. New York: McGraw-Hill.

Ochert, Ayala. 2002. Leaping into the fray. *California Monthly* (December 2002): 20–24.

———. 2003. Saving the forest for the trees. *California Monthly* (September 2003): 14–17.

Ogden, J. C. 1983. Radio-tracking the California condor. *Outdoor California* (September–October 1983): 11–13.

Okamoto, Ariel, R. 1995. *Golden Gate National Recreation Area: Guide to the parks*. Sacramento: Golden Gate Natural History Association.

Olmstead, D. L., and O. C. Stewart. 1978. Achumawi. In *Handbook of North American Indians*, Vol. 8, *California*, by Robert F. Heizer. Washington, D.C.: Smithsonian Institution.

Onuf, C. P. 1987. The ecology of Mugu Lagoon, California: An estuarine profile. U.S. Fish and Wildlife Service Biological Report 85 (7.15). 122 pp.

Ornduff, Robert. 1974. *Introduction to California plant life*. Berkeley: University of California Press.

Orr, R. T. 1950. Early records of Californian mammals. *Journal of Mammalogy* 31 (3): 362.

———. 1950b. Additional records of *Ursus californicus*. *Journal of Mammalogy* 31 (3): 362–363.

Paddison, Joshua. 1999. *A world transformed: Firsthand accounts of California before the gold rush*. Berkeley: Heyday Books.

Page, G. W., F. C. Bidstrup, R. J. Ramer, and L. E. Stenzel. 1986. Distribution of wintering Snowy plovers in California and adjacent states. *Western Birds* 17: 145–170.

Page, G. W., and R. E. Gill, Jr. 1994. Shorebirds of western North America: Late 1800s to late 1900s. In *A century of avifaunal change in western North America*, edited by Joseph R. Jehl and Ned K. Johnson. Proceedings of an International Symposium of the Cooper Ornithological Society at the Centennial Meeting, Sacramento, CA, April 17, 1993. Studies in Avian Biology No. 15. Lawrence, KS: Cooper Ornithological Society.

Page, G. W., and L. E. Stenzel. 1981. The breeding status of the Snowy plover in California. *Western Birds* 12: 1–40.

Paher, Stanley W. 1976. *Colorado River ghost towns*. Las Vegas: Nevada Publications.

Palóu, Francisco. 1926. *Historical memoirs of new California*. 4 Vols. Edited by Herbert E. Bolton. Berkeley: University of California Press.

Parker, K. H. 1928. Growth of Stipa pulchra and Bromus hordeaceus as influenced by herbage removal. Bachelor of Science paper, University of California, Berkeley. 31 pp.

Parmalee, P. W. 1958. New record of California grizzly bear. *Journal of Mammalogy* 39 (1): 151–153.

Parsons, D. J. 1981. The historical role of fire in the foothill communities of Sequoia National Park. *Madrono* 28 (3): 111–120.

Patent, Dorothy H. 1987. *The way of the grizzly*. New York: Clarion Books.

Patten, Duncan T., ed. 1987. The Mono Basin ecosystem: Effects of changing lake level. Washington, D.C.: National Academy Press.

Pattiani, Evelyn C. 1953. *Queen of the hills: The story of Piedmont, a California city*. Fresno, CA: Academy Library Guild.

Pavlik, Bruce M., Pamels C. Muick, Sharon G. Johnson, and Marjorie Popper. 1991. *Oaks of California*. Los Olivos, CA: Cachuma Press.

Pearse, John S. 1098. Intertidal invertebrates. In *The natural history of Año Nuevo*, edited by Burney J. Le Boeuf and Stephanie Kaza. Pacific Grove, CA: Boxwood Press. 2nd printing, 1985.

Pennington, Nat. 2004. Salmon River chinook salmon and steelhead runs: The status of the stocks, the Salmon River's fishery update. Newsletter of the Salmon River Restoration Council, Summer 2004. www.srrc.org. Accessed 2004.

Pennington, Nat, and Amy Stercho. 2004. Un-damming the Klamath? *The River Voice* 1 (2). www.srrc.org (Salmon River Restoration Council). Accessed 2004.

Perkins, Deborah J., Bruce N. Carlsen, Mike Fredstrom, Richard H. Millar, Cindy M. Roper, Gregory T. Ruggerone, and Carolyn S. Zimmerman. 1984. The effects of groundwater pumping on natural spring communities in Owens Valley. In *California riparian systems: Ecology, conservation, and productive management*, edited by Richard E. Warner and Kathleen M. Hendrix. Berkeley: University of California Press.

Perry, Richard. 1970. *Bears*. New York: Arco Publishing Co., Ltd.

Peterson, Martin E. 1991. *Second nature: Four early San Diego landscape painters*. San Diego: San Diego Museum of Art.

Peterson, P. M., and R. J. Soreng. 2007. Systematics of California grasses (Poaceae). In *California grasslands ecology and management*, edited by M. R. Stromberg, J. D. Corbin, and C. M. D'Antonio. Berkeley: University of California Press.

Peterson, Roger Tory, and Edward L. Chalif. 1973. *Mexican birds*. Boston: Houghton Mifflin.

Peterson, Rolf. 1995. *The Wolves of Isle Royale*. Minocqua, WI: Willow Creek Press.

Philpot, C. W. 1977. Vegetative features as determinants of fire frequency and intensity. In *Proceedings of the symposium on the environmental consequences of fire and fuel management in Mediterranean ecosystems, August 1–5, 1977, Palo Alto, California*, edited by H. A. Mooney and C. E. Conrad. USDA Forest Service General Technical Report WO-3.

Piemeisel, R. L., and F. R. Lawson. 1937. Types of vegetation in the San Joaquin Valley of California and their relation to the beet leafhopper. U.S. Department of Agriculture, Washigton, D.C., Technical Bulletin No. 557.

Pierce, Ronnie. 1991. The Klamath River fishery: Early history. In *California's salmon and steelhead: The struggle to restore an imperiled resource*, edited by Alan Lufkin. Berkeley: University of California Press.

Pister, Philip E., and Joanne H. Kerbavaz. 1984. Fish Slough: A case study in management of a desert wetland system. In *California riparian systems: Ecology, conservation, and productive management*, edited by Richard E. Warner and Kathleen M. Hendrix. Berkeley: University of California Press.

Platt, William S. 1984. Riparian system/livestock grazing interaction research in the Intermountain West. In *California riparian systems: Ecology, conservation, and productive management*, edited by Richard E. Warner and Kathleen M. Hendrix. Berkeley: University of California Press.

Poole, William. 1991. For the sake of salmon. In *California's salmon and steelhead: The struggle to restore an imperiled resource*, edited by Alan Lufkin. Berkeley: University of California Press.

Post, Robert. 1989. *Street railways and the growth of Los Angeles*. San Marino. CA: Golden West Books.

Pourade, Richard F. 1963. *The silver dons, 1833–1865*. Vol. 3 of *The History of San Diego*, by Richard F. Pourade. San Diego: Union-Tribune Publishing Co.

——. 1968. *The call to California: The epic journey of the Portola-Serra expedition in 1769*. San Diego: Union-Tribune Publishing Co.

Powell, John Wesley. 1875. The canons of the Colorado: The 1869 discovery voyage down the Colorado River from Wyoming, into Colorado, through Utah, to Arizona and Nevada. *Scribner's Monthly*. Reprint, Golden, CO: Outbooks, 1981.

Power, Dennis M. 1994. Avifaunal changes on California's coastal islands. In *A century of avifaunal change in western North America*, edited by Joseph R. Jehl and Ned K. Johnson. Proceedings of an International Symposium of the Cooper Ornithological Society at the Centennial Meeting, Sacramento, CA, April 17, 1993. Studies in Avian Biology No. 15. Lawrence, KS: Cooper Ornithological Society.

Presnall, C. C. Evidences of bison in southwestern Utah. *Journal of Mammalogy* 20: 111–112.

Preston, William L. 1981. *Vanishing landscapes: Land and life in the Tulare Lake Basin*. Berkeley: University of California Press.

——. 1998. Serpent in the garden: Environmental change in colonial California. In *Contested eden: California before the gold rush*, edited by Ramon A. Gutierrez and Richard J. Orsi. Berkeley: University of California Press.

Price, Kim. 1991. The CCC's Salmon Restoration Project. In *California's salmon and steelhead: The struggle to restore an imperiled resource*, edited by Alan Lufkin. Berkeley: University of California Press.

Priestley, Herbert. 1937. *A historical, political, and natural description of California by Pedro Fages, soldier of Spain*. Berkeley: University of California Press.

Pyle, P., N. Nur, and D. F. Desante. 1994. Trends in nocturnal migrant landbird populations at southeast Farallon Island, California, 1968–1992. In *A century of avifaunal change in western North America*, edited by Joseph R. Jehl and Ned K. Johnson. Proceedings of an International Symposium of the Cooper Ornithological Society at the Centennial Meeting, Sacramento, CA, April 17, 1993. Studies in Avian Biology No. 15. Lawrence, KS: Cooper Ornithological Society.

Quinn, R. D. 1979. Effects of fire on small mammals in the chaparral. *Cal-Neva Wildlife Transactions* 1979: 125–133.

——. 1986. Mammalian herbivory and resilience in Mediterranean-climate ecosystems. In *Resilience in Mediterranean-type ecosystems*, edited by B. Dell, A. J. M. Hopkins, and B. B. Lamont. Dordrecht, Netherlands: Dr. W. Junk, Publishers.

Radtke, K. 1985. First postfire season plant establishment. In *Living in the chaparral of southern California*. Proceedings of the Conference and Public Workshop by the National Foundation for Environmental Safety, National Park Service, October 20, 1984. Los Angeles: Natural History Museum of Los Angeles County.

Raven, Peter, and Henry J. Thompson. 1966. *Flora of the Santa Monica Mountains*. Los Angeles: University of California, Los Angeles.

Ray, Dan, Wayne Woodruff, and R. Chad Roberts. 1984. Management of riparian vegetation in the northcoast region of California's coastal zone. In *California riparian systems: Ecology, conservation, and productive management*, edited by Richard E. Warner and Kathleen M. Hendrix. Berkeley: University of California Press.

Rayl, A. J. S. 2004. Becoming a full-fledged condor. *Smithsonian* (September 2004): 92–97.

Redmond, Kelly T. 2009. Historic climate variability in the Mojave Desert. In *The Mojave Desert: Ecosystem processes and sustainability*, edited by Robert H. Webb, Lynn F. Fenstermaker, Jill S. Heaton, Debra L. Hughson, Eric V. McDonald, and David M. Miller. Reno: University of Nevada Press.

Reed, E. K. 1952. The myth of Montezuma's bison and the type locality of the species. *Journal of Mammalogy* 33 (2): 390–392.

——. 1955. Bison beyond the Pecos. *Texas Journal of Science* 7: 130–135.

Reeves, Kent. 2001. Holistic management and biological planning in California: You be the judge. *Grasslands* 11 (1) Spring 2001: 5–7.

Reiner, R. J. 2007. Fire in California grasslands. In *California grasslands ecology and management*, edited by M. R. Stromberg, J. D. Corbin, and C. M. D'Antonio. Berkeley: University of California Press.

Remsen, J. V., Jr. 1978. Bird species of special concern in California: An annotated list of declining or vulnerable bird species. Administrative Report No. 78-1. California Department of Fish and Game, Wildlife Management Branch.

Reneau, Jack, and Susan C. Reneau. 1993. *Records of North American big game*. 10th edition. Missoula, MT: Boone and Crockett Club.

Renfro, Elizabeth. 1992. *The Shasta Indians of California and their neighbors.* Happy Camp, CA: Naturegraph Publishers, Inc.

Rice, K. J., and E. K. Espeland. 2007. Genes on the range: Population genetics. In *California grasslands ecology and management,* edited by M. R. Stromberg, J. D. Corbin, and C. M. D'Antonio. Berkeley: University of California Press.

Riddell, F. A. 1952. The recent occurrence of bison in northeastern California. *American Antiquity* 18: 168–169.

Ripple, W. J., and R. L. Beschta. 2007. Restoring Yellowstone's aspen with wolves. *Biological Conservation* 138: 514–519.

———. 2008. Trophic cascades involving cougar, mule deer, and black oaks in Yosemite National Park. *Biological Conservation* 141: 1249–1256.

Rising, James D. 1996. *A guide to the identification and natural history of the sparrows of the United States and Canada.* San Diego: Academic Press.

Robbins, Jim. 1998. Return of wolves to Yellowstone affects wide range of species. *San Francisco Chronicle,* January 1, 1998.

Roberts, Fred M., Jr. 1995. *Illustrated guide to the oaks of the southern Californian Floristic Province.* Encinitas, CA: F. M. Roberts Publications.

Roberts, Warren G., J. Greg Howe, and Jack Major. 1977. A survey of riparian flora and fauna in California. In *Riparian forests in California: Their ecology and conservation,* edited by Anne Sands. Institute of Ecology Publication No. 15. Davis: Institute of Ecology, University of California, Davis.

Roberston, Morgan M. 1997. Prescribed burning as a management and restoration tool in wetlands of the upper Midwest. www.hort.agri.umn.edu/h5015/97papers/roberston.html. Accessed 2004.

Robinson, Guy S., David A. Burney, and Lida Pigott Burney. 2003. A palynological approach to the study of megaherbivore extinction in the Hudson Valley. Abstracts in 3rd International Mammoth Conference, May 2003, Dawson City, Yukon Territory, Canada. www.yukonmuseums.ca/mammoth. Accessed 2005.

Robinson, J. W. 1983. *The San Gabriels II: The mountains from Monrovia Canyon to Lytle Creek.* Arcadia, CA: Big Santa Anita Historical Society.

———. 1989. *The San Bernardinos: The mountain country from Cajon Pass to Oak Glen, two centuries of changing use.* Arcadia, CA: Big Santa Anita Historical Society.

Robinson, J. W., and Bruce D. Risher. 1993. *The San Jacintos: The mountain country from Banning to Borrego Valley.* Arcadia, CA: Big Santa Anita Historical Society

Robinson, W. W. 1953. *Panorama: A picture history of southern California.* Los Angeles: Title Insurance and Trust Co.

———. 1981. *Los Angeles from the days of the pueblo: A brief history and a guide to the Plaza area.* San Francisco: California Historical Society and Chronicle Books.

Rogers, Garry F. 1982. *Then and now: A photographic history of vegetation change in the central Great Basin Desert.* Salt Lake City: University of Utah Press.

Ropelewski, C. F., and M. S. Halpert. 1990. Uncovering North American temperature and precipitation patterns associatd with the Southern Oscillation. In *Proceedings of the sixth annual Pacific Climate (PACLIM) Workshop, March 5–8, 1989,* edited by J. L. Betancourt and A. M. Mackay. California Department of Water Resources, Interagency Ecological Studies Program Technical Report 23.

Rose, L. J., Jr. 1959. *L. J. Rose of Sunny Slope, 1827–1899.* San Marino, CA: Huntington Library.

Rosenberg, Kenneth V., Robert D. Ohmart, William C. Hunter, and Bertin W. Anderson. 1991. *Birds of the lower Colorado River Valley.* Tucson: University of Arizona Press.

Rundel, P. W., and J. L. Vankat. 1989. Chaparral communities and ecosystems. In *The California chaparral: Paradigms reexamined,* edited by S. C. Keeley. Science Series No. 34. Los Angeles: Natural History Museum of Los Angeles County.

Russell, Andy. 1967. *Grizzly country.* New York: Nick Lyons Books.

Russell, E. W. B. 1983. Pollen analysis of past vegetation at Point Reyes National Seashore, California. *Madrono* 30 (1): 1–11.

Sacramento County Office of Education. 1973. Environments of the Sacramento region. Geological Society of Sacramento, Annual Field Trip Guidebook, Vol. 1973, 9–21.

Saenz, L., and J. O. Sawyer, Jr. 1986. Grasslands as compared to adjacent *Quercus garryana* woodland understories exposed to different grazing regimes. *Madrono* 33 (1): 40–46.

Safford, H. D. 1995. Woody vegetation and succession in the Garin Woods, Hayward Hills, Alameda County, California. *Madrono* 42 (4): 470–489.

Salsig, Natalie, Marianne Loring, and Katherine Trow. 2000. *Kensington past and present.* Emeryville, CA: Woodford Press.

Salter, John F. 2003. White paper on behalf of the Karuk Tribe of California: A context statement concerning the effect of the Klamath Hydroelectric Project on traditional resource uses and cultural patterns of the Karuk people within the Klamath River corridor. Written under contract with Pacificorp in connection with Federal Energy Relicensing Commission proceedings concerning the relicensing of Iron Gate Dam. Performed under Contract No. 300002057, November 2003.

———. 2004. Fire and forest management: Casting light on the paradigms. Parts 1 and 2. *The River Voice* 1 (2). www.srrc.org (Salmon River Restoration Council). Accessed 2004.

Salwasser, Hal, and Karen Shimamoto. 1984. Pronghorn, cattle, and feral horse use of wetland and upland habitat. In *California riparian systems: Ecology, conservation, and productive management,* edited by Richard E. Warner and Kathleen M. Hendrix. Berkeley: University of California Press.

Sampson, A. W., and A. Chase. 1927. Range grasses of California. Agricultural Experiment Station Bulletin 430. Berkeley: University of California, Berkeley.

Sampson, A. W., A. Chase, and D. W. Hendrick. 1951. California grassland and range forage grasses. Manual 33. California Agricultural Experiment Station Manual. Berkeley: University of California, Berkeley. 162 pp.

Sampson, A. W., and E. C. McCarty. 1930. The carbohydrate metabolism of *Stipa pulchra. Hilgardia* 5 (4): 61–100.

Sampson, Arthur W. 1944. Plant succession on burned chaparral lands in northern California. Agricultural Experiment Station Bulletin 685. Berkeley: University of California, Berkeley.

San Diego County Wildland Fire Task Force. 2003. Mitigation strategies for reducing wildland fire risks. Report to the Board of Supervisors, August 13, 2003.

San Francisco Estuary Institute. 1998. San Francisco Bay Area Wetlands Ecosystem Goals. www.sfei.org/sfbaygoals/docs/goals1998/draft06298/html/chap06.html. Accessed 2003.

San Jose Mercury. 1896. *Santa Clara County and its resources.* Reprinted as *Sunshine, fruit, and flowers: Santa Clara County, California.* San Jose: San Jose Historical Museum Association, 1987.

Sancetta, C., M. Lyle, and J. P. Bradbury. 1992. Late-glacial to Holocene changes in winds, upwelling, and seasonal production of the northern California Current System. *Quaternary Research* 38: 359–370.

Sanchez, H. V. G. 1932. *California and Californians.* Vol. 1, *The Spanish period.* San Francisco: Lewis Publishing.

Sands, Anne, ed. 1977. *Riparian forests in California: Their ecology and conservation.* Institute of Ecology Publication No. 15. Davis: Institute of Ecology, University of California, Davis.

Sandweiss, Dan. 2004. Fish story linked to climate cycle. Earth Observatory, News. http://earthobservatory.nasa.gov/Newsroom/MediaAlerts/2004/2004o6181786.html. Accessed 2007.

Santaelle, L., and A. M. Sada. 1991. A Short-billed albatross observed near San Benedicto Island, Revillagigedo Islands, Mexico. *Western Birds* 22: 33–34.

Saroyan, William. 1937. My name is Aram. New York: Harcourt, Brace.

Sauer, J. D. 1977. Fire history, environmental patterns, and species patterns in Santa Monica mountain chaparral. In *Proceedings of the symposium on the environmental consequences of fire and fuel management in Mediterranean ecosystems, August 1–5, 1977, Palo Alto, California,* edited by H. A. Mooney and C. E. Conrad. USDA Forest Service General Technical Report WO-3.

Savory, A. 1988. *Holistic resource management.* Covelo, CA: Island Press.

Sawyer, Eugene. 1922. *History of Santa Clara County, California.* Los Angeles: Historic Record Co.

Sawyer, John O., and Todd Keeler-Wolf. 1995. *A manual of California vegetation.* Sacramento: California Native Plant Society.

Scammon, C. M. *Marine mammals of the north-western coast of North America.* San Francisco: John H. Carman and Co.

Schenck, W. E. 1926. The Emeryville shellmound final report. *Univeristy of California Publications in American Archaeology and Ethnology* 23 (3): 147–282.

Schiffman, P.M. 2000. Mammal burrowing, erratic rainfall, and the annual lifestyle in the California prairie: Is it time for a paradigm shift? In *Second interface between ecology and land development in California,* edited by J. E. Keeley, M. Baer-Keeley, and C. J. Fotheringham. U.S. Geological Survey Open-File Report 00-62: 153–160.

———. 2007. Ecology of native animals in California grasslands. In *California grasslands ecology and management,* edited by M. R. Stromberg, J. D. Corbin, and C. M. D'Antonio. Berkeley: University of California Press.

Schlorff, R. W., and P. H. Bloom. 1984. Importance of riparian systems to nesting Swainson's hawks in the Central Valley of California. In *California riparian systems: Ecology, conservation, and productive management,* edited by Richard E. Warner and Kathleen M. Hendrix. Berkeley: University of California Press.

Schmidt, Robert H. 1991. Gray wolves in California: Their presence and absence. *California Fish and Game* 77 (2): 79–85.

Schmidts, M. J., D. A. Sims, and J. A. Gamon. 2000. Characterizing stand age of southern California chaparral: Ground validation for landscape-scale remote sensing. http://vcsars.calstatela.edu/eas 00/miriam/miriam esa. Accessed 2003.

Schoenherr, Alan A., C. Robert Feldmeth, and Michael J. Emerson. 1999. *Natural history of the islands of California.* Berkeley: University of California Press.

Schoenman, Theodore, and Helen B. Schoenman, transl. and ed. 1976 (1859). *Travels in southern California,* by John Xantus. Detroit: Wayne State University Press.

Schoonmaker, W. J. 1968. *The world of the grizzly bear.* Philadelphia: J. B. Lippincott Co.

Schulz, Peter D., and Dwight D. Simons. 1973. Fish species diversity in a prehistoric central California Indian midden. *California Fish and Game* 59 (2): 107–113.

Schwartz, Richard. 2000. *Berkeley 1900: Daily life at the turn of the century.* Berkeley: RSB Books.

Schwendinger, Robert J. 1984. *International port of call: An illustrated history of the Golden Gate.* Woodland Hills, CA: Windsor Publications.

Scoffield, N. B. 1918. The salmon catch on the Eel River. *California Department of Fish and Game* 4 (1): 49–50.

———. 1921a. Gear used for salmon trolling in California in 1920. *California Fish and Game* 7 (1): 22–38.

———. 1921b. Salmon conservation and salmon trolling. *California Fish and Game* 7 (1): 55–58.

Scott, Lauren B., and Sandra K. Marquiss. 1984. An historical overview of the Sacramento River. In *California riparian systems: Ecology, conservation, and productive management,* edited by Richard E. Warner and Kathleen M. Hendrix. Berkeley: University of California Press.

Scott, T. A. 1990. The distribution of Engelmann oak (*Quercus engelmannii*) in California. In *Proceedings of the symposium on oak woodlands and hardwood rangeland management, October 31–November 2, 1990, Davis, California.* USDA Forest Service Pacific Southwest Research Station, General Technical Report PSW-126.

Semeniuk, Robert S. 2003. How bears feed salmon to the forest. *Natural History* (April 2003): 22–28.

Seton, Ernest Thompson.1898. *Wild animals I have known.* Reprint, New York: Penguin Books, 1987.

———. 1900. *The biography of a grizzly.* New York: Century Co.

Sharsmith, H. K. 1936. *Flora of the Mount Hamilton Range.* Ph.D. diss., University of California, Berkeley.

Shay, C. Thomas. 1979. "Bison Procurement on the Eastern Margin of the Plains: the Itasca Site." In *Bison Procurement and Utilization: A Symposium,* ed. L. B. Davis and M. Wilson. Lincoln: *Plains Anthropologist Memoir* 14.

Shipek, Florence. 1993. Kumeyaay plant husbandry: Fire, water, and erosion management systems. In *Before the wilderness: Environmental management by Native Californians,* edited by Thomas C. Blackburn and M. Kat Anderson. Menlo Park, CA: Ballena Press.

Short, Lester L. 1982. *Woodpeckers of the world.* Delaware Museum of Natural History Monograph Series No. 4. Greenville, DE.

Show, S. B., and E. I. Kotok. 1924. The role of fire in the California pine forests. USDA Department Bulletin 1294, Washington, D.C.

Shurtleff, Lawton L., and Christopher Savage. *The Wood duck and the Mandarin.* Berkeley: University of California Press.

Sibley, David Allen. 2000. *The Sibley guide to birds.* New York: Alfred A. Knopf.

Sime, Carolyn A., V. Asher, L. Bradley, K. Laudon, M. Ross, J. Trapp, and M. Handegard. 2006. Montana grey wolf conservation and management in the northern Rockies wolf recovery area. Pages 3–63 in Rocky Mountain Wolf Recovery annual report, edited by C. A. Sime and E. E. Bangs. U.S. Fish and Wildlife Service, the Nez Perce Tribe, the National Park Service, and USDA Wildlife Services. USFWS Ecological Services, 585 Shephard Way, Helena, MT 59601. 130 pp. www.westerngraywolf.fws.gov. Published 2005. Accessed 2007.

Simons, D. D. 1983. Interactions between California condors and humans in prehistoric far western North America. In *Vulture biology and management,* edited by S. R. Wilbur and J. A. Jackson. Berkeley: University of California Press.

Simovich, M. A. 1979. Post fire reptile succession. *Cal-Neva Wildlife Transactions* 1979: 104–113.

——. 1998. Crustacean biodiversity and endemism in California's ephemeral wetlands. Pages 107–118 in *Ecology, conservation, and management of vernal pool ecosystems*, edited by C. W. Witham, E. T. Bauder, D. Belk, W. R. Ferren, Jr., and R. Ornduff. Proceedings from a 1996 Conference, Sacramento, California. Sacramento: California Native Plant Society.

Simpson, A. W., A. Chase, and D. W. Hedrick. 1951. California grasslands and range forage grasses. Agricultural Experiment Station Bulletin 724. Berkeley: University of California, Berkeley.

Simpson, J. H. 1876. *Report of explorations across the Great Basin of the territory of Utah for a direct wagon-route from Camp Floyd to Genoa, in Carson Valley, in 1859.* Washington, D.C.: U.S. Government Printing Office. Reprint, Reno: University of Nevada Press, 1983.

Sinclair, A. R. E., and Peter M. Arcese, eds. 1995. *Serengeti II: Dynamics, Management, and Conservation of an Ecosystem.* Chicago: University of Chicago Press.

Sisk, N. R. 2003. Ecology and identification of the Arroyo toad (*Bufo californicus*). Identification and ecology of sensitive amphibians and reptiles of the southern California region. Conference workshop of the Wildlife Society, Western Section, May 8–10, 2003.

Skinner, C. N., and C. Chang. 1996. Fire regimes, past and present. In Sierra Nevada Ecosystem Project. Status of the Sierra Nevada, Vol. 2. Assessments and Scientific Basis for Management Options. Final Report to Congress. Wildlands Resources Center Report No. 37. Centers for Water and Wildland Resources, University of California, Davis.

Skinner, John E. 1962. An historical review of the fish and wildlife resources of the San Francisco Bay Area. Report No. 1. California Department of Fish and Game, Water Projects Branch.

Skinner, Milton P. 1936. Browsing of the Olympic Peninsula elk in early winter. *Journal of Mammalogy* 17: 253–256.

Skolnick, Sharon. 1989. *Dreams of Tamalpais.* San Francisco: Last Gasp of San Francisco Press.

Sleeper, Jim. 1976. *A boy's book of bear stories (not for boys): A grizzly introduction to the Santa Ana Mountains.* Trabuco Canyon, CA: California Classics.

Small, Arnold. 1994. *California Birds: Their Status and Distribution.* Vista, CA: Ibis Press.

Smith, C. F. 1976. *A flora of the Santa Barbara Region, California.* Santa Barbara: Santa Barbara Museum of Natural History.

Smith, Dick. 1978. *Condor journal: The history, mythology and reality of the California condor.* Santa Barbara: Capra Press.

Smith, Douglas W., L. David Mech, Mary Meagher, Wendy E. Clark, Rosemary Jaffe, Michael K. Phillips, and John A. Mack. 2000. Wolf-bison interactions in Yellowstone National Park. *Journal of Mammalogy* 81 (4): 1128–1135.

Smith, G. I., and F. A. Street-Perrott. 1983. Pluvial lakes of the western United States. In *Late Quaternary environments of the United States*, edited by H. E. Wright, Jr. Vol. 2, *The Late Pleistocene.* Minneapolis: University of Minnesota Press.

Smith, Ralph I., and James T. Carlton. 1975. *Light's manual: Intertidal invertebrates of the central California coast.* Berkeley: University of California Press.

Smith, Stanley, Therese Charlet, Lynn Fenstermaker, and Beth Newingham. 2009. Effects of global change on Mojave Desert ecosystems. In *The Mojave Desert: Ecosystem processes and sustainability*, edited by Robert Webb, Lynn Fenstermaker, Jill Heaton, Debra Hughson, Eric McDonald, and David Miller. Reno: University of Nevada Press.

Smith, Wallace. 1925. Spanish exploration of the San Joaquin Valley. *Fresno Republican*, November 29, 1925.

Snow, G. E. 1990. Germination characteristics of Engelmann oak and coast live oak from the Santa Rosa Plateau. In *Proceedings of the symposium on oak woodlands and hardwood rangeland management, October 31–November 2, 1990, Davis, California.* USDA Forest Service Pacific Southwest Research Station, General Technical Report PSW-126.

Snyder, J. O. 1921. Steelhead caught at sea off the coast near Fort Bragg. *California Fish and Game* 7 (1): 9–11.

——. 1921. A royal silver trout caught in Lake Tahoe. *California Fish and Game* 7 (3): 148–149.

——. 1924. Indian methods of fishing on Trinity River and some notes on the king salmon of that stream. *California Fish and Game* 10 (4): 163.

——. 1931. Salmon of the Klamath River, California. *Fish Bulletin* 34: 1–30.

Snyder, L. A. 1951. Cytology of inter-strain hybrids and the probable origin of variability in *Elymus glaucus. American Journal of Botany* 38: 195–202.

Snyder, Noel, and Helen Snyder. 2000. *The California condor: A saga of natural history and conservation.* San Diego: Academic Press.

Snyder, Susan. 2003. *Bear in mind: The California grizzly.* Berkeley: Heyday Books and the Bancroft Library, University of California, Berkeley.

Solomon, Christopher. 2003. An underwater ark. *Audubon* (September 2003): 26–31.

Soltz, D. L., and R. J. Naiman. 1978. The natural history of native fishes in the Death Valley system. Science Series No. 30. Los Angeles: Natural History Museum of Los Angeles County.

Soper, J. D. 1941. History, range, and home life of the northern bison. *Ecological Monographs* 11 (4): 349–412.

Sparling, D. W., G. M. Fellers, and L. L. McConnell. 2001. Pesticides and amphibian population declines in California, USA. *Environmental Toxicology and Chemistry* 20: 1591–1595.

SPAWN (Salmon Protection and Watershed Network). 2002. Stream naturalist training manual. Forest Knolls, CA: Salmon Protection and Watershed Network. www.spawnusa.org.

Speth, J. W. 1971. The status of coastal wetlands in southern California. *Cal-Neva Wildlife* 1971: 51–58.

Spier, R. F. 1978. Monache. In *Handbook of North American Indians*, Vol. 8, *California*, by Robert F. Heizer. Washington, D.C.: Smithsonian Institution.

Spring, Cindy. 2004. Grazing for change: Interview with Joe Morris. *Bay Nature* (April–June 2004): 5, 27.

Stager, K. E. 1964. The role of olfaction in food location by the turkey vulture (*Cathartes aura*). *Los Angeles County Museum Contributions in Science* 81: 1–63.

Standiford, R. N. McDougald, W. Frost, and R. Phillips. 1997. Factors influencing the probability of oak regeneration on southern Sierra Nevada woodlands in California. *Madroño* 44 (2): 170–183.

Starks, Edwin Chapin. 1918. The herrings and herring-like fishes of California. *California Fish and Game* 4 (2): 58–65.

Starr, Kevin. 1976. *Americans and the California dream.* New York: Oxford University Press.

Stebbins, G. L. 1972. The evolution of the grass family. In *The biology and utilization of grasses*, edited by V. B. Youngner and C. M. McKell. New York: Academic Press.

——. 1975. The role of polyploid complexes in the evolution of North American grasslands. *Taxon* 24 (1): 91–106.

Stebbins, G. L., and H. A. Tobgy. 1944. The cytogenetics of hybrids in Bromus. I. Hybrids within the section *Ceratochloa. American Journal of Botany* 31 (1): 1–11.

Steelquist, Robert. 1992. A field guide to the Pacific salmon. Adopt-A-Stream Foundation. Seattle: Sasqatch Books.

Stein, Eric D., Shawna Dark, Travis Longcore, Nicholas Hall, Michael Beland, Robin Grossinger, Jason Casanova, and Martha Sutula. 2007. *Historical ecology and landscape change of the San Gabriel River and floodplain.* Southern California Coastal Water Research Project Technical Report No. 499.

Stein, Mimi. 1984. *A vision acheived: Fifty years of East Bay Regional Park District.* East Bay Regional Park District.

Steinhart, Peter. 1990. *California's wild heritage: Threatened and endangered animals in the Golden Sate.* Sacramento: California Department of Fish and Game.

Stephenson, Nathan L. 1999. Reference conditions for giant sequoia forest restoration: Structure, process, and precision. *Ecological Applications* 9 (4): 1253–1265.

Stewart, B. S., P. K. Yochem, Robert L. DeLong, and G. A. Antonelis. 1993. Trends in abundance and status of pinnipeds on the southern Channel Islands. In *Third California Islands Symposium: Recent advances in research of the California islands,* edited by F. G. Hochberg. Santa Barbara: Santa Barbara Museum of Natural History.

Stiles, Gary F., and Alexander F. Skutch. 1989. *A guide to the birds of Costa Rica.* Ithaca, NY: Comstock Publishing Associates.

Stine, S. 1994. Extreme and persistent drought in California and Patagonia during mediaeval time. *Nature* 369 (6481): 546–549.

——. 1996. Climate, 1650–1850. In Sierra Nevada Ecosystem Project. Status of the Sierra Nevada, Vol. 2. Assessments and Scientific Basis for Management Options. Final Report to Congress. Wildlands Resources Center Report No. 37. Centers for Water and Wildland Resources, University of California, Davis.

Stine, Scott, David Gaines, and Peter Vorster. 1984. Destruction of riparian systems due to water development in the Mono Lake watershed. In *California riparian systems: Ecology, conservation, and productive management,* edited by Richard E. Warner and Kathleen M. Hendrix. Berkeley: University of California Press.

Stolzenburg, William. The jaguar's umbrella. *Nature Conservancy* (March–April 1997): 8–9.

Stone, Livingston. 1880. Report of operations at the United States salmon-hatching station on the M'Cloud River, California, in 1878. U.S. Commission on Fish and Fisheries Report for 1878, Washington, D.C.

Stone, Thomas B. 1976. Observations on furbearers within the riparian habitat of the upper Sacramento River. California Department of Fish and Game Memorandum Report, July 1976.

Storer, Tracy I. 1965a. Animal life of the Sacramento Valley: Past and present. Part 1 of 3. *Outdoor California* 26 (7).

——. 1965b. Fish and wildlife of the Sacramento Valley: Past and present. Part 2 of 3. *Outdoor California* 26 (8).

——. 1965c. Animal life of the Sacramento Valley: Past and present. Part 3 of 3. *Outdoor California* 26 (9).

Storer, Tracy I., and L. P. Tevis, Jr. 1955. *California grizzly.* Berkeley: University of California Press. Reprint, Lincoln: University of Nebraska Press, 1978.

Stowe, Keith S. 1979. *Ocean science.* New York: Wiley.

Strahan, Jan. 1984. Regeneration of riparian forests of the Central Valley. In *California riparian systems: Ecology, conservation, and productive management,* edited by Richard E. Warner and Kathleen M. Hendrix. Berkeley: University of California Press.

Stromberg, M. R., C. M. D'Antonio, T. P. Young, J. Wirka, and P. R. Kephart. 2007. California grassland restoration. In *California grasslands ecology and management,* edited by M. R. Stromberg, J. D. Corbin, and C. M. D'Antonio. Berkeley: University of California Press.

Stubbs, Kevin, and Rolland White. 1993. Lost River sucker and Shortnose sucker recovery plan. U.S. Department of Interior, Fish and Wildlife Service, Region One, Portland, Oregon.

Sudworth, George. 1900. Stanislaus and Lake Tahoe Forest Reserves, California, and adjacent territories. In *Annual reports of the Department of the Interior: Twenty-first annual report of the U.S. Geological Survey.* Part 5, 505–561. Washington, D.C.: U.S. Government Printing Office.

Suisun Ecological Workgroup. 2003. www.iep.water.ca.gov/suisun-eco-workgroup. Accessed March 1, 2003.

Sund, P. N., and J. G. Norton. 1990. Interpreting long-term fish landings records: Environment and/or exploitation? In *Proceedings of the sixth annual Pacific Climate (PACLIM) Workshop, March 5–8, 1989,* edited by J. L. Betancourt and A. M. Mackay. California Department of Water Resources, Interagency Ecological Studies Program Technical Report 23.

Sweeney, J. R. 1985. Fire ecology and plant succession. In *Living in the chaparral of southern California.* Proceedings of the Conference and Public Workshop by the National Foundation for Environmental Safety, National Park Service, October 20, 1984. Los Angeles: Natural History Museum of Los Angeles County.

Sweet, Sam. 1999. Arroyo toad. Exhibit on display at Los Prietos Ranger Station, Los Padres National Forest, in cooperation with University of California, Santa Barbara.

Swetnam, T. W., and C. H. Baisan. 1989. Can a climate record be extracted from giant sequoia tree rings In *Proceedings of the sixth annual Pacific Climate (PACLIM) Workshop, March 5–8, 1989,* edited by J. L. Betancourt and A. M. Mackay. California Department of Water Resources, Interagency Ecological Studies Program Technical Report 23.

Swetnam, T. W., Craig Allen, and Julio Betancourt. 2003. Applied historical ecology: Using the past to manage for the future. www.geog.utah.edu/courses/geog3270/17/INDEX_FILES/FRAME. Accessed March 2003.

Swetnam, Thomas W. 1993. Fire history and climate change in giant sequoia groves. *Science* 262: 885–889.

Sykes, Steve. 2003. The California tiger salamander (*Ambystoma californiense*). Identification and ecology of sensitive amphibians and reptiles of the southern California region. Conference workshop of the Wildlife Society, Western Section, May 8–10, 2003.

Takasuka, A., Y. Oozeki, and H. Kubota. 2005. Contrastive temperature optimums for anchovy and sardine spawning between both sides of the north Pacific: Optimal growth temperature hypothesis extended. Abstracts in CalCOFI Annual Conference 2005, C-13.

Tanner, Ogden. 1976. *Bears and other carnivores.* New York: Time-Life Films, Inc.

Terasmae, J., and N. C. Weeks. 1979. Natural fires as an index of paleoclimate. *Canadian Field Naturalist* 93 (2): 116–125.

Terres, John K. 1980. *The Audubon encyclopedia of North American birds.* New York: Alfred A. Knopf.

Thelander, Carl G., ed. 1994. *Life on the edge: A guide to California's endangered natural resources. Wildlife.* Berkeley: Heyday Books, and Santa Cruz: Biosystems Books.

Thomas, Jack W., and Dale E. Toweill. 1982. *Elk of North America: Ecology and management.* Harrisburg, PA: Stackpole Books.

Thomas, John Hunter. 1961. *Flora of the Santa Cruz Mountains of California*. Stanford, CA: Stanford University Press.

Thomas, T. W. 1987. Population structure of the valley oak in the Santa Monica National Recreation Area. In USDA Forest Service Pacific Southwest Research Station, General Technical Report PSW-100.

Thomasson, J. R. 1978. Epidermal patterns of the lemma in some fossil and living grasses and their phylogenetic significance. *Science* 199: 975–977.

———. 1986. Fossil grasses: 1820–1986 and beyond. In *Grass systematics and evolution*, edited by T. R. Soderstrom, K. W. Hilu, C. S. Campbell, and M. E. Barkworth. Washington, D.C.: Smithsonian Institution.

Thompson, Kenneth. 1977. Riparian forests of the Sacramento Valley, California. In *Riparian forests in California: Their ecology and conservation*, edited by Anne Sands. Institute of Ecology Publication No. 15. Davis: Institute of Ecology, University of California, Davis.

Thompson, L. G. 1991. Initial global perspective of climate for the last thousand years: The ice core record. In *Proceedings of the seventh annual Pacific Climate (PACLIM) Workshop, Asilomar, California, April 1990*, edited by Julio L. Betancourt and Vera L. Tharp. Technical Report 26 of the Interagency Ecological Studies Program for the Sacramento-San Joaquin Estuary.

Thompson, R. A. 1896. *The Russian settlement in California known as Fort Ross*. Santa Rosa, CA: Sonoma Democrat Publishing Co.

———. 1902. Woodland, Yolo County. *Out West: A magazine of the Old Pacific and the New*, edited by Charles F. Lummis. Vol. 17. Los Angeles: Out West Magazine Company.

Thompson, William F. 1920. The grunion at Monterey. *California Fish and Game* 6 (2): 130.

———. 1921. The sardine of California. *California Fish and Game* 7 (4): 193–194.

Thorp, R. W., and J. M. Leong. 1998. Specialist bee pollinators of showy vernal pool flowers. Pages 169–179 in *Ecology, conservation, and management of vernal pool ecosystems*, edited by C. W. Witham, E. T. Bauder, D. Belk, W. R. Ferren, Jr., and R. Ornduff. Proceedings from a 1996 Conference, Sacramento, California. Sacramento: California Native Plant Society.

Timbrook, Jan, John R. Johnson, and David D. Earle. 1993. Vegetation Burning by the Chumash. In *Before the wilderness: Environmental management by Native Californians*, edited by Thomas C. Blackburn and M. Kat Anderson. Menlo Park, CA: Ballena Press.

Tratz, W. M., and R. J. Vogl. 1977. Postfire vegetational recovery, productivity, and herbivore utilization of a chaparral-desert ecotone. In *Proceedings of the symposium on the environmental consequences of fire and fuel management in Mediterranean ecosystems, August 1–5, 1977, Palo Alto, California*, edited by H. A. Mooney and C. E. Conrad. USDA Forest Service General Technical Report WO-3.

Treend, H. 1987. Historical review of *Quercus lobata* and *Quercus agrifolia* in southern California. In USDA Forest Service Pacific Southwest Research Station, General Technical Report PSW-100.

Turbak, Gary. 1995. *Pronghorn: Portrait of the American antelope*. Flagstaff, AZ: Northland Publishing.

Tweed, William. 1986. Kaweah remembered: The story of the Kaweah Colony and the founding of Sequoia National Park. Three Rivers, CA: Sequoia Natural History Association.

Twisselman, E. C. 1967. A flora of Kern County, California. *Wassmann Journal of Biology* 25: 1–395.

U.S. Fish and Wildlife Service. 1998. Draft recovery plan for the Least Bell's vireo (*Vireo bellii pusillus*). Portland, OR: U.S. Fish and Wildlife Service, Ecological Services.

U.S. Fish and Wildlife Service et al. 2000. Rocky Mountain Wolf Recovery Team annual report. A cooperative effort by the U.S. Fish and Wildlife Service, the Nez Perce Tribe, the National Park Service, and USDA Wildlife Services. www.westerngraywolf.fws.gov. Accessed 2007.

U.S. Fish and Wildlife Service. 2007. Initiative areas of California, Nevada, and the Klamath Basin of Oregon. Pamphlet 919/414-6464. Sacramento: U.S. Fish and Wildlife Service, California/Nevada Operations Office.

U.S. Forest Service. 2000. Southern California mountains and foothills assessment. USDA General Technical Report PSW-GTR-172.

U.S. Forest Service Cooperation. 1920. *California Fish and Game* 6 (2): 88–89.

U.S. Forest Service Pacific Southwest Research Station. 1998. Sierra Nevada Science Review, Report of the Science Review Team Charged to Synthesize New Information of Rangewide Urgency to the National Forests of the Sierra Nevada. www.psw.fs.fed.US/sierra/final. Accessed 2003.

Unitt, P. 1987. *Empidonax traillii extimus*: An endangered subspecies. *Western Birds* 18: 137–162.

Urness, P. J. 1981. Food habits and nutrition. In *Mule and Black-tailed deer of North America*, edited by Olof C. Wallmo. Lincoln: University of Nebraska Press and Wildlife Management Institute.

Valdez, Raul, and Paul R. Krausman, eds. 1999. *Mountain sheep of North America*. Tucson: University of Arizona Press.

Vale, T. R. 1979. *Pinus coulteri* and wildfire on Mount Diablo, California. *Madrono* 26 (3): 135–140.

Vale, T. R., and G. R. Vale. 1994. *Time and the Tuolumne landscape: Continuity and change in the Yosemite high country*. Salt Lake City: University of Utah Press.

Valenciennes, P. H. 1820. *Éléments de perspective pratique*. Paris.

Van Devender, T. R. 1977. Holocene woodlands in the southwestern deserts. *Science* 198: 189–192.

Van Dyke, John C. 1980. *The desert*. Salt Lake City: Peregrine Smith, Inc. Originally published in 1901, New York: Scribner.

van Staalduinen, M. A. and M. J. A. Werger. 2006. Vegetation ecological features of dry Inner and Outer Mongolia. *Berichte der Reinhold-Tuexen-Gesellschaft* 18.

Van Valkenburgh, Blaire, Jennifer Leonard, Carles Villa, and Robert Wayne. 2006. Cryptic extinction of a unique wolf ecomorph. Abstract in *Journal of Vertebrate Paleontology* 26 (3): 134A.

Van Wormer, Joe. 1969. *The world of the Pronghorn*. Philadelphia: J. B. Lippincott Co.

Vandor, P. E. 1919. *History of Fresno County, California*. Vol. 1. Los Angeles: Historic Record.

Villeponteaux, Jim. 2004. Fire and rain. Newsletter of the Salmon River Restoration Council, Summer 2004. www.srrc.org. Accessed 2004.

Vincent, Stephen, ed. 1990. *O California: Nineteenth and early twentieth century California landscape and observations*. San Francisco: Bedford Arts, Publishers.

Vogl, R. J. 1977. Fire frequency and site degradation. In *Proceedings of the symposium on the environmental consequences of fire and fuel management in Mediterranean ecosystems, August 1–5, 1977, Palo Alto, California*, edited by H. A. Mooney and C. E. Conrad. USDA Forest Service General Technical Report WO-3.

Vucetich, John A., Douglas W. Smith, Daniel R. Stahler. 2005. Influence of harvest, climate, and wolf predation on Yellowstone elk, 1961–2004. *Oikos* 111 (2): 259–270.

Wallace, W. J. 1978a. Northern valley Yokuts. In *Handbook of North American Indians*, Vol. 8, *California*, by Robert F. Heizer. Washington, D.C.: Smithsonian Institution.

———. 1978b. Southern valley Yokuts. In *Handbook of North American Indians*, Vol. 8, *California*, by Robert F. Heizer. Washington, D.C.: Smithsonian Institution.

Wallace, W. J., and D. W. Lathrop. 1975. West Berkeley (CA-ALA-307): A culturally stratified shellmound on the east shore of San Francisco Bay. Contributions of the University of California (Berkeley) Archaeological Research Facility No. 29.

Waller, Steven, Lowell Moser, Patrick Reece, and George Gates. 1985. *Understanding grass growth: The key to profitable livestock grazing.* Kansas City, MO: Trabon Printing Co., Inc.

Ward, Kennan. 1994. *Grizzlies in the wild.* Minocqua, WI: Northword Press.

Ware, D. M. 1991. "Climate forcing of Pacific herring recruitment and growth in southern British Columbia." In *Proceedings of the seventh annual Pacific Climate (PACLIM) Workshop, Asilomar, California, April 1990*, ed. Julio L. Betancourt and Vera L. Tharp. Technical Report 26, Interagency Ecological Studies Program, Sacramento–San Joaquin Estuary.

Warme, J. E. 1971. Paleoecological aspects of a modern coastal lagoon. *University of California Publications in Geological Sciences* 87: 1–131.

Warner, Richard E., and Kathleen M. Hendrix. 1984. *California riparian systems: Ecology, conservation, and productive management.* Berkeley: University of California Press.

Waszczuk, Henry, and Italo Labignan. 1996. In quest of big fish. Toronto: Key Porter Books Limited.

Watkins, T. H. 1983. *California: An illustrated history.* New York: American West Publishing Co.

Watson, Sereno. 1880. *Botany of California.* Vol. 2. Boston: Little, Brown, and Co.

Wauer, Roland H. 1962. Birds of Death Valley National Monument. Unpublished manuscript in the library of Death Valley National Park.

Webb, Robert H. 1996. *Grand Canyon, a century of change: Rephotography of the 1889–1890 Stanton expedition.* Tucson: University of Arizona Press.

Webb, Robert H., Jayne Belnap, and John S. Weisheit. 2004. *Cataract Canyon: A human and environmental history of the rivers in Canyonlands.* Salt Lake City: University of Utah Press.

Webb, Robert H., Diane E. Boyer, and Kristin H. Berry. 2001. Changes in the riparian vegetation in the southwestern United States: Historical changes along the Mojave River, California. Poster. U.S. Geological Survey Open-File Report of 01-245, 2001.

Weber, Gerald E. 1985. Physical environment. In *The natural history of Año Nuevo*, edited by Burney J. Le Boeuf and Stephanie Kaza. Pacific Grove, CA: Boxwood Press. 2nd printing, 1985.

Webster, George, and J. T. Mills. 1861. Notes on trips of the San Joaquin Valley Agricultural Society's Visiting Committee on Orchards and Vineyards. Transactions and second annual report of the San Joaquin Valley Agricultural Society, Stockton.

Wehausen, John. 1983. Sierra Nevada Bighorn sheep: History and population ecology. Cooperative National Park Resources Studies Unit, Technical Report No. 12, Contribution No. 335/1. Institute of Ecology, University of California, Davis.

Welch, Walter R. 1927. Hunting and fishing reminiscences. *California Fish and Game* 13 (3): 180.

Welles, Ralph E., and Florence B. Welles. 1961. The Bighorn of Death Valley. U.S. Department of the Interior, National Park Service, Fauna Series No. 6. Washington, D.C.: U.S. Government Printing Office.

Wells, I. E. 1990. Holocene history of the El Nino phenomenon as recorded in flood sediments of north coastal Peru. In *Proceedings of the sixth annual Pacific Climate (PACLIM) Workshop, March 5–8, 1989*, edited by J. L. Betancourt and A. M. Mackay. California Department of Water Resources, Interagency Ecological Studies Program Technical Report 23.

Wells, P. V. 1962. Vegetation in relation to geological substratum and fire in the San Luis Obispo Quadrangle, California. *Ecological Monographs* 32 (1): 79–103.

West, James, and Dwight Simons. 1979. The archaeology of VEN-100. California Archaeological Reports No. 17. California Department of Parks and Recreation.

Wester, Lyndon. 1981. Composition of native grasslands in the San Joaquin Valley, California. *Madrono* 28 (4): 231–241.

Westerling, A. L., H. G. Hidalgo, D. R. Cayan, and T. W. Swetnam. 2006. Warming and earlier spring increase western U.S. forest wildfire activity. *Science* 313 (5789): 940–943.

White, K. L. 1967. Native bunchgrass (*Stipa pulchra*) on Hastings Reservation, California. *Ecology* 48 (6): 949–955.

White, Mary E. 1998 (1994). *After the greening: The browning of Australia.* East Roseville, New South Wales, Australia: Kangaroo Press.

White, P. S., and J. L. Walker. 1997. Approximating nature's variation: Selecting and using reference information in restoration ecology. *Restoration Ecology* 5 (4): 338–349.

White, Stewart E. 1937. *Old California, in picture and story.* New York: Doubleday, Doran and Co., Inc.

Whitney, J. D. 1870. Geological survey of California. *Ornithology* 7 (Raptores): 496–503.

Wilbur, Sanford R. 1983. The condor and the Native Americans. *Outdoor California* (September–October 1983): 7–8.

———. 1987. *Birds of Baja California.* Berkeley: University of California Press.

Willett, George. 1933. A revised list of the birds of southwestern California. *Pacific Coast Avifauna* 21. Cooper Ornithological Club.

Williams, B. D. 2001. Purple martins in oak woodlands. Abstract in Oaks in California's changing landscape, 5th Symposium on Oak Woodlands, October 22–25, 2001, Bahia Resort Hotel, San Diego, California. University of California Integrated Harwood Range Management Program, University of California, Berkeley. http://danr.ucop.edu/ihrmp/proceed/symproc49.html. Accessed December 2003.

Williams, Jack E., Gail C. Kobetich, and Carl T. Benz. 1984. Management aspects of relict populations inhabiting the Amargosa Canyon ecosystem. In *California riparian systems: Ecology, conservation, and productive management*, edited by Richard E. Warner and Kathleen M. Hendrix. Berkeley: University of California Press.

Williams, Jack E., and Cindy Deacon Williams. 1991. The Sacramento River winter Chinook salmon: Threatened with extinction. In *California's salmon and steelhead: The struggle to restore an imperiled resource*, edited by Alan Lufkin. Berkeley: University of California Press.

Williams, Ted. 2003. Salmon stakes. *Audubon* (March 2003).

Wilson, N. L., and A. H. Towne. 1978. Nisenan. In *Handbook of North American Indians*, Vol. 8, *California*, by Robert F. Heizer. Washington, D.C.: Smithsonian Institution.

Winterhalder, Bruce. 1994. Concepts in historical ecology: The view from evolutionary ecology. In *Historical ecology: Cultural knowledge and changing landscapes*, edited by Carole Crumley. Santa Fe, NM: School of American Research Press.

Wirtz, W. O. 1979. Effects of fire on birds in chaparral. *Cal-Neva Wildlife Transactions* 1979: 114–124.

Witham, C. W., E. T. Bauder, D. Belk, W. R. Ferren, Jr., and R. Orduff, eds. 1998. *Ecology, conservation, and management of vernal pool ecosystems*. Proceedings from a 1996 Conference, Sacramento, California. Sacramento: California Native Plant Society.

Wolf, Edward C. 2004. *Klamath heartlands: A guide to the Klamath Reservation forest plan*. Portland, OR: Ecotrust.

Wood, R. Coke. 1968. *Big Tree–Carson Valley Turnpike, Ebbets Pass, and Highway Four*. Murphys, CA: Old Timers Museum.

Woodward, Lucinda, and Jesse M. Smith, eds. 1977. A history of the Lower American River. Sacramento: County of Sacramento, Department of Parks and Recreation, and Natomas County. Revised and updated by William C. Dillinger, 1991, Carmichael, CA: American River Natural History Association.

Woolfenden, Wallace B. 1996. Quaternary vegetation history. In Sierra Nevada Ecosystem Project. Status of the Sierra Nevada, Vol. 2. Assessments and Scientific Basis for Management Options. Final Report to Congress. Wildlands Resources Center Report No. 37. Centers for Water and Wildland Resources, University of California, Davis.

Wrangler, Michael. 2003. Discussion on San Diego Fire Recovery Network forum, message posted on December 10, 2003. http://groups.yahoo.com/group/SanDiegoFireRecovery. Accessed December 2003.

Wright, Albert H., and Anna A. Wright. 1949. *Handbook of frogs and toads of the United States and Canada*. Ithaca, NY: Cornell University Press.

Wright, H. E., Jr. 1972. Interglacial and postglacial climates: The pollen record. *Quaternary Research* 2: 274–282.

Wuerthner, George, and Mollie Matteson. 2002. *Welfare ranching: The subsidized destruction of the American West*. Washington, D.C.: Island Press.

Yoshiyama, R. M., E. R. Gerstung, F. W. Moyle, and P. B. Moyle. 2001. Historical and present distribution of Chinook salmon in the Central Valley drainage of California. In Contributions to the biology of Central Valley salmonids, edited by R. L. Brown. California Department of Fish and Game Fish Bulletin 179.

Young, Richard P. 1986. Fire ecology and management in plant communities of Malheur National Wildlife Refuge, Southeastern Oregon. M.S. thesis, Oregon State University.

Zauner, Phyllis. 1982. *Lake Tahoe: The way it was then—and now*. Sacramento, CA: Spilman Printing Co.

Zedler, J. B., C. S. Nordby, and B. E. Kus. 1992. The ecology of Tijuana Estuary, California: A National Estuarine Research Reserve. Washington, D.C.: NOAA (National Oceanic and Atmospheric Administration) Office of Coastal Resource Management, Sanctuaries and Reserves Division.

Zedler, P. H. 1977. Life history attributes of plants and the fire cycle: A case study in chaparral dominated by *Cupressus forbesii*. In *Proceedings of the symposium on the environmental consequences of fire and fuel management in Mediterranean ecosystems, August 1–5, 1977, Palo Alto, California*, edited by H. A. Mooney and C. E. Conrad. USDA Forest Service General Technical Report WO-3.

Zedler, P. H., C. R. Gautier, and G. S. McMaster. 1983. Vegetation change in response to extreme events: The effect of a short interval between fires in California chaparral and coastal scrub. *Ecology* 64: 809–818.

Zedler, P. H., and C. A. Zammit. 1989. A population-based critique of concepts of change in chaparral. In *The California chaparral: Paradigms reexamined*, edited by S. C. Keeley. Science Series No. 34. Los Angeles: Natural History Museum of Los Angeles County.

Zeiner, David C., William F. Laudenslayer, Jr., Kenneth E. Mayer, and Marshall White. 1990. *California's wildlife*. Vol. 2, *Birds*. Sacramento: California Department of Fish and Game.

Zeiner, David C., William F. Laudenslayer, Jr., Kenneth E. Mayer, and Marshall White. 1990. *California's wildlife*. Vol. 3, *Mammals*. Sacramento: California Department of Fish and Game.

Zembal, R., and B. W. Massey. 1981. A census of the Light-footed Clapper rail in California. *Western Birds* 12: 87–99.

Zimmer, C. 1994. Cows were in the air. *Discover* (September 1994): 29.

Zwinger, Ann. 1986. *John Xantus: The Fort Tejon letters, 1857–1859*. Tucson: University of Arizona Press.

INDEX

HEYDAY
into California

About Heyday

Heyday is an independent, nonprofit publisher and unique cultural institution. We promote widespread awareness and celebration of California's many cultures, landscapes, and boundary-breaking ideas. Through our well-crafted books, public events, and innovative outreach programs we are building a vibrant community of readers, writers, and thinkers.

Thank You

It takes the collective effort of many to create a thriving literary culture. We are thankful to all the thoughtful people we have the privilege to engage with. Cheers to our writers, artists, editors, storytellers, designers, printers, bookstores, critics, cultural organizations, readers, and book lovers everywhere!

We are especially grateful for the generous funding we've received for our publications and programs during the past year from foundations and hundreds of individual donors. Major supporters include:

Alliance for California Traditional Arts; Anonymous (6); Arkay Foundation; Judith and Phillip Auth; Judy Avery; Paul Bancroft III; Richard and Rickie Ann Baum; BayTree Fund; S. D. Bechtel, Jr. Foundation; Jean and Fred Berensmeier; Berkeley Civic Arts Program and Civic Arts Commission; Joan Berman; Nancy Bertelsen; Barbara Boucke; Beatrice Bowles, in memory of Susan S. Lake; John Briscoe; David Brower Center; Lewis and Sheana Butler; California Historical Society; California Indian Heritage Center Foundation; California State Parks Foundation; Joanne Campbell; The Campbell Foundation; Graham Chisholm; The Christensen Fund; Jon Christensen; Community Futures Collective; Compton Foundation; Creative Work Fund; Lawrence Crooks; Lauren B. Dachs; Nik Dehejia; Topher Delaney; Chris Desser and Kirk Marckwald; Lokelani Devone; Frances Dinkelspiel and Gary Wayne; Doune Fund; The Durfee Foundation; Megan Fletcher and J.K. Dineen; Richard and Gretchen Evans; Flow Fund Circle; The Fred Gellert Family Foundation; Friends of the Roseville Library; Furthur Foundation; The Wallace Alexander Gerbode Foundation; Patrick Golden; Nicola W. Gordon; Wanda Lee Graves and Stephen Duscha; The Walter and Elise Haas Fund; Coke and James Hallowell; Theresa Harlan and Ken Tiger; Cindy Heitzman; Carla Hills; Historic Resources Group; Sandra and Charles Hobson; Nettie Hoge; Donna Ewald Huggins; JiJi Foundation; Claudia Jurmain; Kalliopeia Foundation; Marty and Pamela Krasney; Robert and Karen Kustel; Guy Lampard and Suzanne Badenhoop; Thomas Lockard and Alix Marduel; Thomas J. Long Foundation; Sam and Alfreda Maloof Foundation for Arts & Crafts; Michael McCone; Giles W. and Elise G. Mead Foundation; Moore Family Foundation; Michael J. Moratto, in memory of Major J. Moratto; Stewart R. Mott Foundation; The MSB Charitable Fund; Karen and Thomas Mulvaney; Richard Nagler; National Wildlife Federation; Native Arts and Cultures Foundation; Humboldt Area Foundation, Native Cultures Fund; The Nature Conservancy; Nightingale Family Foundation; Northern California Water Association; Ohlone-Costanoan Esselen Nation; Panta Rhea Foundation; David Plant; Restore Hetch Hetchy; Spreck and Isabella Rosekrans; Alan Rosenus; The San Francisco Foundation; Santa Barbara Museum of Natural History; Sierra College; Stephen M. Silberstein Foundation; Ernest and June Siva, in honor of the Dorothy Ramon Learning Center; William Somerville; Martha Stanley; John and Beverly Stauffer Foundation; Radha Stern, in honor of Malcolm Margolin and Diane Lee; Roselyne Chroman Swig; Sedge Thomson and Sylvia Brownrigg; Tides Foundation; Sonia Torres; Michael and Shirley Traynor; The Roger J. and Madeleine Traynor Foundation; Lisa Van Cleef and Mark Gunson; Patricia Wakida; John Wiley & Sons, Inc.; Peter Booth Wiley and Valerie Barth; Bobby Winston; Dean Witter Foundation; Yocha Dehe Wintun Nation; and Yosemite Conservancy.

Board of Directors

Getting Involved

To learn more about our publications, events, membership club, and other ways you can participate, please visit www.heydaybooks.com.

ABOUT THE AUTHOR

Laura Cunningham is an artist-naturalist who studied paleontology and biology at the University of California, Berkeley, and has worked at field biology jobs for the California Department of Fish and Game, U.S. Geological Survey, and various universities, gaining experience with such species as the Owens Valley pupfish, the southern California steelhead trout, the Yosemite toad, and the Panamint alligator lizard. Simultaneously, she taught herself the arts of sketching and oil painting and pursued studies of California's historic and living wildlife, flora, and unique landscapes. Her studio is next to Death Valley National Park. She cofounded the group Basin and Range Watch to explore the historical ecology of the desert ecosystems of California and Nevada and work to protect them.